THE WEB COLLECTION
MACROMEDIA® DREAMWEAVER® 8, FLASH® 8, AND FIREWORKS® 8
REVEALED
DELUXE EDUCATION EDITION

Sherry Bishop, Jim Shuman, Barbara Waxer

THOMSON
COURSE TECHNOLOGY

The Web Collection: Macromedia® Dreamweaver® 8, Flash® 8, and Fireworks® 8 Revealed, Deluxe Education Edition

by Sherry Bishop, Jim Shuman, and Barbara Waxer

Managing Editor:
Marjorie Hunt

Product Manager:
Jane Hosie-Bounar

Associate Product Manager:
Shana Rosenthal

Editorial Assistant:
Janine Tangney

Production Editors:
Kelly Robinson, Summer Hughes, Pamela Elizian

Developmental Editors:
Ann Fisher, Rachel Biheller Bunin, M.T. Cozzola, Barbara Waxer

Marketing Manager
Joy Stark

QA Manuscript Reviewers:
Jeff Schwartz, Ashlee Welz, Chris Carvalho, Susan Whelan, Marc Spoto, Danielle Shaw

Composition House:
Integra—Pondicherry, India

Illustrator:
Philip Brooker

Cover Design:
Steve Deschene

Revealed Series Vision

The Revealed Series is your guide to today's hottest multimedia applications. These comprehensive books teach the skills behind the application, showing you how to apply smart design principles to multimedia products, such as dynamic graphics, animation, Web sites, software authoring tools, and digital video.

A team of design professionals, including multimedia instructors, students, authors, and editors, worked together to create this series. We recognized the unique needs of the multimedia market and created a series that gives you comprehensive step-by-step instructions and offers an in-depth explanation of the "why" behind a skill, all in a clear, visually-based layout. It was our goal to create a book that speaks directly to the multimedia and design community—one of the most rapidly growing computer fields today. We feel that *The Web Collection: Macromedia Dreamweaver® 8, Flash® 8, and Fireworks® 8—Revealed* does just that, with sophisticated content and an instructive book design.

—The Revealed Series

Authors' Vision

What a joy it has been to be a part of such a creative and energetic team. The Revealed Series is a great format for teaching and learning Macromedia Flash 8, Dreamweaver 8, and Fireworks 8. We would like to thank Nicole Pinard who provided the vision for the project, Marjorie Hunt and Jane Hosie-Bounar for their management expertise, and everyone at Thomson Course Technology for their professional guidance.

A special thanks to Ann Fisher, M.T. Cozzola, Rachel Biheller Bunin, and Barbara Waxer for their editorial expertise and encouragement. Our sincere appreciation goes out to Anita Quintana and Deborah van Rooyen for their help with some of the graphic images used in the book.

—The authors

I would like to give special thanks to my family and friends for their constant encouragement. My husband, Don, has been supportive in so many ways. Thank you is so inadequate.

—Sherry Bishop

I would like to thank my co-authors, Barbara and Sherry. I also want to give a heartfelt thanks to my wife, Barbara, for her patience and support.

—Jim Shuman

Huge thanks to my partner, Lindy, and to a house full of animals who deserve the utmost acknowledgement for their spontaneous contributions that never once bordered on combustion.

—Barbara Waxer

SERIES & AUTHORS' VISIONS

iii

Introduction to Macromedia Dreamweaver 8, Flash 8, and Fireworks 8

Welcome to *The Web Collection: Macromedia® Dreamweaver® 8, Flash® 8, and Fireworks® 8—Revealed, Deluxe Education Edition.* This book offers creative projects, concise instructions, and complete coverage of basic to intermediate Dreamweaver, Flash, and Fireworks skills, helping you create dynamic Web sites. Use this book both in the classroom and as your own reference guide.

This text is organized into 14 chapters. In these chapters, you will learn many skills, including how to develop a Dreamweaver Web site, add Flash and Fireworks interactivity and animation, and integrate the tools of each application.

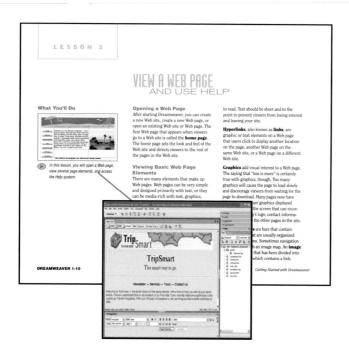

What You'll Do

A What You'll Do figure begins every lesson. This figure gives you an at-a-glance look at the skills covered in the chapter and shows you the completed Data File of the lesson. Before you start the lesson, you will know—both on a technical and artistic level—what you will be creating.

Comprehensive Conceptual Lessons

Before jumping into instructions, in-depth conceptual information tells you why skills are applied. This book provides the "how" and "why" through the use of professional examples. Also included in the text are helpful tips and sidebars to help you work more efficiently and creatively.

Step-by-Step Instructions

This book combines in-depth conceptual information with concise steps to help you learn Dreamweaver, Fireworks, and Flash. Each set of steps guides you through a lesson where you will apply either Flash, Dreamweaver, or Fireworks tasks to a dynamic and professional Data File. Step references to large, colorful images and quick step summaries round out the lessons.

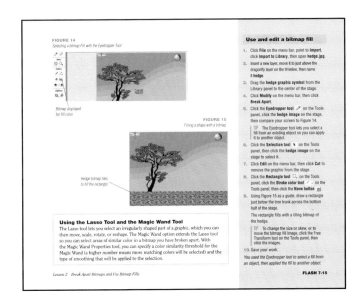

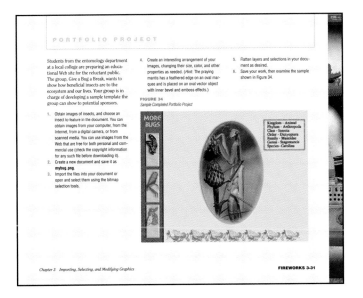

Projects

This book contains a variety of end-of-chapter material for additional practice and reinforcement. The Skills Review contains hands-on practice exercises that mirror the progressive nature of the lesson material. The chapter concludes with four projects: two Project Builders, one Design Project, and one Portfolio Project. The Project Builder cases require you to apply the skills you've learned in the chapter to create movies, Web sites, and animations. Design Projects examine Web site design and send students to the Web to research these issues. Portfolio Projects encourage you to create a project to save in your own portfolio.

What Instructor Resources Are Available with this Book?

The Instructor Resources CD-ROM is Course Technology's way of putting the resources and information needed to teach and learn effectively into your hands. All the resources are available for both Macintosh and Windows operating systems, and many of the resources can be downloaded from *www.course.com*.

Instructor's Manual

Available as an electronic file, the Instructor's Manual is quality-assurance tested and includes chapter overviews and detailed lecture topics for each chapter, with teaching tips. The Instructor's Manual is available on the Instructor Resources CD-ROM, or you can download it from *www.course.com*.

Syllabus

Prepare and customize your course easily using this sample course outline (available on the Instructor Resources CD-ROM).

PowerPoint Presentations

Each chapter has a corresponding PowerPoint presentation that you can use in lecture, distribute to your students, or customize to suit your course.

Figure Files

Figure Files contain all the figures from the book in bitmap format. Use the figure files to create transparency masters or PowerPoint presentations.

Solutions to Exercises

Solution Files are Data Files completed with comprehensive sample answers. Use these files to evaluate your students' work. Or, you can distribute them electronically or in hard copy so students can verify their work.

ExamView Test Bank and Test Engine

ExamView is a powerful testing software package that allows instructors to create and administer printed, computer (LAN-based), and Internet exams. ExamView includes hundreds of questions that correspond to the topics covered in this text, enabling students to generate detailed study guides that include page references for further review. The computer-based and Internet testing components allow students to take exams at their computers and also save the instructor time by grading each exam automatically.

Data Files for Students

To complete most of the chapters in this book, your students will need the Data Files provided on the CD at the back of this book. Instruct students to use the Data Files List at the end of the book. This list gives instructions on copying and organizing files.

viii

Dreamweaver

CHAPTER 2 DEVELOPING A WEB PAGE

CHAPTER 3   WORKING WITH TEXT AND GRAPHICS

CONTENTS

CHAPTER 4 WORKING WITH LINKS

CHAPTER 5 — WORKING WITH TABLES

CONTENTS

Flash

CHAPTER 1   GETTING STARTED WITH MACROMEDIA FLASH

CHAPTER 3   WORKING WITH SYMBOLS AND INTERACTIVITY

CONTENTS

CHAPTER 1   **GETTING STARTED WITH MACROMEDIA FIREWORKS**

CONTENTS

Integration

CHAPTER 1 INTEGRATING MACROMEDIA STUDIO 8

Intended Audience

This text is designed for the beginner or intermediate user who wants to learn how to use Dreamweaver 8, Flash 8, and Fireworks 8. The book is designed to provide basic and in-depth material that not only educates, but also encourages you to explore the nuances of these exciting programs.

Approach

The text allows you to work through step-by-step tutorials at your own pace. A concept is presented and the process is explained, followed by the actual steps. To learn the most from the use of the text, you should adopt the following habits:

- Proceed slowly: Accuracy and comprehension are more important than speed.
- Understand what is happening with each step before you continue to the next step.
- After finishing a skill, ask yourself if you could do it on your own, without referring to the steps. If the answer is no, review the steps.

Icons, Buttons, and Pointers

Symbols for icons, buttons, and pointers are shown in the step each time they are used.

Fonts

The Data Files contain a variety of commonly used fonts, but there is no guarantee that these fonts will be available on your computer. In a few cases, fonts other than those common to a PC or a Macintosh are used. If any of the fonts in use is not available on your computer, you can make a substitution, realizing that the results may vary from those in the book.

Windows and Macintosh

Macromedia Studio 8 works virtually the same on Windows and Macintosh operating systems. In those cases where there is a significant difference, the abbreviations (Win) and (Mac) are used.

Data Files

To complete the lessons in this book, you need the Data Files on the CD located on the inside back cover. Your instructor will tell you where to store the files as you work, such as to the hard drive, a network server, or a USB storage device. The instructions in the lessons will refer to "the drive and folder where your Data Files are stored" when referring to the Data Files for the book.

Creating a Portfolio

The Portfolio Project and Project Builders allow students to use their creativity to come up with original Dreamweaver Web sites, Flash animations and screen designs, and Fireworks graphics. Your instructor might suggest that students create a portfolio in which they can store their original work.

Macromedia Dreamweaver 8

System Requirements

For a Windows operating system, Dreamweaver 8 requires at least an 800 MHz Intel Pentium III processor (or equivalent); Windows 2000 or Windows XP; 256 MB RAM (1 GB recommended to run more than one Studio 8 product simultaneously); 1024 × 768, 16-bit display (32-bit recommended); and 1.8 GB available disk space.

For a Macintosh operating system, Dreamweaver 8 requires at least 600 MHz PowerPC G3; Mac OS X 10.3 or 10.4; 256 MB RAM (1 GB recommended to run more than one Studio 8 product simultaneously); 1024 × 768, thousands of colors display (millions of colors recommended); and 1.2 GB available disk space.

Dreamweaver 8 Workspace

If you are starting Dreamweaver for the first time after installing it, you will see the Workspace Setup dialog box, which asks you to choose between two workspace layouts. This book uses the Designer workspace layout throughout.

Building a Web Site

You will create and develop a Web site called The Striped Umbrella in the lesson material in this book. Because each chapter builds off of the previous chapter, it is recommended that you work through the chapters in consecutive order.

Preference Settings

The learning process will be much easier if you can see the file extensions for the files you will use in the lessons. To do this in Windows, open Windows Explorer, click Tools, Folder Options, View, then uncheck the box Hide Extensions for Known File Types. To do this for a Mac, go to the Finder, click the Finder menu, and then click Preferences. Click the Advanced tab, then select the Show all file extensions check box.

To view the Flash content that you will be creating, you must set a preference in your browser to allow active content to run. Otherwise, you will not be able to view objects, such as Flash buttons. To set this preference in Internet Explorer, click Tools, Internet Options, Advanced, then check the box Allow active content to run in files on My Computer. Your browser settings may be slightly different, so look for similar wording.

Macromedia Flash 8

Flash Basic versus Flash Professional

Macromedia Flash 8 is available in two versions, Flash Basic 8 and Flash Professional 8. The underlying program is the same for both versions. However, several features in Professional are not available in Basic. These include custom easing controls, filters, blend modes, bitmap smoothing, some components and data binding, and several video features. In addition to screen-based visual development environment features, Flash Professional 8 provides tools for managing data interactively and for fostering team productivity. This book was developed using Flash Professional 8. If there are any steps that won't work in Flash Basic 8, we have provided alternate steps or instructions in the Student Online Companion for the book. To access the Online Companion, please go to *www.course.com/revealed/flash8dee*.

Windows System Requirements

Macromedia Flash 8 runs under Windows 2000 and Windows XP, and requires an Intel 800 MHz Pentium III (or equivalent) or later processor, 256 MB of RAM (1 GB recommended to run more than one Studio 8 product simultaneously), 1024 x 768, 16-bit display (32-bit recommended), and 710 MB of disk space.

Macintosh System Requirements

Macromedia Flash 8 requires Mac OS X version 10.2.6 or above, a 600 MHz PowerPC G3 processor or later, 256 MB of RAM (1 GB recommended to run more than one Studio 8 product simultaneously), 1024 x 768, thousands of colors display (millions of colors recommended), and 360 MB of disk space.

Projects

Several projects are presented at the end of each chapter that allow students to apply the skills they have learned in the unit. Two projects, Ultimate Tours and the Portfolio, build from chapter to chapter. You will need to contact your instructor if you plan to work on these without having completed the previous chapter's project.

Macromedia Fireworks 8

Windows System Requirements

Fireworks 8 runs under Windows® 2000 or Windows XP. Fireworks 8 requires an Intel® 800 MHz Pentium® III or equivalent processor, 256 MB RAM (1 GB recommended to run more than one Studio 8 product simultaneously), and 880 MB of disk space (1.8 GB if you are installing the complete Studio 8). Monitor resolution of 1024 x 768, 16-bit display required (32-bit recommended). Netscape Navigator, Mozilla Firefox 1.0, or Microsoft® Internet Explorer 5.0 or later recommended.

Macintosh System Requirements

Fireworks 8 runs under Mac OS X® 10.3 or 10.4. Fireworks 8 requires a 600 MHz PowerPC® G3 processor or later, 256 MB RAM (1 GB recommended to run more than one Studio 8 product simultaneously), and 320 MB of disk space (1.2 GB if you are installing the complete Studio 8). Monitor resolution of 1024 x 768, thousands of colors display required (millions of colors recommended). Safari 2.0 or Mozilla Firefox 1.0 recommended.

GETTING STARTED WITH
DREAMWEAVER

1. Explore the Dreamweaver workspace.

2. View a Web page and use Help.

3. Plan and define a Web site.

4. Add a folder and pages and set the home page.

5. Create and view a site map.

GETTING STARTED WITH
DREAMWEAVER

Introduction

Macromedia Dreamweaver 8 is a Web development tool that lets you create dynamic, interactive Web pages containing text, images, hyperlinks, animation, sounds, video, and other elements. You can use Dreamweaver to create individual Web pages or complex Web sites consisting of many Web pages. A **Web site** is a group of related Web pages that are linked together and share a common interface and design. You can use Dreamweaver to create some Web page elements such as text, tables, and interactive buttons, or you can import elements from other software programs. You can save Dreamweaver files in many different file formats including XHTML, HTML, JavaScript, CSS, or XML to name a few. **XHTML** is the acronym for eXtensible HyperText Markup Language, the current standard language used to create Web pages. You can still use **HTML** (HyperText Markup Language) in Dreamweaver; however, it is no longer considered the standard language. In Dreamweaver you can easily convert existing HTML code to XHTML-compliant code. You use a browser to view your Web pages on the Internet. A **browser** is a program, such as Microsoft Internet Explorer

or Netscape Communicator, that lets you display HTML-developed Web pages.

Using Dreamweaver Tools

Creating a good Web site is a complex task. Fortunately, Dreamweaver has an impressive number of tools that can help. Using Dreamweaver's design tools, you can create dynamic and interactive Web pages without writing a word of code. However, if you prefer to write code, Dreamweaver makes it easy to enter and edit the code directly and see the visual results of the code instantly. Dreamweaver also contains organizational tools that help you work with a team of people to create a Web site. You can also use Dreamweaver's management tools to help you manage a Web site. For instance, you can use the **Files panel** to create folders to organize and store the various files for your Web site, add pages to your Web site, and set the **home page**, the first page that viewers will see when they visit the site. You can also use the **site map**, a graphical representation of how the pages within a Web site relate to each other, to view and edit the navigation structure of your Web site. The **navigation structure** is the way viewers navigate from page to page in your Web site.

Tools You'll Use

Property inspector

Browse for File icon

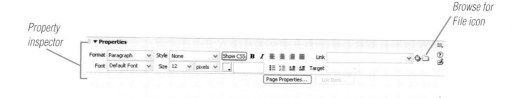

Refresh button

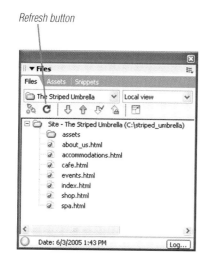

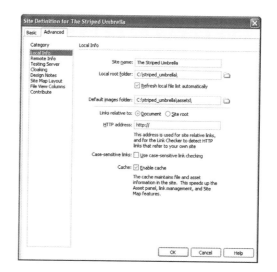

Show Code view button

Show Code and Design views button

Show Design view button

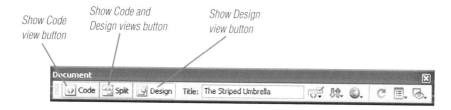

EXPLORE THE DREAMWEAVER WORKSPACE

What You'll Do

In this lesson, you will start Dreamweaver, examine the components that make up the Dreamweaver workspace, and change views.

Examining the Dreamweaver Workspace

The **Dreamweaver workspace** is designed to provide you with easy access to all the tools you need to create Web pages. Refer to Figure 1 as you locate the components described below.

The **document window** is the large white area in the Dreamweaver program window where you create and edit Web pages. The **menu bar**, located above the document window, includes menu names, each of which contains Dreamweaver commands. To choose a menu command, click the menu name to open the menu, then click the menu command. Directly below the menu bar is the Insert bar. The **Insert bar** includes eight groups of buttons displayed in a drop-down menu. They are Common, Layout, Forms, Text, HTML, Application, Flash elements, and Favorites. Clicking a group name on the Insert bar displays the buttons and menus associated with that group. For example, if you click Layout, you will find the Table button, used for

inserting a table, and the Frames menu, used for selecting one of thirteen different frame layouts.

QUICKTIP

You can also display the categories using tabs, as in previous versions of Dreamweaver, by clicking the current Insert bar list arrow, then clicking Show as Tabs.

The **Document toolbar** contains buttons and drop-down menus you can use to change the current work mode, preview Web pages, debug Web pages, choose visual aids, and view file-management options. The **Standard toolbar** contains buttons you can use to execute frequently used commands also available on the File and Edit menus. The Style Rendering toolbar contains buttons that can be used to render different media types. The Coding toolbar contains buttons that are used when working directly in the code. These, along with the Standard toolbar, are not part of the default workspace setup and might not show when you open Dreamweaver.

The **Property inspector**, located at the bottom of the Dreamweaver window, lets you view and change the properties of a selected object. The Property inspector is context sensitive, which means it changes according to what is selected in the document window. The **status bar** is located below the document window. The left end of the status bar displays the **tag selector**, which shows the HTML tags used at the insertion point location. The right side displays the window size and estimated download time for the current page as well as the Select tool used for page editing, the Hand tool used for panning, and the Zoom tool used for magnifying.

A **panel** is a window that displays information on a particular topic or contains related commands. **Panel groups** are sets of related panels that are grouped together. To view the contents of a panel in a panel group, click the panel. Panel groups can be collapsed and docked on the right side of the screen, or undocked by dragging the gripper on the left side of the panel group title bar. To collapse or expand a panel group, click the expander arrow on the left side of the panel group title bar, as shown in Figure 2, or just click the name of the panel group. When you use Dreamweaver for the first time, the CSS Application, Tag Inspector, and Files panel groups are displayed by default. Panels can be opened using the Window menu commands or the corresponding shortcut keys.

Working with Dreamweaver Views

A **view** is a particular way of displaying page content. Dreamweaver has three working views. **Design view** shows the page as it would appear in a browser and is primarily used for designing and creating a Web page. **Code view** shows the underlying HTML code for the page; use this view to read or edit the underlying code. **Code and Design view** is a combination of Code view and Design view. Code and Design view is the best view for **debugging** or correcting errors because you can immediately see how code modifications change the appearance of the page. The view buttons are located on the Document toolbar.

FIGURE 1

Dreamweaver 8 workspace

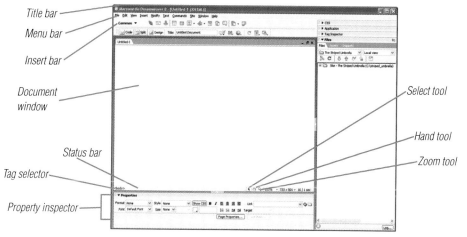

Title bar
Menu bar
Insert bar
Document window
Status bar
Tag selector
Property inspector
Select tool
Hand tool
Zoom tool

FIGURE 2

Panels in Files panel group

Expander arrow
Gripper
Active panel tab

Start Dreamweaver (Windows)

1. Click the **Start button** 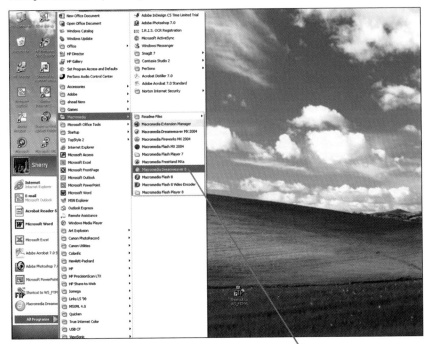 on the taskbar.

2. Point to **Programs** or **All Programs**, point to **Macromedia**, then click **Macromedia Dreamweaver 8**, as shown in Figure 3.

You started Dreamweaver 8 for Windows.

FIGURE 3

Starting Dreamweaver 8 (Windows)

Click Macromedia
Dreamweaver 8

Choosing a workspace layout (Windows)

If you are starting Dreamweaver in Windows for the first time after installing it, you will see the Workspace Setup dialog box, which asks you to choose between the Designer or Coder layout. Both layouts are built with an integrated workspace using the Multiple Document Interface (MDI). The **Multiple Document Interface** means that all document windows and panels are positioned within one large application window. In the Designer workspace layout, the panels are docked on the right side of the screen and the Design view is the default view. In the Coder workspace layout, the panels are docked on the left side of the screen and the Code view is the default view. To change the workspace layout, click Window on the menu bar, point to Workspace Layout, then click the desired layout.

FIGURE 4

Starting Dreamweaver 8 (Macintosh)

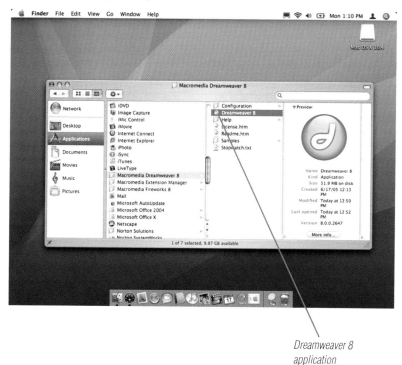

Dreamweaver 8
application

Start Dreamweaver (Macintosh)

1. Click **Finder** in the Dock, then click **Applications**.

2. Click the **Macromedia Dreamweaver 8 folder**, then double-click the **Dreamweaver 8 application,** as shown in Figure 4.

   TIP   Once Dreamweaver is running, you can add it to the Dock permanently by [control]-clicking the Dreamweaver icon, then clicking Keep In Dock.

You started Dreamweaver 8 for Macintosh.

Change views and view panels

1. Click the **HTML link** in the Create New category on the Dreamweaver Start page.

   The Dreamweaver Start page provides shortcuts for opening files or for creating new files or Web sites.

   TIP If you do not want the Dreamweaver Start page to appear each time you start Dreamweaver, click the Don't show again check box on the Start page or remove the check mark next to Show start page in the General category of the Preferences dialog box.

2. Click the **Show Code view button** Code on the Document toolbar.

   The default code for a new document appears in the document window, as shown in Figure 5.

   TIP The Coding toolbar is available only in Code view.

3. Click the **Show Code and Design views button** Split on the Document toolbar.

4. Click the **Show Design view button** Design on the Document toolbar.

   (continued)

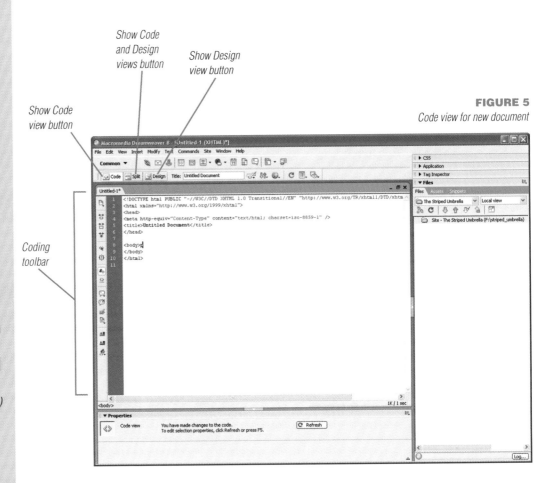

Show Code and Design views button

Show Design view button

Show Code view button

Coding toolbar

FIGURE 5
Code view for new document

Getting Started with Dreamweaver

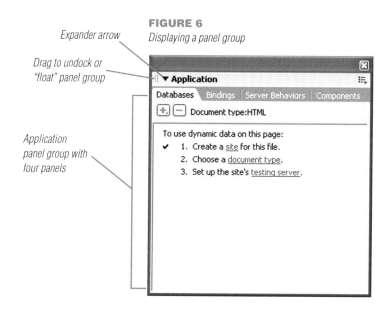

FIGURE 6
Displaying a panel group

Expander arrow

*Drag to undock or
"float" panel group*

*Application
panel group with
four panels*

5. Click **Application** on the panel group title bar, then compare your screen to Figure 6.

 TIP If the Application panel group is not displayed, click Window on the menu bar, then click Server Behaviors.

6. Click each panel name tab to display the contents of each panel.

7. Click **Application** on the panel group title bar to collapse the Application panel group.

8. View the contents of the CSS and Files panel groups, then collapse the CSS panel group.

 TIP If you are a Mac user, you first need to open the panel groups. To open each panel group, click Window on the menu bar, then click Server Behaviors (for the Application panel group) or Assets (for the Files panel group).

9. Close the open XHTML document.

You viewed a new Web page using three views, opened panel groups, viewed their contents, then closed panel groups.

VIEW A WEB PAGE
AND USE HELP

What You'll Do

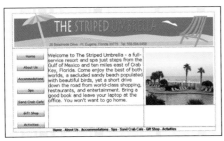

 In this lesson, you will open a Web page, view several page elements, and access the Help system.

Opening a Web Page

After starting Dreamweaver, you can create a new Web site, create a new Web page, or open an existing Web site or Web page. The first Web page that appears when viewers go to a Web site is called the **home page**. The home page sets the look and feel of the Web site and directs viewers to the rest of the pages in the Web site.

Viewing Basic Web Page Elements

There are many elements that make up Web pages. Web pages can be very simple and designed primarily with text, or they can be media-rich with text, graphics, sound, and movies. Figure 7 is an example of a Web page with several different page elements that work together to create a simple and attractive page.

Most information on a Web page is presented in the form of **text**. You can type text directly onto a Web page in Dreamweaver or import text created in other programs. You can then use the Property inspector to format text so that it is attractive and easy

to read. Text should be short and to the point to prevent viewers from losing interest and leaving your site.

Hyperlinks, also known as **links**, are graphic or text elements on a Web page that users click to display another location on the page, another Web page on the same Web site, or a Web page on a different Web site.

Graphics add visual interest to a Web page. The saying that "less is more" is certainly true with graphics, though. Too many graphics will cause the page to load slowly and discourage viewers from waiting for the page to download. Many pages now have **banners**, which are graphics displayed across the top of the screen that can incorporate a company's logo, contact information, and links to the other pages in the site.

Navigation bars are bars that contain multiple links that are usually organized in rows or columns. Sometimes navigation bars are used with an image map. An **image map** is a graphic that has been divided into sections, each of which contains a link.

Flash button objects are Flash objects that can be created in Dreamweaver that can serve as links to other files or Web pages. You can insert them onto a Web page without requiring the Macromedia Flash program to be installed. They add "pizzazz" to a Web page.

Getting Help

Dreamweaver has an excellent Help feature that is both comprehensive and easy to use.

When questions or problems arise, you can use the commands on the Help menu to find the answers you need. Clicking the Using Dreamweaver command opens the Dreamweaver 8 Help window that contains four tabs you can use to search for answers in different ways. The Contents tab lists Dreamweaver Help topics by category. The Index tab lets you view topics in alphabetical order, and the Search tab lets you enter a keyword to search for a specific topic. You

can use the Favorites tab to bookmark topics that you might want to view later. On a Macintosh you can choose between Index or Table of Contents view, and the Search field is always present at the top of the window. You can also use the Getting Started and Tutorials command on the Help menu to get step-by-step instructions on how to complete various tasks. Context-specific help can be accessed by clicking the question mark button on the Property inspector.

FIGURE 7
Common Web page elements

Graphics

Navigation structure includes several sets of text links

Small form used to join the mailing list

Search form

Open a Web page and view basic page elements

1. Click the **Open link** at the bottom of the first column on the Dreamweaver Start page.

2. Click the **Look in list arrow** (Win), or **navigation list arrow** (Mac), locate the drive and folder where your Data Files are stored, then double-click the **chapter_1 folder** (Win), or click the **chapter_1 folder** (Mac).

3. Click **dw1_1.html**, then click **Open**.

4. Locate each of the Web page elements shown in Figure 8.

5. Click the **Show Code view button** <kbd></> Code</kbd> to view the code for the page.

6. Scroll down to view all the code, then click the **Show Design view button** <kbd>Design</kbd> to return to Design view.

   TIP To view the code for a particular page element, select the page element in Design view, then click the Show Code view button.

7. Click **File** on the menu bar, then click **Close** to close the page without saving it.

You opened a Web page, located several page elements, viewed the code for the page, then closed the Web page without saving it.

FIGURE 8
Striped Umbrella Web page elements

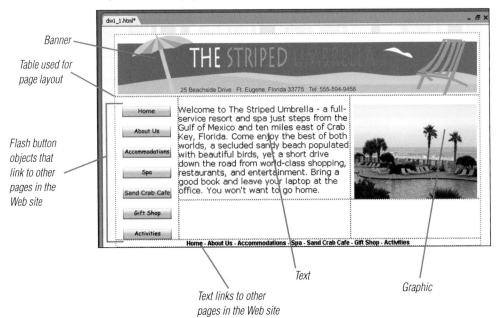

Banner

Table used for page layout

Flash button objects that link to other pages in the Web site

Text links to other pages in the Web site

Text

Graphic

FIGURE 9
Dreamweaver 8 Help window

Keywords

Click to
see topics

Topics found
with keywords

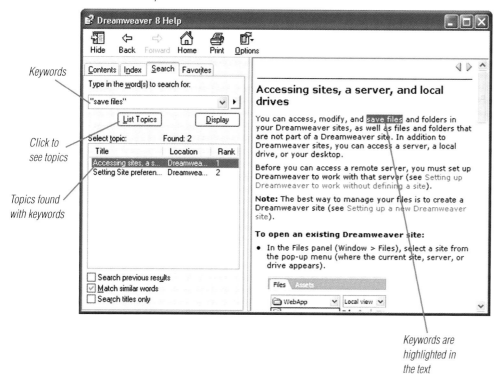

Keywords are
highlighted in
the text

1. Click **Help** on the menu bar, then click **Using Dreamweaver**.

2. Click the **Search tab** (Win).

3. Type **saving** in the Type in the word(s) to search for text box (Win) or the Ask a Question text box (Mac).

4. Press **[Enter]** or click **List Topics** (Win) or press **[return]** (Mac), then scroll down to view the topics.

5. Continue to Step 6 (Win) or close the Dreamweaver 8 Help window (Mac).

6. If necessary, select **saving** in the Type in the word(s) to search for text box, type **"save files"** (be sure to type the quotation marks), then press **[Enter]** or click **List Topics**.

   Because you placed the keywords in quotation marks, Dreamweaver shows only the topics that contain the exact phrase "save files".

7. Double-click the first topic in the topic list.

   Information on accessing sites, a server, and local drives appears in the right frame, as shown in Figure 9.

8. Scroll down and scan the text.

   The search words you used are highlighted in the Help text.

9. Close the Dreamweaver 8 Help window.

You used the Dreamweaver Help files to read information about connecting to a server to edit files.

PLAN AND DEFINE A
WEB SITE

What You'll Do

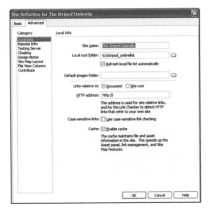

 In this lesson, you will review a Web site plan for The Striped Umbrella, a full-service beach resort and spa. You will also create a root folder for The Striped Umbrella Web site, and then define the Web site.

Understanding the Web Site Creation Process

Creating a Web site is a complex process. It can often involve a large team of people working in various roles to ensure that the Web site contains accurate information, looks good, and works smoothly. Figure 10 illustrates the phases in a Web site development project.

Planning a Web Site

Planning is probably the most important part of any successful project. Planning is an *essential* part of creating a Web site, and is a continuous process that overlaps the subsequent phases. To start planning your Web site, you need to create a checklist of questions and answers about the site. For example, what are your goals for

FIGURE 10

Phases of a Web site development project

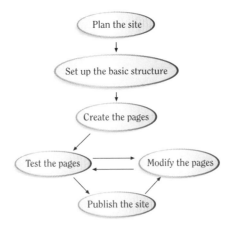

the Web site? Who is the audience you want to target? Teenagers? Senior citizens? How can you design the site to appeal to the target audience? The more questions you can answer about the site, the more prepared you will be when you begin the developmental phase. Because of the public demand for "instant" information, your plan should include not just how to get the site up and running, but how to keep it current. Table 1 lists some of the basic

questions you need to answer during the planning phase for almost any type of Web site. From your checklist, you should create a statement of purpose and scope, a timeline for all due dates, a budget, a task list with work assignments, and a list of resources needed. You should also include a list of deliverables such as a preliminary storyboard, page drafts, and art work for approval. The due dates for each deliverable should be included in the timeline.

Setting Up the Basic Structure

Once you complete the planning phase, you need to set up the structure of the site by creating a storyboard. A **storyboard** is a small sketch that represents every page in a Web site. Like a flowchart, a storyboard shows the relationship of each page in the Web site to all the other pages. Storyboards are very

TABLE 1: Web Site Planning Checklist

question	examples
1. Who is the target audience?	Seniors, teens, children
2. How can I tailor the Web site to reach that audience?	Specify an appropriate reading level, decide the optimal amount of multimedia content, use formal or casual language
3. What are the goals for the site?	Sell a product, provide information
4. How will I gather the information?	Recruit other company employees, write it myself, use content from in-house documents
5. What are my sources for multimedia content?	Internal production department, outside production company, my own photographs
6. What is my budget?	Very limited, well financed
7. How long do I have to complete the project?	Two weeks, 1 month, 6 months
8. Who is on my project team?	Just me, a complete staff of designers
9. How often should the site be updated?	Every 10 minutes, once a month
10. Who is responsible for updating the site?	Me, other team members

helpful when planning a Web site, because they allow you to visualize how each page in the site is linked to others. You can sketch a storyboard using a pencil and paper or using a graphics program on a computer. The storyboard shown in Figure 11 shows all the pages that will be contained in The Striped Umbrella Web site that you will create in this book. Notice that the home page appears at the top of the storyboard, and that it has four pages linked to it. The home page is called the **parent page**, because it is at a higher level in the Web hierarchy and has pages linked to it. The pages linked to it below are called **child pages**. The Activities page, which is a child page to the home page, is also a parent page to the Cruises and Fishing pages. You can refer to this story-board as you create the actual links in Dreamweaver. More detailed storyboards will also include all document names, images, text files, and link information.

QUICKTIP

You can create a storyboard on a computer using a software program such as Word, PowerPoint, Paint, Paintshop Pro, or Macromedia Freehand. You might find it easier to make changes to a computer-generated storyboard than to one created on paper.

In addition to creating a storyboard for your site, you should also create a folder hierarchy for all of the files that will be used in the Web site. Start by creating a folder for the Web site with a descriptive name, such as the name of the company.

This folder, known as the **root folder** or **local root folder**, will store all the Web pages or HTML files for the site. Then create a subfolder called **assets** in which you store all of the files that are not Web pages, such as images and video clips. You should avoid using spaces, special characters, or uppercase characters in your folder names to ensure that all your files can be read and linked successfully on all Web servers.

After you create the root folder, you need to define your Web site. When you **define** a Web site, the root folder and any folders and files it contains appear in the **Files**

panel, the panel you use to manage your Web site's files and folders. Using the Files panel to manage your files ensures that the site links work correctly when the Web site is published. You also use the Files panel to add or delete pages.

Creating the Web Pages and Collecting the Page Content

This is the fun part! After you create your storyboard, you need to gather the files that will be used to create the pages, including text, graphics, buttons, video, and animation. Some of these files will come

FIGURE 11

The Striped Umbrella Web site storyboard

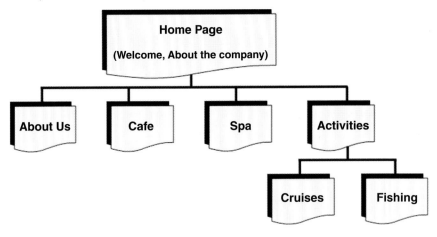

from other software programs, and some will be created in Dreamweaver. For example, you can create text in a word-processing program and insert it into Dreamweaver, or you can create and format text in Dreamweaver. Graphics, tables, colors, and horizontal rules all contribute to making a page attractive and interesting. In choosing your elements, however, you should always carefully consider the file size of each page. A page with too many graphical elements might take a long time to load, which could cause visitors to leave your Web site. Before you actually add content to each page, however, it is a good idea to use the Files panel to add all the pages to the site according to the structure you specified in your storyboard. Once all the blank pages are in place, you can add the content you collected. This will allow you to create and test the navigation links you will need for the site. The blank pages will act as placeholders. Some designers prefer to add pages as they are created and build the links as they go. It is a personal preference.

Testing the Pages

Once all your pages are completed, you need to test the site to make sure all the links work and that everything looks good.

It is important to test your Web pages using different browser software. The two most common browsers are Microsoft Internet Explorer and Netscape Navigator, although the Firefox browser is quickly gaining popularity. You should also test your Web site using different versions of each browser. Older versions of Internet Explorer and Netscape Navigator do not support the latest Web technology. You should also test your Web site using a variety of screen sizes. Some viewers may have small monitors, while others may have large, high-resolution monitors. You should also consider modem speed. Although more people use cable modems or DSL (Digital Subscriber Line) these days, some still use slower dial-up modems. Testing is a continuous process, for which you should allocate plenty of time.

Modifying the Pages

After you create a Web site, you'll probably find that you need to keep making changes to it, especially when information on the site needs to be updated. Each time you make a change, such as adding a new button or graphic to a page, you should test the site again. Modifying and testing pages in a Web site is an ongoing process.

Publishing the Site

Publishing a Web site means that you transfer all the files for the site to a **Web server**, a computer that is connected to the Internet with an IP (Internet Protocol) address, so that it is available for viewing on the Internet. A Web site must be published or users of the Internet cannot view it. There are several options for publishing a Web site. For instance, many Internet Service Providers (ISPs) provide space on their servers for customers to publish Web sites, and some commercial Web sites provide limited free space for their viewers. Although publishing happens at the end of the process, it's a good idea to set up Web server access in the planning phase. Use the Files panel to transfer your files using the FTP (File Transfer Protocol) capability. **FTP** is the process of uploading and downloading files to and from a remote site. Dreamweaver 8 also gives you the ability to transfer files using the FTP process without creating a Web site first. You simply enter login information to an FTP site to establish a connection by clicking New in the Manage Sites dialog box, then clicking the FTP & RDS Server option.

Create a root folder (Windows)

1. Click the **Start button** 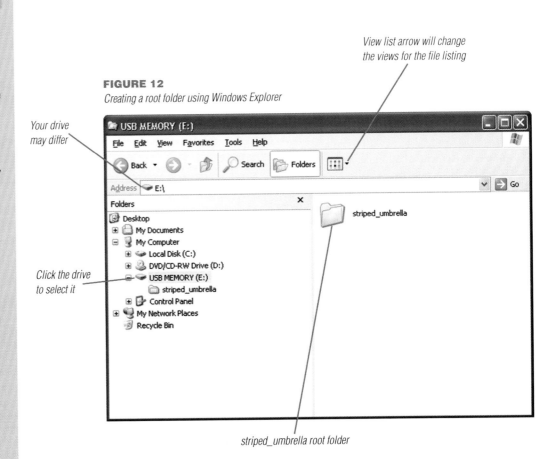 on the taskbar, point to **All Programs**, point to **Accessories**, then click **Windows Explorer**.

2. Navigate to the drive and folder where you will create a folder to store your files for The Striped Umbrella Web site.

3. Click **File** on the menu bar, point to **New**, then click **Folder**.

4. Type **striped_umbrella** to rename the folder, then press **[Enter]**.

   The folder is renamed striped_umbrella as shown in Figure 12.

   TIP   Your desktop will look different than Figure 12 if you are not using Windows XP.

5. Close Windows Explorer.

   TIP   You can also use the Files panel to create a new folder by clicking the Site list arrow, selecting the drive and folder where you want to create the new folder, right-clicking, selecting New Folder, then typing the new folder name.

You created a new folder to serve as the root folder for The Striped Umbrella Web site.

FIGURE 12
Creating a root folder using Windows Explorer

View list arrow will change the views for the file listing

Your drive may differ

Click the drive to select it

striped_umbrella root folder

FIGURE 13

Creating a root folder using a Macintosh

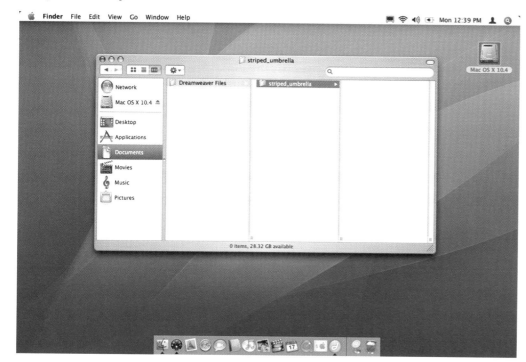

Create a root folder (Macintosh)

1. Double-click the **hard drive icon**, then navigate to the drive and folder where you will create a folder to store your files for The Striped Umbrella Web site.

2. Click **File** on the menu bar, then click **New Folder**.

3. Type **striped_umbrella** to rename the folder, as shown in Figure 13.

   TIP If you cannot type a new folder name, click the current folder name once to highlight it, then type a new folder name.

You created a new folder to serve as the root folder for The Striped Umbrella Web site.

Define a Web site

1. Return to Dreamweaver, then click the **Dreamweaver Site link** in the Create New category on the Start page.

2. Click the **Advanced tab** (if necessary), then type **The Striped Umbrella** in the Site name text box.

   The Basic tab can be used instead of the Advanced tab if you prefer to use a wizard approach.

   TIP It is acceptable to use uppercase letters in the site name because it is not the name of a folder or a file.

3. Click the **Browse for File icon** 📁 next to the Local root folder text box, click the **Select list arrow** (Win) or the **navigation list arrow** (Mac) in the Choose local root folder for site The Striped Umbrella dialog box, click the drive and folder where your Web site files will be stored, then click the **striped_umbrella folder**.

4. Click **Open** (Win) or **Choose** (Mac), then click **Select** (Win).

5. Verify that the Refresh local file list automatically and the Enable cache check boxes are both checked, as shown in Figure 14.

6. Verify that the Links relative to option button is set to Document.

   This is very important to make sure your links work correctly.

You created a Web site and defined it with the name The Striped Umbrella. You then verified that the correct options were selected in the Site Definition dialog box.

FIGURE 14
Site Definition for The Striped Umbrella dialog box

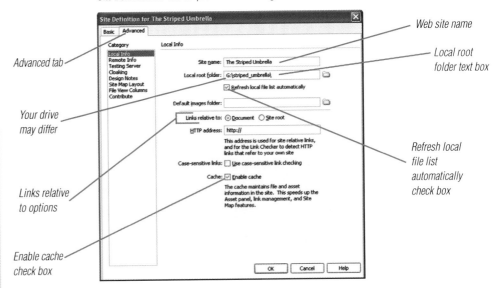

Advanced tab

Your drive may differ

Links relative to options

Enable cache check box

Web site name

Local root folder text box

Refresh local file list automatically check box

Understanding IP addresses and domain names

To be accessible over the Internet, a Web site must be published to a Web server with a permanent IP address. An **IP address** is an assigned series of numbers, separated by periods, that designate an address on the Internet. To access a Web page, you can enter either an IP address or a domain name in the address text box of your browser window. A **domain name** is a Web address that is expressed in letters instead of numbers and usually reflects the name of the business represented by the Web site. For example, the domain name of the Macromedia Web site is *www.macromedia.com*, but the IP address would read something like 123.456.789.123. Because domain names use descriptive text instead of numbers, they are much easier to remember. Compare an IP address to your Social Security number and a domain name to your name. Both your Social Security number and your name are used to refer to you as a person, but your name is much easier for your friends and family to use than your Social Security number. You can type the IP address or the domain name in the address text box of the browser window to access a Web site. The domain name is also referred to as a URL, or Uniform Resource Locator.

FIGURE 15

Setting the remote access for The Striped Umbrella Web site

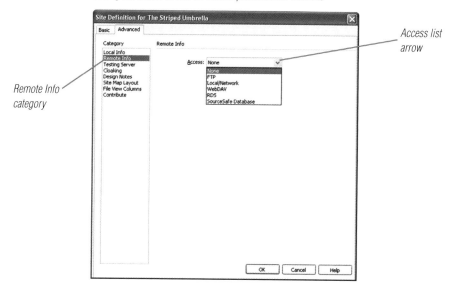

Remote Info category

Access list arrow

Set up Web server access

1. Click **Remote Info** in the Category list, click the **Access list arrow**, then choose the method you will use to publish your Web site, as shown in Figure 15.

   TIP If you do not have the information to publish your Web site, choose None. You can specify this information later.

2. Enter any necessary information in the Site Definition dialog box based on the setting you chose in Step 1, click **OK**, then click **Done**.

You set up the remote access information to prepare you for publishing your Web site.

Understanding the process of publishing a Web site

Before publishing a Web site so that viewers of the Web can access it, you should first create a local root folder, called the **local site**, to house all the files for your Web site. This folder usually resides on your hard drive. Next, you need to gain access to a remote server. A **remote server** is a Web server that hosts Web sites and is not directly connected to the computer housing the local site. Many Internet Service Providers, or ISPs, provide space for publishing Web pages on their servers. Once you have access to a remote server, you can then use the Remote Info category in the Site Definition dialog box to enter information such as the FTP host, host directory, login, and password. After entering this information, you can then use the Put File(s) button in the Files panel to transfer the files to the designated remote server. Once the site is published to a remote server, it is called a **remote site**.

ADD A FOLDER AND PAGES
AND SET THE HOME PAGE

What You'll Do

 In this lesson, you will set the home page. You'll also create a new folder and new pages for the Web site, using the Files panel.

Adding a Folder to a Web Site

After defining a Web site, you need to create folders to organize the files that will make up the Web site. Creating a folder called **assets** is a good beginning. You can use the assets folder to store all non-HTML files, such as images or sound files. After you create the assets folder, it is a good idea to set it as the default location to store the Web site images. This saves a step when you import new images into the Web site.

DESIGNTIP   **Creating an effective navigation structure**

When you create a Web site, it's important to consider how your viewers will navigate from page to page within the site. A navigation bar is a critical tool for moving around a Web site, so it's important that all text, buttons, and icons used in a navigation bar have a consistent look across all pages. If a complex navigation bar is used, such as one that incorporates JavaScript or Flash, it's a good idea to include plain text links in another location on the page for accessibility. Otherwise, viewers might become confused or lost within the site. A navigation structure can include more links than those included in a navigation bar, however. For instance, it can contain other sets of links that relate to the content of a specific page and which are placed at the bottom or sides of a page in a different format. No matter what navigation structure you use, make sure that every page includes a link back to the home page. Don't make viewers rely on the Back button on the browser toolbar to find their way back to the home page. It's possible that the viewer's current page might have opened as a result of a search and clicking the Back button will take the viewer out of the Web site.

Getting Started with Dreamweaver

Setting the Home Page

The home page of a Web site is the first page that viewers see when they visit your Web site. Most Web sites contain many other pages that all connect back to the home page. Dreamweaver uses the home page that you have designated as a starting point for creating a **site map**, a graphical representation of the Web pages in a Web site. When you **set** the home page, you tell Dreamweaver which page you have designated to be your home page. The home page filename usually has the name index.html (.htm), or default.html (.htm).

Adding Pages to a Web Site

Web sites might be as simple as one page or might contain hundreds of pages. When you create a Web site, you need to add all the pages and specify where they should be placed in the Web site folder structure in the root folder. Once you add and name all the pages in the Web site, you can then add the content, such as text and graphics, to each page. It is better to add as many blank pages as you think you will need in the beginning, rather than adding them one at a time with all the content in place. This will enable you to set up the navigation structure of the Web site at the beginning of the development process and view how each page is linked to others. When you are satisfied with the overall structure, you can then add the content to each page. This is strictly a personal preference, however. You can also choose to add and link pages as they are created, and that will work just fine, too.

You have a choice of several default document types you can generate when you create new HTML pages. The default document type is designated in the Preferences dialog box. XHTML 1.0 Transitional is the default document type when you install Dreamweaver and will be used throughout this book. It's important to understand the terminology—the pages are still called HTML pages and the file extension is still HTML, but the document type will be XHTML 1.0 Transitional.

Using the Files panel for file management

You should definitely use the Files panel to add, delete, move, or rename files and folders in a Web site. It is very important that you perform these file maintenance tasks in the Files panel rather than in Windows Explorer (Win) or in the Finder (Mac). Working outside of Dreamweaver, such as in Windows Explorer, will cause linking errors. You cannot take advantage of Dreamweaver's simple yet powerful site-management features unless you use the Files panel for all file-management activities. You may choose to use Windows Explorer (Win) or the Finder (Mac) only to create the root folder or to move or copy the root folder of a Web site to another location. If you move or copy the root folder to a new location, you will have to define the Web site again in the Files panel, as you did in Lesson 3 of this chapter. Defining a Web site is not difficult and will become routine for you after you practice a bit.

Add a folder to a Web site (Windows)

1. Right-click **The Striped Umbrella site** in the Files panel, then click **New Folder**.

2. Type **assets** in the folder text box, then press **[Enter]**.

3. Compare your screen with Figure 16.

You used the Files panel to create a new folder in the striped_umbrella folder and named it assets.

Add a folder to a Web site (Macintosh)

1. Click **Window** on the menu bar, click **Files** to open the Files panel (if necessary), press and hold **[control]**, click the **striped_umbrella folder**, then click **New Folder**.

2. Click the triangle to the left of the striped_umbrella folder to open it (if necessary), then click untitled on the new folder, type **assets** as the folder name, then press **[return]**.

   TIP You will not see the new folder until you expand the striped_umbrella folder by clicking the triangle to the left of the striped_umbrella folder.

3. Compare your screen with Figure 17.

You used the Files panel to create a new folder under the striped_umbrella folder and named it assets.

FIGURE 16
The Striped Umbrella site in Files panel with assets folder created (Windows)

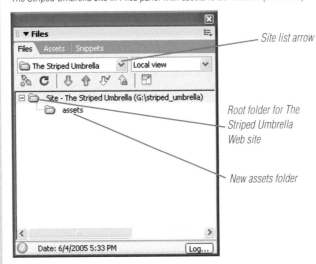

Site list arrow

Root folder for The Striped Umbrella Web site

New assets folder

FIGURE 17
The Striped Umbrella site in Files panel with assets folder created (Macintosh)

Getting Started with Dreamweaver

FIGURE 18

Site Definition for The Striped Umbrella with assets folder set as the default images folder

Default images
folder text box

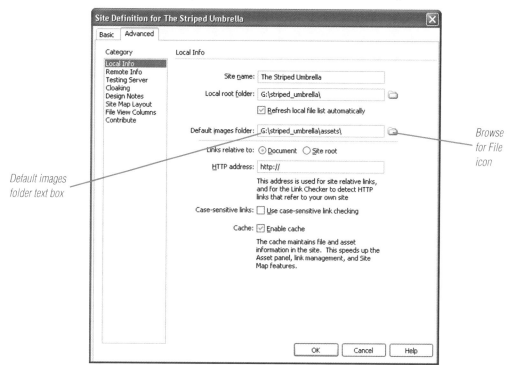

Browse
for File
icon

1. Click the **Site list arrow** next to The Striped Umbrella in the Site text box on the Files panel, click **Manage Sites**, then click **Edit**.

2. Click the **Browse for File icon** 🗀 next to the Default images folder text box.

3. Navigate to the folder where your Web site files will be stored, double-click the **striped_umbrella folder** (Win) or click the **striped_umbrella folder** (Mac), double-click the **assets folder** (Win) or click the **assets folder** (Mac), then click **Select** (Win) or **Choose** (Mac).

   Compare your screen to Figure 18.

4. Click **OK**, then click **Done**.

You set the assets folder as the default images folder so that imported images will be automatically saved in it.

Set the home page

1. Open dw1_2.html from the location where your Data Files are stored.

2. Click **File** on the menu bar, click **Save As**, click the **Save in list arrow** (Win) or the **Where list arrow** (Mac), navigate to the striped_umbrella folder, type **index** in the File name text box (Win) or Save As text box (Mac), then click **Save**.

   TIP If you are asked if you want to update links, click Yes.

   The file extension .html is automatically added to the filename. As shown in Figure 19, the title bar displays the page title, The Striped Umbrella followed by the root folder (striped_umbrella) and the name of the page (index.html) in parentheses. The information within the parentheses is called the **path**, or location of the open file in relation to other folders in the Web site.

3. Right-click (Win) or [control]-click (Mac) the **index.html filename** in the Files panel, then click **Set as Home Page**.

   TIP If you want your screen to match the figures in this book, make sure the document window is maximized.

You opened a file, saved it with the filename index, then set it as the home page.

FIGURE 19
index.html placed in the striped_umbrella root folder

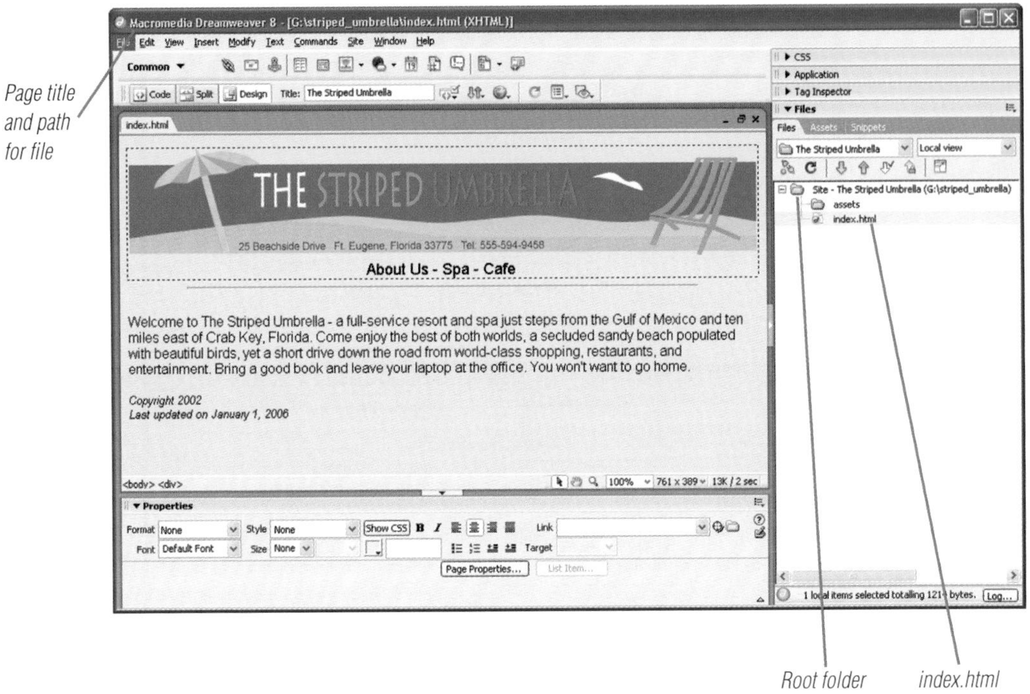

Page title and path for file

Root folder   *index.html*

FIGURE 20

Property inspector showing properties of The Striped Umbrella banner

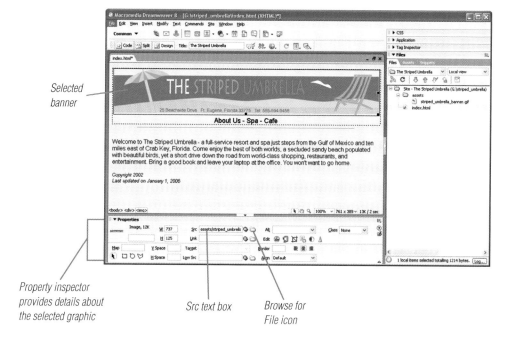

Selected banner

Property inspector provides details about the selected graphic

Src text box

Browse for File icon

1. Click **The Striped Umbrella banner** to select it.

   The Src text box in the Property inspector displays the current location of the selected banner. The banner is linked to the data files folder, which is the original source for this file. You need to copy the banner to your assets folder and reset the link to your site. Otherwise, you will have linking problems when you publish the Web site.

2. Click the **Browse for File icon** next to the Src text box in the Property inspector, click the **Look in list arrow** (Win) or **navigation list arrow** (Mac), navigate to the assets folder in your Data Files folder for this chapter, click **striped_umbrella_banner.gif**, then click **OK** (Win) or **Choose** (Mac).

   The Striped Umbrella banner is automatically copied to the assets folder of The Striped Umbrella Web site, the folder that you designated as the default images folder. The Src text box now shows the path of the banner to the assets folder in the Web site.

3. Compare your screen to Figure 20.

   TIP   If you do not see the striped_umbrella_banner.gif file listed in the Files panel, click the Refresh button ⟳ on the Files panel toolbar.

   Until you copy a graphic from an outside folder to your Web site, the graphic is not part of the Web site and the image will appear as a broken link on the page when the Web site is copied to a remote site.

You saved The Striped Umbrella banner in the assets folder.

Add pages to a Web site (Windows)

1. Click the **plus sign** to the left of the assets folder (if necessary) to open the folder and view its contents, striped_umbrella_banner.gif.

   TIP If you do not see any contents in the assets folder, click the Refresh button **C** on the Files panel toolbar.

2. Right-click the **striped_umbrella root folder**, click **New File**, type **about_us.html** to replace untitled.html, then press **[Enter]**.

   TIP If you create a new file in the Files panel, you must type the filename extension (.html) manually. If you create a new file using the File menu or the Start page, the filename extension will be added automatically.

3. Repeat Step 2 to add five more blank pages to The Striped Umbrella Web site, then name the new files **spa.html**, **cafe.html**, **activities.html**, **cruises.html**, and **fishing.html**.

   TIP Make sure to add the new files to the root folder, not the assets folder. If you accidentally add them to the assets folder, just drag them to the root folder.

4. Click the **Refresh button** **C** on the Files panel to list the files alphabetically, then compare your screen to Figure 21.

You added the following six pages to The Striped Umbrella Web site: about_us, activities, cafe, cruises, fishing, index, and spa.

FIGURE 21
New pages added to The Striped Umbrella Web site (Windows)

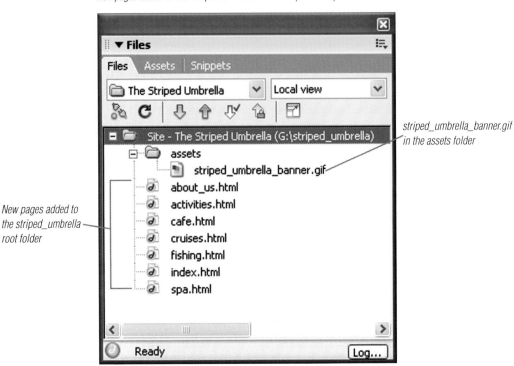

striped_umbrella_banner.gif in the assets folder

New pages added to the striped_umbrella root folder

FIGURE 22

New pages added to The Striped Umbrella Web site (Macintosh)

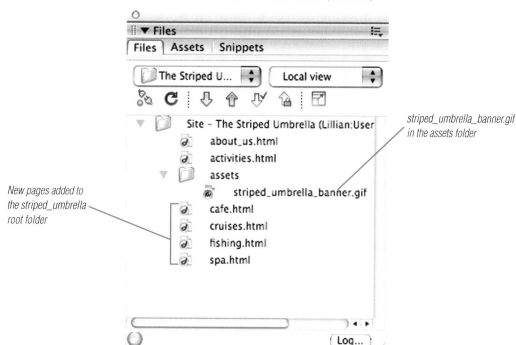

New pages added to the striped_umbrella root folder

striped_umbrella_banner.gif in the assets folder

1. Click **Window** on the menu bar, then click **Files** to open the Files panel, if necessary.

2. Click the triangle to the left of the assets folder to open the folder and view its contents.

   TIP If you do not see any contents in the assets folder, click the Refresh button 🔁 on the Files panel.

3. [control]-click the **striped_umbrella root folder**, click **New File**, type **about_us.html** to replace untitled.html, then press **[return]**.

   TIP If you create a new file in the Files panel, you must type the filename extension (.html) manually.

4. Repeat Step 3 to add five more blank pages to The Striped Umbrella Web site, then name the new files **spa.html**, **cafe.html**, **activities.html**, **cruises.html**, and **fishing.html**.

5. Click the **Refresh button** 🔁 to list the files alphabetically, then compare your screen to Figure 22.

You added six pages to The Striped Umbrella Web site: about_us, activities, cafe, cruises, fishing, spa.

CREATE AND VIEW
A SITE MAP

What You'll Do

 In this lesson, you will create and view a site map for The Striped Umbrella Web site.

Creating a Site Map

As you add new Web pages to a Web site, it is easy to lose track of how they all link together. You can use the site map feature to help you keep track of the relationships between pages in a Web site. A **site map** is a graphical representation of the pages in the Web site and shows the folder structure for the Web site. You can find out details about each page by viewing the visual clues in the site map. For example, the site map uses icons to indicate pages with broken links, e-mail links, and links to external Web sites. It also indicates which pages are currently **checked out,** or being used by other team members.

Viewing a Site Map

You can view a site map using the Map view in the Files panel. You can expand the Files panel to display both the site map and the Web site file list. You can specify that the site map show a filename or a page title for each page. You can also edit page titles in the site map. Figure 23 shows the site map and file list for The Striped Umbrella Web site. Only the home page and pages that are linked to the home page will display in the site map. As more child pages are added, the site map will display them using a **tree structure**, or a diagram that visually represents the way the pages are linked to each other.

DESIGNTIP **Verifying page titles**

When you view a Web page in a browser, its page title is displayed in the browser window title bar. The page title should reflect the page content and set the tone for the page. It is especially important to use words in your page title that are likely to match keywords viewers may enter when using a search engine. Search engines compare the text in page titles to the keywords typed into the search engine. When a title bar displays "Untitled Document", the designer has neglected to give the page a title. This is like giving up free "billboard space" and looks very unprofessional.

Using Site Map Images in Web Pages

It is very helpful to include a graphic of the site map in a Web site to help viewers understand the navigation structure of the site. Using Dreamweaver, you have the options of saving a site map for printing purposes or for displaying a site map on a page in a Web site. Windows users can save site maps as either a BMP (bitmapped) file or as a PNG (Portable Network Graphics) file. The BMP format is the best format to use for printing the site map or inserting it into a page layout program or slide show. The PNG format is best for inserting the site map on a Web page. Macintosh users can save site maps as PICT or JPEG file. The PICT format is the best format for printing the site map and inserting it into a page layout program or a slide show. The JPEG format is best for inserting the site map on a Web page. Though gaining in popularity, PNG files are not supported by older versions of browsers. However, they are capable of showing millions of colors, are small in size, and compress well without losing image quality.

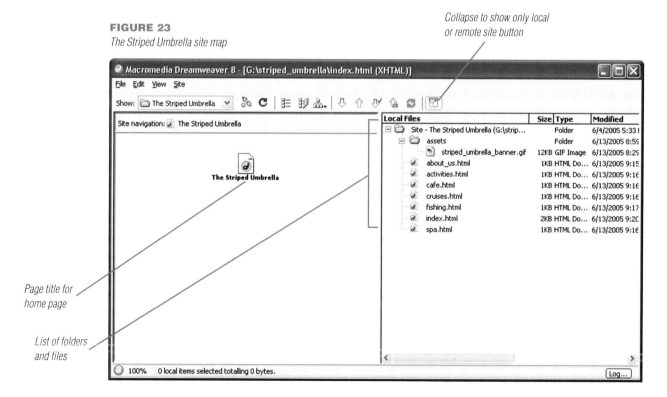

FIGURE 23
The Striped Umbrella site map

Collapse to show only local or remote site button

Page title for home page

List of folders and files

Select site map options

1. Click the **Site list arrow** next to The Striped Umbrella in the Files panel, click **Manage Sites**, click **The Striped Umbrella** (if necessary), then click **Edit** to open the Site Definition dialog box.

2. Click **Site Map Layout** in the Category list.

3. Verify that index.html is specified as the home page in the Home page text box, as shown in Figure 24.

   TIP   If the index.html file is not specified as your home page, click the Browse for File icon next to the Home page text box, then locate and double-click index.html.

4. Click the **Page titles option button**.

5. Click **OK**, then click **Done**.

You designated index.html as the home page for The Striped Umbrella Web site to create the site map. You also specified that page titles display in the site map instead of filenames.

FIGURE 24

Options for the site map layout

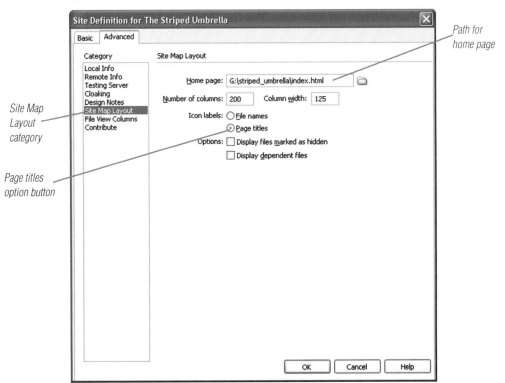

Path for home page

Site Map Layout category

Page titles option button

FIGURE 25

Expanding the site map

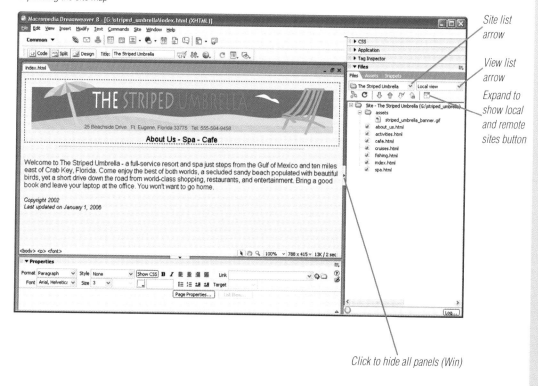

Site list arrow

View list arrow

Expand to show local and remote sites button

Click to hide all panels (Win)

View a site map

1. Click the **Expand to show local and remote sites button** [▣] on the Files panel toolbar, as shown in Figure 25, to display the expanded site map.

   The site map shows the home page and pages that are linked to it. Because there are no pages linked to the home page, the site map shows only the home page.

   | TIP You can drag the border between the two panes on the screen to resize them.

2. Click the **Site map button**, then click **Map and Files** if you don't see the index page icon on the site map.

3. Click the **Collapse to show only local or remote site button** [▣] on the toolbar to collapse the site map.

   The file list appears again in the Files panel.

4. Click **File** on the menu bar, then click **Exit** (Win) or click **Dreamweaver** on the menu bar, and then click **Quit Dreamweaver** (Mac).

   | TIP If you are prompted to save changes, click No.

You opened and closed The Striped Umbrella site map in the Files panel.

Explore the Dreamweaver workspace.

1. Start Dreamweaver.
2. Create a new HTML document.
3. Change the view to Code view.
4. Change the view to Code and Design views.
5. Change the view to Design view.
6. Expand the Application panel group.
7. View each panel in the Application panel group.
8. Collapse the Application panel group.
9. Close the page without saving it.

View a Web page and use Help.

1. Open dw1_3.html from the folder where your Data Files are stored.
2. Locate the following page elements: a table, a banner, a graphic, and some formatted text.
3. Change the view to Code view.
4. Change the view to Design view.
5. Use the Dreamweaver Help feature to search for information on panel groups.
6. Display and read one of the topics you find.
7. Close the Dreamweaver 8 Help window.
8. Close the page without saving it.

Plan and define a Web site.

1. Select the drive and folder where you will store your Web site files using Windows Explorer or the Macintosh Finder.
2. Create a new root folder called **blooms**.
3. Close Windows Explorer or the Finder (Mac), then activate the Dreamweaver window.
4. Create a new site called **blooms & bulbs**.
5. Specify the blooms folder as the Local root folder.
6. Verify that the Refresh local file list automatically and the Enable cache check boxes are both selected.
7. Use the Remote Info category in the Site Definition for blooms & bulbs dialog box to set up Web server access. (Specify None if you do not have the necessary information to set up Web server access.)
8. Click OK, then click Done to close the Site Definition for blooms & bulbs dialog box.

Add a folder and pages and set the home page.

1. Create a new folder in the blooms root folder called **assets**.
2. Edit the site to set the assets folder as the default location for the Web site graphics.
3. Open dw1_4.html from the folder where your Data Files are stored, save this file in the blooms root folder as **index.html**, then click Yes to update the links.
4. Set index.html as the home page.
5. Select the blooms & bulbs banner on the page.
6. Use the Property inspector to browse for blooms_banner.jpg, then save it in the assets folder of the blooms & bulbs Web site.
7. Create seven new pages in the Files panel, and name them: **plants.html**, **classes.html**, **newsletter.html**, **annuals.html**, **perennials.html**, **water_plants.html**, and **tips.html**.
8. Refresh the view to list the new files alphabetically.

Create and view a site map.

1. Use the Site Definition dialog box to verify that the index.html file is shown as the home page.
2. View the expanded site map for the Web site.
3. Show the page titles.
4. Compare your screen to Figure 26.
5. Collapse the site map, save your work, then close index.html.

FIGURE 26
Completed Skills Review

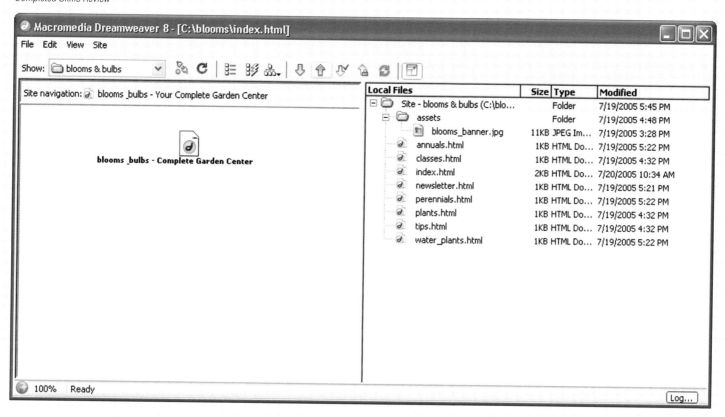

You have been hired to create a Web site for a travel outfitter called TripSmart. TripSmart specializes in travel products and services. In addition to selling travel products, such as luggage and accessories, they sponsor trips and offer travel advice. Their clients range from college students to families to vacationing professionals. The owner, Thomas Howard, has requested a dynamic Web site that conveys the excitement of traveling.

1. Using the information in the paragraph above, create a storyboard for this Web site, using either a pencil and paper or a software program such as Microsoft Word. Include the home page with links to four child pages named **catalog.html**, **newsletter.html**, **services.html**, and **destinations.html**. Include two child pages under the destinations page named **amazon.html** and **kenya.html**.

2. Create a new root folder named **tripsmart** in the drive and folder where you store your Web site files.

3. Start Dreamweaver, then create a Web site with the name **TripSmart**.

4. Create an assets folder and set it as the default location for images.

5. Open dw1_5.html from the location where your Data Files are stored, then save it in the tripsmart root folder as **index.html**.

6. Save the tripsmart_banner.jpg file in the assets folder.

7. Set index.html as the home page.

8. Create six additional pages for the site, and name them as follows: **catalog.html**, **newsletter.html**, **services.html**, **destinations.html**, **amazon.html**, and **kenya.html**. Use your storyboard and Figure 27 as a guide.

9. Refresh the Files panel.

10. View the site map for the Web site.

FIGURE 27
Completed Project Builder 1

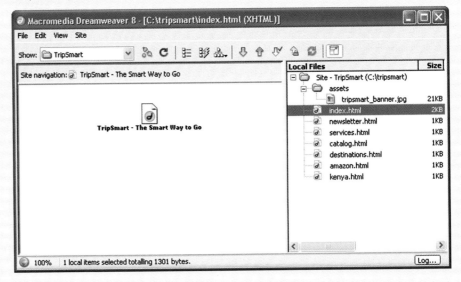

Your company has been selected to design a Web site for "emma's book bag," a small bookstore in rural Virginia. The owner of the bookstore, Emma Claire, specializes in children's books, although she stocks a large variety of other books. She has a small cafe in the store that serves drinks and light snacks.

1. Create a storyboard for this Web site that includes a home page and child pages named **events.html**, **books.html**, **cafe.html**, and **corner.html**. Create two more child pages under the events.html page called **signings.html** and **seasonal.html**.

2. Create a new root folder for the Web site in the drive and folder where you save your Web site files, then name it **book_bag**.

3. Create a Web site with the name **emma's book bag**.

4. Create an assets folder for the Web site and set the assets folder as the default location for images.

5. Open dw1_6.html from the chapter_1 Data Files folder, then save it as **index.html** in the book_bag folder.

6. Save the book_bag_banner.jpg file in the assets folder.

7. Set index.html as the home page, then add the title **emma's book bag** to the page.

8. Using Figure 28 and your storyboard as guides, create the additional pages shown for the Web site.

9. View the site map that displays page titles.

FIGURE 28
Completed Project Builder 2

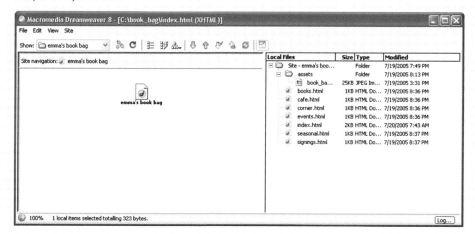

Figure 29 shows the Audi Web site, a past selection for the Macromedia Site of the Day. To visit the current Audi Web site, connect to the Internet, go to *www.course.com*, navigate to the page for this book, click the Online Companion link, then click the link for this chapter. The current page might differ from the figure because dynamic Web sites are updated frequently to reflect current information. If you are viewing the Web page on a screen whose resolution is set to 800 × 600, you will see that the design fits very well. The main navigation structure is accessed through the images along the right side of the page. The page title is Audi World Site.

Go to the Macromedia Web site at *www.macromedia.com*, click the Showcase link, then click the current Site of the Day. Explore the site and answer the following questions:

1. Do you see page titles for each page you visit?
2. Do the page titles accurately reflect the page content?
3. View the pages using more than one screen resolution, if possible. For which resolution does the site appear to be designed?
4. Is the navigation structure clear?
5. How is the navigation structure organized?
6. Why do you think this site was chosen as a Site of the Day?

FIGURE 29
Design Project

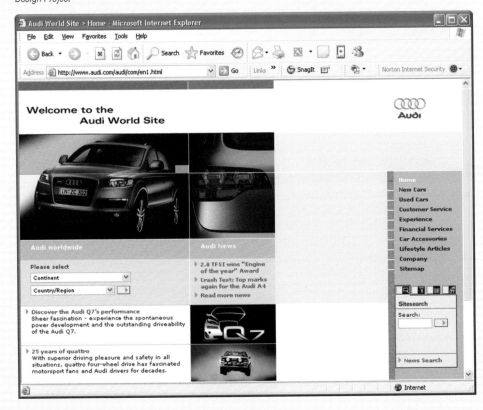

The Portfolio Project will be an ongoing project throughout the book, in which you will plan and create an original Web site without any data files. The focus of the Web site can be on any topic, organization, sports team, club, or company that you would like. You will build on this Web site from chapter to chapter, so you must do each Portfolio Project assignment in each chapter to complete your Web site. When you finish, you should have a completed Web site that would be an excellent addition to a professional portfolio.

1. Decide what type of Web site you would like to create. It can be a personal Web site about you, a business Web site that promotes a fictitious or real company, or an informational Web site that provides information about a topic, cause, or organization.

2. Write a list of questions and answers about the Web site you have decided to create.

3. Create a storyboard for your Web site to include at least four pages. The storyboard should include the home page with at least three child pages under it.

4. Create a root folder and an assets folder to house the Web site assets, then set it as the default location for images.

5. Create a blank page named **index.html** as a placeholder for the home page, then set it as the home page.

6. Begin collecting content, such as pictures or text to use in your Web site. You can use a digital camera to take photos, scan pictures, or create your own graphics using a program such as Macromedia Fireworks. Gather the content in a central location that will be accessible to you as you develop your site.

2

DEVELOPING A
WEB PAGE

1. Create head content and set page properties.

2. Create, import, and format text.

3. Add links to Web pages.

4. Use the History panel and edit code.

5. Modify and test Web pages.

Introduction

The process of developing a Web page requires several steps. If the page is a home page, you need to decide on the head content. The head content contains information used by search engines to help viewers find your Web site. You also need to choose the colors for the page background and the links. You then need to add the page content and format it attractively, and add links to other spages in the Web site or to other Web sites. To ensure that all links work correctly and are current, you need to test them regularly.

Understanding Page Layout

Before you add content to a page, consider the following guidelines for laying out pages:

Use White Space Effectively. A living room crammed with too much furniture makes it difficult to appreciate the individual pieces. The same is true of a Web page. Too many text blocks, links, and images can be distracting. Consider leaving some white space on each page. White space, which is not necessarily white, is the area on a Web page that contains no text or graphics.

Limit Multimedia Elements. Too many multimedia elements, such as graphics, video clips, or sounds, may result in a page that takes too much time to load. Viewers may leave your Web site before the entire page finishes loading. Use multimedia elements only if you have a good reason to.

Keep It Simple. Often the simplest Web sites are the most appealing and are also the easiest to create and maintain. A simple Web site that works well is far superior to a complex one that contains errors.

Use an Intuitive Navigation Structure. Make sure the navigation structure is easy to use. Viewers should always know where they are in the site and be able to find their way back to the home page. If viewers get lost, they may leave the site rather than struggle to find their way around.

Apply a Consistent Theme. To help give pages in your Web site a consistent appearance, consider designing your pages using elements that relate to a common theme. Consistency in the use of color and fonts, the placement of the navigation links, and the overall page design gives a Web site a unified look and promotes greater ease-of-use and accessibility. Template-based pages make this task much easier.

Tools You'll Use

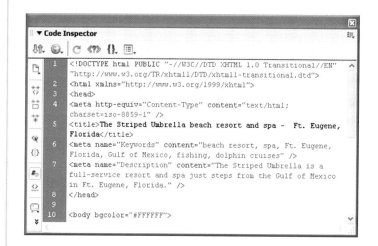

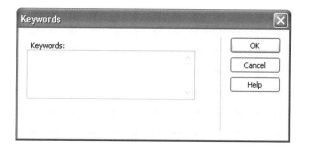

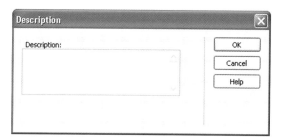

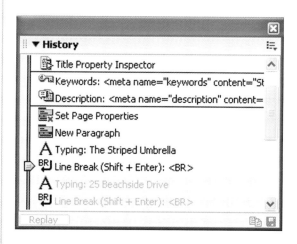

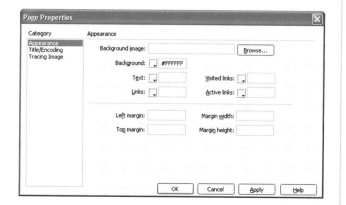

CREATE HEAD CONTENT AND
SET PAGE PROPERTIES

What You'll Do

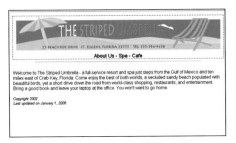

In this lesson, you will learn how to enter titles, keywords, and descriptions in the head content section of a Web page. You will also change the background color for a Web page.

Creating the Head Content

A Web page is composed of two distinct sections: the head content and the body. The **head content** includes the page title that is displayed in the title bar of the browser and some important page elements, called meta tags, that are not visible in the browser. Page titles are not to be confused with filenames, the name used to store each file on the server. **Meta tags** are HTML codes that include information about the page, such as keywords and descriptions. Meta tags are read by screen readers and are also used to provide the server information such as the PICS rating for the page. PICS is the acronym for **Platform for Internet Content Selection**. This is a rating system for Web pages that is similar to rating systems used for movies. **Keywords** are words that relate to the content of the Web site.

DESIGNTIP **Using Web-safe colors**

Before 1994, colors appeared differently on different types of computers. For instance, if a designer chose a particular shade of red in a document created on a Windows computer, he or she could not be certain that the same shade of red would appear on a Macintosh computer. In 1994, Netscape developed the first **Web-safe color palette**, a set of colors that appears consistently in all browsers and on Macintosh, Windows, and UNIX platforms. If you want your Web pages to be viewed across a wide variety of computer platforms, choose Web-safe colors for all your page elements. Dreamweaver has two Web-safe color palettes, Color Cubes and Continuous Tone, each of which contains 216 Web-safe colors. Color Cubes is the default color palette. To choose a different color palette, click Modify on the menu bar, click Page Properties, click the Appearance category, click the Background, Text, or Links color box to open the color picker, click the color picker list arrow, then click the color palette you want. This issue has become much less important today, however, with most computers capable of displaying millions of colors.

A **description** is a short paragraph that describes the content and features of the Web site. For instance, "beach" and "resort" would be appropriate keywords for The Striped Umbrella Web site. It is important to include concise, useful information in the head content, because search engines find Web pages by matching the title, description, and keywords in the head content of Web pages with keywords that viewers enter in search engine text boxes. The **body** is the part of the page that appears in a browser window. It contains all the page content that is visible to viewers, such as text, graphics, and links.

Setting Web Page Properties

When you create a Web page, one of the first design decisions that you should make is choosing the **background color**, or the color that fills the entire Web page. The background color should complement the colors used for text, links, and graphics that are placed on the page. Many times images are used for backgrounds for either the entire page or a part of the page, such as a table background. A strong contrast between the text color and the background color makes it easier for viewers to read the text on your Web page. You can choose a light background color and a dark text color, or a dark background color and a light text color. A white background with dark text, though not terribly exciting, provides good contrast and is the easiest to read for most viewers. Another design decision you need to make is whether to change the **default font** and **default link colors**, which are the colors used by the browser to display text, links,

and visited links. The default color for **unvisited links**, or links that the viewer has not clicked yet, is blue. In Dreamweaver, unvisited links are simply called **links**. The default color for **visited links**, or links that have been previously clicked, is purple. You change the background color, text, and link colors using the color picker in the Page Properties dialog box. You can choose colors from one of the five Dreamweaver color palettes, as shown in Figure 1.

QUICKTIP

Many design decisions are implemented through the use of Cascading Style Sheets, or CSS. We will initially use the Page Properties dialog box to set page properties such as the background color. Later we will learn to do this through the use of Cascading Style Sheets.

FIGURE 1
Color picker showing color palettes

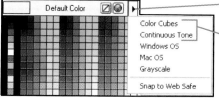

Click list arrow to choose a color palette

Web-safe palettes

DESIGNTIP **Making pages accessible to viewers of all abilities**

Not all of your viewers will have perfect vision and hearing or full use of both hands. There are several techniques you can use to ensure that your Web site is accessible to individuals with disabilities. These techniques include using alternate text with graphic images, avoiding certain colors on Web pages, and supplying text as an alternate source for information that is presented in an audio file. Macromedia provides much information about Web site compliance with Section 508 accessibility guidelines. For more information, visit the Macromedia Web site at *www.macromedia.com/resources/accessibility/*.

Edit a page title

1. Start Dreamweaver, click the **Site list arrow** on the Files panel, then click **The Striped Umbrella** (if necessary).

2. Double-click **index.html** in the Files panel to open The Striped Umbrella home page, click **View** on the menu bar, then click **Head Content**.

   The Title icon and Meta icon are now visible in the head content section, as shown in Figure 2.

3. Click the **Title icon** in the head content section.

   The page title The Striped Umbrella appears in the Title text box in the Property inspector.

4. Click at the end of The Striped Umbrella in the Title text box in the Property inspector, press **[Spacebar]**, type **beach resort and spa, Ft. Eugene, Florida**, then press **[Enter]** (Win) or **[return]** (Mac).

   Compare your screen with Figure 3. The new title is better, because it incorporates the words "beach resort" and "spa" and the location of the resort—words that potential customers might use as keywords when using a search engine.

   TIP   You can also change the page title using the Title text box on the Document toolbar.

You opened The Striped Umbrella Web site, opened the home page in Design view, opened the head content section, and changed the page title.

FIGURE 2
Viewing the head content

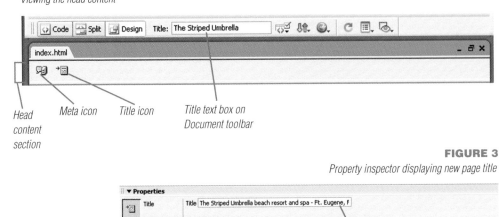

Head content section
Meta icon   Title icon   Title text box on Document toolbar

FIGURE 3
Property inspector displaying new page title

Scroll with arrow key to see the rest of the title

DESIGNTIP   **Planning the page layout**

When you begin developing the content for your Web site, you need to decide what content to include and how to arrange each element on each page. You must design the content with the audience in mind. What is the age group of your audience? What reading level is appropriate? Should you use a formal or informal tone? Should the pages be simple, containing mostly text, or rich with images and multimedia files? Your content should fit your target audience. Look at the font sizes used, the number and size of graphics used, the reading level, and the amount of technical expertise needed to navigate your site, then evaluate them to see if they fit your audience. If they do not, you will be defeating your purpose. Usually the first page that your audience will see when they visit your Web site is the home page. The home page should be designed so that viewers will feel "at home" and comfortable finding their way around the pages in your site. To ensure that viewers do not get lost in your Web site, make sure you design all the pages with a consistent look and feel. You can use templates to maintain a common look for each page. **Templates** are Web pages that contain the basic layout for each page in the site, including the location of a company logo or a menu of buttons.

FIGURE 4

Insert bar displaying the HTML category

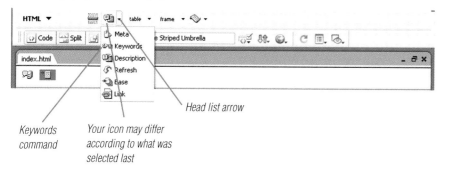

Head list arrow

Keywords
command

Your icon may differ
according to what was
selected last

Enter keywords

1. Click the **Insert bar list arrow**, then click **HTML**.

2. Click the **Head list arrow**, as shown in Figure 4, then click **Keywords**.

   TIP Some buttons on the Insert bar include a list arrow indicating that there is a menu of choices beneath the current button. The button that you select last will appear on the Insert bar until you select another.

3. Type **beach resort, spa, Ft. Eugene, Florida, Gulf of Mexico, fishing, dolphin cruises** in the Keywords text box, as shown in Figure 5, then click **OK**.

You added keywords relating to the beach to the head content of The Striped Umbrella home page.

FIGURE 5

Keywords dialog box

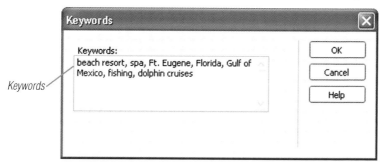

Keywords

DESIGNTIP **Entering keywords and descriptions**

Search engines use keywords, descriptions, and titles to find pages after a user enters search terms. Therefore, it is very important to anticipate the search terms your potential customers would use and include these words in the keywords, description, and title. Many search engines display page titles and descriptions in their search results. Some search engines limit the number of keywords that they will index, so make sure you list the most important keywords first. Keep your keywords and description short and concise to ensure that all search engines will include your site.

Lesson 1   Create Head Content and Set Page Properties

Enter a description

1. Click the **Head list arrow** on the Insert bar, then click **Description**.

2. Type **The Striped Umbrella is a full-service resort and spa just steps from the Gulf of Mexico in Ft. Eugene, Florida**.

   Your screen should resemble Figure 6.

3. Click **OK**.

4. Click the **Show Code view button** [⟨⟩ Code] on the Document toolbar.

   Notice the title, keywords, and description appear in the HTML code in the document window, as shown in Figure 7.

   | TIP   You can also enter and edit the meta tags directly in the code in Code view.

5. Click the **Show Design view button** [⊞ Design] to return to Design view.

6. Click **View** on the menu bar, then click **Head Content** to close the head content section.

You added a description of The Striped Umbrella resort to the head content of the home page. You then viewed the home page in Code view and examined the HTML code for the head content.

FIGURE 6
Description dialog box

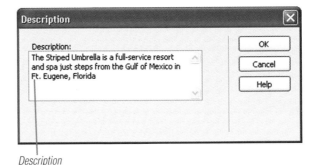

Description

FIGURE 7
Head content displayed in Code view

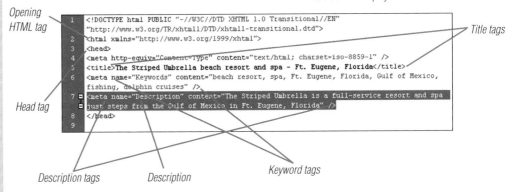

Opening HTML tag

Head tag

Title tags

Description tags   Description   Keyword tags

FIGURE 8
Page Properties dialog box

Background
color box

Hexadecimal
number for
white

Strikethrough
button

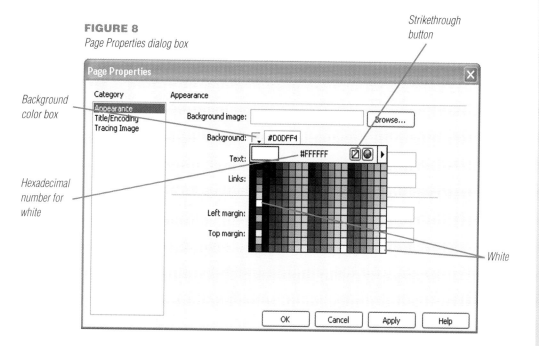

White

1. Click **Modify** on the menu bar, then click **Page Properties** to open the Page Properties dialog box.

2. Click the **Background color box** [↓] to open the color picker, as shown in Figure 8.

3. Click the last color in the bottom row (white).

4. Click **Apply**, then click **OK**.

   Clicking Apply lets you see the changes you made to the Web page without closing the Page Properties dialog box.

   TIP   If you don't like the color you chose, click the Strikethrough button [⊘] in the color picker to switch back to the default color.

   The background color of the Web page is now white. The black text against the white background provides a nice contrast and makes the text easy to read.

You used the Page Properties dialog box to change the background color to white.

Understanding hexadecimal values

Each color is assigned a **hexadecimal value**, a value that represents the amount of red, green, and blue present in the color. For example, white, which is made of equal parts of red, green, and blue, has a hexadecimal value of FFFFFF. Each pair of characters in the hexadecimal value represents the red, green, and blue values. The hexadecimal number system is based on 16, rather than 10 in the decimal number system. Because the hexadecimal number system includes only numbers up to 9, values after 9 use the letters of the alphabet. "A" represents the number 10 in the hexadecimal number system. "F" represents the number 15.

CREATE, IMPORT, AND
FORMAT TEXT

What You'll Do

 In this lesson, you will apply HTML heading styles and HTML text styles to text on The Striped Umbrella home page. You will also import an XHTML file and set text properties for the text on the new page.

Creating and Importing Text

Most information in Web pages is presented in the form of text. You can type text directly in Dreamweaver or copy and paste it from another software program. To import text from a Microsoft Word file, you use the Import Word Document command. Not only will the formatting be preserved, but clean HTML code will be generated. When you import text, it is important to keep in mind that visitors to your site must have the same fonts installed on their computers as the fonts applied to the imported text. Otherwise, the text may appear incorrectly. Some software programs may be able to convert text into graphics so that the text retains the same appearance no matter what fonts are installed. However, text converted into graphics is no longer editable. If text does

Using keyboard shortcuts

When working with text, the standard Windows keyboard shortcuts for Cut, Copy, and Paste are very useful. These are [Ctrl][X] (Win) or ⌘ [X] (Mac) for Cut, [Ctrl][C] (Win) or ⌘ [C] (Mac) for Copy, and [Ctrl][V] (Win) or ⌘ [V] (Mac) for Paste. You can view all Dreamweaver keyboard shortcuts using the Keyboard Shortcuts dialog box, which lets you view existing shortcuts for menu commands, tools, or miscellaneous functions, such as copying HTML or inserting an image. You can also create your own shortcuts or assign shortcuts that you are familiar with from using in other software programs. To view or modify keyboard shortcuts, click the Keyboard Shortcuts command on the Edit menu (Win) or Dreamweaver menu (Mac), then select the shortcut key set you want. The Keyboard Shortcuts feature is also available in Macromedia Fireworks and Flash. A printable version of all Dreamweaver keyboard shortcuts can be downloaded from the Dreamweaver Support Center at *www.macromedia.com/support/ dreamweaver/documentation/dwmx_shortcuts/.*

not have a font specified, the default font will apply. This means that the default font on the user's computer will be used to display the text. Keep in mind that some fonts may not be displayed the same on both a Windows and Macintosh computer. It is wise to stick to the standard fonts that work well with both systems.

Formatting Text Using the Property Inspector

Because text is more difficult and tiring to read on a computer screen than on a printed page, you should make the text in your Web site attractive and easy to read. You can format text in Dreamweaver by changing its font, size, and color, just as you would in other software programs. To apply formatting to text, you first select the text you want to enhance, and then use the Property inspector to apply formatting attributes, such as font type, size, color, alignment, and indents.

Changing Fonts

You can format your text with different fonts by choosing a font combination from the Font list in the Property inspector. A **font combination** is a set of three fonts that specify which fonts a browser should use to display the text of your Web page. Font combinations are used so that if one font is not available, the browser will use the next

one specified in the font combination. For example, if text is formatted with the font combination Arial, Helvetica, sans serif, the browser will first look on the viewer's system for Arial. If Arial is not available, then it will look for Helvetica. If Helvetica is not available, then it will look for a sans-serif font to apply to the text. Using fonts within the default settings is wise, as fonts set outside the default settings may not be available on all viewers' computers.

Changing Font Sizes

There are two ways to change the size of text using the Property inspector. You can select a font size between 1 and 7 (where 1 is the smallest and 7 is the largest), or you can change the font size relative to the default base font. The **default base font** is size 3. For example, choosing +1 in the Size list increases the font size from 3 to 4. Choosing –1 decreases the font size from 3 to 2. Font sizes on Windows and Macintosh computers may differ slightly, so it's important to view your page on both platforms, if possible.

Formatting Paragraphs

You can format blocks of text as paragraphs or as different sizes of headings. To format a paragraph as a heading, click anywhere in the paragraph, then select the heading size you want from the Format list in

the Property inspector. The Format list contains six different heading formats. Heading 1 is the largest size, and Heading 6 is the smallest size. Browsers display text formatted as headings in bold, setting them off from paragraphs of text. You can also align paragraphs with the alignment buttons on the Property inspector and indent paragraphs using the Text Indent and Text Outdent buttons on the Property inspector.

QUICKTIP

Avoid mixing too many different fonts and formatting attributes on a Web page. This can result in pages that are visually confusing and that may be difficult to read.

Using HTML Tags or Using CSS

The standard practice today is to use Cascading Style Sheets (CSS) to handle most of the formatting and placement of Web page objects. In fact, the default preference in Dreamweaver is to use CSS rather than HTML tags. However, this is a lot to learn when you are just beginning, so we are going to disable this preference temporarily until we study CSS in depth. At that point, we will select the default preference by clicking Edit (Win) or Dreamweaver (Mac) on the menu bar, then clicking Preferences.

Enter text

1. Position the insertion point directly after "want to go home." at the end of the paragraph, press **[Enter]** (Win) or **[return]** (Mac), then type **The Striped Umbrella**.

   Pressing [Enter] (Win) or [return] (Mac) creates a new paragraph. The HTML code for a paragraph break is <p>. The tag is closed with </p>.

2. Press and hold **[Shift]**, press **[Enter]** (Win) or **[return]** (Mac), then type **25 Beachside Drive**.

   Pressing and holding [Shift] while you press [Enter] (Win) or [return] (Mac) creates a line break. A line break places a new line of text on the next line down without creating a new paragraph. Line breaks are useful when you want to add a new line of text directly below the current line of text and keep the same formatting.

3. Add the following text below the 25 Beachside Drive text, using line breaks after each line:

   Ft. Eugene, Florida 33775

   (555) 594-9458

4. Compare your screen with Figure 9.

   You entered text for the address and telephone number on the home page.

FIGURE 9

Entering the address and telephone number on The Striped Umbrella home page

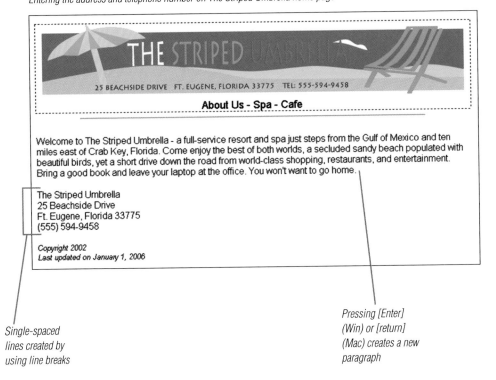

Single-spaced lines created by using line breaks

Pressing [Enter] (Win) or [return] (Mac) creates a new paragraph

FIGURE 10

Formatting the address on The Striped Umbrella home page

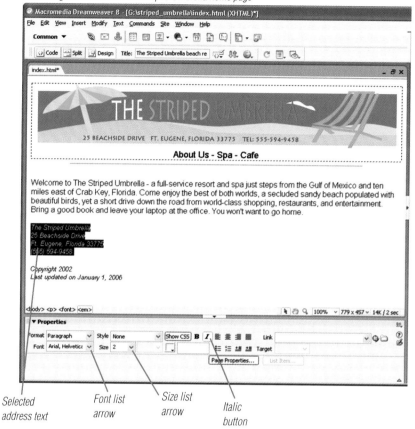

Selected
address text

Font list
arrow

Size list
arrow

Italic
button

1. Select the entire address and telephone number, as shown in Figure 10, then click the **Italic button** *I* in the Property inspector to italicize the text.

   When you have applied the italic style to selected text, the HTML code is <em>.

   TIP To create bold text, the HTML tag is <strong></strong>; to underline text the HTML code is <u></u>.

2. With the text still selected, click the **Size list arrow**, click **2**, then compare your screen to Figure 10.

3. Save your work, then close the document.

You formatted the address and phone number for The Striped Umbrella by changing the font style to Italic and changing the size to 2.

Preventing data loss

When you are ready to stop working with a file in Dreamweaver, it is a good idea to save your changes, close the page or pages on which you are working, and exit Dreamweaver. Doing this will prevent the loss of data if power is interrupted. In some cases, loss of power can corrupt an open file and render it unusable.

Save graphics in the assets folder

1. Open dw2_1.html from your Data Files folder, save it as **spa.html** in the striped_umbrella folder, overwriting the existing file, then click **No** in the Update Links dialog box.

2. Select The Striped Umbrella banner.

   If you update the links, any links to graphics or hyperlinks on the page will remain linked to the data files location. Because you have the banner file in your Web site, the banner will correctly link to your folder, instead.

3. Click the broken link placeholder to select it, click the **Browse for File icon** next to the Src text box in the Property inspector, navigate to the chapter_2 assets folder, click **the_spa.jpg**, then click **OK** (Win) or **Choose** (Mac).

   Because you did not have this graphic in your Web site, it displayed as a broken link. You must use the Browse for File icon to select the source of the original graphic file. The file will automatically be copied to the assets folder of the Web site and be displayed on the page. You may have to deselect the new graphic to see it replace the broken placeholder.

4. Click the **Refresh button** on the Files panel toolbar, then click the **plus sign** (Win) or **expander arrow** (Mac) next to the assets folder in the Files panel, (if necessary).

   A copy of the_spa.jpg file is now in the assets folder, as shown in Figure 11.

   You opened a new file and saved it as the new spa page. You changed the path of the new graphic to The Striped Umbrella assets folder.

FIGURE 11
Graphic file added to The Striped Umbrella assets folder

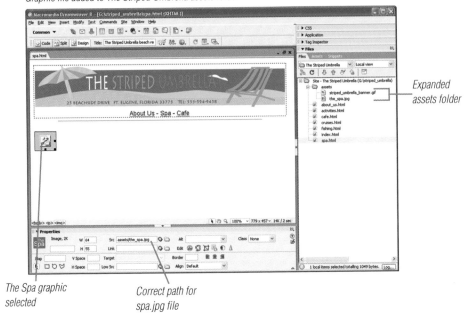

The Spa graphic selected

Correct path for spa.jpg file

Expanded assets folder

Choosing filenames for Web pages

When you choose a name for a Web page, you should use a descriptive name that reflects the contents of the page. For example, if the page is about your company's products, you could name it products.html. You should also follow some general rules for naming Web pages. For example, you should name the home page **index.html**. Most file servers look for the file named index.html to use as the initial page for a Web site. Do not use spaces, special characters, or punctuation in Web page filenames or the names of any graphics that will be inserted in your Web site. Spaces in filenames can cause errors when a browser attempts to read a file, and may cause your graphics to load incorrectly. You should also never use a number for the first character of a filename. To ensure that everything will load properly on all platforms, including UNIX, assume the filenames are case-sensitive and use lowercase characters. Files are saved with the .htm or .html file extension. Although either file extension is appropriate, the default file extension is .html. Use underscores in place of spaces. Forbidden characters include * & ^ % $ # @ ! / and \.

FIGURE 12
Clean Up Word HTML dialog box

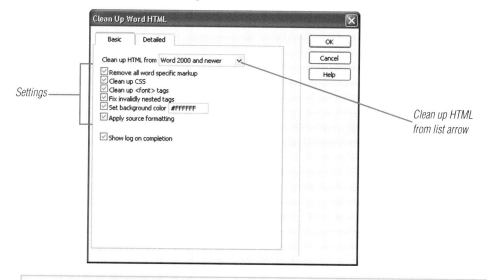

Settings

Clean up HTML
from list arrow

Importing and Linking Microsoft Office documents

Macromedia has made enormous strides in providing for easy transfer of data between Microsoft Office documents and Dreamweaver Web pages. When importing a Word or Excel document, you click File on the menu bar, point to Import, then click either Word Document or Excel Document. Select the file you want to import, then click the Formatting list arrow to choose between importing Text only (unformatted text); Text with structure (unformatted text with structure intact); Text, structure, basic formatting (retains structure and simple HTML-formatted text); and Text, structure, full formatting (formatted text with structure intact and CSS styles) before you click Open. The option you choose depends on the importance of the original structure and formatting. Always use the Clean Up Word HTML command after importing a Word file. You can also create a link to a Word or Excel document on your Web page. To do so, drag the Word or Excel document from its current location to the location on the Web page where you would like the link to appear. (If the document is located outside the Web site, you can browse for it using the Site list arrow on the Files panel.) Next, select the Create a link option button in the Insert Document dialog box, then save the file in your root folder so it will be uploaded when you publish your site. If it is not uploaded, the link will be broken.

Import text

1. Click **Edit** (Win) or **Dreamweaver** (Mac) on the menu bar, click **Preferences**, then click **General** on the left (if necessary).

2. Verify that the Use CSS instead of HTML tags check box is not checked, then click **OK**.

   TIP   It is very important to remove the check mark in the Use CSS instead of HTML tags check box at this time. After we explore CSS, we will restore this default preference. This is not a recommended practice. It is being suggested only to facilitate the learning process for a beginning Web designer.

3. Click to the right of the spa graphic on the spa.html page, then press **[Enter]** (Win) or **[return]** (Mac).

4. Click **File** on the menu bar, point to **Import**, click **Word Document**, navigate to the drive and folder where your Data Files are stored, double-click the **chapter_2 folder** (Win), then double-click **spa.doc** (Win), or navigate to the chapter_2 folder, double-click **spa.doc**, select all, copy, close spa.doc, and paste the copied text on the spa page in Dreamweaver (Mac).

5. Click **Commands** on the menu bar, then click **Clean Up Word HTML**.

   TIP   If a dialog box appears stating that Dreamweaver was unable to determine the version of Word used to generate this document, click OK, click the Clean up HTML from list arrow, then choose a version of Word.

6. Make sure each check box in the Clean Up Word HTML dialog box is checked, as shown in Figure 12, click **OK**, then click **OK** again to close the Clean Up Word HTML Results window.

You imported a Word document then used the Clean Up Word HTML command.

Set text properties

1. Click the **Insert bar list arrow**, click **Common**, then place the insertion point anywhere within the words "Spa Services".

2. Click the **Format list arrow** in the Property inspector, then click **Heading 4**.

   The Heading 4 format is applied to the paragraph. Even a single word is considered a paragraph if there is a hard return, or paragraph break, after it. The HTML code for a Heading 4 tag is <h4>. The tag is then closed with </h4>. The level of the heading tag follows the h, so the code for a Heading 1 tag is <h1>.

3. Click the **Align Center button** ≣ in the Property inspector to center the heading.

   When the paragraph is centered, the HTML code align="center" is added to the <p> tag.

4. Select the words "Spa Services", click the **Font list arrow**, then click **Arial, Helvetica, sans-serif**.

   Because setting a font is a character command, you must select all the characters you want to format before applying a font.

   > TIP You can modify the font combinations in the Font list by clicking Text on the menu bar, pointing to Font, then clicking Edit Font List.

5. With the heading still selected, click the **Text Color button** ☐ in the Property inspector to open the color picker, then click the dark blue color in the third row of the first column (#000066). The HTML code

   (continued)

FIGURE 13

Formatted Spa Services text

THE STRIPED UMBRELLA

25 BEACHSIDE DRIVE   FT. EUGENE, FLORIDA 33775   TEL: 555-594-9458

About Us - Spa - Cafe

The Spa

Spa Services

Our spa services include numerous skin care treatments, body treatments, and Massages. We also have several spa packages that combine several spa services into economical packages.

Skin Care

added when the font color is designated is <font color="#000066">. The tag is closed with </font>.

> TIP You can also type #000066 in the color text box in the Property inspector to select the color in Step 5.

6. Click to the left of the O in Our spa services, press and hold **[Shift]**, scroll to the end of the text, click to place the insertion point after the end of the last sentence on the page, then release **[Shift]**.

7. Click the **Font list arrow** in the Property inspector, click **Arial, Helvetica, sans-serif**, click the **Size list arrow** in the Property inspector, then click **3**.

> TIP To change the size of selected text, use either the Format list arrow or the Size list arrow, but not both.

8. Click anywhere on the page to deselect the text, save your work, then compare your screen to Figure 13.

9. Close the spa page.

You formatted the Spa Services text using the Heading 4 style and the Arial, Helvetica, sans-serif font combination. Next, you centered the heading on the page and changed the text color to a dark blue. You then selected the rest of the text on the page and changed it to the Arial, Helvetica, sans-serif font combination with a text size of 3.

DESIGNTIP **Choosing fonts**

There are two classifications of fonts: sans-serif and serif. **Sans-serif fonts** are block-style characters that are often used for headings and subheadings. The headings in this book use a sans-serif font. Examples of sans-serif fonts include Arial, Verdana, and Helvetica. **Serif fonts** are more ornate and contain small extra strokes at the beginning and end of the characters. Some people consider serif fonts easier to read in printed material, because the extra strokes lead your eye from one character to the next. This paragraph you are reading uses a serif font. Examples of serif fonts include Times New Roman, Times, and Georgia. Many designers feel that a sans-serif font is preferable when the content of a Web site is primarily intended to be read on the screen, but that a serif font is preferable if the content will be printed. When you choose fonts, you need to keep in mind the amount of text each page will contain and whether most viewers will read the text on-screen or print it out. A good rule of thumb is to limit each Web site to no more than three font variations. Using more than three may make your Web site look unprofessional and suggest the "ransom note effect." The phrase **ransom note effect** implies that fonts have been randomly used in a document without regard to style, similar to a ransom note made up of words cut from various sources and pasted onto a page.

ADD LINKS TO
WEB PAGES

What You'll Do

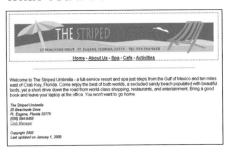

 In this lesson, you will open the home page and add links to the navigation bar that link to the About Us, Spa, Cafe, and Activities pages. You will then insert an e-mail link at the bottom of the page and create page titles for the untitled pages in the site map.

Adding Links to Web Pages

Links provide the real power for Web pages. Links make it possible for viewers to navigate through all the pages in a Web site and to connect to other pages anywhere on the Web. Viewers are more likely to return to Web sites that have a user-friendly navigation structure. Viewers also enjoy Web sites that have interesting links to other Web pages or other Web sites.

To add links to a Web page, first select the text or graphic that you want to serve as a link, then specify a path to the page to which you want to link in the Link text box in the Property inspector. After you add all your links, you can open the site map to see a diagram of how the linked pages relate to each other.

When you create links on a Web page, it is important to avoid **broken links**, or links that cannot find their intended destinations. You can accidentally cause a broken link by typing the incorrect address for the link in the Link text box. Broken links are often caused by companies merging, going out of business, or simply moving their Web site addresses.

In addition to adding links to your pages, you should provide a **point of contact**, or a place on a Web page that provides viewers with a means of contacting the company. A common point of contact is a **mailto: link**, which is an e-mail address that viewers with questions or problems can use to contact someone at the company's headquarters.

Using Navigation Bars

A **navigation bar** is an area on a Web page that contains links to the main pages of a Web site. Navigation bars are usually located at the top or side of the main pages of a Web site and can be created with text, graphics, or a combination of the two. To make navigating through a Web site as easy as possible, you should place navigation bars in the same position on each Web page. Navigation bars are the backbone of a Web site's navigation structure, which includes all navigation aids for moving around a Web site. You can, however, include additional links to the main pages of the Web site elsewhere on the page. The Web page in Figure 14 shows an example of a navigation bar that contains both text and graphic links that use JavaScript. Notice that when the mouse is placed on an item at the top of the navigation bar, a menu appears.

Navigation bars can also be simple and contain only text-based links to the pages in the site. You can create a simple navigation bar by typing the names of your Web site's pages at the top of your Web page, formatting the text, and then adding links to each page name. It is always a good idea to provide plain text links for accessibility regardless of the type of navigation structure you choose to use.

FIGURE 14
Coca-Cola Web site

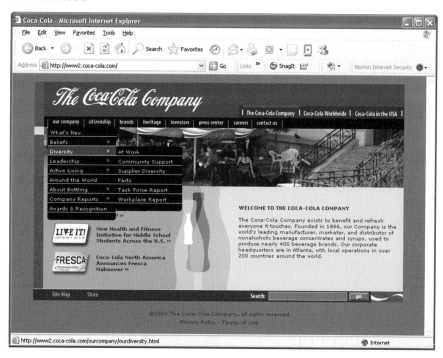

Create a navigation bar

1. Open index.html (the home page).

2. Position the insertion point to the left of "A" in About Us then drag to select About Us - Spa - Cafe.

3. Type **Home - About Us - Spa - Cafe - Activities,** as shown in Figure 15.

   These five text labels will serve as a navigation bar. You will add the links later.

You created a new navigation bar using text, replacing the original navigation bar.

Format a navigation bar

1. Select **Home - About Us - Spa - Cafe - Activities**, click the **Size list arrow** in the Property inspector, then click **None**.

   None is equal to size 3, the default text size. The None setting eliminates any prior size formatting that was applied to the text.

   TIP If your Property inspector is not displayed, click Window on the menu bar, then click Properties to open it.

2. Click the **Format list arrow** in the Property inspector, then click **Heading 4**.

3. Click the **Font list arrow** in the Property inspector, click **Arial, Helvetica, sans-serif** (if necessary), deselect the text, then compare your screen to Figure 16.

   TIP An asterisk after the filename in the title bar indicates that you have altered the page since you last saved it. After you save your work, the asterisk will disappear.

You formatted the new navigation bar, using a heading and a font combination.

FIGURE 15
Viewing the new navigation bar

New navigation bar

FIGURE 16
Formatting the navigation bar

New navigation bar

Format list arrow

Font list arrow

Property inspector

Size list arrow

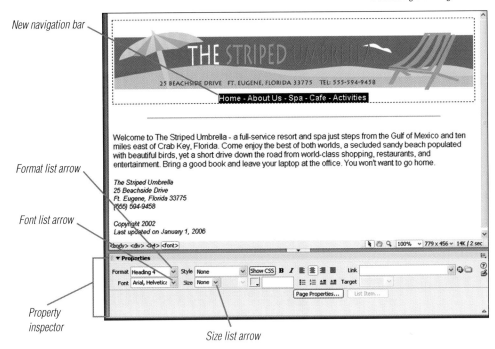

FIGURE 17

Selecting the Home link

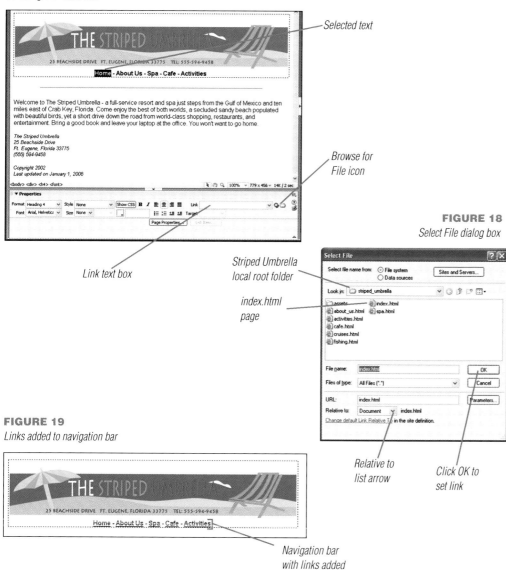

Selected text

Browse for File icon

Link text box

FIGURE 18

Select File dialog box

Striped Umbrella local root folder

index.html page

Relative to list arrow

Click OK to set link

FIGURE 19

Links added to navigation bar

Navigation bar with links added

Add links to Web pages

1. Double-click **Home** to select it, as shown in Figure 17.

2. Click the **Browse for File icon** next to the Link text box in the Property inspector, then navigate to the striped_umbrella root folder (if necessary).

3. Verify that the link is set Relative to Document in the Select File dialog box.

4. Click **index.html** as shown in Figure 18, click **OK** (Win) or **Choose** (Mac), then click anywhere on the page to deselect Home.

   Home now appears in blue with an underline, indicating it is a link. However, clicking Home will not open a new page because the link is to the home page. It might seem odd to create a link to the same page on which the link appears, but this will be helpful when you copy the navigation bar to other pages in the site. Always provide viewers a link to the home page.

5. Repeat Steps 1–4 to create links for About Us, Spa, Cafe, and Activities to their corresponding pages in the striped_umbrella root folder.

6. When you finish adding the links to the other four pages, deselect all, then compare your screen to Figure 19.

You created a link for each of the five navigation bar elements to their respective Web pages in The Striped Umbrella Web site.

Create an e-mail link

1. Place the insertion point after the last digit in the telephone number, then insert a line break.

2. Click the **Insert bar list arrow**, click **Common** (if necessary), then click the **Email Link button** 📧 on the Insert bar to insert an e-mail link.

3. Type **Club Manager** in the Text text box, type **manager@stripedumbrella.com** in the E-Mail text box, as shown in Figure 20, then click **OK** to close the Email Link dialog box.

4. Save your work.

    Notice that the link in the Property inspector for the e-mail link shows mailto: manager@striped_umbrella.com. When clicked, this link will automatically open the default e-mail software on the viewer's computer for him to type his e-mail message. See Figure 21.

    > TIP You must enter the correct e-mail address in the E-Mail text box for the link to work. However, you can enter any descriptive name, such as customer service or Bob Smith in the Text text box. You can also enter the e-mail address as the text if you want to show the actual e-mail address on the Web page.

You inserted an e-mail link to serve as a point of contact for The Striped Umbrella.

FIGURE 20
Email Link dialog box

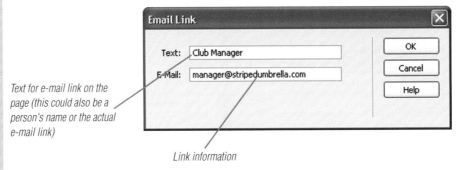

Text for e-mail link on the page (this could also be a person's name or the actual e-mail link)

Link information

FIGURE 21
mailto: link on the Property inspector

mailto: link

FIGURE 22

The Striped Umbrella site map

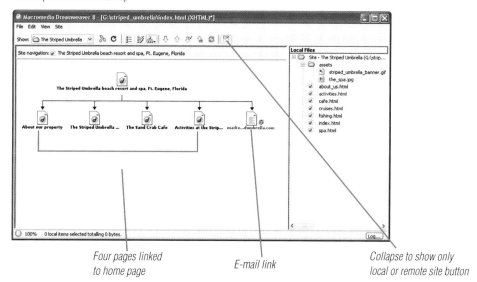

Four pages linked to home page

E-mail link

Collapse to show only local or remote site button

View the linked pages in the site map

1. Click the **Expand to show local and remote sites button** on the Files panel to expand the site map.

The site map shows the home page, the four pages that are linked to it, and the e-mail link on the home page.

> TIP If you don't see the site map on the left window, click the Site Map button, then click Map and Files.

2. Click **View** on the Files panel menu bar, point to **Site Map Options**, then click **Show Page Titles** (Win), or click the **Files panel list arrow**, point to **View**, point to **Site Map Options**, then click **Show Page Titles** (Mac) (if necessary).

3. Select the first Untitled Document page in the site map, click the words **Untitled Document**, type **About our property**, then press **[Enter]** (Win) or **[return]** (Mac).

When you select a page title in the site map, the corresponding file is selected in the Local Files panel. Be careful before entering a new page title in the Site map. If the option is set to file names rather than page titles, you will accidentally change the filename.

4. Repeat Step 3 for the other two Untitled Document pages, naming them **The Sand Crab Cafe** and **Activities at The Striped Umbrella**, as shown in Figure 22.

5. Click the **Collapse to show only local or remote site button** on the toolbar to collapse the site map.

You viewed the site map and added page titles to the untitled pages.

USE THE HISTORY
PANEL AND EDIT CODE

What You'll Do

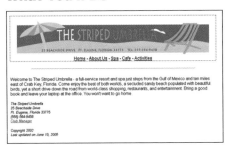

 In this lesson, you will use the History panel to undo formatting changes you make to a horizontal rule. You will then use the Code Inspector to view the HTML code for the horizontal rule. You will also insert a date object and then view its code in the Code Inspector.

Using the History Panel

Throughout the process of creating a Web page, it's likely that you will make mistakes along the way. Fortunately, you have a tool named the History panel to undo your mistakes. The **History panel** records each editing and formatting task performed and displays them in a list in the order in which they were completed. Each task listed in the History panel is called a **step**. You can drag the **slider** on the left side of the History panel to undo or redo steps, as shown in Figure 23. You can also click in the gray bar to the left of a step to undo all steps below it. If you click on the step itself, you will select that step. By default, the History panel records 50 steps. You can change the number of steps the History panel records in the General category of the Preferences dialog box. However, keep in mind that setting this number too high might require additional memory and could hinder the way Dreamweaver operates.

Understanding other History panel features

Dragging the slider up and down in the History panel is a quick way to undo or redo steps. However, the History panel offers much more. It has the capability to "memorize" certain tasks and consolidate them into one command. This is a useful feature for steps that are executed repetitively on Web pages. Some Dreamweaver features, such as drag and drop, cannot be recorded in the History panel and have a red "x" placed next to them. The History panel does not show steps performed in the Files panel.

Viewing HTML Code in the Code Inspector

If you enjoy writing code, you occasionally might want to make changes to Web pages by entering the code rather than using the panels and tools in Design view. You can view the code in Dreamweaver using Code view, Code and Design views, or the Code Inspector. The **Code Inspector**, shown in Figure 24, is a separate window that displays the current page in Code view. The advantage of using the Code Inspector is that you can see a full-screen view of your page in Design view while viewing the underlying code in a floating window that you can resize and position wherever you want.

You can add advanced features, such as JavaScript functions, to Web pages by copying and pasting code from one page to another in the Code Inspector. A **JavaScript** function is a block of code that adds dynamic content such as rollovers or interactive forms to a Web page. A **rollover** is a special effect that changes the appearance of an object when the mouse "rolls over" it.

FIGURE 23

The History panel

Slider

Click in the gray bar next to a step to undo to that step

FIGURE 24

Code Inspector

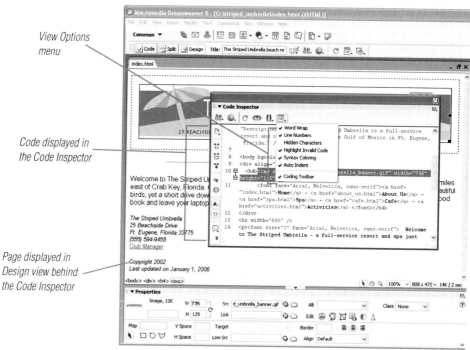

View Options menu

Code displayed in the Code Inspector

Page displayed in Design view behind the Code Inspector

Use the History panel

1. Click **Window** on the menu bar, then click **History**.

   The History panel opens and displays steps you have recently performed.

2. Click the **History panel list arrow**, click **Clear History**, as shown in Figure 25, then click **Yes** to close the warning box (if necessary).

3. Select the horizontal rule on the home page.

   A **horizontal rule** is a line used to separate page elements or to organize information on a page.

4. Select the number in the W text box, type **90**, click the list arrow next to the W text box, click **%**, press **[Tab]**, then compare your screen to Figure 26.

5. Using the Property inspector, change the width of the horizontal rule to 80%, click the **Align list arrow**, then click **Left**.

6. Drag the **slider** on the History panel up to Set Width: 90%, as shown in Figure 27.

   The bottom two steps in the History panel appear gray, indicating that these steps have been undone.

7. Click the **History panel list arrow**, then click **Close panel group** to close the History panel.

You formatted the horizontal rule, made changes to it, then used the History panel to undo some of the changes.

FIGURE 25
Clearing the History panel

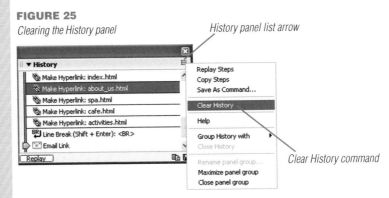

History panel list arrow

Clear History command

FIGURE 26

Property inspector settings for horizontal rule

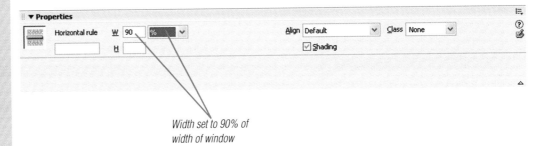

Width set to 90% of width of window

FIGURE 27

Undoing steps using the History panel

Set Width: 90%

Slider

Steps that have been undone

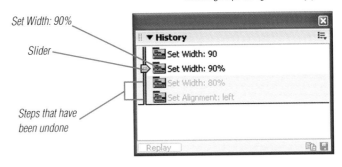

Developing a Web Page

FIGURE 28

Viewing the View Options menu in the Code Inspector

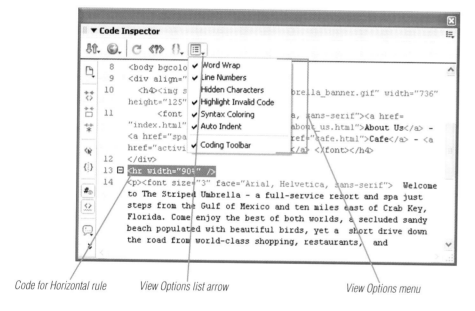

Code for Horizontal rule   View Options list arrow   View Options menu

1. Click the **horizontal rule** to select it (if necessary), click **Window** on the menu bar, then click **Code Inspector**.

   The Code Inspector highlights the code for the horizontal rule.

   TIP You can also press [F10] to display the Code Inspector.

2. Click the **View Options list arrow** on the Code Inspector toolbar to display the View Options menu, then click **Word Wrap** (if necessary), to activate Word Wrap.

   The Word Wrap feature forces text to stay within the confines of the Code Inspector window, allowing you to read without scrolling sideways.

3. Click the **View Options list arrow**, then verify that the Word Wrap, Line Numbers, Highlight Invalid Code, Syntax Coloring, Auto Indent, and the Coding Toolbar menu items are checked, as shown in Figure 28.

4. Replace the 90% horizontal rule width in the code with 80%.

5. Click **Refresh** in the Property inspector.

   After typing in the Code Inspector, you must refresh your changes to see them.

You changed the width of the horizontal rule by changing the code in the Code Inspector.

Use the Reference panel

1. Click the **Reference button** 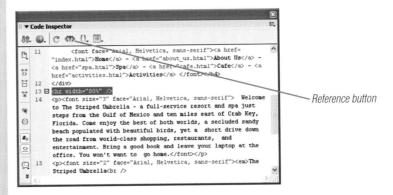 on the Code Inspector toolbar, as shown in Figure 29, to open the Results panel group with the Reference panel displayed.

   TIP   Verify that the horizontal rule is still selected, or you will not see the horizontal rule description in the Reference panel.

2. Read the information about horizontal rules in the Reference panel, as shown in Figure 30, right-click the **Results panel group title bar**, then click **Close panel group** (Win) or click the **Results panel option list** in the Results panel title bar, then click **Close panel group** (Mac) to close the Results panel group.

3. Close the Code Inspector.

You read information about horizontal rule settings in the Reference panel.

FIGURE 29
Reference button on the Code Inspector toolbar

Reference button

FIGURE 30
Viewing the Reference panel

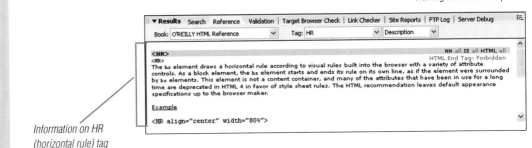

Information on HR (horizontal rule) tag

Inserting comments

A handy Dreamweaver feature is the ability to insert comments into HTML code. Comments can provide helpful information describing portions of the code, such as a JavaScript function. You can create comments in any Dreamweaver view, but you must turn on Invisible Elements to see them in Design view. To create a comment, click the Insert bar list arrow, click Common, click the Comment button, type a comment in the Comment dialog box, then click OK. Comments are not visible in browser windows.

Developing a Web Page

FIGURE 31

Insert Date dialog box

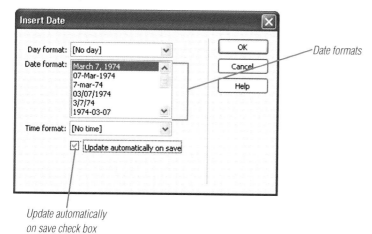

Date formats

*Update automatically
on save check box*

Insert a date object

1. Scroll down, if necessary, to select January 1, 2006, then press **[Delete]** (Win) or **[delete]** (Mac).

2. Click the **Date button** 🗓 on the Insert bar, then click **March 7, 1974** in the Date format text box.

3. Click the **Update automatically on save check box**, as shown in Figure 31, then click **OK**.

4. Click the **Show Code and Design views button** 🔲 Split.

   Notice that the code has changed to reflect the date object, which is set to today's date, as shown in Figure 32. (Your date will be different.)

5. Return to Design view.

You inserted a date object that will be updated automatically when you open and save the home page.

FIGURE 32

Viewing the date object in Code view

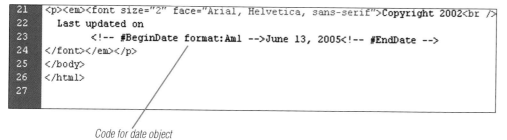

```
21  <p><em><font size="2" face="Arial, Helvetica, sans-serif">Copyright 2002<br />
22     Last updated on
23        <!-- #BeginDate format:Am1 -->June 13, 2005<!-- #EndDate -->
24  </font></em></p>
25  </body>
26  </html>
27
```

Code for date object

MODIFY AND TEST
WEB PAGES

What You'll Do

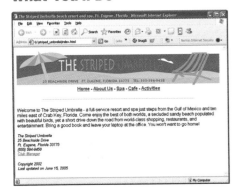

In this lesson, you will preview the home page in the browser to check for typographical errors, grammatical errors, broken links, and overall appearance. After previewing, you will make slight formatting adjustments to the page to improve its appearance.

Testing and Modifying Web Pages

Testing Web pages is a continuous process. You never really finish a Web site, as there are always additions and corrections to make. As you add and modify pages, you must test each page as part of the development process. The best way to test a Web page is to preview it in a browser window to make sure that all text and graphic elements appear the way you expect them to. You should also test your links to make sure they work properly. You also need to proofread your text to make sure it contains all the necessary information for the page and no typographical or grammatical errors. Designers typically view a page in a browser, return to Design view to make necessary changes, then view the page in a browser again. This process may be repeated many times before the page is ready for publishing. In fact, it is sometimes difficult to stop making improvements to a page and move on to another project. You need to strike a balance among quality, creativity, and productivity.

DESIGNTIP **Using "Under Construction" pages**

Many people are tempted to insert an unfinished page as a placeholder for a page that will be finished later. Rather than have real content, these pages usually contain text or a graphic that indicates the page is not finished, or "under construction." You should not publish a Web page that has a link to an unfinished page. It is frustrating to click a link for a page you want to open only to find an "under construction" note or graphic displayed. You want to make the best possible impression on your viewing audience. If you cannot complete a page before publishing it, at least provide enough information on it to make it "worth the trip."

Testing a Web Page Using Different Browsers

Because users access the Internet using a wide variety of computer systems, it is important to design your pages so that all browsers and screen sizes can display them well. You should test your pages using different browsers and a wide variety of screen sizes and resolutions to ensure the best view of your page by all types of computer equipment. Although the most common screen size that designers use today is 800×600, many viewers view at 1024×768. A page that is designed for a screen resolution of 800×600 will look much better at that setting than at a higher one. Many designers place a statement such as "this Web site is best viewed at 800×600" on the home page. To view your page using different screen sizes, click the Window Size pop-up menu in the middle of the status bar (Win) or at the bottom of the document window (Mac), then choose the setting you want to use. Table 1 lists the Dreamweaver default window screen sizes. Remember also to check your pages using Windows and Macintosh platforms. Some page elements such as fonts, colors, table borders, layers, and horizontal rules may not appear consistently in both.

TABLE 1: Dreamweaver Default Window Screen Sizes

window size (inside dimensions of the browser window without borders)	monitor size
592W	
536×196	640×480, default
600×300	640×480, maximized
760×420	800×600, maximized
795×470	832×624, maximized
955×600	1024×768, maximized
544×378	Web TV

Modify a Web page

1. Click the **Restore Down button** on the index.html title bar to decrease the size of the home page window (Win) or skip to Step 2 (Mac).

2. Click the **Window Size list arrow** on the status bar, as shown in Figure 33, then click **600 × 300 (640 × 480, Maximized)**, if necessary.

   A viewer using this setting will be forced to use the horizontal scroll bar to view the entire page. This should be avoided, but very few people view at this resolution anymore.

   TIP   You cannot use the Window Size options if your document window is maximized (Win).

3. Click the **Window Size list arrow**, click **760 × 420 (800 × 600, Maximized)**.

4. Replace the period after the last sentence, "You won't want to go home." with an exclamation point.

5. Shorten the horizontal rule to 75%.

6. Click the **Maximize button** on the index.html title bar to maximize the home page window.

7. Save your work.

You viewed the home page using two different window sizes and you made simple formatting changes to the page.

FIGURE 33
Window screen sizes

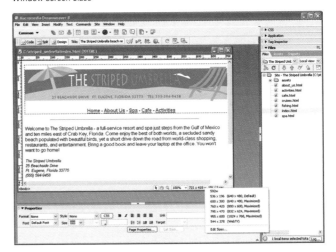

Using design principles in Web page layout

As you view your pages in the browser, take a critical look at the symmetry of the page. Is it balanced? Are there too many graphics compared to text or vice versa? Does everything "heavy" seem to be on the top or bottom of the page, or do the page elements seem to balance with the weight evenly distributed between the top, bottom, and sides of the page? There are many design principles that will help guide you to create a site-wide consistency for your pages. Horizontal symmetry means that the elements are balanced across the page. Vertical symmetry means that they are balanced down the page. Diagonal symmetry balances page elements along the invisible diagonal line of the page. Radial symmetry runs from the center of the page outward, like the petals of a flower. These principles all deal with balance; however, too much balance is not good, either. Sometimes it adds interest to place page elements a little off center or to have an asymmetric layout. Color, white space, text, and graphics should all complement each other and provide a natural flow across and down the page. The rule of thirds—dividing a page into nine squares like a tic-tac-toe grid—states that interest is increased when your focus is on one of the intersections in the grid.

Developing a Web Page

FIGURE 34

Viewing The Striped Umbrella home page in the Firefox browser

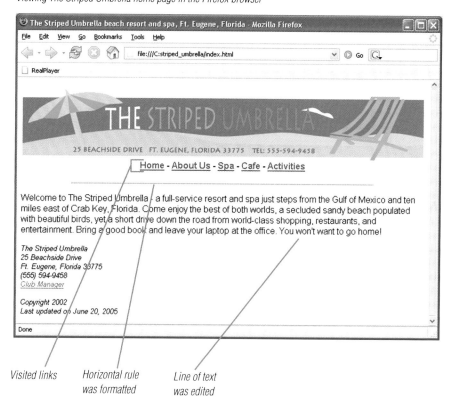

Visited links

Horizontal rule
was formatted

Line of text
was edited

1. Click the **Preview/Debug in browser button** 🌐, on the Document toolbar, then choose your browser from the menu that opens.

   The Striped Umbrella home page opens in your default browser.

2. Click all the links on the navigation bar, then after each click, use the Back button on the browser toolbar to return to the home page.

   Pages with no content at this point will appear as blank pages. Compare your screen to Figure 34.

3. Close your browser window.

You viewed The Striped Umbrella home page in your browser and tested each link on the navigation bar.

DESIGNTIP   **Choosing a window size**

The 640 × 480 window size is not used by many viewers today. The 800 × 600 window setting is used on 15-inch monitors and some 17-inch monitors. Most consumers have at least a 15-inch monitor at their homes or offices, making this window size a good choice for a Web page. However, because more viewers are viewing at a 1024 resolution or higher, even if you are designing to an 800 × 600 window size, you can make sure that the pages will still view well at a higher resolution by placing the page content in a table with a fixed width. This will keep the content from spreading out too much when viewed in a larger window.

Create head content and set Web page properties.

1. Open the blooms & bulbs Web site.
2. Open the index page and view the head content.
3. Change the page title to **blooms & bulbs - Your Complete Garden Center**.
4. Insert the following keywords: **garden**, **plants**, **nursery**, **flowers**, **landscape**, and **blooms & bulbs**.
5. Insert the following description: **blooms & bulbs is a premier supplier of garden plants for both professional and home gardeners.**
6. Switch to Code view to view the HTML code for the head content, then switch back to Design view.
7. Open the Page Properties dialog box to view the current page properties.
8. Change the background color to a color of your choice.
9. Change the background color to white again, then save your work.

Create, import, and format text.

1. Select the current navigation bar and replace it with **Home**, **Featured Plants**, **Garden Tips**, and **Classes**. Use the [Spacebar] and a hyphen to separate the items.
2. Using the Property inspector, apply the Heading 4 format to the navigation bar.

3. Create a new paragraph after the paragraph of text and type the following text, inserting a line break after each line.
   blooms & bulbs
   Highway 43 South
   Alvin, Texas 77511
   (555) 248-0806
4. Italicize the address and phone number lines and change the font to Arial, Helvetica, sans-serif and the size to 2.
5. Change the copyright and last updated statements to size 2.
6. Save your work, then close the home page.
7. Open dw2_2.html and save it as **tips.html** in the blooms & bulbs Web site, overwriting the existing file, but not updating links.
8. Click the broken image link below the blooms & bulbs banner, browse to the chapter_2 Data Files folder, find the garden_tips.jpg in the assets folder of the blooms folder, then click OK to save it in the blooms & bulbs Web site.
9. Place the insertion point under the Garden Tips graphic.
10. Import gardening_tips.doc from the drive and folder where your chapter 2 Data Files are stored, using the Import Word Document command, then use the Clean Up Word HTML command. (*Hint*: The Use CSS instead of HTML tags should be turned off before executing the following steps.)
11. Format all of the text on the page using the following attributes: Font: Arial, Helvetica, sans-serif, Alignment: Align Left, and Style: None.

12. Select the Seasonal Gardening Checklist heading, then use the Property inspector to center the text.
13. Use the Property inspector to format the selected text with a Heading 3 format.
14. Apply the color #003366 (the second color in the third row) to the text.
15. Select the rest of the text on the page except for the Seasonal Gardening Checklist heading, then set the size to 3.
16. Select the Basic Gardening Tips heading, then format this text in bold, with the color #003366.
17. Save your work and close the tips page.

Add links to Web pages.

1. Open the index page, then use the Property inspector to link Home on the navigation bar to the index.html page in the blooms & bulbs Web site.
2. Link Featured Plants on the navigation bar to the plants.html page.
3. Link Garden Tips on the navigation bar to the tips.html page.
4. Link Classes on the navigation bar to the classes.html page.
5. Using the Insert bar, create an e-mail link under the telephone number.
6. Type **Customer Service** in the Text text box and **mailbox@blooms.com** in the E-Mail text box.
7. Open the plants.html page, add a page title called **Our Featured Plants**, then save the page.
8. Open the classes.html page and add the page title **Classes Offered**, then save your work.

Use the History panel and edit code.

1. Open the History panel, then clear its contents.
2. Delete the current date in the Last updated on statement on the home page and replace it with a date that will update automatically when the file is saved.
3. Change the font for the last updated on statement using the font of your choice.
4. Use the History panel to go back to the original font and style settings for the last updated on statement.
5. Close the History panel.

6. Examine the code for the last updated on statement.
7. Save your work.

Modify and test Web pages.

1. Using the Window Size pop-up menu, view the home page at 600 × 300 (640 × 480, Maximized) and 760 × 420 (800 × 600, Maximized), then maximize the document window.
2. View the page in your browser.

3. Verify that all links work correctly, then close the browser.
4. On the home page, change the text "Stop by and see us soon!" to **We ship overnight**.
5. Save your work, then view the pages in your browser, comparing your screens to Figure 35 and Figure 36.
6. Close your browser.
7. Adjust the spacing (if necessary), save your work, then preview the home page in the browser again.
8. Close the browser, then close all open pages.

FIGURE 35
Completed Skills Review, home page

FIGURE 36
Completed Skills Review, tips page

Home - Featured Plants - Garden Tips - Classes

Welcome to blooms & bulbs. We carry a variety of plants and shrubs along with a large inventory of gardening supplies. Our four greenhouses are full of healthy young plants just waiting to be planted in your yard. Our staff includes a certified landscape architect, three landscape designers, and six master gardeners. We offer detailed landscape plans tailored to your location as well as planting and regular maintenance services. We ship overnight.

blooms & bulbs
Highway 43 South
Alvin, Texas 77511
(555) 248-0806
<u>*Customer Service*</u>

©Copyright 2001
Last updated on July 20, 2005

We have some planting tips we would like to share with you as you prepare your gardens this season. Remember, there is always something to be done for your gardens, no matter what the season. Our experienced staff is here to help you plan your gardens, select your plants, prepare your soil, assist you in the planting, and maintain your beds. Check out our calendar for a list of our scheduled classes. All classes are free of charge and on a first-come, first-served basis!

Seasonal Gardening Checklist:

Fall – The time to plant trees and spring blooming bulbs.
Winter – The time to prune fruit trees and finish planting your bulbs.
Spring – The time to prepare your beds, plant annuals, and apply fertilizer to established plants.
Summer – The time to supplement rainfall so that plants get one inch of water per week.

Basic Gardening Tips

You have been hired to create a Web site for a TripSmart, a travel outfitter. You have created the basic framework for the Web site and are now ready to format and edit the home page to improve the content and appearance.

1. Open the TripSmart Web site, then open the home page.
2. Enter the following keywords: **travel**, **traveling**, **trips**, and **vacations**.
3. Enter the following description: TripSmart is a comprehensive travel store. We can help you plan trips, make travel arrangements, and supply you with travel gear.
4. Change the page title to **TripSmart - Serving All Your Travel Needs**.
5. Create a centered navigation bar below the TripSmart logo with the following text links: **Home**, **Catalog**, **Services**, **Destinations**, and **Newsletter**. Place hyphens between each text link.
6. Apply the Arial, Helvetica, sans-serif font combination to the text links.
7. Type the following address two lines below the paragraph about the company, using line breaks after each line:
TripSmart
1106 Beechwood
Fayetteville, AR 72704
(555) 848-0807

8. Insert an e-mail link in the line below the telephone number, using **Customer Service** for the Text text box and **mailbox@tripsmart.com** for the E-mail text box in the Email Link dialog box.
9. Italicize the address, phone number, and e-mail link and format it to size 2, Arial, Helvetica, sans-serif.
10. Link the navigation bar entries to index.html, catalog.html, services.html, destinations.html, and newsletter.html.
11. View the HTML code for the page.
12. View the page using two different window sizes, then test the links in your browser window.

13. View the site map.
14. Create the following page titles:
catalog.html = **TripSmart Catalog**
services.html = **TripSmart Services**
destinations.html = **TripSmart Featured Destinations**
newsletter.html = **TripSmart Newsletter**
15. Verify that all the page titles are entered correctly, then save your work.
16. Preview the home page in your browser, then test all the links.
17. Compare your page to Figure 37, close the browser, then close all open pages.

FIGURE 37
Completed Project Builder 1

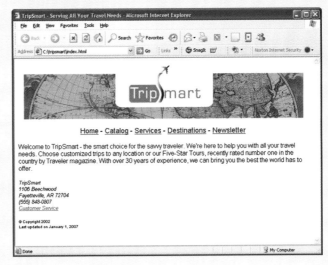

Your company has been selected to design a Web site for emma's book bag, a small bookstore that specializes in children's books. You are now ready to add content to the home page and apply formatting options to improve the page appearance, using Figure 38 as a guide.

1. Open the emma's book bag Web site, then open the home page.

2. Enter a line break after "emma's book bag - a unique bookshop", then add the following sentence: **Store hours - Monday through Saturday from 9:00 til 5:00**.

3. Center the two lines of text.

4. Change the navigation bar to the Heading 5 format.

5. Add the following address below the store hours text using line breaks after each line:
   emma's book bag
   496 Maple Street
   Seven Falls, Virginia 52404
   (555) 958-9684

6. Enter another line break after the telephone number and type **E-mail**, then add an e-mail link using **Emma Claire** for the text and **mailbox@emmasbookbag.com** for the e-mail address.

7. Apply the Verdana, Arial, Helvetica, sans-serif font to the contact information then apply any other formatting of your choice.

8. Create links from each navigation bar element to its corresponding Web page.

9. Replace the date that follows the text "Last updated on" with a date object, then save your work.

10. View the completed page in your default browser, then test each link.

11. Close your browser.

12. View the site map, then title any untitled pages with appropriate titles.

13. Save your work, then close all pages.

FIGURE 38
Completed Project Builder 2

Angela Lou is a freelance photographer. She is searching the Internet looking for a particular type of paper to use in processing her prints. She knows that Web sites use keywords and descriptions in order to receive "hits" with search engines. She is curious about how they work. Follow the steps below and write your answers to the questions.

1. Connect to the Internet, go to *www.course.com,* navigate to the page for this book, click the Online Companion link, then click the link for this chapter to see the Kodak Web site's home page, as shown in Figure 39.

2. View the page source by clicking View on the menu bar, then clicking Source (Internet Explorer) or Page Source (Netscape Navigator or Communicator).

3. Can you locate a description and keywords? If so, what are they?

4. How many keywords do you find?

5. Is the description appropriate for the Web site? Why or why not?

6. Look at the numbers of keywords and words in the description. Is there an appropriate number? Or are there too many or not enough?

7. Use a search engine such as Google at *www.google.com* and search for "photography" and "paper" in the Search text box.

FIGURE 39
Design Project

8. Click the first link in the list of results and view the source code for that page. Do you see keywords and a description? Do any of them match the words you used in the search?

In this assignment, you will continue to work on the Web site you defined in Chapter 1. In Chapter 1, you created a storyboard for your Web site with at least four pages. You also created a local root folder for your Web site and an assets folder to store the Web site asset files. You set the assets folder as the default storage location for your images. You began to collect information and resources for your Web site and started working on the home page.

1. Add the title, keywords, and description. Think about to the head content for the home page.

2. Create the main page content for the home page and format it attractively.

3. Add the address and other contact information to the home page, including an e-mail address.

4. Consult your storyboard and design the navigation bar.

5. Link the navigation bar items to the appropriate pages.

6. Add a last updated on statement to the home page with a date that will automatically update when the page is saved.

7. Edit and format the page content until you are satisfied with the results.

8. Verify that each page has a page title by viewing the site map.

9. Verify that all links, including the e-mail link, work correctly.

10. When you are satisfied with the home page, review the check list questions shown in Figure 40, then make any necessary changes.

11. Save your work.

FIGURE 40
Portfolio Project check list

Web Site Check List

1. Do all pages have a page title?
2. Does the home page have a description and keywords?
3. Does the home page contain contact information, including an e-mail address?
4. Do all completed pages in the Web site have consistent navigation links?
5. Does the home page have a "last updated on" statement that will automatically update when the page is saved?
6. Do all pages have attractively formatted text?
7. Do all paths for links and images work correctly?
8. Does the home page view well using at least two different screen resolutions?

Developing a Web Page

WORKING WITH TEXT
AND GRAPHICS

1. Create unordered and ordered lists.

2. Create, apply, and edit Cascading Style Sheets.

3. Add styles and attach Cascading Style Sheets.

4. Insert and align graphics.

5. Enhance an image and use alternate text.

6. Insert a background image and perform site maintenance.

3 WORKING WITH TEXT
AND GRAPHICS

Introduction

Most Web pages contain a combination of text and graphics. Dreamweaver provides many tools for working with text and graphics that you can use to make your Web pages attractive and easy to read. Dreamweaver also has tools that help you format text quickly and ensure a consistent appearance of text elements across all your Web pages.

Formatting Text as Lists

If a Web page contains a large amount of text, it can be difficult for viewers to digest it all. You can break up the monotony of large blocks of text by creating lists. You can create three types of lists in Dreamweaver: unordered lists, ordered lists, and definition lists.

Using Cascading Style Sheets

You can save time and ensure that all your page elements have a consistent appearance by using Cascading Style Sheets (CSS). You can use Cascading Style Sheets to define formatting attributes for page elements such as text and tables. You can

then apply the formatting attributes you define to any element in a single document or to all of the pages in a Web site.

Using Graphics to Enhance Web Pages

Graphics make Web pages visually stimulating and more exciting than pages that contain only text. However, you should use graphics sparingly. If you think of text as the meat and potatoes of a Web site, the graphics would be the seasoning. You should add graphics to a page just as you would add seasoning to food. A little seasoning enhances the flavor and brings out the quality of the dish. Too much seasoning overwhelms the dish and masks the flavor of the main ingredients. Too little seasoning results in a bland dish. There are many ways to work with graphics so that they complement the content of pages in a Web site. There are specific file formats that should be used to save graphics for Web sites to ensure maximum quality with minimum file size. You should store graphics in a Web site's assets folder in an organized fashion.

Tools You'll Use

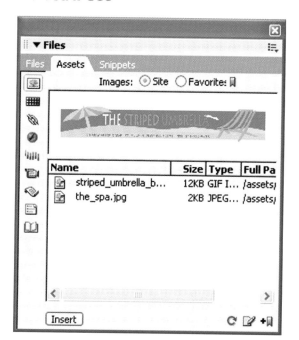

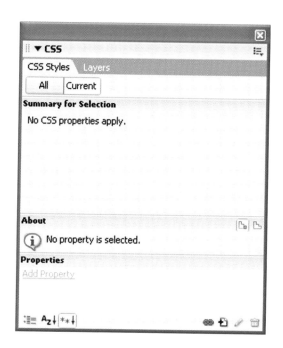

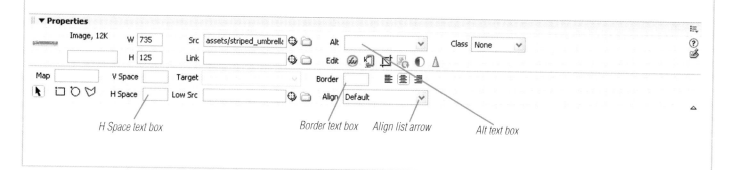

H Space text box   Border text box   Align list arrow   Alt text box

CREATE UNORDERED AND ORDERED LISTS

What You'll Do

Massages

- Sports Massage
  Our deepest massage for tense and sore muscles.
- Swedish Massage
  A gentle, relaxing massage.
- Hot Stone Massage
  Good for tight, sore muscles. Advance notice required.

Packages

- Spa Sampler
  Mix and match any three of our services.
- Girl's Day Out
  One hour massage, a facial, a manicure, and a pedicure.
- Call the Spa desk for prices and reservations. Our desk is open from 7:00 a.m. until 5:00 p.m.

Questions you may have

1. How do I schedule Spa services?
   Please make appointments by calling The Club desk at least 24 hours in advance. Please arrive 15 minutes before your appointment to allow enough time to shower or use the sauna.
2. Will I be charged if I cancel my appointment?
   Please cancel 24 hours before your service to avoid a cancellation charge. No-shows and cancellations without adequate notice will be charged for the full service.
3. Are there any health safeguards I should know about?
   Please advise us of medical conditions or allergies you have. Heat treatments like hydrotherapy and body wraps should be avoided if you are pregnant, have high blood pressure, or any type of heart condition or diabetes.
4. What about tipping?
   Gratuities are at your sole discretion, but are certainly appreciated.

 In this lesson, you will create an unordered list of spa services on the spa page. You will also import text with questions and format them as an ordered list.

Creating Unordered Lists

Unordered lists are lists of items that do not need to be placed in a specific order. A grocery list that lists items in a random order is a good example of an unordered list. Items in unordered lists are usually preceded by a **bullet**, or a small raised dot or similar icon. Unordered lists that contain bullets are sometimes called **bulleted lists**. Though you can use paragraph indentations to create an unordered list, bullets can often make lists easier to read. To create an unordered list, first select the text you want to format as an unordered list, then use the Unordered List button in the Property inspector to insert bullets at the beginning of each paragraph of the selected text.

Formatting Unordered Lists

In Dreamweaver, the default bullet style is a round dot. To change the bullet style to square, you need to expand the Property inspector to its full size, as shown in Figure 1, click List Item in the Property inspector to open the List Properties dialog box, then set the style for bulleted lists to Square. Be aware, however, that not all browsers display square bullets correctly, in which case the bullets will appear as round dots.

Creating Definition Lists

Definition lists are similar to unordered lists but do not have bullets. They are often used with terms and definitions, such as in a dictionary or glossary. To create a definition list, select the text to use for the list, click Text on the menu bar, point to List, then click Definition List.

Creating Ordered Lists

Ordered lists, which are sometimes called **numbered lists**, are lists of items that are presented in a specific order and that are preceded by numbers or letters in sequence. An ordered list is appropriate for a list in which each item must be executed according to its specified order. A list that provides numbered directions for driving from Point A to Point B or a list that provides instructions for assembling a bicycle are both examples of ordered lists.

Formatting Ordered Lists

You can format an ordered list to show different styles of numbers or letters using the List Properties dialog box, as shown in Figure 2. You can apply numbers, Roman numerals, lowercase letters, or capital letters to an ordered list.

FIGURE 1
Expanded Property inspector

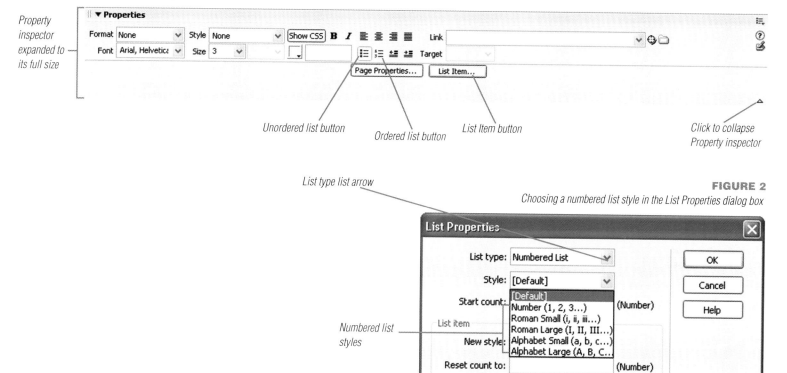

Property inspector expanded to its full size

Unordered list button
Ordered list button
List Item button
Click to collapse Property inspector

List type list arrow

FIGURE 2
Choosing a numbered list style in the List Properties dialog box

Numbered list styles

Create an unordered list

1. Open the spa page in The Striped Umbrella Web site.

2. Select the three items under the Skin Care Treatments heading.

3. Click the **Unordered List button** in the Property inspector to format the selected text as an unordered list, click anywhere to deselect the text, then compare your screen to Figure 3.

   Each spa service item and its description is separated by a line break. That is why each description is indented under its corresponding item, rather than creating a new list item. You must enter a paragraph break to create a new list item.

4. Repeat Step 3 to create unordered lists of the items under the Body Treatments, Massages, and Spa Packages headings.

   TIP Be careful not to include the last sentence on the page as part of your list. It is the contact information.

   TIP Pressing [Enter] (Win) or [return] (Mac) once at the end of an unordered list creates another bulleted item. To end an unordered list, press [Enter] (Win) or [return] (Mac) twice.

You opened the spa page in Design view and formatted four spa services lists as unordered lists.

FIGURE 3
Creating an unordered list

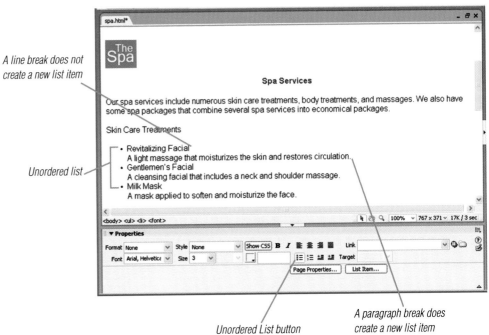

A line break does not create a new list item

Unordered list

Unordered List button

A paragraph break does create a new list item

Working with Text and Graphics

FIGURE 4
List Properties dialog box

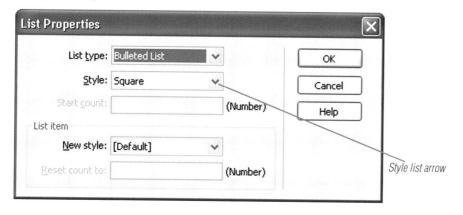

FIGURE 5
HTML tags in Code view for unordered list

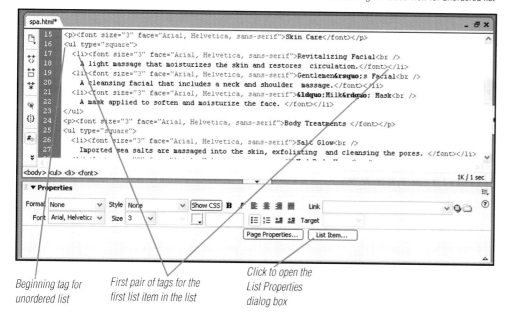

Beginning tag for unordered list

First pair of tags for the first list item in the list

Click to open the List Properties dialog box

Format an unordered list

1. Click any of the items in the first unordered list to place the insertion point in the list.

2. Expand the Property inspector (if necessary), click **List Item** in the Property inspector to open the List Properties dialog box, click the **Style list arrow**, click **Square**, as shown in Figure 4, then click **OK**.

   The bullets in the unordered list now have a square shape.

3. Repeat Step 2 to format the other three unordered lists.

4. Position the insertion point to the left of the first item in the first unordered list, then click the **Show Code view button** on the toolbar to view the code for the unordered list, as shown in Figure 5.

   Notice that there is a pair of HTML codes, or tags, surrounding each type of element on the page. The first tag in each pair begins the code for a particular element, and the last tag ends the code for the element. For instance, the tags <ul></ul> surround the unordered list. The tags <li> and </li> surround each item in the list.

5. Click the **Show Design view button** on the toolbar.

   TIP To ensure that you do not have trouble with your lists being displayed correctly, it is wise to stick to unordered or ordered lists. This assures that you will have backward and forward compatibility with different versions of HTML.

You used the List Properties dialog box to apply the Square bullet style to the unordered lists. You then viewed the HTML code for the unordered lists in Code view.

Create an ordered list

1. Place the insertion point at the end of the page.

2. Use the Import Word Document command to import questions.doc from the chapter_3 folder where your Data Files are stored (Win) or open questions.doc from the chapter_3 folder, select all, copy, then paste the copied text on the page (Mac).

   TIP   Remember to remove the check mark in the Use CSS instead of HTML tags check box in the General section of the Preferences dialog box before importing Word text.

3. Click the **Insert bar list arrow**, click **HTML**, place the insertion point to the left of the text "Questions you may have", then click the **Horizontal Rule button** 🔲 on the Insert bar.

   A horizontal rule appears and helps to separate the unordered list from the text you just imported.

4. Select the text beginning with "How do I schedule" and ending with the last sentence on the page.

5. Click the **Ordered List button** ☷ in the Property inspector to format the selected text as an ordered list.

6. Deselect the text, then compare your screen to Figure 6.

You imported text onto the spa page. You also added a horizontal rule to help organize the page. Finally, you formatted selected text as an ordered list.

FIGURE 6
Creating an ordered list

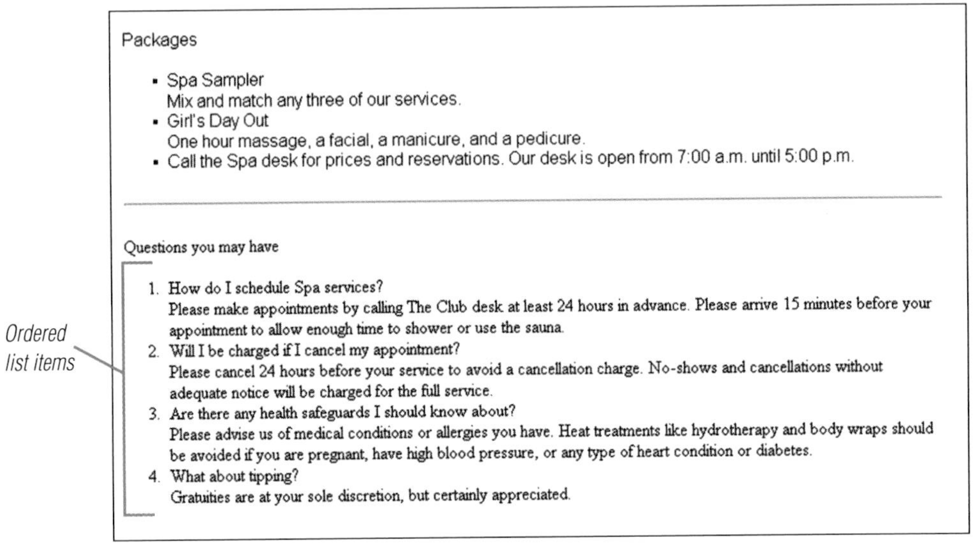

Packages

- Spa Sampler
  Mix and match any three of our services.
- Girl's Day Out
  One hour massage, a facial, a manicure, and a pedicure.
- Call the Spa desk for prices and reservations. Our desk is open from 7:00 a.m. until 5:00 p.m.

Questions you may have

Ordered list items

1. How do I schedule Spa services?
   Please make appointments by calling The Club desk at least 24 hours in advance. Please arrive 15 minutes before your appointment to allow enough time to shower or use the sauna.
2. Will I be charged if I cancel my appointment?
   Please cancel 24 hours before your service to avoid a cancellation charge. No-shows and cancellations without adequate notice will be charged for the full service.
3. Are there any health safeguards I should know about?
   Please advise us of medical conditions or allergies you have. Heat treatments like hydrotherapy and body wraps should be avoided if you are pregnant, have high blood pressure, or any type of heart condition or diabetes.
4. What about tipping?
   Gratuities are at your sole discretion, but certainly appreciated.

FIGURE 7
Spa page with ordered list

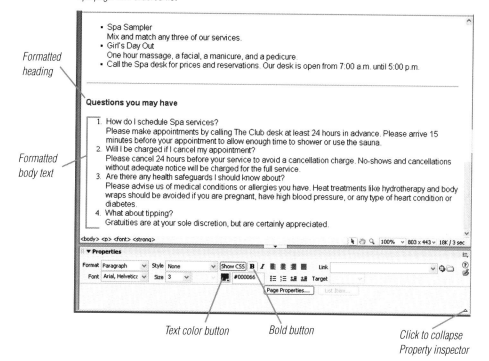

Formatted
heading

Formatted
body text

Text color button   Bold button

Click to collapse
Property inspector

1. Select all the text below the horizontal rule, then change the font to Arial, Helvetica, sans-serif, size 3.

2. Select the heading "Questions you may have", then click the **Bold button B** in the Property inspector.

3. Click the **Text Color button** in the Property inspector to open the color picker, click the first square in the third row, color #000066, deselect, then compare your screen to Figure 7.

   TIP If you want to see more of your Web page in the document window, you can collapse the Property inspector.

5. Save your work.

You applied a new font and font size to the ordered list. You also formatted the "Questions you may have" heading.

CREATE, APPLY, AND EDIT
CASCADING STYLE SHEETS

What You'll Do

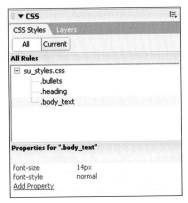

 In this lesson, you will create a Cascading Style Sheet file for The Striped Umbrella Web site. You will also create styles called bullets and heading and apply them to the spa page.

Using Cascading Style Sheets
When you want to apply the same formatting attributes to page elements such as text, objects, and tables, you can save a significant amount of time by using Cascading Style Sheets. A **Cascading Style Sheet (CSS)** is made up of sets of formatting attributes called rules and are either saved with a descriptive name as a separate file or are part of the code for an individual page. External CSS style sheets are saved as individual files with the .css extension and stored in the directory structure of a Web site, as shown in Figure 8. Internal CSS style sheets are embedded in the code on an individual page. CSS style sheets contain **styles**, or **rules**, which are formatting attributes that can be applied to page elements.

You use the buttons on the CSS Styles panel to create, edit, and apply styles. To add a style, use the New CSS Rule dialog box to name the style and specify whether to add it to a new or existing style sheet. You then use the CSS Rule definition dialog box to set the formatting attributes for

the style. Once you add a new style to a style sheet, it appears in a list in the CSS Styles panel. To apply a style, you select the text to which you want to apply the style, then choose a style from the Style list in the Property inspector. You can apply CSS styles to any element on a Web page or to all of the pages in a Web site. When you make a change to a style, all page elements formatted with that style are automatically updated. Once you create a CSS style sheet, you can attach it to other pages in your Web site.

The CSS Styles panel is used for managing styles. If you select a style in the CSS Styles panel, the properties are displayed in the Properties pane, the bottom part of the panel. A drop-down list can be accessed next to each property value to enable you to make quick changes, such as increasing the font size.

You can use CSS styles to save an enormous amount of time. Being able to define a rule and then apply it to page elements on all the pages of your Web site means that you can make hundreds of formatting changes in a few minutes. Be aware, however, that not all browsers can read CSS styles. Versions of Internet Explorer that are 4.0 or lower do not support CSS styles. As for Netscape Navigator, version 6.0 or higher supports CSS styles.

QUICKTIP

You can also use CSS styles to format other page content such as backgrounds, borders, lists, and boxes.

Understanding CSS Style Sheet Settings

If you open a style sheet file, you will see the code for the CSS styles. A CSS style consists of two parts: the selector and the declaration. The **selector** is the name of the tag to which the style declarations have been assigned. The **declaration** consists of the property and the value. For example, Figure 9 shows the code for the su_styles.css style sheet. In this example,

the first property listed for the .bullets style is font-family. The value for this property is Arial, Helvetica, sans-serif. When you create a new Cascading Style Sheet, you will see it as an open document in the Dreamweaver document window. Save this file as you make changes to it.

QUICKTIP

For more information about Cascading Style Sheets, visit www.w3.org.

FIGURE 8
Cascading Style Sheet file created in striped_umbrella root folder

New Cascading Style Sheet file

FIGURE 9
su_styles.css style sheet file

```
1   .bullets {
2       font-family: Arial, Helvetica, sans-serif;
3       font-size: 14px;
4       font-style: normal;
5       font-weight: bold;
6       color: #000066;
7   }
8   .heading {
9       font-family: Arial, Helvetica, sans-serif;
10      font-size: 16px;
11      font-style: normal;
12      font-weight: bold;
13      color: #000066;
14      text-align: center;
15  }
16  .body_text {
17      font-family: Arial, Helvetica, sans-serif;
18      font-size: 14px;
19      font-style: normal;
20  }
21
```

Create a Cascading Style Sheet and a style

1. Click **Edit** (Win) or **Dreamweaver** (Mac) on the menu bar, click **Preferences**, click the **General category**, if necessary, click the **Use CSS instead of HTML tags check box**, then click **OK** to turn this default option back on.

   From this point forward, we will use CSS rather than HTML tags to format text. The Property inspector font sizes will be shown in pixels rather than HTML text sizes, as shown in Figure 10.

2. Expand the CSS panel group, then click the **CSS Styles panel tab** (if necessary).

3. Click the **Switch to All (Document) Mode button** , click the **New CSS Rule button** in the CSS Styles panel to open the New CSS Rule dialog box, verify that the Class option button is selected, then type **bullets** in the Name text box.

   TIP Class names are preceded by a period. If you don't enter a period when you type the name, Dreamweaver will add the period for you.

4. Click the **Define in list arrow**, click **(New Style Sheet File)**, if necessary, compare your screen with Figure 11, then click **OK**.

5. Type **su_styles** in the File name text box (Win) or the Save As text box (Mac), then click **Save** to open the CSS Rule Definition for .bullets in su_styles.css dialog box.

   The .bullets rule will be stored within the su_styles.css file.

(continued)

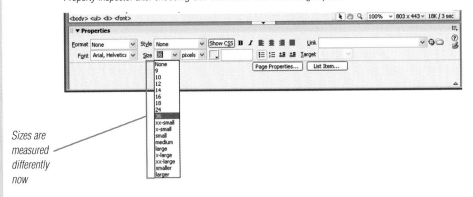

Sizes are measured differently now

FIGURE 11
New CSS Rule dialog box

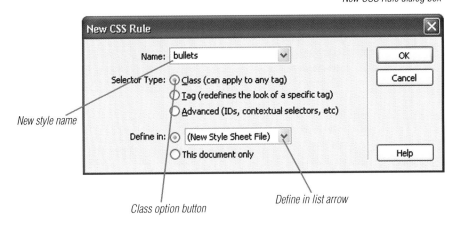

New style name

Class option button

Define in list arrow

Working with Text and Graphics

FIGURE 12

CSS Rule Definition for .bullets in su_styles.css dialog box

Type category selected

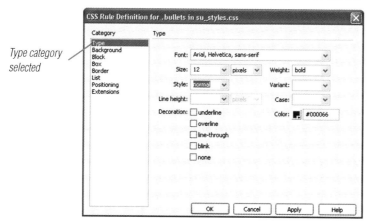

FIGURE 13

CSS Styles panel with .bullets style added

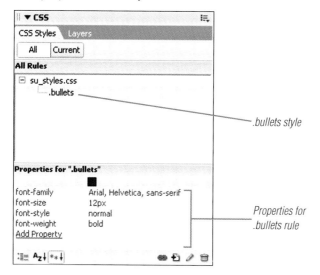

.bullets style

Properties for .bullets rule

6. Verify that Type is selected in the Category list, set the Font to Arial, Helvetica, sans-serif, set the Size to 12 pixels, set the Weight to bold, set the Color to #000066, set the Style to normal, compare your screen to Figure 12, then click **OK**.

7. Click the **plus sign** (Win) or the **expander arrow** (Mac) next to su_styles.css in the CSS Styles panel (if necessary) to list the .bullets rule.

   The CSS rule named .bullets appears in the CSS Styles panel, as shown in Figure 13.

You created a Cascading Style Sheet file named su_styles.css and a rule called .bullets.

Apply a Cascading Style Sheet

1. Click **View** on the menu bar, point to **Toolbars**, then click **Style Rendering**.

2. Verify that the **Toggle Displaying of CSS Styles button** on the Style Rendering toolbar is activated, as shown in Figure 14.

   The Toggle Displaying of CSS Styles button can be used to see how your styles are affecting your page.

3. Select the text "Revitalizing Facial" as shown in Figure 15, then use the Property inspector to set the Font to Default Font, the Size to None, and the Style to bullets.

   TIP   Before you apply a style to selected text, you need to remove all formatting attributes such as font and color from it, or the style will not be applied correctly.

4. Repeat Step 1 to apply the bullets style to each of the spa services names in the unordered lists, then compare your screen to Figure 16.

You applied the bullets style to each item in the Spa Services category lists.

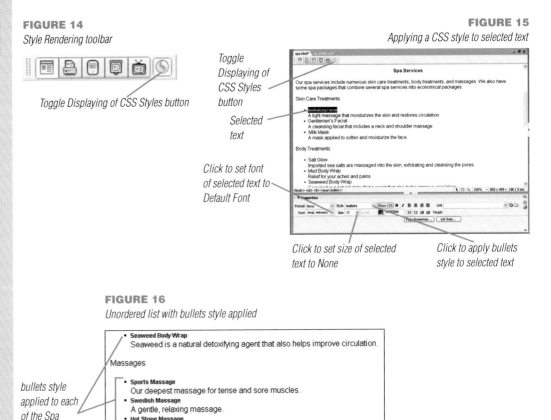

FIGURE 14
Style Rendering toolbar

Toggle Displaying of CSS Styles button

FIGURE 15
Applying a CSS style to selected text

Toggle Displaying of CSS Styles button

Selected text

Click to set font of selected text to Default Font

Click to set size of selected text to None

Click to apply bullets style to selected text

FIGURE 16
Unordered list with bullets style applied

bullets style applied to each of the Spa Services items

Using the Style Rendering toolbar

The Style Rendering toolbar is a new Dreamweaver 8 feature. It can be displayed by clicking View on the menu bar, pointing to Toolbars, then clicking Style Rendering, when a page is open. The buttons on the Style Rendering toolbar allow you to render your page as different media types, such as print or handheld. The last button on the toolbar is the Toggle Displaying of CSS Styles button. Its purpose is to show you how styles applied to your page will display. It works independently from the other buttons and acts as a toggle between viewing and not viewing the styles.

FIGURE 17
Editing a CSS style

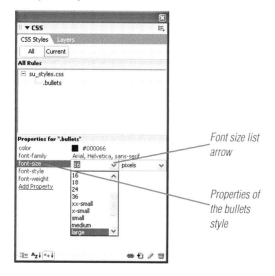

Font size list arrow

Properties of the bullets style

FIGURE 18
Viewing the changes made to the bullets style

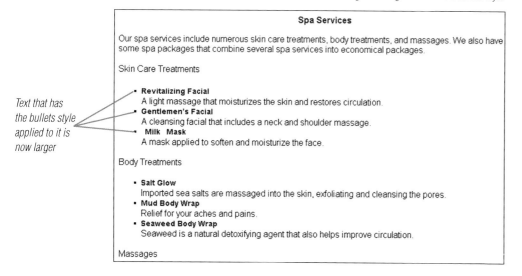

Text that has the bullets style applied to it is now larger

1. Click **.bullets** in the CSS Styles panel.

   The style's properties and values are displayed in the Properties pane, the bottom part of the CSS Styles panel, as shown in Figure 17. You can also click the **Edit Style button** ✎ in the CSS Styles panel to open the CSS Rule Definition for .bullets dialog box.

   TIP Click the plus sign (Win) or expander arrow (Mac) to the left of su_styles.css in the CSS Styles panel if you do not see .bullets. Click the plus sign (Win) or expander arrow (Mac) to the left of <style> if you do not see su_styles.css

2. Click **12px** in the CSS Styles panel, click the **font-size list arrow**, click **14**, then compare your screen to Figure 18.

   The text is much bigger than before, reflecting the changes you made to the bullets style.

   TIP If you position the insertion point in text that has a CSS style applied to it, that style is displayed in the Style text box on the Property inspector.

You edited the bullets style to change the font size to 14 pixels. You then viewed the results of the edited style in the unordered list.

ADD STYLES AND ATTACH
CASCADING STYLE SHEETS

What You'll Do

 In this lesson, you will add a style to a Cascading Style Sheet. You will then attach the style sheet file to the index page and apply one of the styles to text on the page.

Understanding External and Embedded Style Sheets

When you are first learning about Cascading Style Sheets, the terminology can be very confusing. In the last lesson, you learned that external style sheets are a separate file in a Web site saved with the .css file extension. You also learned that Cascading Style Sheets can be part of an html file, rather than a separate file. These are called embedded style sheets. External CSS files are created by the Web designer. Embedded style sheets are created automatically by Dreamweaver when the Preference is set to Use CSS instead of HTML tags. When this preference is set, any formatting choices you make using the Property inspector will automatically create a style. The code for these styles will reside in the head content for that page. These styles will be named style1, style2, etc. You can rename the styles as they are created to make them more recognizable for you to use such as body, heading, or address. Embedded style sheets apply only to a single page. Remember that style sheets can be used to format much more than text objects. They can be used to set the page background, link properties, tables, or almost any object on the page. Figure 19 shows the code for some embedded styles. The code resides in the head content of the Web page.

When you have several pages in a Web site, you will probably want to use the same CSS style sheet for each page to ensure that all your elements have a consistent appearance. To attach a style sheet to another document, click the Attach Style Sheet button on the CSS Styles panel to open the Attach External Style Sheet dialog box, make sure the Add as Link option is selected, browse to locate the file you want to attach, then click OK. The styles contained in the attached style sheet will appear in the CSS Styles panel, and you can use them to apply styles to text on the page. External style sheets can be attached, or linked, to any page. This is an extremely powerful tool. If you decide to make a change in a style, it will automatically be made to every object that it formats.

FIGURE 19

Code for embedded styles shown in Code view

```
1   <!DOCTYPE html PUBLIC "-//W3C//DTD XHTML 1.0 Transitional//EN"
    "http://www.w3.org/TR/xhtml1/DTD/xhtml1-transitional.dtd">
2   <html xmlns="http://www.w3.org/1999/xhtml">
3   <head>
4   <meta http-equiv="Content-Type" content="text/html; charset=iso-8859-1" />
5   <title>Welcome to the Striped Umbrella</title>
6   <style type="text/css">
7   <!--
8   .style1 {
9       font-size: 18px;
10      font-family: Arial, Helvetica, sans-serif;
11  }
12  .style2 {
13      font-family: Verdana, Arial, Helvetica, sans-serif;
14      font-size: 16px;
15  }
16  body {
17      background-color: #FFFFFF;
18  }
19  a:link {
20      color: #0033CC;
21  }
22  -->
23  </style>
24  </head>
```

Add a style to a Cascading Style Sheet

1. Click the **New CSS Rule button** [+] in the CSS Styles Panel.

2. Type **heading** in the Name text box, as shown in Figure 20, then click **OK**.

3. Set the Font to Arial, Helvetica, sans-serif, set the Size to 16, set the Style to normal, set the Weight to bold, set the Color to #000066, compare your screen to Figure 21, then click **OK**.

4. Click the **Edit Style button** [✎].

5. Click the **Block category** in the CSS Rule Definition for .heading in su_styles.css dialog box, click the **Text align list arrow**, click **center**, as shown in Figure 22, then click **OK**.

6. Select the heading "Spa Services" then use the Property inspector to set the Format to None and the Font to Default Font.

7. With the heading still selected, click the **Text Color button** [▢] to open the color picker, then click the **Strikethrough button** [▨].

8. Click the **Style list arrow** in the Property inspector, then click **heading** to apply it to the Spa Services heading.

9. Repeat Steps 1 through 3 to add another style called **body_text** with the Arial, Helvetica, sans-serif font, size 14, and normal style.

10. Repeat Steps 5 through 7 to apply the body_text style to the rest of the text on the page except for the text that already has the bullets style applied to it and the text "Questions you may have".

FIGURE 20

Adding a style to a CSS style sheet

New style name

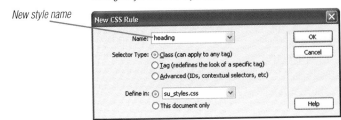

FIGURE 21

Formatting options for heading style

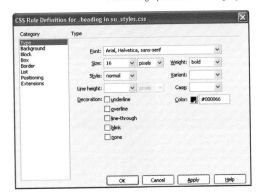

FIGURE 22

Setting text alignment for heading style

Block category selected

Text align list arrow

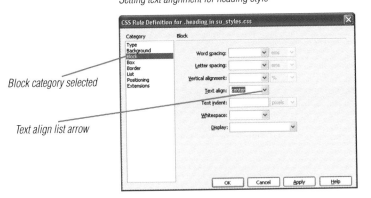

Working with Text and Graphics

FIGURE 23

Attaching a style sheet to a page

Link option button

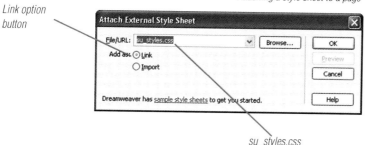

su_styles.css

FIGURE 24

Viewing the code to link the CSS style sheet file

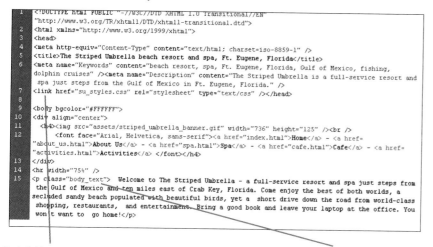

Code linking external style sheet file to the index page   Code that applies the body_text style to the paragraph

11. Click **File** on the menu bar, then click **Save All**, to save both the spa page and the su_styles.css file.

> TIP You must save the open su_styles.css file after editing it, or you will lose your changes.

You added two new styles called heading and body_text to the su_styles.css file. You then applied the two styles to selected text.

Attach a style sheet

1. Close the spa page and open the index page.

2. Click the **Attach Style Sheet button** on the CSS Styles panel.

3. Click the **Link option button**, if necessary, as shown in Figure 23, then click **OK**.

4. Select the paragraph of text and set the Font to Default and the Size to None to clear prior formatting.

5. Click the **Style list arrow**, then click **body_text**.

6. Click the **Show Code view button** and view the code that links the su_styles.css file to the index page as shown in Figure 24.

7. Click the **Show Design view button**, then save your work.

You attached the su_styles.css file to the index.html page.

INSERT AND ALIGN
GRAPHICS

What You'll Do

In this lesson, you will insert five graphics on the about us page in The Striped Umbrella Web site. You will then stagger the alignment of the images on the page to make the page more visually appealing.

Understanding Graphic File Formats

When you add graphics to a Web page, it's important to choose the appropriate graphic file format. The three primary graphic file formats used in Web pages are **GIF** (Graphics Interchange Format), **JPEG** (Joint Photographic Experts Group), and **PNG** (Portable Network Graphics). GIF files download very quickly, making them ideal to use on Web pages. Though limited in the number of colors they can represent, GIF files have the ability to show transparent areas. JPEG files can display many colors. Because they often contain many shades of the same color, photographs are often saved in JPEG format. Files saved with the PNG format share advantages of both GIFs and JPEGs, but are not universally recognized by older browsers.

> QUICKTIP
>
> The status bar displays the download time for the page. Each time you add a new graphic to the page, you can see how much additional time is added to the total download time.

Understanding the Assets Panel

When you add a graphic to a Web site, it is automatically added to the Assets panel. The **Assets panel**, located in the Files panel group, displays all the assets in a Web site. The Assets panel contains nine category buttons that you use to view your assets by category. These include Images, Colors, URLs, Flash, Shockwave, Movies, Scripts, Templates, and Library. To view a particular type of asset, click the appropriate category button. The Assets panel is split into two panes. When you click the Images button, as shown in Figure 25, the lower pane displays a list of all the images in your site and contains four columns. The top pane displays a thumbnail of the selected image in the list. You can view assets in each category in two ways. You can use the Site option button to view all the assets in a Web site, or you can use the Favorites option button to view those assets that you have designated as **favorites**, or assets that you expect to use repeatedly while you work on the site. You can use the Assets panel to add an asset to a Web page by dragging the asset from the Assets panel to the page or by using the Insert button on the Assets panel.

Aligning Images

When you insert an image on a Web page, you need to position it in relation to other elements on the page. Positioning an image is referred to as **aligning** an image. By default, when you insert an image in a paragraph, its bottom edge aligns with the baseline of the first line of text or any other element in the same paragraph. When you select an image, the Align text box in the Property inspector displays the

alignment setting for the image. You can change the alignment setting using the options in the Align menu in the Property inspector.

FIGURE 25
The Assets panel

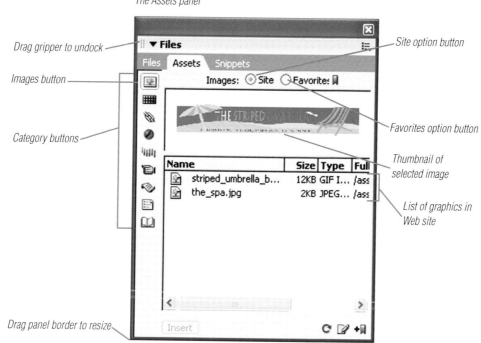

Drag gripper to undock

Images button

Category buttons

Drag panel border to resize

Site option button

Favorites option button

Thumbnail of selected image

List of graphics in Web site

Insert a graphic

1. Open dw3_1.html from the chapter_3 folder where your Data Files are stored, then save it as **about_us.html** in the striped_umbrella root folder.

2. Click **Yes** (Win) or **Replace** (Mac) to overwrite the existing file, then click **No** to Update Links.

    Clicking No to Update Links will keep the links from linking to the original Data Files location.

3. Click the **Attach Style Sheet button** 🔗 in the CSS Styles panel, attach the su_styles.css style sheet, then apply the body_text style to all of the paragraph text on the page.

4. Position the insertion point in front of "When" in the first paragraph, click the **Insert bar list arrow**, click **Common**, click the **Images list arrow**, then click **Image** to open the Select Image Source dialog box, navigate to the chapter_3 assets folder, double-click **club_house.jpg**, insert the alternate text **The Striped Umbrella Club House**, then verify that the file was copied to your assets folder in the striped_umbrella root folder.

    Compare your screen to Figure 26.

5. Click the **Assets panel tab** in the Files panel group, click the **Images button** 🖼 on the Assets panel (if necessary), then click the **Refresh Site List button** C on the Assets panel to update the list of images in The Striped Umbrella Web site.

    The Assets panel displays a list of all the images in The Striped Umbrella Web site, as shown in Figure 27. A thumbnail of the club house image appears above the list.

    (continued)

FIGURE 26
The Striped Umbrella about us page with inserted image

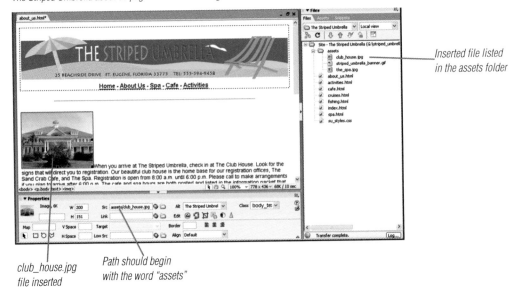

Inserted file listed
in the assets folder

club_house.jpg
file inserted

Path should begin
with the word "assets"

FIGURE 27

Image files for The Striped Umbrella Web site listed in the Assets panel

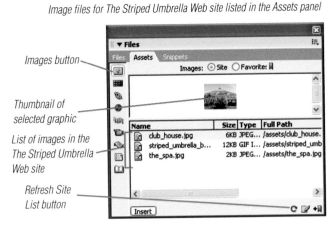

Images button

Thumbnail of
selected graphic

List of images in the
The Striped Umbrella
Web site

Refresh Site
List button

Working with Text and Graphics

FIGURE 28

Assets panel with seven images

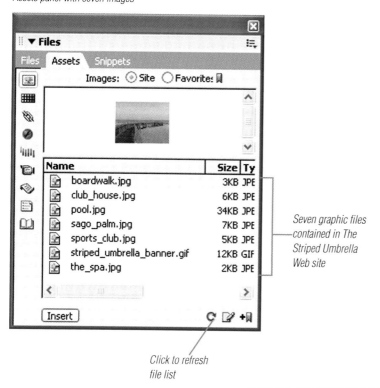

Click to refresh
file list

Seven graphic files
contained in The
Striped Umbrella
Web site

6. Insert boardwalk.jpg to the left of "After" at the beginning of the second paragraph, then refresh the Assets panel to verify that the boardwalk.jpg file was copied to the assets folder of The Striped Umbrella Web site.

> TIP The file boardwalk.jpg is located in the assets folder in the chapter_3 folder where your Data Files are stored.

7. Repeat Step 5 to insert the pool.jpg, sago_palm.jpg, and sports_club.jpg files at the beginning of each of the next paragraphs.

After refreshing, your Assets panel should resemble Figure 28.

You inserted five images on the about us page and copied each image to the assets folder of The Striped Umbrella Web site.

Using Favorites in the Assets panel

The assets in the Assets panel can be listed two ways: Site and Favorites. The Site option lists all of the assets in the Web site in the selected category in alphabetical order. As your list of assets grows, you can designate some of the assets that are used more frequently as Favorites for quicker access. To add an asset to the Favorites list, right-click (Win) or [control]-click (Mac) the asset name in the Site list, then click Add to Favorites. When an asset is placed in the Favorites list, it is still included in the Site list. To delete an asset from the Favorites list, select the asset you want to delete, then press [Delete] or the Remove from Favorites button on the Assets panel. You can further organize your Favorites list by creating folders for similar assets and grouping them inside the folders.

Align a graphic

1. Scroll to the top of the page, click the **club house image**, then expand the Property inspector (if necessary).

   Because an image is selected, the Property inspector displays tools for setting the properties of an image.

2. Click the **Align list arrow** in the Property inspector, then click **Left**.

   The club house photo is now left-aligned and the paragraph text flows around its right edge, as shown in Figure 29.

   (continued)

FIGURE 29
Left-aligned club house image

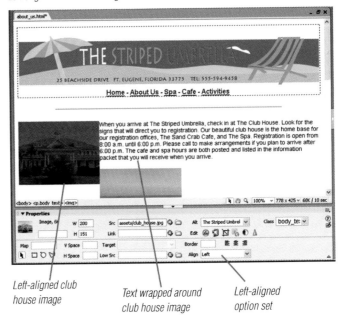

Left-aligned club house image

Text wrapped around club house image

Left-aligned option set

FIGURE 30

Aligned images on the about us page

3. Select the boardwalk image, click the **Align list arrow** in the Property inspector, then click **Right**.

4. Align the pool image, using the Left Align option.

5. Align the sago palm image, using the Right Align option.

6. Align the sports club image, using the Left Align option.

7. Save your work.

8. Preview the Web page in your browser, compare your screen to Figure 30, then close your browser.

You used the Property inspector to set the alignment for the five images. You then previewed the page in your browser.

ENHANCE AN IMAGE AND
USE ALTERNATE TEXT

What You'll Do

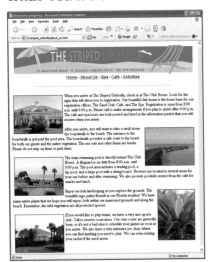

In this lesson you will add borders to images, add horizontal and vertical space to set them apart from the text, and then add alternate text to each image on the page.

Enhancing an Image

After you place an image on a Web page, you have several options for **enhancing** it, or improving its appearance. To make changes to the image itself, such as removing scratches from it, or making it lighter or darker, you need to use an image editor such as Macromedia Fireworks or Adobe Photoshop. To edit a graphic directly in Fireworks from Dreamweaver, first select the graphic, then click Edit on the Property inspector. This will open the Fireworks program. Complete your editing, then click Done to return to Dreamweaver. However, you can use Dreamweaver to enhance certain aspects of how images appear on a page. For example, you can add borders around an image or add horizontal and vertical space. **Borders** are frames that surround an image. Horizontal and vertical space is blank space above, below, and on the sides of an image that separates the image from text or other elements on the page. Adding horizontal or vertical space, which is the same as adding white space, helps images

---

DESIGNTIP **Resizing graphics using an external editor**

Each image on a Web page takes a specific number of seconds to download, depending on the size of the file. Larger files (in kilobytes, not width and height) take longer to download than smaller files. It's important to figure out the smallest acceptable size for an image on your Web page. Then, if you need to resize an image to reduce the file size, use an external image editor to do so, *instead* of resizing it in Dreamweaver. Although you can adjust the width and height settings of an image in the Property inspector to change the size of the image as it appears on your screen, these settings do not affect the file size. Decreasing the size of an image using the H (height) and W (width) settings in the Property inspector does *not* reduce the time it will take the file to download. Ideally you should use graphics that have the smallest file size and the highest quality possible, so that each page downloads in eight seconds or less.

---

stand out on a page. In the Web page shown in Figure 31, the horizontal and vertical space around the images in the center column helps make these images more prominent. Adding horizontal or vertical space does not affect the width or height of the image. Spacing around Web page objects can also be created by using "spacer" images, or clear images that act as placeholders.

Using Alternate Text

One of the easiest ways to make your Web page viewer-friendly and handicapped-accessible is to use alternate text. **Alternate text** is descriptive text that appears in place of an image while the image is downloading or when the mouse pointer is placed over it. You can program some browsers to display only alternate text and to download images manually. Alternate text can be "read" by a **screen reader**, a device used by the visually impaired to convert written text on a computer monitor to spoken words. Screen readers and alternate text make it possible for visually impaired viewers to have an image described to them in detail. You can also set up Dreamweaver to prompt you to enter alternate text whenever you insert an image on a page.

The use of alternate text is the first checkpoint listed in the World Wide Web Consortium (W3C) list of Priority 1 checkpoints. The Priority 1 checkpoints dictate the most basic level of accessibility standards to be used by Web developers today. The complete list of these and the other priority level checkpoints are listed on the W3C Web site, *www.w3.org*. You should always strive to meet these criteria for all Web pages.

FIGURE 31
Lands' End Web site

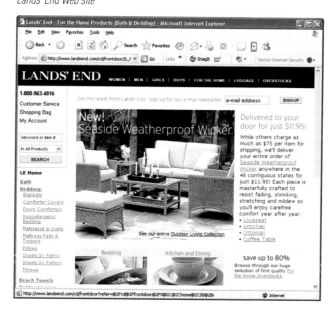

Add a border

1. Select the club house image, then expand the Property inspector (if necessary).
2. Type **1** in the Border text box, then press **[Tab]** to apply the border to the club house image, as shown in Figure 32.
3. Repeat Step 2 to add borders to the rest of the images.

You added a 1-pixel border to each image on the about us page.

Add horizontal space

1. Select the club house image, type **7** in the V Space text box in the Property inspector, press **[Tab]**, type **7** in the H Space text box, then compare your screen to Figure 33.

   The text is more evenly wrapped around the image and is easier to read, because it is not so close to the edge of the image.
2. Repeat Step 1 to set the V Space and H Space to 7 for the other four images.

   The spacing under each picture differs because of the difference in the lengths of the paragraphs.

You added horizontal spacing and vertical spacing around each image on the about us page.

FIGURE 32
Using the Property inspector to add a border

Selected image
with 1-pixel border

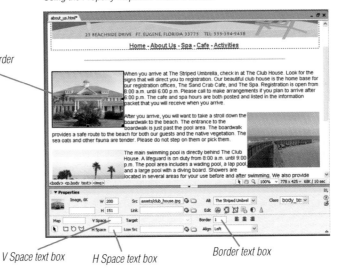

V Space text box   H Space text box   Border text box

FIGURE 33
Comparing images with and without horizontal and vertical space

Image with horizontal
and vertical space

Image without
horizontal and
vertical space

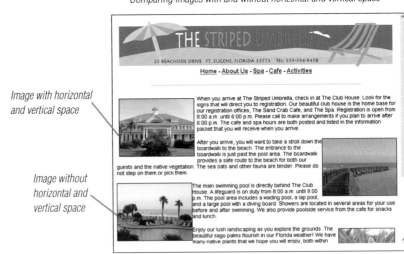

FIGURE 34

Brightness and contrast settings for the boardwalk image

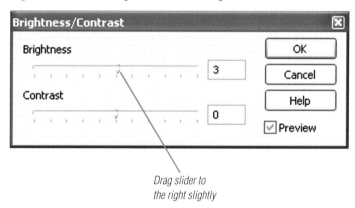

Drag slider to
the right slightly

1. Select the boardwalk image.

2. Click the **Brightness and Contrast button** in the Property inspector, then click **OK** to close the warning dialog box and open the Brightness/Contrast dialog box.

3. Compare your screen to Figure 34, then drag the **Brightness slider** slightly to the right to lighten the image, as shown in Figure 34.

4. Repeat Step 3 to adjust any of the other images if desired, then click **OK**.

   TIP To scale an image, first select the image, then drag one of the borders toward the center of the image to reduce it, or drag away from the center of the image to enlarge it.

You used the Brightness/Contrast dialog box to lighten an image.

Use alternate text

1. Select the club house image, type **The Striped Umbrella Club House** in the Alt text box in the Property inspector, as shown in Figure 35, then press **[Enter]** (Win) or **[return]** (Mac).

2. Save your work, preview the page in your browser, then point to the **club house image** until the alternate text appears, as shown in Figure 36.

3. Close your browser.

4. Select the boardwalk image, type **The boardwalk to the beach** in the Alt text box in the Property inspector, then press **[Enter]** (Win) or **[return]** (Mac).

5. Repeat Step 4 to add the alternate text **The pool area** to the pool image.

6. Repeat Step 4 to add the alternate text **Sago palm** to the sago palm image.

7. Repeat Step 4 to add the alternate text **The Sports Club** to the sports club image.

8. Save your work.

9. Preview the page in your browser, view the alternate text for each image, then close your browser.

You added alternate text to five images on the page, then you viewed the alternate text in your browser.

FIGURE 35
Alternate text setting in the Property inspector

Alt text box

FIGURE 36
Alternate text displayed in browser

Alternate text displayed on top of image

FIGURE 37

Preferences dialog box with Accessibility category selected

Accessibility category

Check boxes for Form objects, Frames, Media, and Images

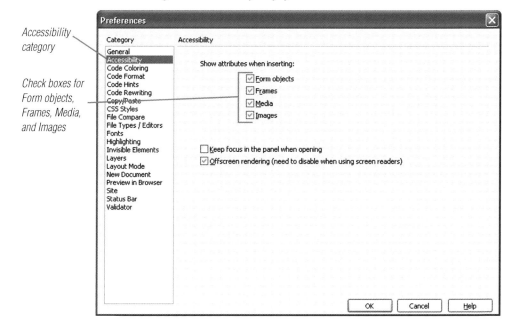

1. Click **Edit** (Win) or **Dreamweaver** (Mac) on the menu bar, click **Preferences** to open the Preferences dialog box, then click the **Accessibility category**.

2. Click the **four check boxes**, if necessary, as shown in Figure 37, then click **OK**.

   TIP Once you set the Accessibility preferences, they will be in effect for all Web sites that you develop, not just the one that's open when you set them.

You set the Accessibility preferences to prompt you to enter alternate text each time you insert a form object, frame, or media or image object on a Web page.

INSERT A BACKGROUND IMAGE
AND PERFORM SITE MAINTENANCE

What You'll Do

 In this lesson, you will insert two types of tiled background images. You will then use the Assets panel to delete them both from the Web site. You will also check for Non-Websafe colors in the Assets panel and delete one that you locate on the home page.

Inserting a Background Image

You can insert a background image on a Web page to provide depth and visual interest to the page, or to communicate a message or mood. **Background images** are graphic files used in place of background colors. Although you can use background images to create a dramatic effect, you should avoid inserting them on Web pages that have lots of text and other elements. Even though they might seem too plain, standard white backgrounds are usually the best choice for Web pages. If you choose to use a background image on a Web page, it should be small in file size, and preferably in GIF format. You can insert either a small graphic file that is tiled, or repeated, across the page or a larger graphic that is not repeated across the page. A tiled image will download much faster than a large image. A **tiled image** is a small graphic that repeats across and down a Web page, appearing as individual squares or rectangles. When you create a Web page, you should use either a background color or a background image, but not both, unless you have a need for the background color to be displayed while the background image finishes downloading. The background in the Web page shown in Figure 38 contains several images arranged in a table format.

Managing Graphics

As you work on a Web site, you might find that you accumulate files in your assets folder that are not used in the site. To avoid accumulating unnecessary files, it's a good idea to look at a graphic on a page first, before you copy it to the assets folder. If you inadvertently copy an unwanted file to the assets folder, you should delete it or move it to another location. This is a good Web-site management practice that will prevent the assets folder from filling up with unwanted graphics.

Removing a graphic from a Web page does not remove it from the assets folder in the local root folder of the Web site. To remove an asset from a Web site, you first locate the file you want to remove in the Assets panel. You then use the Locate in Site command to open the Files panel with the unwanted file selected. You then use the Delete command to remove the file from the site.

QUICKTIP

You cannot use the Assets panel to delete a file. You must use the Files panel to delete files and perform all file-management tasks.

Removing Colors from a Web Site

You can use the Assets panel to locate Non-Websafe colors in a Web site. **Non-Websafe** colors are colors that may not be displayed uniformly across computer platforms. After you remove colors from a Web site, you should use the Refresh Site List button on the Assets panel to verify that these colors have been removed. Sometimes it's necessary to press [Ctrl]

(Win) or [⌘] (Mac) while you click the Refresh Site List button. If refreshing the Assets panel does not work, try recreating the site cache, then refreshing the Assets panel again

QUICKTIP

To recreate the site cache, click Site on the menu bar, point to Advanced, then click Recreate Site Cache.

FIGURE 38
The Mansion on Turtle Creek home page

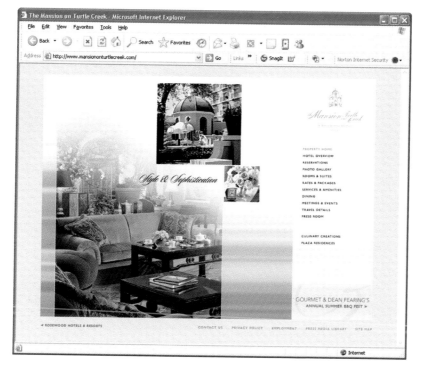

Lesson 6   Insert a Background Image and Perform Site Maintenance

Insert a background image

1. Click **Modify** on the menu bar, then click **Page Properties** to open the Page Properties dialog box.

2. Click the **Appearance category**, if necessary.

3. Click **Browse** next to the Background image text box, navigate to the chapter_3 assets folder, then double-click **umbrella_back.gif**.

   The umbrella_back.gif file is automatically copied to The Striped Umbrella assets folder.

4. Click **OK** to close the Page Properties dialog box, then click the **Refresh Site List button** [C] to refresh the file list in the Assets panel.

   A file with a single umbrella forms a background made up of individual squares, replacing the white background, as shown in Figure 39. It is much too busy and makes it difficult to read the page.

5. Repeat Steps 1 through 4 to replace the umbrella_back.gif background image with stripes_bak.gif, located in the chapter_3 assets folder.

   As shown in Figure 40, the striped background is still being tiled, but with vertical stripes you aren't aware of the small squares making up the pattern. It is still too busy, though.

You applied a tiled background to the about us page. Then you replaced the tiled background with another tiled background that was not as busy.

FIGURE 39
The about us page with a busy tiled background

Each umbrella is a small square that forms a tiled background

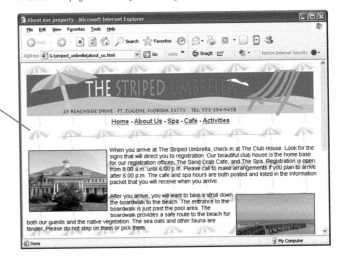

FIGURE 40
The about us page with a more subtle tiled background

It is harder to tell where each square ends

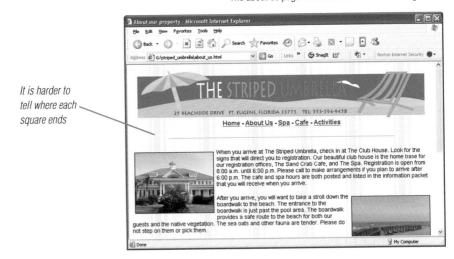

Working with Text and Graphics

FIGURE 41
Removing a background image

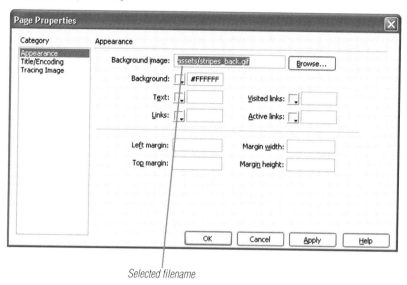

Selected filename

1. Click **Modify** on the menu bar, click **Page Properties**, then click **Appearance**.

2. Select the text in the Background image text box, as shown in Figure 41, press **[Delete]**, then click **OK**.

   The background of the about us page is white again.

You deleted the link to the background image file to change the about us page background back to white.

Understanding HTML body tags

When you are setting page preferences, it is handy to understand the HTML tags that are being generated. Sometimes it's much easier to make changes to the code, rather than through menus and dialog boxes. The <body> </body> tags define the beginning and end of the body section of a Web page. The page content falls between those two tags. If you want to change the page properties, additional codes will be added to the <body> tag. The tag to add a color to the page background is bgcolor, so the tag will read <body bgcolor="#000000">, where the numbers following the pound sign indicate a color. If you insert an image for a background, the code will read <body background="assets/stripes.gif">. The filename between the quotes is the name of the graphic file used for the background.

Delete files from a Web site

1. Click the **Assets panel tab** (if necessary).

2. Right-click (Win) or [control]-click (Mac) **stripes_back.gif** in the Assets panel, click **Locate in Site** to open the Files panel, click the **Refresh button** ⟳ , select **stripes_back.gif** in the Files panel (if necessary), press **[Delete]**, then click **Yes** in the dialog box that appears.

3. Repeat Step 2 to remove umbrella_back.gif from the Web site, open the Assets panel, then refresh the Assets panel.

   TIP If you delete a file in the Files panel that has an active link to it, you will receive a warning message. If you rename a file in the Files panel that has a link to it, the Files panel will update the links to correctly link to the renamed file. To rename a file, right-click (Win) or [control]-click (Mac) the file you want to rename, point to Edit, click Rename, then type the new name.

Your Assets panel should resemble Figure 42.

You removed two image files from The Striped Umbrella Web site, then refreshed the Assets panel.

FIGURE 42
Images listed in Assets panel

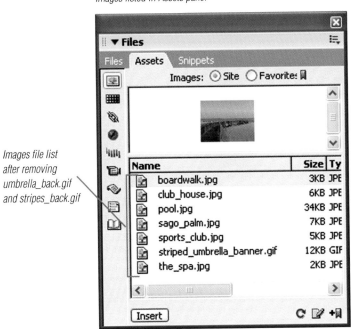

Images file list after removing umbrella_back.gif and stripes_back.gif

Managing graphic files

It is a good idea to store copies of your original Web site graphic files in a separate folder, outside the assets folder of your Web site. If you edit the original files, save them again using different names. Doing this ensures that you will be able to find a file in its original, unaltered state. You might have no need for certain files now, but you might need them later. Storing currently unused files also helps to keep your assets folder free of clutter. Storing copies of original Web site graphic files in a separate location also ensures that you have back-up copies in the event that you accidentally delete a file from the Web site that you need later.

FIGURE 43

Colors listed in Assets panel

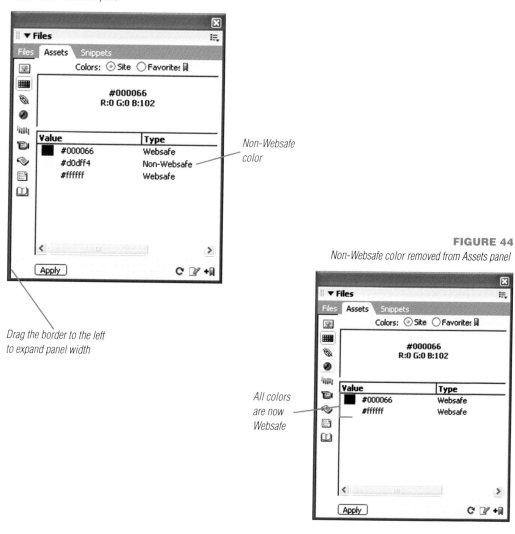

Non-Websafe color

Drag the border to the left to expand panel width

FIGURE 44

Non-Websafe color removed from Assets panel

All colors are now Websafe

Remove Non-Websafe colors from a Web site

1. Click the **Colors button** ▦ in the Assets panel to display the colors used in the Web site, then drag the left border of the Assets panel (if necessary) to display the second column.

   The Assets panel shows that color d0dff4 is Non-Websafe, as shown in Figure 43. This color was the original background color on the home page. We removed it, but it is still listed in the list of colors used in the Web site.

   > TIP If you do not see any Non-Websafe colors in your Assets panel, your cache has already been cleared and you can skip Steps 2 and 3.

2. Click the **Refresh Site List button** ⟳.

3. Press and hold [**control**] (Win) or ⌘ (Mac) while you click the **Refresh Site List button**.

   The color is removed, as shown in Figure 44. Sometimes the Refresh Site List button doesn't work. If it doesn't, try pressing and holding [control] (Win) or ⌘ (Mac). If that doesn't work, recreate the site cache.

4. Save your work, preview the page in your browser, close your browser, then close all open files.

You removed one Non-Websafe color from the Assets panel list of colors.

Create unordered and ordered lists.

1. Open the blooms & bulbs Web site.
2. Open the tips page.
3. Select the four lines of text below the Seasonal Gardening Checklist heading and format them as an unordered list. (*Hint*: If each line does not become a separate list item, enter a paragraph break between each line, then remove any extra spaces.)
4. Select the lines of text below the Basic Gardening Tips heading and format them as an ordered list.
5. Save your work.

Create, apply, and edit Cascading Style Sheets.

1. Create a new CSS rule named **seasons**, making sure that the Class option button is selected in the Selector Type section and that the (New Style Sheet File) option button is selected in the Define in section of the New CSS Rule dialog box.
2. Click OK, name the style sheet file **blooms_styles** in the Save Style Sheet File As dialog box, then click Save.
3. Choose the following settings for the seasons style: Font = Arial, Helvetica, sans-serif, Size = 12 pixels, Style = normal, Weight = bold, and Color = #003366.
4. Change the Font setting to Default Font and the Size setting to None for the following words in the Seasonal Gardening Checklist: Fall, Winter,

Spring, and Summer. Then, apply the seasons style to Fall, Winter, Spring, and Summer.
5. Edit the seasons style by changing the font size to 16 pixels.
6. Add an additional style called **headings** in the blooms_styles.css file and define this style choosing the following type settings: Font = Arial, Helvetica, sans-serif, Size = 18 pixels, Style = normal, Weight = bold, and Color = #003366.
7. Apply the headings style to the two sub-headings on the page: Seasonal Gardening Checklist and Basic Gardening Tips. (Make sure you remove any manual formatting before applying the style.)
8. Click File on the menu bar, click Save All, view the page in the browser, then compare your screen to Figure 45.
9. Close the browser and all open pages.

Insert and align graphics.

1. Open dw3_2.html from the chapter_3 Data Files folder, save it as **plants.html** in the blooms & bulbs Web site, overwriting the existing plants.html file, and do not update links.
2. Verify that the path of the blooms & bulbs banner is set correctly to the assets folder in the blooms root folder.
3. Set the Accessibility preferences to prompt you to add alternate text to images (if necessary).

4. Insert the petunias.jpg file from the assets folder located in the chapter_3 Data Files folder to the left of the words Pretty petunias and add **Petunias** as alternate text.
5. Insert the verbena.jpg file from the chapter_3 Data Files folder in front of the words Verbena is one and add **Verbena** as alternate text.
6. Insert the lantana.jpg file from the chapter_3 assets folder in front of the words Dramatic masses and add **Lantana** as alternate text.
7. Refresh the Files panel to verify that all three images were copied to the assets folder.
8. Left-align the petunias image.
9. Right-align the verbena image.
10. Left-align the lantana image.
11. Save your work, then compare your screen to Figure 46.

Enhance an image and use alternate text.

1. Apply a 1-pixel border and horizontal spacing of 20 pixels around the petunias image.
2. Apply a 1-pixel border and horizontal spacing of 20 pixels around the verbenas image.
3. Apply a 1-pixel border and horizontal spacing of 20 pixels around the lantanas image.
4. Open the index page and add appropriate alternate text to the banner.
5. Save your work.

Working with Text and Graphics

Insert a background image and manage graphics.

1. Switch to the plants page, then insert the daisies.jpg file from the chapter_3 assets folder as a background image.
2. Save your work.
3. Preview the Web page in your browser, then close your browser.
4. Remove the daisies.jpg file from the background.
5. Open the Assets panel, then refresh the Files list.
6. Use the Files panel to delete the daisies.jpg file from the list of images.
7. Refresh the Assets panel, then verify that the daisies.jpg file has been removed from the Web site.
8. View the colors used in the site in the Assets panel, then verify that all are Websafe.
9. Save your work, then close all open pages.

FIGURE 45
Completed Skills Review

We have some planting tips we would like to share with you as you prepare your gardens this season. Remember, there is always something to be done for your gardens, no matter what the season. Our experienced staff is here to help you plan your gardens, select your plants, prepare your soil, assist you in the planting, and maintain your beds. Check out our calendar for a list of our scheduled classes. All classes are free of charge and on a first-come, first-served basis!

Seasonal Gardening Checklist:

- **Fall** – The time to plant trees and spring blooming bulbs.
- **Winter** – The time to prune fruit trees and finish planting your bulbs.
- **Spring** – The time to prepare your beds, plant annuals, and apply fertilizer to established plants.
- **Summer** – The time to supplement rainfall so that plants get one inch of water per week.

Basic Gardening Tips

1. Select plants according to your climate.
2. In planning your garden, consider the composition, texture, structure, depth, and drainage of your soil.
3. Use compost to improve the structure of your soil.
4. Choose plant foods based on your garden objectives.
5. Generally, plants should receive one inch of water per week.
6. Use mulch to conserve moisture, keep plants cool, and cut down on weeding.

FIGURE 46
Completed Skills Review

Drop by to see our Featured Spring Plants

Pretty petunias blanket your beds with lush green leaves and bright blooms in assorted colors. Shown is the Moonlight White Petunia (Mini-Spreading). This variety is fast-growing and produces spectacular blooms. Cut them back in July for blooms that will last into the fall. Full sun to partial shade. Great for border plants or hanging baskets.

Verbena is one of our all-time favorites. The variety shown is Blue Silver. Verbena grows rapidly and is a good choice for butterfly gardens. The plants can spread up to two feet wide, so it makes excellent ground cover. Plant in full sun. Heat resistant. Beautiful also in rock gardens. We have several other varieties equally as beautiful.

Dramatic masses of Lantana display summer color for your beds or containers. The variety shown is Golden Dream. Blooms late spring through early fall. This variety produces outstanding color. Plant in full sun with well-drained soil. We carry tall, dwarf, and trailing varieties. You can also overwinter with cuttings.

Stop by to see us soon. We will be happy to help you with your selections.

Use Figures 47 and 48 as guides to continue your work on the TripSmart Web site that you began in Project Builder 1 in Chapter 1. You are now ready to format text on the newsletter page and begin work on the destinations page that showcases one of the featured tours to Kenya. You want to include some colorful pictures and attractively formatted text on the page.

1. Open the TripSmart Web site.
2. Open dw3_3.html from the chapter_3 Data Files folder and save it in the tripsmart root folder as **newsletter.html**, overwriting the existing newsletter.html file and do not update the links.
3. Verify that the path for the banner is correctly set to the assets folder of the TripSmart Web site. Create an unordered list from the text beginning "Expandable clothesline" to the end of the page.
4. Create a new CSS Rule called **bodytext**, making sure that the Class option button is selected in the Selector Type section and that the (New Style Sheet File) option button is selected in the Define in section of the New CSS Rule dialog box.
5. Save the style sheet file as **tripsmart_styles.css** in the TripSmart Web site root folder.
6. Choose a font, size, style, color, and weight of your choice for the bodytext style.
7. Apply the bodytext style to all of the text on the page except the "Ten Packing Essentials" heading on the newsletter page.

8. Create another style called **heading** with a font, size, style, color, and weight of your choice and apply it to the "Ten Packing Essentials" heading.
9. Type **Travel Tidbits** in the Title text box on the Document toolbar, then save and close the newsletter page.
10. Open dw3_4.html from the chapter_3 Data Files folder and save it in the tripsmart root folder as **destinations.html**, overwriting the existing destinations.html file, and do not update links.
11. Insert zebra_mothers.jpg from the chapter_3 assets folder to the left of the sentence beginning "Our next", then add appropriate alternate text.
12. Insert lion.jpg from the chapter_3 assets folder to the left of the sentence beginning "This lion", then add appropriate alternate text.

13. Align both images using the Align list arrow in the Property inspector, then add horizontal spacing, vertical spacing, or borders if desired.
14. Apply the heading style to the "Destination: Kenya" heading and the bodytext style to the rest of the text on the page.
15. Apply any additional formatting to enhance the page appearance, then add the page title **Destination: Kenya**.
16. Verify that the Accessibility Preference option is turned on.
17. Save your work, then preview the destinations page in your browser.
18. Close your browser, then close all open files.

FIGURE 47
Sample Project Builder 1

FIGURE 48
Sample Project Builder 2

Working with Text and Graphics

In this exercise you will continue your work on the emma's book bag Web site that you started in Project Builder 2 in Chapter 1. You are now ready to add two new pages to the Web site. One page will display a list of featured books and another page will describe the story hour that the bookstore sponsors each Saturday morning. Figures 49 and 50 show possible solutions for this exercise. Your finished pages will look different if you choose different formatting options.

1. Open the emma's book bag Web site.
2. Open dw3_5.html from the chapter_3 Data Files folder, save it to the book_bag root folder as **books.html**, overwriting the existing file and not updating the links.
3. Format the list of books as an ordered list.
4. Create a CSS rule named **bodytext** and save the style sheet file as **book_bag_styles.css** in the emma's book bag Web site root folder. Use any formatting options that you like, and then apply the bodytext style to the first paragraph and the list of books.
5. Create another style called **heading** using appropriate formatting options and apply it to the line of text beginning with "Featured books".

6. Add appropriate alternate text to the banner, then save and close the file.
7. Open dw3_6.html from the chapter_3 Data Files folder and save it as **corner.html**, overwriting the existing file and not updating the links.
8. Apply the bodytext style to the paragraph text.

FIGURE 49
Completed Project Builder 1

9. Insert the reading.jpg image from the chapter_3 assets folder next to the paragraph, choosing an alignment and spacing of your choice and adding appropriate alternate text.
10. Add the page title **Caroline's Corner** to the page, save all pages, then preview both new pages in the browser.
11. Close your browser, then close all open pages.

FIGURE 50
Completed Project Builder 2

Don Chappell is a new sixth-grade history teacher. He is reviewing educational Web sites for information he can use in his classroom.

1. Connect to the Internet, navigate to the Online Companion, then select the link for this chapter. The Library of Congress Web site is shown in Figure 51.
2. Which fonts are used for the main content on the home page? Are the same fonts used consistently on the other pages in the Web site?
3. Do you see ordered or unordered lists on any pages in the Web site? If so, how are they used?
4. Use the Source command on the View menu to view the source code to see if a set of fonts was used. If so, which one?
5. Do you see the use of Cascading Style Sheets noted in the source code?
6. Select another site from the list and compare the use of text on the two sites.

FIGURE 51
Design Project

Working with Text and Graphics

In this assignment, you will continue to work on the Web site that you started in Chapter 1. There will be no data files supplied. You are building this Web site from chapter to chapter, so you must do each Portfolio Project assignment in each chapter to complete your Web site.

You will continue building your Web site by designing and completing a page that contains a list, headings, body text, graphics, and a background. During this process, you will develop a style sheet and add several styles to it. You will insert appropriate graphics on your page and enhance them for maximum effect. You will also check for Non-Websafe colors and remove any that you find.

1. Consult your storyboard and decide which page to create and develop for this chapter.
2. Plan the page content for the page and make a sketch of the layout. Your sketch should include at least one ordered or unordered list, appropriate headings, body text, several graphics, and a background color or image. Your sketch should also show where the body text and headings should be placed on the page and what styles should be used for each type of text. You should plan on creating at least two styles.
3. Create the page using your sketch for guidance.
4. Create a Cascading Style Sheet for the Web site and add to it the styles you decided to use. Apply the styles to the appropriate content.
5. Access the graphics you gathered in Chapter 1, and place the graphics on the page so that the page matches the sketch you created in Step 2. Add a background image if you want to and appropriate alternate text for each graphic.
6. Remove any Non-Websafe colors.
7. Identify any files in the Assets panel that are currently not used in the Web site. Decide which of these assets should be removed, then delete these files.
8. Preview the new page in a browser, then check for page layout problems and broken links. Make any necessary fixes in Dreamweaver, then preview the page again in the browser. Repeat this process until you are satisfied with the way the page looks in the browser.
9. Use the check list in Figure 52 to check all the pages in your site.
10. Close the browser, save your changes to the page, then close the page.

FIGURE 52
Portfolio Project check list

Web Site Check List

1. Does each page have a page title?
2. Does the home page have a description and keywords?
3. Does the home page contain contact information?
4. Does every page in the Web site have consistent navigation links?
5. Does the home page have a last updated statement that will automatically update when the page is saved?
6. Do all paths for links and images work correctly?
7. Do all images have alternate text?
8. Are all colors Websafe?
9. Are there any unnecessary files you can delete from the assets folder?
10. Is there a style sheet with at least two styles?
11. Did you apply the styles to page content?
12. Do all pages view well using at least two different browsers?

Working with Text and Graphics

4 WORKING WITH
LINKS

1. Create external and internal links.

2. Create internal links to named anchors.

3. Insert rollovers with Flash text.

4. Create, modify, and copy a navigation bar.

5. Manage Web site links.

4 WORKING WITH
LINKS

Introduction

What makes Web sites so powerful are the links that connect one page to another within a Web site or to any page on the Web. Though you can add graphics, animations, movies, and other enhancements to a Web site to make it visually attractive, the links you include are often the most essential components of a Web site. Links that connect the pages within a Web site are always very important because they help viewers navigate between the pages of the site. However, if one of your goals is to keep viewers from leaving your Web site, you might want to avoid including links to other Web sites. For example, most e-commerce sites include only links to other pages in the site to discourage shoppers from leaving the site. In this chapter you will create links to other pages in The Striped Umbrella Web site and to other sites on the Web. You will also insert a navigation bar that contains graphics instead of text, and check the links

in The Striped Umbrella Web site to make sure they all work correctly.

Understanding Internal and External Links

Web pages contain two types of links: internal links and external links. **Internal links** are links to Web pages in the same Web site, and **external links** are links to Web pages in other Web sites or to e-mail addresses. Both internal and external links have two important parts that work together. The first part of a link is the element that viewers see and click on a Web page, for example, text, a graphic, or a button. The second part of a link is the **path**, or the name and location of the Web page or file that will open when the element is clicked. Setting and maintaining the correct paths for all your links is essential to avoid having broken links in your site.

Tools You'll Use

Named Anchor button

Named anchor

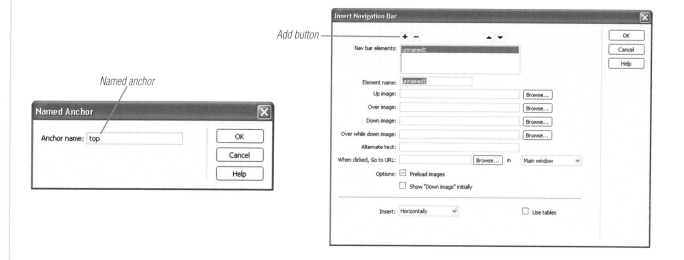

Add button

CREATE EXTERNAL AND
INTERNAL LINKS

What You'll Do

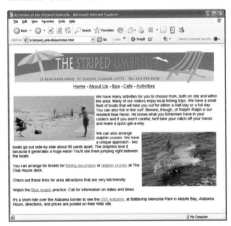

 In this lesson, you will create external links on The Striped Umbrella activities page that link to Web sites related to area attractions. You will also create internal links to other pages within The Striped Umbrella Web site.

Creating External Links

A good Web site usually includes a variety of external links to other related Web sites so that viewers can get more information on a particular topic. To create an external link, you first select the text or object that you want to serve as a link, then you type the absolute path to the destination Web page in the Link text box in the Property inspector. An **absolute path** is a path used for external links that includes the complete address for the destination page, including the protocol (such as http://) and the complete **URL** (Uniform Resource Locator), or address, of the destination page. When necessary, the Web page filename and folder hierarchy are also part of an absolute path. Figure 1 shows an example of an absolute path showing the protocol, URL, and filename. After you enter external links on a Web page, you can view them in the site map. An example for the code for an external link would be <a href="http://www.macromedia.com" Macromedia Web site </a>.

FIGURE 1

An example of an absolute path

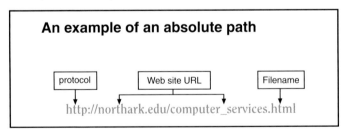

An example of an absolute path

| protocol | Web site URL | Filename |

http://northark.edu/computer_services.html

Creating Internal Links

Each page in a Web site usually focuses on an individual category or topic. You should make sure that the home page provides links to each page in the site, and that all pages in the site contain numerous internal links so that viewers can move easily from page to page. To create an internal link, you first select the text element or graphic object that you want to make a link, then you use the Browse for File icon next to the Link text box in the Property inspector to specify the relative path to the destination page. A **relative path** is a type of path used to reference Web pages and graphic files within the same Web site. Relative paths include the filename and folder location of a file. Figure 2 shows an example of a relative path. Table 1 describes absolute paths and relative paths. Relative paths can either be site root relative or document relative. You can also use the Point to File icon in the Property inspector to point to the file you want to use for the link, or drag the file you want to use for the link from the Files panel into the Link text box on the Property inspector.

You should take great care in managing your internal links to make sure they work correctly and are timely and relevant to the page content. You should design the navigation structure of your Web site so that viewers are never more than three or four clicks away from the page they are seeking. An example for the code for an internal link would be <a href="activities.html" Activities page </a>.

FIGURE 2
An example of a relative path

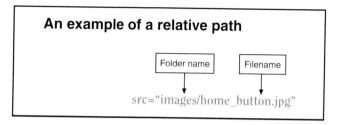

TABLE 1: Description of absolute and relative paths

type of path	description	examples
Absolute path	Used for external links and specifies protocol, URL, and filename of destination page	*http://www.yahoo.com/recreation*
Relative path	Used for internal links and specifies location of file relative to the current page	spa.html or assets/heron.gif
Root-relative path	Used for internal links when publishing to a server that contains many Web sites or where the Web site is so large it requires more than one server	/striped_umbrella/activities.html
Document-relative path	Used in most cases for internal links and specifies the location of file relative to current page	cafe.html or assets/heron.gif

Create an external link

1. Open The Striped Umbrella Web site that you completed in Chapter 3, open dw4_1.html from the chapter_4 folder where your Data Files are stored, then save it as **activities** in the striped_umbrella root folder, overwriting the existing activities page, but not updating links.

2. Attach the su_style.css file, then apply the body text style to the paragraphs of text on the page (not to the navigation bar).

3. Select the first broken image, click the **Browse for File icon** next to the Src text box, then select the heron_waiting_small.jpg in the Data Files folder to save the graphic in your assets folder.

4. Repeat Step 3 for the second image, two_dolphins_small.jpg.

5. Scroll down, then select the text "Blue Angels".

6. Click in the Link text box in the Property inspector, type **http://www.blueangels. navy.mil**, press **[Enter]** (Win) or **[return]** (Mac), then compare your screen to Figure 3.

7. Repeat Steps 5 and 6 to create a link for the USS Alabama site in the next paragraph: http://www.ussalabama.com.

8. Save your work, preview the page in your browser, test all the links to make sure they work, then close your browser.

   TIP You must have an active Internet connection to test the links. If clicking a link does not open a page, make sure you typed the URL correctly in the Link text box.

You opened The Striped Umbrella Web site, replaced the existing activities page, attached the su_styles.css.file, applied the body text style to the text, then added two external links to other sites on the page. You also tested each link in your browser.

FIGURE 3

Creating an external link to the Blue Angels Web site

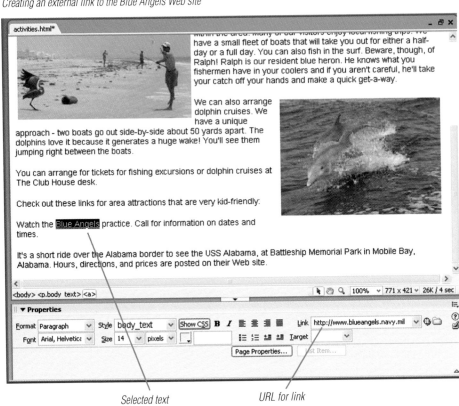

Selected text   URL for link

FIGURE 4
Site map displaying external links on the activities page

Click to collapse window

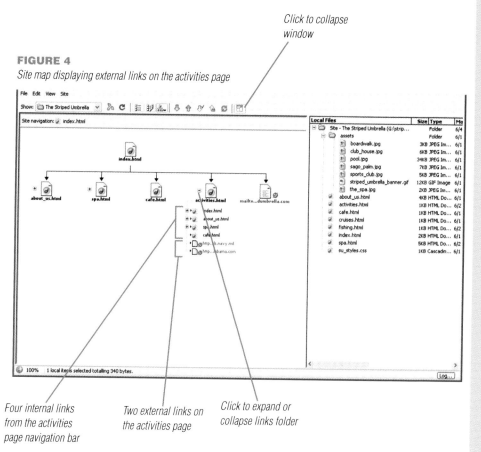

Four internal links from the activities page navigation bar

Two external links on the activities page

Click to expand or collapse links folder

1. Click the **Expand to show local and remote sites button** on the Files panel to expand the Files panel.

2. Click the **Site Map list arrow** on the toolbar then click **Map and Files**.

   Four links from the navigation bar appear as internal links.

   TIP If you want to view or hide page titles in the site map, click View on the menu bar, point to Site Map Options, then click Show Page Titles (Win) or click the Options button in the Files panel group title bar, point to View, then click Show Page Titles (Mac).

3. Click the **plus sign** to the left of the activities page icon in the site map (if necessary) to view a list of the two external links you created, as shown in Figure 4.

4. Click the **minus sign** to the left of the activities page icon in the site map to collapse the list of links.

5. Click the **Collapse to show only local or remote site button** , on the toolbar.

You viewed The Striped Umbrella site map and expanded the view of the activities page to display the two external links you added.

Create an internal link

1. Select the text "fishing excursions" in the third paragraph.

2. Click the **Browse for File icon** 📁 next to the Link text box in the Property inspector, then double-click **fishing.html** in the Select File dialog box to set the relative path to the fishing page.

   Notice that fishing.html appears in the Link text box in the Property inspector, as shown in Figure 5.

   TIP To collapse all open panels below the document window, such as the Link Checker or the Property inspector, click the expander arrow in the center of the bottom border of the Document window. Pressing [F4] will hide all panels, including the ones on the right side of the screen.

3. Select the text "dolphin cruises" in the same sentence.

4. Click the **Browse for File icon** 📁 next to the Link text box in the Property inspector, then double-click **cruises.html** in the Select File dialog box to specify the relative path to the cruises page.

   The words "dolphin cruises" are now a link to the cruises page.

5. Save your work, preview the page in your browser to verify that the internal links work correctly, then close your browser.

   The fishing and cruises pages do not have page content yet, but serve as placeholders until they do.

   You created two internal links on the activities page, and then tested the links in your browser.

FIGURE 5
Creating an internal link on the activities page

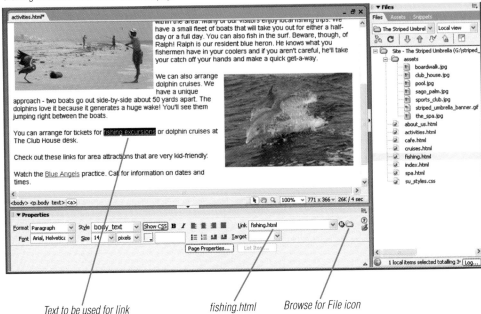

Text to be used for link   fishing.html   Browse for File icon

Typing URLs

Typing URLs in the Link text box in the Property inspector can be very tedious. When you need to type a long and complex URL, it is easy to make mistakes and create a broken link. You can avoid such mistakes by copying and pasting the URL from the Address text box (Internet Explorer) or Location text box (Netscape Navigator and Communicator) to the Link text box in the Property inspector. Copying and pasting a URL ensures that the URL is entered correctly.

FIGURE 6

Site map displaying external and internal links on the activities page

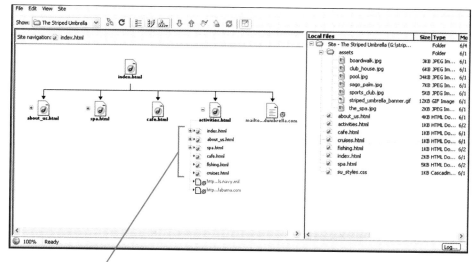

Six internal links, four from the navigation bar and two from text links

1. Click the **Expand to show local and remote sites button** 🖹 on the Files panel.

2. Click the **Site Map list arrow**, then click **Map and Files**, if necessary.

3. Click the **plus sign** to the left of the activities page icon.

   A list of eight links appears below the activities page icon, as shown in Figure 6. Two are external links, and six are internal links.

   TIP If your links do not display correctly, recreate the site cache. To recreate the site cache, click Site on the menu bar, click Advanced, then click Recreate Site Cache.

4. Click the **Collapse to show only local or remote site button** 🖹 .

5. Close the activities page.

You viewed the links on the activities page in the site map.

CREATE INTERNAL LINKS
TO NAMED ANCHORS

What You'll Do

In this lesson, you will insert five named anchors on the spa page: one for the top of the page and four for each of the spa services lists. You will then create internal links to each named anchor.

Inserting Named Anchors

Some Web pages have so much content that viewers must scroll repeatedly to get to the bottom of the page and then back up to the top of the page. To make it easier for viewers to navigate to specific areas of a page without scrolling, you can use a combination of internal links and named anchors. A **named anchor** is a specific location on a Web page that has a descriptive name. Named anchors act as targets for internal links and make it easy for viewers to jump to a particular place on the same page quickly. A **target** is the location on a Web page that a browser displays when an internal link is clicked. For example, you can insert a named anchor called "top" at the top of a Web page, then create a link to it at the bottom of the page. You can also insert named anchors in strategic places on a Web page, such as at the beginning of paragraph headings.

You insert a named anchor using the Named Anchor button on the Common category of the Insert bar, as shown in Figure 7. You then enter the name of the anchor in the Named Anchor dialog box. You should choose short names that describe the named anchor location on the page. Named anchors are represented by yellow anchor icons on a Web page. Selected anchors are represented by blue icons. You can show or hide named anchor icons by clicking View on the menu bar, pointing to Visual Aids, then clicking Invisible Elements.

Creating Internal Links to Named Anchors

Once you create a named anchor, you can create an internal link to it using one of two methods. You can select the text or graphic on the page that you want to make a link, then drag the Point to File icon from the Property inspector to the named anchor icon on the page. Or, you can select the text or graphic to which you want to make a link, then type # followed by the named anchor name (such as #top) in the Link text box in the Property inspector.

QUICKTIP

To avoid possible errors, you should create a named anchor before you create a link to it.

FIGURE 7
Named Anchor button on the Insert bar

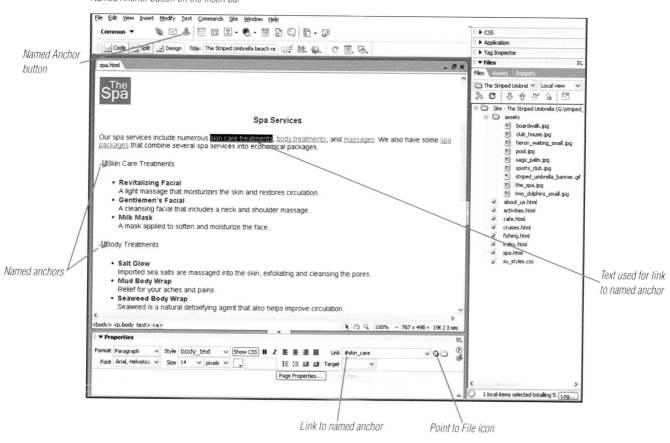

Named Anchor button

Named anchors

Text used for link to named anchor

Link to named anchor

Point to File icon

Insert a named anchor

1. Open the spa page, click the **banner** to select it, then press [←] to place the insertion point to the left of the banner.

2. Click **View** on the menu bar, point to **Visual Aids**, then verify that Invisible Elements is checked.

   TIP If there is no check mark next to Invisible Elements, this feature is turned off. Click Invisible Elements to turn this feature on.

3. Click the **Insert bar list arrow**, then click **Common**, if necessary.

4. Click the **Named Anchor button** 🔱 on the Insert bar to open the Named Anchor dialog box, type **top** in the Anchor name text box, compare your screen with Figure 8, then click **OK**.

   An anchor icon now appears before The Striped Umbrella banner.

   TIP Use lowercase letters, no spaces, and no special characters in named anchor names. You should also avoid using a number as the first character in a named anchor name.

   (continued)

FIGURE 8
Named Anchor dialog box

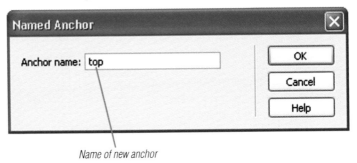

Name of new anchor

5. Click to the left of the Skin Care Treatments heading, then insert a named anchor called **skin_care**.

6. Insert named anchors to the left of the Body Treatments, Massages, and Packages headings using the following names: **body_treatments**, **massages**, and **packages**.

Your screen should resemble Figure 9.

You created five named anchors on the activities page; one at top of the page, and four that will help viewers quickly access the Spa Services headings on the page.

FIGURE 9

Named anchors on the spa page

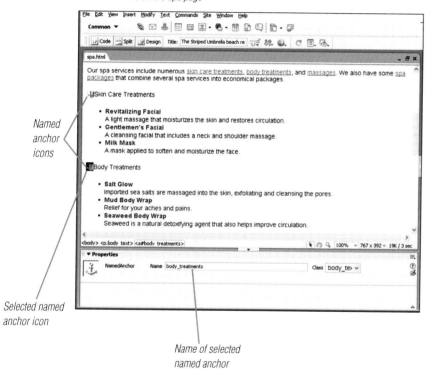

Named anchor icons

Selected named anchor icon

Name of selected named anchor

Create an internal link to a named anchor

1. Select the words "skin care treatments" in the first paragraph, then drag the **Point to File icon** 🕹️ from the Property inspector to the anchor named skin_care, as shown in Figure 10.

   The words "skin care treatments" are now linked to the skin_care named anchor. When viewers click the words "skin care treatments" the browser will display the Skin Care Treatments heading at the top of the browser window.

   TIP The name of a named anchor is always preceded by a pound (#) sign in the Link text box in the Property inspector.

2. Create internal links for body treatments, massages, and spa packages in the first paragraph by first selecting each of these words or phrases, then dragging the **Point to File icon** 🕹️ to the appropriate named anchor icon.

   The words body "treatments," "massages," and "spa packages" are now links that connect to the Body Treatments, Massages, and Spa Packages headings.

   TIP Once you select the text you want to link, you might need to scroll down to view the named anchor on the screen. Once you see the named anchor on your screen, you can drag the Point to File icon on top of it.

   (continued)

FIGURE 10

Dragging the Point to File icon to a named anchor

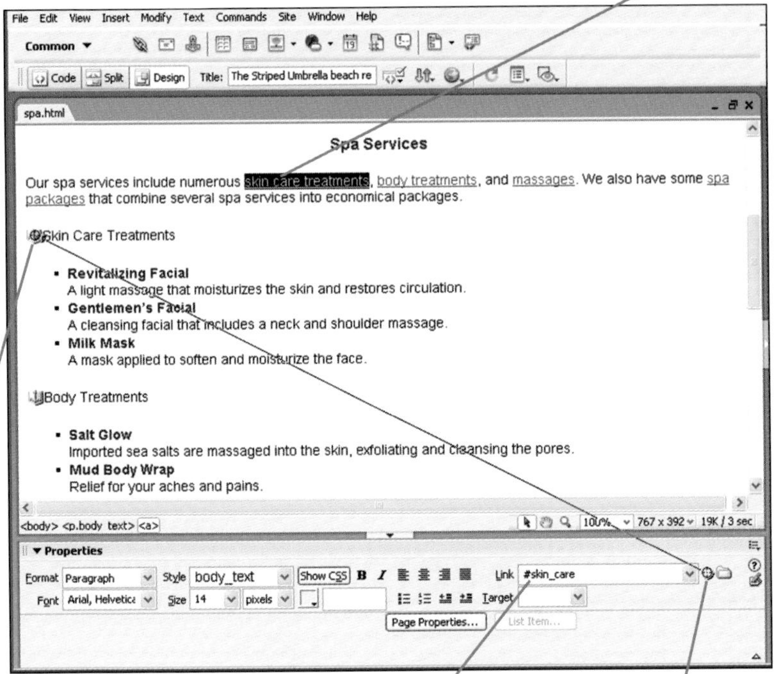

Selected text to link to named anchor

Point to File icon dragged to named anchor

Named anchor name preceded by # sign

Point to File icon

Working with Links

FIGURE 11

Spa page in Internet Explorer with internal links to named anchors

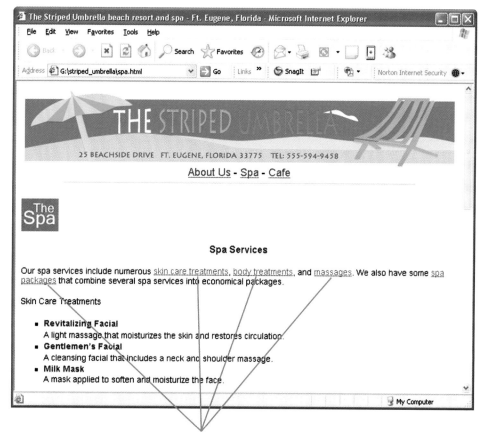

Internal links to named anchors

3. Save your work, preview the page in your browser, as shown in Figure 11, then test the links to each named anchor.

   Notice that when you click the spa packages link in the browser, the associated named anchor appears in the middle of the page instead of at the top. This happens because the spa page is not long enough to position this named anchor at the top of the page.

4. Close your browser.

You created internal links to the named anchors next to the Spa Services headings on the spa page. You then previewed the page in your browser and tested each link.

INSERT ROLLOVERS
WITH FLASH TEXT

What You'll Do

 In this lesson, you will use the Insert Flash Text dialog box to create a button that links to the top named anchor on the spa page. You will copy this button to several locations on the spa page, and then change the alignment of each button.

Understanding Flash Text

Flash is a Macromedia software program that you can use to create vector-based graphics and animations. **Vector-based graphics** are graphics that are based on mathematical formulas, as opposed to other types of graphic files such as JPG and BMP, which are based on pixels. Vector-based graphics have a smoother look and are smaller in file size than pixel-based graphics. Because they download quickly, vector-based graphics are ideal for Web sites. **Flash text** is a vector-based graphic file that contains text. You can insert Flash text to add visual interest to an otherwise dull Web page or to help deliver or reinforce a message. You can use Flash text to create internal or external links. Flash text files are saved with the .swf filename extension.

QUICKTIP

In order to view Flash animations, you must have the Flash player installed on your computer. The Flash player is free software that lets you view movies created with Macromedia software.

Inserting Flash Text on a Web Page

You can create Flash text in Dreamweaver without opening the Flash program. To insert Flash text on a Web page, you choose Common from the Insert bar, click the Media list arrow, then click Flash Text, as shown in Figure 12. Clicking this button opens the Insert Flash Text dialog box, which you use to specify the settings for the Flash text. You first need to specify the text you want to create as Flash text by typing it in the Text text box. You can then specify the font, size, and color of the Flash text, apply bold or italic styles to it, and align it using left, center, or right alignment options. You can also specify a **rollover color**, or the color in which the text will appear when the mouse pointer is placed on it. You also need to enter the path for the destination link in the Link text box. The destination link can be an internal link to another page in the site or to a named anchor on the same page, or an external link

to a page on another Web site. You then use the Target list to specify how to open the destination page. The four options are described in Table 2.

QUICKTIP

Notice that the _parent option in the table specifies to display the page in the parent frameset. A **frameset** is a group of Web pages displayed using more than one **frame** or window.

Before you close the Insert Flash Text dialog box, you need to type a descriptive name for your Flash text file in the Save as text box. Flash text files must be saved in the same folder as the page that contains the Flash text. For this reason, you should save your Flash text files in the root folder of the Web site.

FIGURE 12
Media menu on the Insert bar

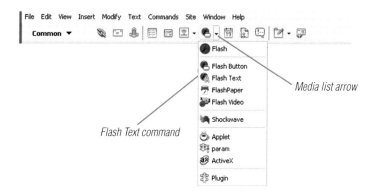

Flash Text command

Media list arrow

TABLE 2: Options in the Target list

target	result
_blank	Displays the destination page in a separate browser window
_parent	Displays the destination page in the parent frameset (replaces the frameset)
_self	Displays the destination page in the same frame or window
_top	Displays the destination page in the whole browser window

Create Flash text

1. Click after the last word on the spa page, then press **[Enter]** (Win) or **[return]** (Mac) twice to end the ordered list.

2. Click the **Insert bar list arrow**, click **Common**, click the **Media list arrow**, then click **Flash Text** to open the Insert Flash Text dialog box.

3. Type **Top of page** in the Text text box, set the Font to Arial, set the Size to 14, set the Color to #000066, set the Rollover color to #66CCFF, type **spa.html#top** in the Link text box, use the Target list arrow to set the Target to _top, type **top.swf** in the Save as text box, as shown in Figure 13, then click **OK**.

4. Type **Link to top of page** in the Flash Accessibility Attributes dialog box, then click **OK**.

   The Top of page Flash text now appears as a button at the bottom of the page. When a viewer clicks this button, the browser will display the top of the page.

5. Click **Assets** in the Files panel group to open the Assets panel, click the **Flash button** on the Assets panel, as shown in Figure 14, then click the **play button** to see the Flash text preview.

6. Drag **top.swf** from the Assets panel to the end of each of the spa services groups to insert four more links to the top of the page, adding the alternate text **Link to top of page** for each one.

   TIP Drag top.swf directly after the period in each section.

7. Click the **Files panel tab**, then refresh the Files panel (if necessary).

(continued)

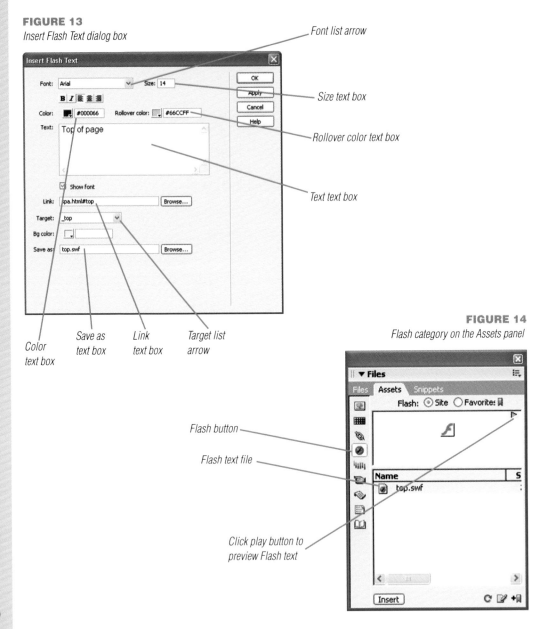

FIGURE 13
Insert Flash Text dialog box

Font list arrow

Size text box

Rollover color text box

Text text box

Color text box

Save as text box

Link text box

Target list arrow

FIGURE 14
Flash category on the Assets panel

Flash button

Flash text file

Click play button to preview Flash text

FIGURE 15
Flash text aligned to top

Spa Services

Our spa services include numerous skin care treatments, body treatments, and massages. We also have some spa packages that combine several spa services into economical packages.

Skin Care Treatments

- **Revitalizing Facial**
  A light massage that moisturizes the skin and restores circulation.
- **Gentlemen's Facial**
  A cleansing facial that includes a neck and shoulder massage.
- **Milk Mask**
  A mask applied to soften and moisturize the face. Top of page

Body Treatments

Flash text aligned with top of paragraph text line

Using Flash Player

To play Flash movies in Dreamweaver and in your browser, you must have the Flash Player installed on your computer. If the Flash Player is not installed, you can download it from the Macromedia Web site at (*www.macromedia.com*). In addition, you need to choose a specific setting in your browser. If you are using Internet Explorer, click Tools on the menu bar, click Internet Options, click the Advanced tab, click the Allow active content to run in files on my computer check box, then click OK. If you are using another browser, look for a similar setting in your Options or Preferences dialog boxes.

8. Save your work, preview the spa page in your browser, test each Top of page link, then close your browser.

    TIP If the top of the page is already displayed, the window will not move when you click the Flash text.

You used the Insert Flash Text dialog box to create a Top of page button that links to the top named anchor on the spa page. You also inserted the Top of page button at the end of each separate list of spa services, so viewers will be able to go quickly to the top of the page without scrolling.

Change the alignment of Flash text

1. Click the **Top of page button** at the end of the Skin Care Treatments section, expand the Property inspector, click the **Align list arrow** in the Property inspector, then click **Top**.

    The Top of page button is now aligned with the top of the line of text, as shown in Figure 15.

2. Apply the Top alignment setting to the Top of page button located at the end of the Body Treatments, Massages, and Spa Packages sections.

3. Collapse the Property inspector, turn off Invisible Elements, then save your work.

4. Preview the spa page in your browser, test each Top of page button, then close your browser.

You aligned the Flash text to improve its appearance on the page.

CREATE, MODIFY, AND COPY
A NAVIGATION BAR

What You'll Do

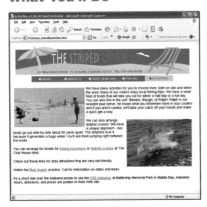

In this lesson, you will create a navigation bar on the spa page that can be used to link to each major page in the Web site. The navigation bar will have five elements: home, about us, cafe, spa, and activities. You will also copy the new navigation bar to other pages in the Web site. On each page you will modify the appropriate element state to reflect the current page.

Creating a Navigation Bar Using Images

To make your Web site more visually appealing, you can create a navigation bar with graphics rather than text. Any graphics you use in a navigation bar must be created in a graphics software program, such as Macromedia Fireworks or Adobe Illustrator. In order for a browser to display a navigation bar correctly, all graphic links in the navigation bar must be exactly the same size. You insert a navigation bar by clicking Insert on the menu bar, pointing to Image Objects, then clicking Navigation Bar. The Insert Navigation Bar dialog box appears. You use this dialog box to specify the appearance of each graphic link, called an **element**, in each of four possible states. A **state** is the condition of the element in relation to the mouse pointer. The four states are as follows: **Up image** (the state when the mouse pointer is not on top of the element), **Over image** (the state when the mouse pointer is positioned on top of the element), **Down image** (the state when you click the element), and **Over while down image**

(the state when you click the element and continue pressing and holding the mouse button). You can create a rollover effect by using different colors or images to represent each element state. You can add many special effects to navigation bars or to links on a Web page. For instance, the Web site shown in Figure 16 contains a navigation bar that uses rollovers and also contains images that link to featured items in the Web site.

> QUICKTIP
>
> You can place only one navigation bar on a Web page using the Insert Navigation Bar dialog box. Another way to insert a navigation bar is to choose Navigation Bar from the Images menu when the Common category is chosen on the Insert bar.

Copying and Modifying a Navigation Bar

After you create a navigation bar, you can copy and paste it to the other main pages in your site to save time. Make sure you place the navigation bar in the same position on each page. This practice ensures that the navigation bar will look the same on each page, making it much easier for viewers to navigate to all the pages in a Web site.

You can then use the Modify Navigation Bar dialog box to customize the appearance of the copied navigation bar on each page. For example, you can change the appearance of the spa navigation bar element on the spa page so that it appears in a different color. Highlighting the navigation element for the current page provides a visual reminder so that viewers can quickly tell which page they are viewing. This process ensures that the navigation bar will look consistent across all pages, but will be customized for each page.

FIGURE 16
Ohio Historical Society Web site

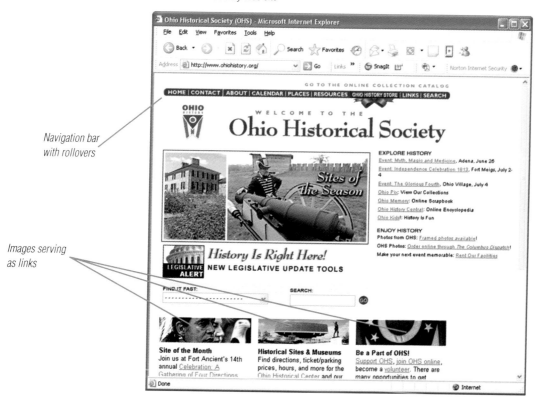

Navigation bar
with rollovers

Images serving
as links

Create a navigation bar using images

1. Select the navigation bar (About Us - Spa - Cafe) on the spa page, then delete it.

   The insertion point is now positioned between the banner and the horizontal rule.

2. Click the **Insert bar list arrow**, click **Common**, click the **Images list arrow**, then click **Navigation Bar**.

3. Type **home** in the Element name text box, click the **Insert list arrow** in the dialog box, click **Horizontally** (if necessary), to specify that the navigation bar be placed horizontally on the page, then remove the check mark in the Use tables check box.

4. Click **Browse** next to the Up image text box, navigate to the drive and folder where your Data Files are stored, double-click (Win) or click (Mac) the **chapter_4 folder**, double-click (Win) or click (Mac) the **assets folder**, then double-click **home_up.gif**.

   The path to the file home_up.gif appears in the Up image text box, as shown in Figure 17.

5. Click **Browse** next to the Over image text box to specify a path to the file home_down.gif located in the chapter_4 assets folder.

(continued)

FIGURE 17
Insert Navigation Bar dialog box

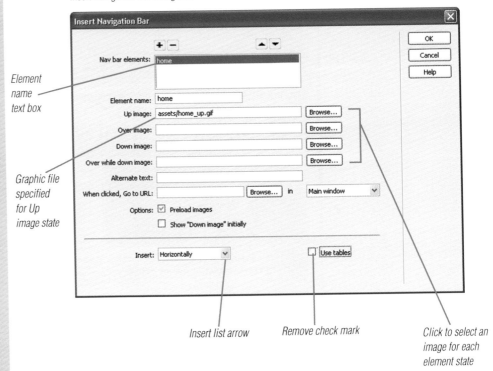

Element name text box

Graphic file specified for Up image state

Insert list arrow

Remove check mark

Click to select an image for each element state

FIGURE 18
Home element of the navigation bar

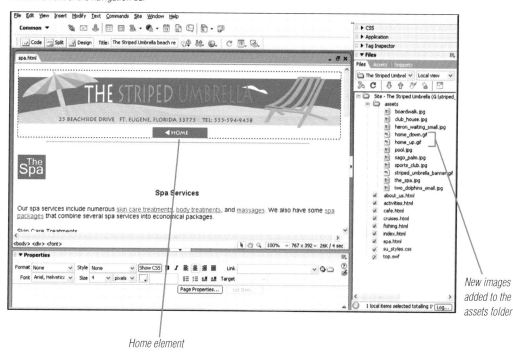

*New images
added to the
assets folder*

Home element

6. Click **Browse** next to the Down image text box to specify a path to the file home_down.gif located in the chapter_4 assets folder, overwriting the existing file.

   TIP Instead of clicking Browse in Steps 6 and 7, you could copy the path of the home_down.gif file in the Over image text box and paste it to the Down image and Over while down image text boxes. You could also reference the home_down.gif file in The Striped Umbrella assets folder once it is copied there in Step 5.

7. Click **Browse** next to the Over while down image text box to specify a path to the file home_down.gif located in the chapter_4 assets folder, overwriting the existing file.

   By specifying one graphic for the Up image state, and another graphic for the Over image, Down image, and Over while down image states, you will create a rollover effect.

8. Type **Navigation button linking to home page** in the Alternate text text box, click **Browse** next to the When clicked, Go to URL text box, then double-click **index.html** in the striped_umbrella root folder.

9. Click **OK**, refresh the Files panel to view the new images you added to The Striped Umbrella assets folder, deselect the button, place the insertion point in front of the button, press **[Backspace]** (Win) or **[delete]** (Mac), press **[Shift][Enter]** (Win) or **[Shift][return]** (Mac), compare your screen to Figure 18, then save your work.

You used the Insert Navigation Bar dialog box to create a navigation bar for the spa page and added the home element to it. You used two images for each state, one for the Up image state and one for the other three states.

Add elements to a navigation bar

1. Click **Modify** on the menu bar, then click **Navigation Bar**.

2. Click the **Add button** ⊞ in the Modify Navigation Bar dialog box, type **about_us** in the Element name text box, then compare your screen with Figure 19.

   > TIP You use the Add button ⊞ to add a new navigation element to the navigation bar, and the Delete button ⊟ to delete a navigation element from the navigation bar.

3. Click **Browse** next to the Up image text box, navigate to the chapter_4 assets folder, click **about_us_up.gif**, then click **OK** (Win) or **Choose** (Mac).

   > TIP If a dialog box appears asking if you would like to copy the file to the root folder, click Yes, then click Save (Mac).

4. Click **Browse** next to the Over image text box to specify a path to the file about_us_down.gif located in the chapter_4 assets folder.

5. Click **Browse** next to the Down image text box to specify a path to the file about_us_down.gif located in the chapter_4 assets folder, overwriting the existing file.

6. Click **Browse** next to the Over while down image text box to specify a path to the file about_us_down.gif located in the chapter_4 assets folder, overwriting the existing file.

(continued)

FIGURE 19

Add elements to a navigation bar

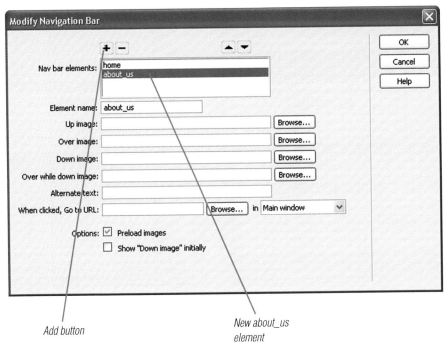

Add button

New about_us element

FIGURE 20

Navigation bar with all elements added

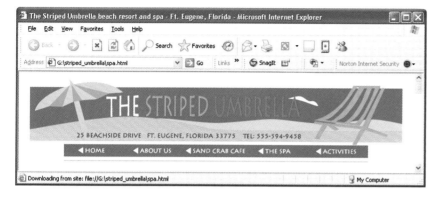

TABLE 3: Settings to use in the Modify Navigation Bar dialog box for each new element

dialog box item	cafe element	spa element	activities element
Up image file	cafe_up.gif	spa_up.gif	activities_up.gif
Over image file	cafe_down.gif	spa_down.gif	activities_down.gif
Down image file	cafe_down.gif	spa_down.gif	activities_down.gif
Over while down image file	cafe_down.gif	spa_down.gif	activities_down.gif
Alternate text	Navigation button linking to cafe page	Navigation button linking to spa page	Navigation button linking to activities page
When clicked, Go to URL	cafe.html	spa.html	activities.html

7. Type **Navigation button linking to the about us page** in the Alternate text text box, click **Browse** next to the When clicked, Go to URL text box, then double-click **about_us.html**.

8. Using the information provided in Table 3, add three more navigation bar elements in the Modify Navigation Bar dialog box called **cafe**, **spa**, and **activities**.

   TIP All files listed in the table are located in the assets folder of the chapter_4 folder where your Data Files are stored.

9. Click **OK** to close the Modify Navigation Bar dialog box.

10. Save your work, preview the page in your browser, compare your screen to Figure 20, check each link to verify that each element works correctly, then close your browser.

You completed The Striped Umbrella navigation bar by adding four more elements to it, each of which contain links to four pages in the site. All images added to the navigation bar are now stored in the assets folder of The Striped Umbrella Web site.

Copy and paste a navigation bar

1. Place the insertion point to the left of the navigation bar, press and hold **[Shift]**, then click to the right of the navigation bar.
2. Click **Edit** on the menu bar, then click **Copy**.
3. Double-click **activities.html** in the Files panel to open the activities page.
4. Select the original navigation bar on the page, click **Edit** on the menu bar, click **Paste**, then compare your screen to Figure 21.
5. Click in front of the navigation bar, then press **[Backspace]** (Win) or **[delete]** (Mac), then press **[Shift][Enter]** (Win) or **[Shift][return]** (Mac).

You copied the navigation bar from the spa page and pasted it on the activities page.

Customize a navigation bar

1. Click **Modify** on the menu bar, then click **Navigation Bar** to open the Modify Navigation Bar dialog box.
2. Click **activities** in the Nav bar elements text box, then click the **Show "Down image" initially check box**, as shown in Figure 22.

   An asterisk appears next to activities in the Nav bar elements text box, indicating that this element will be displayed in the Down image state initially. The sand-colored activities navigation element normally used for the Down image state of the activities navigation bar element will remind viewers that they are on the activities page.

(continued)

FIGURE 21

Navigation bar copied to the activities page

FIGURE 22

Changing settings for the activities element

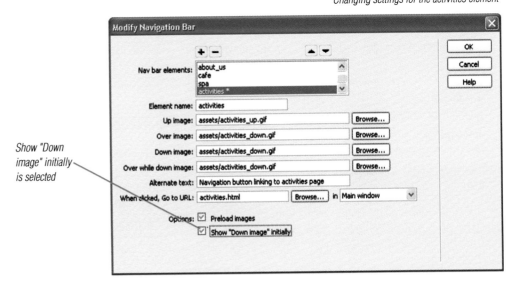

Show "Down image" initially is selected

Working with Links

FIGURE 23
about us page with the modified navigation bar

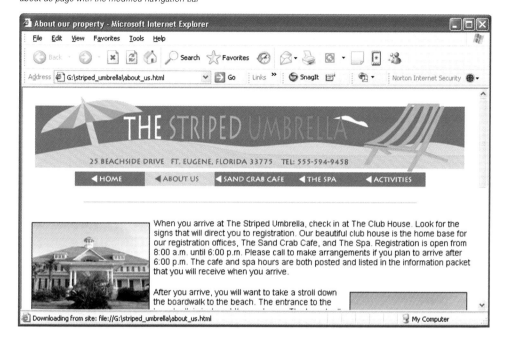

Creating an image map

Another way to create navigation links for Web pages is to create an image map. An **image map** is a graphic that has one or more hotspots placed on top of it. A **hotspot** is an area on a graphic that, when clicked, links to a different location on the page or to another Web page. For example, a map of the United States could have a hotspot placed on each state so that viewers could click a state to link to information about that state. To create a hotspot on an image, select the image on which you want to place the hotspot, then create the hotspot using one of the hotspot tools in the Property inspector.

3. Click **OK** to save the new settings and close the Modify Navigation Bar dialog box, then save and close the activities page.

4. Repeat Steps 1 through 3 to modify the navigation bar on the spa page to show the Down image initially for the spa element, then save and close the spa page.

   > TIP The Show "Down image" initially check box should be checked only for the element that links to the current page.

5. Open the home page, paste the navigation bar on top of the original navigation bar, then modify the navigation bar to show the Down image initially for the home element.

6. Save and close the home page.

7. Open the about us page, paste the navigation bar on top of the original navigation bar, then use the Modify Navigation Bar dialog box to specify that the Down image be displayed initially for the about_us element, then compare your screen to Figure 23.

8. Save your work, preview the current page in your browser, test the navigation bar on the home, about us, spa, and activities pages, then close your browser.

You modified the navigation bar on the activities page to show the activities element in the Down state initially. You then copied the navigation bar to two additional pages in The Striped Umbrella Web site, modifying the navigation bar elements each time to show the Down image state initially.

MANAGE WEB
SITE LINKS

What You'll Do

In this lesson, you will use some of Dreamweaver's reporting features to check The Striped Umbrella Web site for broken links and orphaned files.

Managing Web Site Links

Because the World Wide Web changes constantly, Web sites may be up one day and down the next. To avoid having broken links on your Web site, you need to check external links frequently. If a Web site changes server locations or goes down due to technical difficulties or a power failure, the links to it become broken. An external link can also become broken when an Internet connection fails to work properly. Broken links, like misspelled words on a Web page, indicate that a Web site is not being maintained diligently.

Checking links to make sure they work is an ongoing and crucial task you need to

perform on a regular basis. You must check external links manually by reviewing your Web site in a browser and clicking each link to make sure it works correctly. The Check Links Sitewide feature is a helpful tool for managing your internal links. You can use it to check your entire Web site for the total number of links and the number of links that are okay, external, or broken, and then view the results in the Link Checker panel. The Link Checker panel also provides a list of all of the files used in a Web site, including those that are **orphaned files**, or files that are not linked to any pages in the Web site.

DESIGNTIP   **Considering navigation design issues**

As you work on the navigation structure for a Web site, you should try to limit the number of links on each page to no more than is necessary. Too many links may confuse visitors to your Web site. You should also design links so that viewers can reach the information they want within three or four clicks. If finding information takes more than three or four clicks, the viewer may become discouraged or lost in the site. It's a good idea to provide visual clues on each page to let viewers know where they are, much like a "You are here" marker on a store directory at the mall.

FIGURE 24

Link Checker panel displaying external links

External links
displayed

Show list arrow

FIGURE 25

Link Checker panel displaying no orphaned files

No orphaned
files shown

Show list arrow

FIGURE 26

Assets panel displaying links

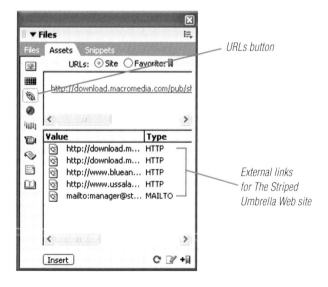

URLs button

External links
for The Striped
Umbrella Web site

Manage Web site links

1. Click **Site** on the menu bar, point to **Advanced**, then click **Recreate Site Cache**.

2. Click **Site** on the menu bar, then click **Check Links Sitewide**.

   The Results panel group opens with the Link Checker panel displayed. By default the Link Checker panel initially displays any broken internal links found in the Web site. The Striped Umbrella Web site has no broken links.

3. Click the **Show list arrow** in the Link Checker panel, click **External Links**, then compare your screen to Figure 24.

   Some external links are listed more than once because the Link Checker displays each instance of an external link.

4. Click the **Show list arrow**, then click **Orphaned Files** to view the orphaned files in the Link Checker panel, as shown in Figure 25.

   The Striped Umbrella Web site has no orphaned files.

5. Click the **Options button** ⚏ in the Results panel group title bar, then click **Close panel group**.

6. Display the Assets panel (if necessary), then click the **URLs button** ⚐ in the Assets panel to display the list of links in the Web site.

   The Assets panel displays the external links used in the Web site, as shown in Figure 26.

7. Close all open pages.

You used the Link Checker panel to check for broken links, external links, and orphaned files in The Striped Umbrella Web site.

Update a page

1. Open dw4_2.html from the chapter_4 folder where your Data Files are stored, then save it as **fishing.html** in the striped_umbrella root folder, overwriting the existing fishing page, but not updating the links.

2. Click the broken link graphic placeholder, click the **Browse for File icon** next to the Src text box on the Property inspector, then browse to the chapter_4 assets folder and select the file heron_small.jpg to copy the file to the striped_umbrella assets folder.

3. Deselect the image placeholder and the image will appear as shown in Figure 27.

   Notice that the text is automatically updated with the body text style. The code was already in place on the page linking the su_styles.css to the file.

4. Save and close the page.

FIGURE 27
Fishing page updated

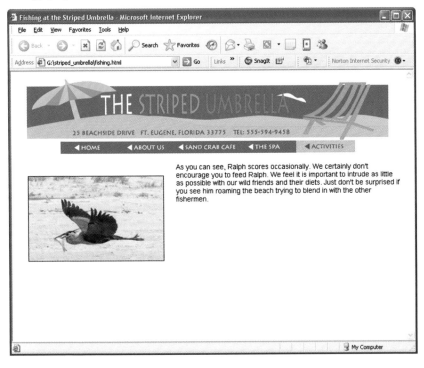

FIGURE 28

Cruises page updated

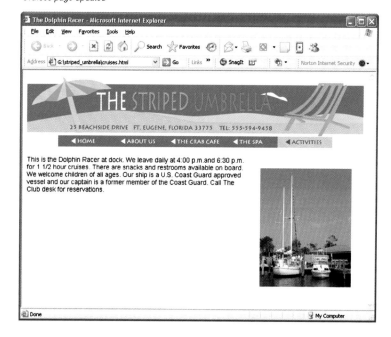

3. Open dw4_3.html from the chapter_4 folder where your Data Files are stored, then save it as **cruises.html** in the striped_umbrella root folder, overwriting the existing cruises page, but not updating the links.

4. Click the broken link graphic placeholder, click the **Browse for File icon** next to the Src text box on the Property inspector, then browse to the chapter_4 assets folder and select the file boats.jpg to copy the file to the striped_umbrella assets folder.

5. Deselect the image placeholder and the image will appear as shown in Figure 28.

   Notice that the text is automatically updated with the body text style. The code was already in place on the page linking the su_styles.css to the file.

6. Save and close the page.

Create external and internal links.

1. Open the blooms & bulbs Web site.
2. Open dw4_4.html from the chapter_4 Data Files folder, then save it as **newsletter.html** in the blooms & bulbs Web site, overwriting the existing file without updating the links.
3. Verify that the banner path is set correctly to the assets folder in the Web site and correct it, if it is not.
4. Scroll to the bottom of the page, then link the National Gardening Association text to *http://www.garden.org*.
5. Link the Better Homes and Gardens Gardening Home Page text to *http://bhg.com/gardening*.
6. Link the Southern Living text to *http://www.southernliving.com/southern*.
7. Save the file, then preview the page in your browser, verifying that each link works correctly.
8. Close your browser, then return to the newsletter page in Dreamweaver.
9. Scroll to the paragraph about gardening issues, select the gardening tips text in the last sentence, then link the selected text to the tips.html file in the blooms root folder.
10. Add a new rule to the blooms_styles.css file called **bodytext** using the following formatting choices: Font: Arial, Helvetica, sans-serif; Style: normal; Weight: normal; and Size: 14.

11. Apply the headings style to the text "Gardening Matters", the seasons style to the subheadings on the page, and the bodytext style to the descriptions under each subheading.
12. Center the "Gardening Matters" text.
13. Change the page title to **Gardening Matters**, save all open files, test the links in your browser, then close your browser.
14. Open the plants page and add the following sentence to the end of the last paragraph: **We have many annuals, perennials, and water plants that have just arrived**.
15. Link the "annuals" text to the annuals.html file, link the "perennials" text to the perennials.html file, and the "water plants" text to the water_plants.html file.
16. Save your work, test the links in your browser, then close your browser.

Create internal links to named anchors.

1. Show Invisible Elements (if necessary).
2. Click the Insert bar list arrow, then click Common.
3. Switch to the newsletter page, if necessary, then insert a named anchor in front of the Grass heading named **grass**.
4. Insert a named anchor in front of the Plants heading named **plants**.

5. Insert a named anchor in front of the Trees heading named **trees**.
6. Insert a named anchor at the top of the page named **top**.
7. Click the Point to File icon in the Property inspector to create a link from the word grass in the Gardening Issues paragraph to the grass named anchor.
8. Create a link from the word trees in the Gardening Issues paragraph to the trees named anchor.
9. Create a link from the word plants in the Gardening Issues paragraph to the plants named anchor.
10. Save your work, view the page in your browser, test all the links to make sure they work, then close your browser.

Insert Flash text.

1. Insert Flash text at the bottom of the page that will take you to the top of the page. Use the following settings: Font: Arial, Size: 16, Color: #000066, Rollover color: #3366FF, Text: Top of page, Link: newsletter.html#top, Target: _top.
2. Save the Flash text file as **top.swf** and enter the title **Link to top of page** in the Flash Accessibility Attributes dialog box.
3. Save all open files, view the page in your browser, test the Flash text link, then close your browser.

Create, modify, and copy a navigation bar.

1. Place your insertion point right under the banner, click the Images list arrow on the Insert bar, then click Navigation Bar to insert a horizontal navigation bar at the top of the newsletter page below the banner.

2. Type **home** as the first element name, then use the b_home_up.jpg file for the Up image state. This file is in the assets folder of the chapter_4 Data Files folder.

3. Specify the file b_home_down.jpg file for the three remaining states. This file (and all files for the remainder of this exercise) are in the assets folder of the chapter_4 Data Files folder.

4. Enter **Link to home page** as the alternate text, then set the index.html file as the link for the home element.

5. Create a new element named **plants** and use the b_plants_up.jpg file for the Up image state and the b_plants_down.jpg file for the remaining three states.

6. Enter **Link to plants page** as the alternate text, then set the plants.html file as the link for the plants element.

7. Create a new element named **tips** and use the b_tips_up.jpg file for the Up image state and the b_tips_down.jpg file for the remaining three states.

8. Enter **Link to tips page** as the alternate text, then set the tips.html file as the link for the tips element.

9. Create a new element named **classes** and use the b_classes_up.jpg file for the Up image state and the b_classes_down.jpg file for the remaining three states.

10. Enter **Link to classes page** as the alternate text, then set the classes.html file as the link for the classes element.

11. Create a new element named **newsletter**, then use the b_newsletter_up.jpg file for the Up image state and the b_newsletter_down.jpg file for the remaining three states.

12. Enter the alternate text **Link to newsletter page**, then set the newsletter.html file as the link for the newsletter element.

13. Center the navigation bar (if necessary), save the page and test the links in your browser, then close the browser.

14. Select and copy the navigation bar, then open the home page.

15. Delete the current navigation bar on the home page, then paste the new navigation bar under the banner. (*Hint*: Insert a line break after the banner before you paste so that the navigation bar is directly below the banner.)

16. Modify the home element on the navigation bar to show the Down image state initially.

17. Save the page, test the links in your browser, then close the browser and the page.

18. Modify the navigation bar on the newsletter page so the Down image is shown initially for the newsletter element, then save and close the newsletter page.

19. Paste the navigation bar on the plants page and the tips page, making the necessary modifications so that the Down image is shown initially for each element.

20. Save your work, preview all the pages in your browser, compare your newsletter page to Figure 29, test all the links, then close your browser.

Manage Web site links.

1. Use the Link Checker panel to view and fix broken links, external links, and orphaned files in the blooms & bulbs Web site.

2. Open dw4_5.html from the chapter_4 Data Files folder, then save it as **annuals.html**, replacing the original file. Do not update links, but save the file fuschia.jpg in the assets folder of the Web site.

3. Repeat Step 2 using dw4_6.html to replace perennials.html, saving the iris.jpg file in the assets folder and using dw4_7.html to replace water_plants.html, saving the water_hyacinth.jpg file in the assets folder.

4. Save your work, then close all open pages.

FIGURE 29
Completed Skills Review

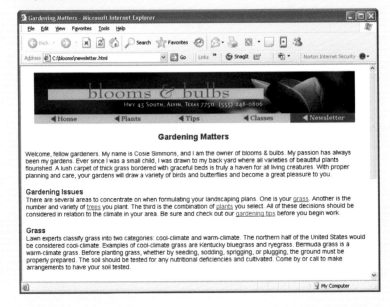

Use Figure 30 as a guide to continue your work on the TripSmart Web site that you began in Project Builder 1 in Chapter 1. You have been asked to create a new page for the Web site that lists helpful links for customers. You will also add content to the destinations, kenya, and amazon pages.

1. Open the TripSmart Web site.
2. Open dw4_8.html from the chapter_4 Data Files folder, then save it as **services.html** in the TripSmart Web site root folder, not updating links.
3. Verify that the TripSmart banner is in the assets folder of the root folder.
4. Apply the bodytext style to the paragraphs of text and the heading style to the paragraph headings.
5. Create named anchors named **reservations, outfitters, tours**, and **links** in front of the respective headings on the page, then link each named anchor to "Reservations", "Travel Outfitters", "Escorted Tours", and "Helpful Links in Travel Planning" in the first paragraph.
6. Link the text "on-line catalog" in the Travel Outfitters paragraph to the catalog.html page.
7. Link the text "CNN Travel Channel" under the heading Travel Information Sites to http://www.cnn.com/TRAVEL.
8. Repeat Step 7 to create links for the rest of the Web sites listed:
   US Department of State:
   http://travel.state.gov
   Yahoo! : http://yahoo.com/Recreation/Travel
   MapQuest:
   http://www.mapquest.com
   Rand McNally:
   http://www.randmcnally.com
   AccuWeather:
   http://www.accuweather.com
   The Weather Channel:
   http://www.weather.com
9. Reformat the navigation bar on the home page with a style of your choice, then place it on each completed page of the Web site. If you decide to use graphics for the navigation bar, you will have to create your own graphic files using a graphics program. There are no data files for you to use. (*Hint*: If you create your own graphic files, be sure to create two graphic files for each element: one for the Up image state and one for the Down image state.) To design a navigation bar using text, you simply type the text for each navigation bar element, format the text appropriately, and insert links to each text element as you did in Chapter 2. The navigation bar should contain the following elements: Home, Catalog, Services, Destinations, and Newsletter.

10. Save each page, then check for broken links and orphaned files. (*Hint*: The two orphaned files will be removed after completing the next steps.)

11. Open the destinations.html file in your root folder and save it as **kenya.html**, overwriting the existing file, then close the file.

12. Open dw4_9.html from the chapter_4 Data Files folder, then save it as **amazon.html**, overwriting the existing file. Do not update links, but save the water_lily.jpg and sloth.jpg files in the assets folder of the Web site, then save and close the file.

13. Open dw4_10.html from the chapter_4 Data Files folder, then save the file as **destinations.html**, overwriting the existing file. Do not update links, but save the parrot.jpg and giraffe.jpg files in the assets folder of the Web site.

14. Link the text "Amazon" in the second sentence of the first paragraph to the amazon.html file.

15. Link the text "Kenya" in the first sentence in the second paragraph to the kenya.html file.

16. Copy your customized navigation bar to the two new pages so they will match the other pages.

17. Save all files.

18. Test all links in your browser, close your browser, then close all open pages.

FIGURE 30

Sample Project Builder 1

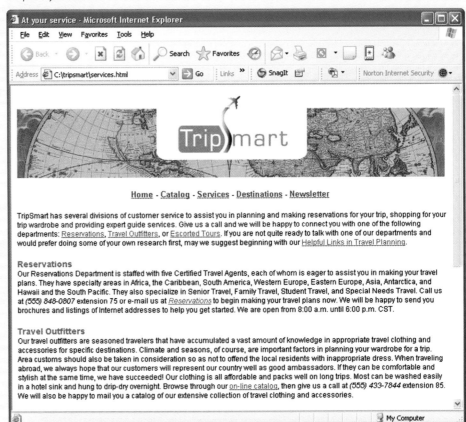

Working with Links

Use Figure 31 as a guide to continue your work on the emma's book bag Web site that you started in Project Builder 2 in Chapter 1. Emma Claire has asked you to create a page describing the upcoming book sale and a book signing event. You will create the content for that page and individual pages describing each event.

1. Open the emma's book bag Web site.
2. Open dw4_11.html from the chapter_4 Data Files folder, save it as **events.html** in the root folder of the emma's book bag Web site, overwriting the existing file and not updating the links.
3. Check the path of the book_bag banner to make sure it is linking to the banner in the assets folder of the Web site, then check the path for each link in the navigation bar to make sure each text link is linking to the files in the root folder.
4. Select the text "annual book sale" in the first paragraph, then link it to the seasonal.html page. (*Hint*: This page has not been developed yet.)
5. Select the text "book signing" in the second paragraph and link it to the signings.html page. (*Hint*: This page has not been developed yet.)
6. Add the page title **book bag happenings**.
7. Insert the file grif_stockley.jpg from the chapter_4 assets folder at the beginning of

the second paragraph, add appropriate alternate text, then choose your own alignment and formatting settings.
8. Save and close the file.
9. Open dw4_12.html from the chapter_4 Data Files folder, then save it as **seasonal.html**, overwriting the existing file and not updating links. Save the image books.jpg from the chapter_4 assets folder in the Web site assets folder.
10. Save and close the file.

11. Repeat Steps 9 and 10 to open the dw4_13.html file and save it as **signings.html**, overwriting the existing file and saving the salted_with_fire.jpg in the assets folder.
12. Save all the pages, then check for broken links and orphaned files.
13. Preview all the pages in your browser, check to make sure the links work correctly, close your browser, then close all open pages.

FIGURE 31
Completed Project Builder 2

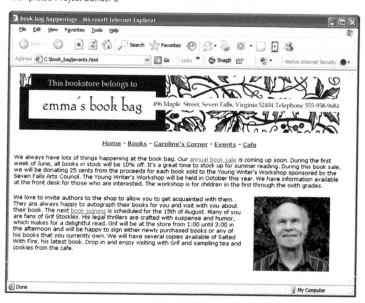

Grace Keiko is a talented young water-color artist who specializes in botanical works. She wants to develop a Web site to advertise her work but isn't sure what she would like to include in a Web site or how to tie the pages together. She decides to spend several hours looking at other artists' Web sites to help her get started.

1. Connect to the Internet, navigate to the Online Companion, and review the links for this chapter. The Web site pictured in Figure 32 is *www.katenessler.com*.
2. Spend some time looking at several of the artist Web sites that you find to familiarize yourself with the types of content that each contains.
3. What categories of page content would you include on your Web site if you were Grace?
4. What external links would you consider including?
5. Describe how you would place external links on the pages and list examples of ones you would use.
6. Would you use text or graphics for your navigation bar?
7. Would you include rollover effects on the navigation bar elements? If so, describe how they might look.

8. How could you incorporate named anchors on any of the pages?
9. Sketch a Web site plan for Grace, including the pages that you would use as links from the home page.

10. Refer to your Web site sketch, then create a home page for Grace that includes a navigation bar, a short introductory paragraph about her art, and a few external links.

FIGURE 32
Design Project

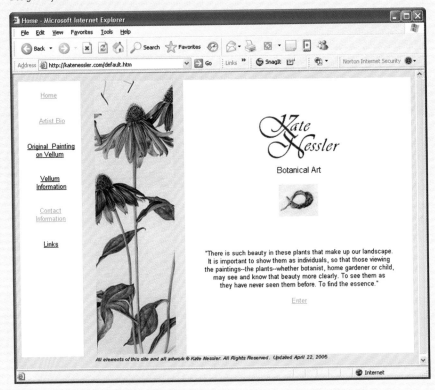

PORTFOLIO PROJECT

In this assignment, you will continue to work on the Web site that you started in Chapter 1 and developed in Chapters 2 and 3.

You will continue building your Web site by designing and completing a page with a navigation bar. After creating the navigation bar, you will copy it to each completed page in the Web site. In addition to the navigation bar, you will add several external links and several internal links to other pages as well as to named anchors. You will also link Flash text to a named anchor. After you complete this work, you will check for broken links and orphaned files.

1. Consult your storyboard to decide which page or pages you would like to develop in this chapter. Decide how to design and where to place the navigation bar, named anchors, Flash text, and any additional page elements you decide to use. Decide which reports should be run on the Web site to check for accuracy.

2. Research Web sites that could be included on one or more of your pages as external links of interest to your viewers. Create a list of the external links you want to use. Using your storyboard as a guide, decide where each external link should be placed in the site.

3. Add the external links to existing pages or create any additional pages that contain external links.

4. Create named anchors for key locations on the page, such as the top of the page, then link appropriate text on the page to them.

5. Insert at least one Flash text object that links to either a named anchor or an internal link.

6. Decide on a design for a navigation bar that will be used on all pages of the Web site.

7. Create the navigation bar and copy it to all finished pages on the Web site. If you decided to use graphics for the navigation bar, create the graphics that will be used.

8. Use the Link Checker panel to check for broken links and orphaned files.

9. Use the check list in Figure 33 to make sure your Web site is complete, save your work, then close all open pages.

FIGURE 33
Portfolio Project check list

Web Site Check List
1. Do all pages have a page title?
2. Does the home page have a description and keywords?
3. Does the home page contain contact information?
4. Does every page in the Web site have consistent navigation links?
5. Does the home page have a last updated statement that will automatically update when the page is saved?
6. Do all paths for links and images work correctly?
7. Do all images have alternate text?
8. Are all colors Websafe?
9. Are there any unnecessary files that you can delete from the assets folder?
10. Is there a style sheet with at least two styles?
11. Did you apply the style sheet to page content?
12. Does at least one page contain links to one or more named anchors?
13. Does at least one page contain Flash text that links to either a named anchor or an internal link?
14. Do all pages view well using at least two different browsers?

Working with Links

WORKING WITH
TABLES

1. Create a table.

2. Resize, split, and merge cells.

3. Insert and align graphics in table cells.

4. Insert text and format cell content.

5. Perform Web site maintenance.

Introduction

You have learned how to place and align elements on a page and enhance them using various formatting options. However, page layout options are fairly limited without the use of tables. Tables offer another solution for organizing text and graphics on a page. **Tables** are placeholders made up of small boxes called **cells**, into which you can insert text and graphics. Cells in a table are arranged horizontally in **rows** and vertically in **columns**. Using tables on a Web page gives you total control over the placement of each object on the page. In this chapter, you will learn how to create and format tables, work with table rows and columns, and format the contents of table cells. You will also learn how to select and format table cells using table tags on the tag selector. Clicking a table tag on the tag selector selects the table element associated with that tag.

Inserting Graphics and Text in Tables

Once you insert a table on a Web page, it becomes very easy to place text and graphics exactly where you want them on the page. You can use a table to control both the placement of elements in relation to each other and the amount of space between each page element. Before you insert a table, however, you should always plan how your table will look with all the text and graphics in it. Even a rough sketch before you begin will save you time as you add content to the page.

Maintaining a Web Site

You already know how to check for broken links and Non-Websafe colors in your Web site. Dreamweaver also provides many other management tools to help you identify other problems. For instance, you can run a report to check for pages that have no page titles, or to search for images that are missing alternate text. It's a good idea to set up a schedule to run these and other reports on a regular basis.

Tools You'll Use

Table properties

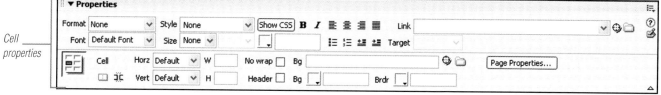

Cell properties

Row properties

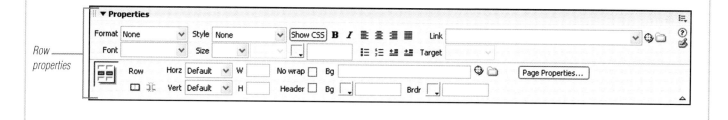

CREATE A TABLE

What You'll Do

In this lesson, you will create a table for the cafe page in The Striped Umbrella Web site to provide the framework for the page layout.

Understanding Table Modes

There are two ways to create a table in Dreamweaver. Each method requires working in Design view. The first method is to click the Table button on the Insert bar. The Table button is available in the Common category of the Insert bar and in the Layout category of the Insert bar, whenever the Standard mode button is enabled. The second method is to click the Insert bar list arrow, click Layout, click the Layout mode button on the Insert bar, then click the Layout Table button or the Draw Layout Cell button. You can choose Standard mode, Expanded Tables mode, or Layout mode by clicking the appropriate button on the Insert bar, when the Layout category of the Insert bar is displayed.

Creating a Table in Standard Mode

Creating a table in Standard mode is useful when you want to create a table with a specific number of columns and rows. To create a table in Standard mode, click the Table button on the Insert bar to open the Table dialog box. Enter values for the number of rows and columns, the border thickness, table width, cell padding, and cell spacing. The **border** is the outline or frame around the table and the individual cells and is measured in pixels. The table width, which can be specified in pixels or as a percentage, refers to the width of the table. When the table width is specified as a percentage, the table width will adjust to the width of the browser window. When the table width is specified in pixels, the table width stays the same, regardless of the size of the browser window. **Cell padding** is the distance between the cell content and the **cell walls**, the lines inside the cell borders. **Cell spacing** is the distance between cells.

Working with Tables

Setting Table Accessibility Preferences for Tables

You can make a table more accessible to visually handicapped viewers by adding a table caption and a table summary that can be read by screen readers. The table caption appears on the screen. The table summary does not. These features are especially useful for tables that are used for tabular data. **Table headers** are another way to provide accessibility. Table headers can be placed at the top or sides of a table with data. They are automatically centered and bold and are used by screen readers to help viewers identify the table content. Table captions, summaries, and headers are all created in the Table dialog box.

Drawing a Table in Layout Mode

You use Layout mode when you want to draw your own table. Drawing a table is ideal when you want to place page elements on a Web page and have no need for a specific number of rows and columns. You can use the Draw Layout Cell button or the Layout Table button in the Layout category of the Insert bar to draw a cell or a table. After you draw the first cell, Dreamweaver plots a table for you automatically.

Planning a Table

Before you create a table, you should sketch a plan for it that shows its location on the Web page and the placement of text and graphics in its cells. You should also decide whether to include borders around the tables and cells. Setting the border value to 0 causes the table to appear invisible, so that viewers will not realize that you used a table for the page layout unless they look at the code. Figure 1 shows a sketch of the table you will create on The Striped Umbrella cafe page to organize graphics and text.

FIGURE 1

Sketch of table on cafe page

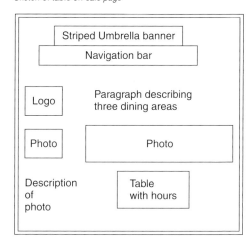

Create a table

1. Open The Striped Umbrella Web site that you completed in Chapter 4.

2. Double-click **cafe.html** in the Files panel to open the cafe page in Design view.

   The cafe page is blank.

3. Click the **Insert bar list arrow**, click **Layout**, click the **Standard mode button** `Standard`, then click the **Table button** ⊞.

4. Type **7** in the Rows text box, type **3** in the Columns text box, type **750** in the Table width text box, click the **Table width list arrow**, click **pixels**, then type **0** in the Border thickness text box, as shown in Figure 2.

   > TIP   It is better to add more rows than you think you will need when you create your table. It is far easier to delete rows than to add rows if you decide later to split or merge cells in the table.

   (continued)

FIGURE 2
Table dialog box

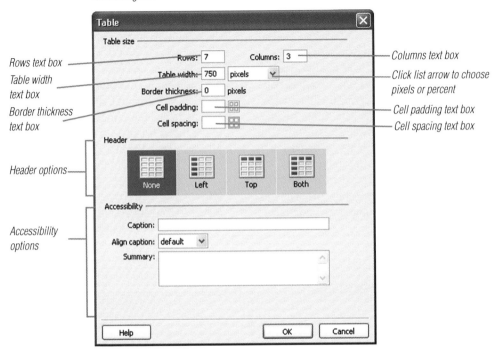

Rows text box
Table width text box
Border thickness text box
Header options
Accessibility options

Columns text box
Click list arrow to choose pixels or percent
Cell padding text box
Cell spacing text box

Expanded Tables mode

Expanded Tables mode is a feature that allows you to change to a table view with expanded table borders and temporary cell padding and cell spacing. This mode makes it much easier to actually see how many rows and columns you have in your table. Many times, especially after splitting empty cells, it is difficult to place the insertion point precisely in a table cell. The Expanded Tables mode allows you to see each cell clearly. However, most of the time you will want to work in Standard mode to maintain the WYSIWYG environment. **WYSIWYG** is the acronym for What You See Is What You Get. This means that your Web page should look the same in the browser as it does in the Web editor. You can toggle between Expanded Tables mode and Standard mode by pressing [F6]. You can access Layout mode by pressing and holding [Ctrl] [F6] (Win) or ⌘ [F6] (Mac).

FIGURE 3

Table dialog box

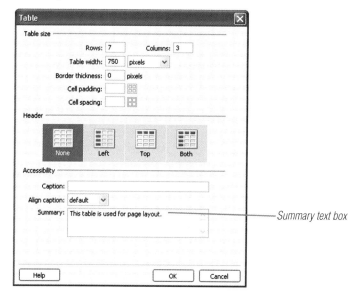

— *Summary text box*

5. Type **This table is used for page layout.** in the Summary text box, then compare your screen to Figure 3.

6. Click **OK**.

   The table appears on the page, but the table summary is not visible. The summary will not appear in the browser but will be read by screen readers.

   TIP To edit accessibility preferences for a table, switch to Code view to edit the code directly.

7. Click the **Expanded Tables mode button** Expanded , then click **OK** in the Getting Started in Expanded Tables Mode dialog box, as shown in Figure 4.

   The Expanded Tables mode makes it easier to select and edit tables.

8. Click the **Standard mode button** Standard to return to Standard mode.

   TIP You can also return to Standard mode by clicking [exit] at the top of the table.

You opened the cafe page in The Striped Umbrella Web site. You then created a table containing seven rows and three columns and set the width to 750 pixels so it will appear in the same size regardless of the browser window size. Finally, you entered a table summary that will be read by screen readers.

FIGURE 4

Expanded Tables mode

Click to exit Expanded Tables mode

Expanded Tables mode displays more space between cells for easier editing

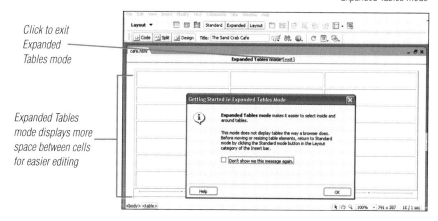

Set table properties

1. Move the pointer slowly to the edge of the table until you see the pointer change to a table pointer ⊞, then click the table border to select the table.

   TIP You can also select a table by (1) clicking the insertion point in the table, then clicking Modify, Table, Select Table; (2) selecting a cell in the table, then clicking Edit, Select All; or (3) clicking the table tag <table> on the tag selector.

2. Expand the Property inspector (if necessary) to display the current properties of the new table.

   TIP The Property inspector will display information about the table only if the table is selected.

3. Click the **Align list arrow** on the Property inspector, then click **Center** to center the table on the page, as shown in Figure 5.

   The center alignment formatting ensures that the table will be centered in all browser windows, regardless of the screen size.

   You selected and center-aligned the table.

FIGURE 5
Property inspector showing properties of selected table

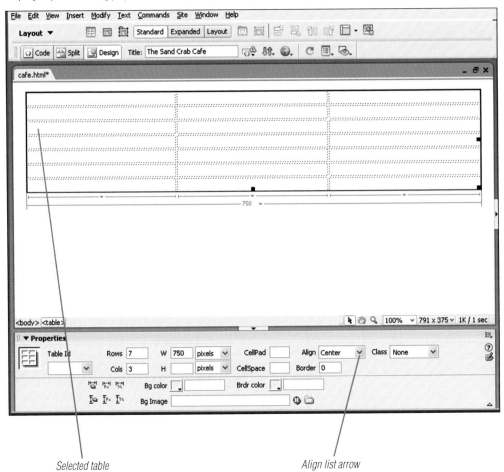

Selected table

Align list arrow

Working with Tables

FIGURE 6

Table in Layout mode

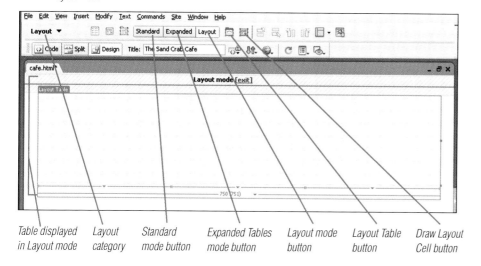

Table displayed in Layout mode   Layout category   Standard mode button   Expanded Tables mode button   Layout mode button   Layout Table button   Draw Layout Cell button

View the table in Layout mode

1. Click the **Layout mode button** Layout on the Insert bar.

   The table appears in Layout mode, as shown in Figure 6.

   TIP The Getting Started in Layout Mode dialog box might open, providing instructions on creating and editing a table in Layout mode.

2. Click **OK** (if necessary) to close the Getting Started in Layout Mode dialog box.

3. Click the **Standard mode button** Standard to return to Standard mode.

4. Click the **Insert bar list arrow**, then click **Common**.

You viewed the table in Layout mode, then returned to Standard mode.

DESIGNTIP   Setting table and cell widths

If you use a table to place all the text and graphics contained on a Web page, it is wise to set the width of the table in pixels. This ensures that the table will not resize itself proportionally if the browser window size is changed. If you set the width of a table using pixels, the table will remain one size, regardless of the browser window size. For instance, if the width of a table is set to slightly less than 800, the table will stretch across the whole width of a browser window set at a resolution of 800×600. The same table would be the same size on a screen set at 1024×768 and therefore would not stretch across the entire screen. Most designers use a resolution of 800×600. Be aware, however, that if you set the width of your table at 800 pixels, your table will be too wide to print the entire width of the page, and part of the right side of the page will be cut off. If you are designing a table layout for a page that is likely to be printed by the viewer, you should make your table narrower to fit on a printed page. If you set a table width as a percentage, however, the table would resize itself proportionally in any browser window, regardless of the resolution. You can also set each cell width as either a percentage of the table or as fixed pixels.

RESIZE, SPLIT, AND MERGE CELLS

What You'll Do

In this lesson, you will set the width of the table cells to be split across the table in predetermined widths. You will then split one cell. You will also merge some cells to provide space for the banner.

Resizing Table Elements

You can resize the rows or columns of a table manually. To resize a table, row, or column, you must first select the table, then drag one of the table's three selection handles. To change all the columns in a table so that they are the same size, drag the middle-right selection handle. To resize the height of all rows simultaneously, drag the middle-bottom selection handle. To resize the entire table, drag the right-corner selection handle. To resize a row or column individually, drag the interior cell borders up, down, to the left, or to the right. You can also resize selected columns, rows, or individual cells by entering specific measurements in the W and H text boxes in the Property inspector specified either in pixels or as a percentage. Cells whose width or height is specified as a percentage will maintain that percentage in relation to the width or height of the entire table if the table is resized.

Resetting table widths and heights

After resizing columns and rows in a table, you might want to change the sizes of the columns and rows back to their previous sizes. To reset columns and rows to their previous widths and heights, click Modify on the menu bar, point to Table, then click Clear Cell Heights or Clear Cell Widths. Using the Clear Cell Heights command also forces the cell border to snap to the bottom of any inserted graphics, so you can also use this command to tighten up extra white space in a cell.

Splitting and Merging Cells

Using the Table button creates a new table with evenly spaced columns and rows. Sometimes you might want to adjust the cells in a table by splitting or merging them. To split a cell means to divide it into multiple rows or columns. To merge cells means to combine multiple cells into one cell. Using split and merged cells gives you more flexibility and control in placing page elements on a page and can help you create a more visually exciting layout. When you merge cells, the HTML tag used to describe the merged cell changes from a width size tag to a column span or row span tag. For example, <td colspan="2"> is the code for two cells that have been merged into one cell that spans two columns.

QUICKTIP
You can split merged cells and merge split cells.

DESIGNTIP   **Using nested tables**

A nested table is a table inside a table. To create a nested table, you place the insertion point in the cell where you want to insert the nested table, then click the Table button on the Insert bar. The nested table is a separate table that can be formatted differently from the table in which it is placed. Nested tables are useful when you want part of your table data to have visible borders and part to have invisible borders. For example, you can nest a table with red borders inside a table with invisible borders. You need to plan carefully when you insert nested tables. It is easy to get carried away and insert too many nested tables, which makes it more difficult to apply formatting and rearrange table elements. Before you insert a nested table, consider whether you could achieve the same result by adding rows and columns or by splitting cells.

Resize columns

1. Click inside the first cell in the bottom row, then click the **cell tag <td>** on the tag selector, as shown in Figure 7.

   Clicking the cell tag (the HTML tag for that cell) selects the corresponding cell in the table.

   TIP You can also click inside a cell to select it. To select the entire table, click the <table> tag on the tag selector.

2. Type **30%** in the W text box in the Property inspector, then press **[Enter]** (Win) or **[return]** (Mac) to change the width of the cell to 30 percent of the table width.

   Notice that the column width is displayed at the bottom of the first column in the table, along with the table width of 750 pixels.

   TIP You need to type the % sign next to the number you type in the W text box. Otherwise, the width will be expressed in pixels.

3. Repeat Steps 1 and 2 for the next two cells in the last row, using **30%** for the middle cell and **40%** for the last cell.

   The combined widths of the three cells add up to 100 percent. As you add content to the table, the columns will remain in this proportion unless you insert a graphic that is larger than the table cell. If a larger graphic is inserted, the cell width will expand to display it.

   TIP Changing the width of a single cell changes the width of the entire column.

   You set the width of each of the three cells in the bottom row to set the column sizes for the table. This will keep the table from resizing when you add content.

FIGURE 7
Selecting a cell

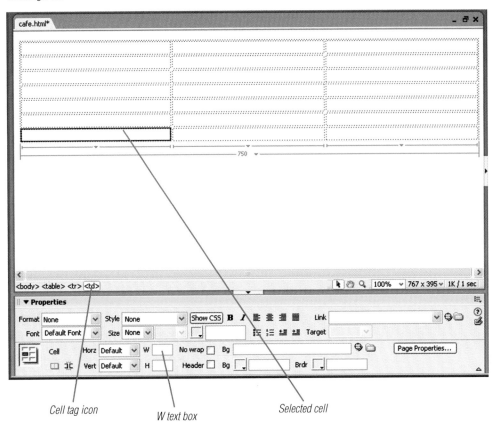

Cell tag icon   W text box   Selected cell

FIGURE 8

Resizing the height of a row

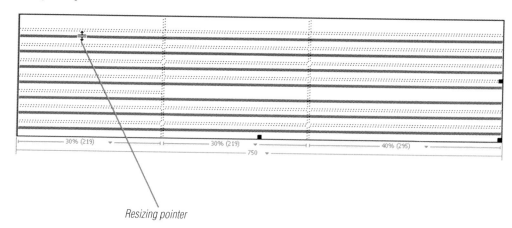

Resizing pointer

Resize rows

1. Place the pointer over the bottom border of the first row until it changes to a resizing pointer ⇻ , as shown in Figure 8, then click and drag down about ¼ of an inch to increase the height of the row.

   The border turns darker when you select and drag it.

2. Click **Window** on the menu bar, click **History**, then drag the **slider** in the History panel up one line to return the row to its original height.

3. Close the History panel group.

You changed the height of the top row, then used the History panel to change it back it to its original height.

HTML table tags

When formatting a table, it is important to understand the basic HTML table tags. The tags used for creating a table are <table> </table>. The tags used to create table rows are <tr></tr>. The tags used to create table cells are <td></td>. Dreamweaver places the   code into each empty table cell at the time it is created. The   code represents a nonbreaking space, or a space that a browser will display on the page. Some browsers will collapse an empty cell, which can ruin the look of a table. The nonbreaking space will hold the cell until content is placed in it, at which time it will be automatically removed.

Split cells

1. Click inside the first cell in the fifth row, then click the **cell tag <td>** in the tag selector.

2. Click the **Splits cell into rows or columns button** ⬓ in the Property inspector.

3. Click the **Split cell into Rows option button** (if necessary), type **2** in the Number of rows text box (if necessary), as shown in Figure 9, then click **OK**.

   TIP   To create a new row identical to the one above it, place the insertion point in the last cell of a table, then press [Tab].

You split a cell into two rows.

FIGURE 9
Splitting a cell into two rows

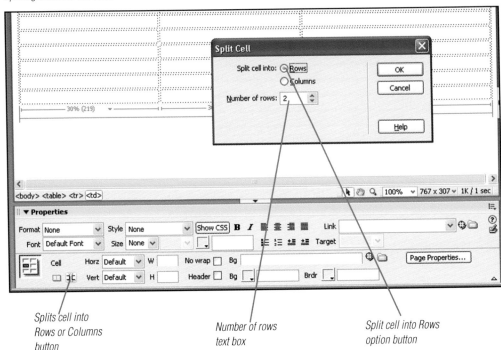

Splits cell into Rows or Columns button

Number of rows text box

Split cell into Rows option button

Adding or deleting a row

As you add new content to your table, you might find that you have too many or too few rows or columns. You can add or delete one row or column at a time or several at once. You use commands on the Modify menu to add and delete table rows and columns. When you add a new column or row, you must first select the existing column or row to which the new column or row will be adjacent. The Insert Rows or Columns dialog box lets you choose how many rows or columns you want to insert or delete, and where you want them placed in relationship to the selected row or column. The new column or row will have the same formatting and number of cells as the selected column or row.

FIGURE 10
Merging selected cells into one cell

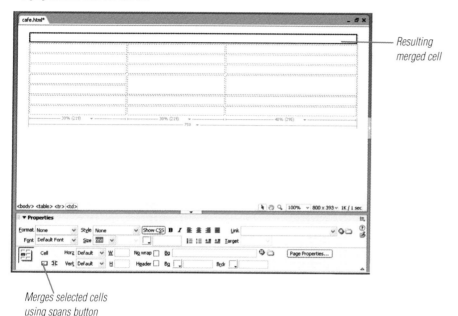

Resulting merged cell

Merges selected cells using spans button

FIGURE 11
Code view for merged cells

colspan tag

```
1   <!DOCTYPE html PUBLIC "-//W3C//DTD XHTML 1.0 Transitional//EN"
    "http://www.w3.org/TR/xhtml1/DTD/xhtml1-transitional.dtd">
2   <html xmlns="http://www.w3.org/1999/xhtml">
3   <head>
4   <meta http-equiv="Content-Type" content="text/html; charset=iso-8859-1" />
5   <title>The Sand Crab Cafe</title>
6   </head>
7
8   <body>
9   <table width="750" border="0" align="center" summary="This table is used for page layout.">
10  <tr>
11      <td colspan="3"> </td>
12  </tr>
13  <tr>
14      <td> </td>
15      <td> </td>
16      <td> </td>
17  </tr>
```

Merge cells

1. Click the insertion point in the first cell in the top row, then click and drag to the right to select the second and third cells in the top row.

2. Click the **Merges selected cells using spans button** ⊡ in the Property inspector.

   The three cells are merged into one cell, as shown in Figure 10. Merged cells are good placeholders for banners or page headings.

   TIP   You can only merge cells that are adjacent to each other.

3. Click the **Show Code view button** ⟨⟩ Code, then view the code for the merged cells, as shown in Figure 11.

   Notice the table tags denoting the column span (td colspan="3") and the nonbreaking spaces ( ) inserted in the empty cells.

4. Click the **Show Design view button** Design, then save your work.

You merged three cells in the first row to make room for The Striped Umbrella banner.

INSERT AND ALIGN
GRAPHICS IN TABLE CELLS

What You'll Do

In this lesson, you will insert The Striped Umbrella banner in the top row of the table. You will then insert three graphics in three different cells. After placing the three graphics, you will align them within their cells.

Inserting Graphics in Table Cells

You can insert graphics in the cells of a table using the Image command in the Images menu on the Insert bar. If you already have graphics saved in your Web site that you would like to insert in a table, you can drag them from the Assets panel into the table cells. When you add a large graphic to a cell, the cell expands to accommodate the inserted graphic. If you select the Show attributes when inserting Images check box in the Accessibility category of the Preferences dialog box, the Image Tag Accessibility Attributes dialog box will open after you insert a graphic, prompting you to enter alternate text. Figure 12 shows the John Deere Web site, which uses a table for page layout and contains several images in its table cells. Notice that some images appear in cells by themselves, and some appear in cells containing text or other graphics. Some cells have a white background, and some have a green background.

Aligning Graphics in Table Cells

You can align graphics both horizontally and vertically within a cell. You can align a graphic horizontally using the Horz (horizontal) alignment options in the Property inspector. This option is used to align the entire contents of the cell, whether there is one object, or several. You can also align a graphic vertically by the top, middle, bottom, or baseline of a cell. To align a graphic vertically within a cell, use the Vert (vertical) Align list arrow in the Property inspector, then choose an alignment option, as shown in Figure 13. To control spacing between cells, you can use cell padding and cell spacing. **Cell padding** is the space between a cell's border and its contents. **Cell spacing** is the distance between adjacent cells.

FIGURE 12

John Deere Web site (courtesy of Deere & Company)

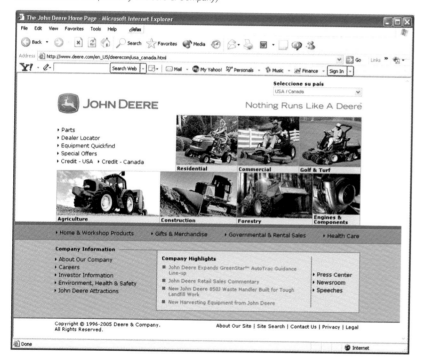

FIGURE 13

Vertical alignment options in the Property inspector

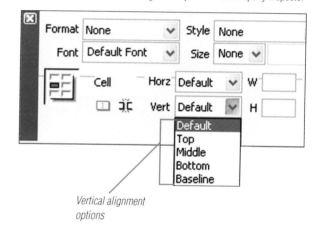

Vertical alignment options

Insert graphics in table cells

1. Open the index page, click the **banner** to select it, press and hold **[Shift]**, then click to the right of the navigation bar to select both the banner and the navigation bar.

2. Click **Edit** on the menu bar, click **Copy**, then close the index page.

3. Click in the top cell on the cafe page, click **Edit** on the menu bar, then click **Paste**.

   The Image Description (Alt Text) dialog box opens showing that alt text is missing from the banner graphic.

   | TIP If you are working on a Macintosh computer, the Image Description (Alt Text) dialog box may not appear.

4. Click the pointer in the blank space under the Description heading, as shown in Figure 14, type **Striped Umbrella banner**, then click **OK**.

   (continued)

FIGURE 14
Image Description (Alt Text) dialog box

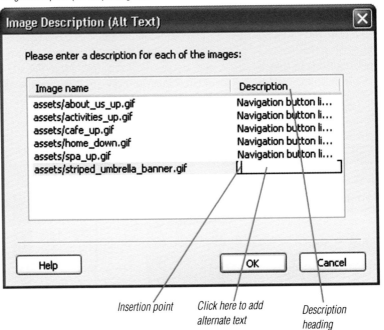

Insertion point

Click here to add alternate text

Description heading

Using visual aids

There is an option in Dreamweaver for turning on and off various borders that are displayed in Design view but are not displayed in the browser. This tool is called Visual Aids and can be accessed through the View menu or through the Visual Aids button on the Document toolbar. Most of the time these borders are very helpful while you are editing and formatting a page. However, turning them off is a quick way to see how the page will be viewed in the browser without having to open it in the browser window.

5. Click in the first cell in the third row and insert cafe_logo.gif from the chapter_5 assets folder, then type **Sand Crab Cafe logo** as the alternate text.

6. Compare your screen to Figure 15.

7. Repeat Step 5 to insert cheesecake.jpg in the first cell in the fifth row (the top row in the set of split cells), using **Banana Chocolate Cheesecake** for the alternate text.

(continued)

FIGURE 15

Sand Crab Cafe logo imported into table cell

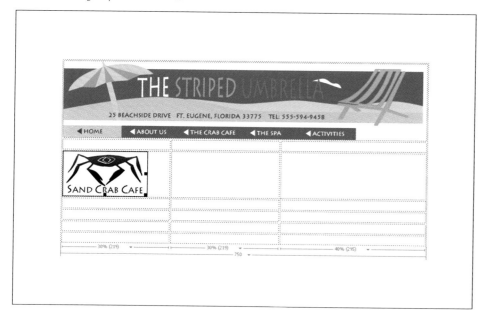

8. Merge the two cells to the right of the cheesecake graphic, repeat Step 5 to insert the cafe_photo.jpg in the newly merged cells, using **The Sand Crab Cafe** as the alternate text, then compare your screen to Figure 16.

> TIP Press [Tab] to move the insertion point to the next cell in a row. Press [Shift][Tab] to move the insertion point to the previous cell.

9. Refresh the Assets panel to verify that the three new graphics were copied to The Striped Umbrella Web site assets folder.

10. Save your work, then preview the page in your browser.

Notice that the page would look better if the new graphics had better placement on the page.

11. Close your browser.

You inserted images into four cells of the table on the cafe page.

FIGURE 16
Graphics inserted into table cells

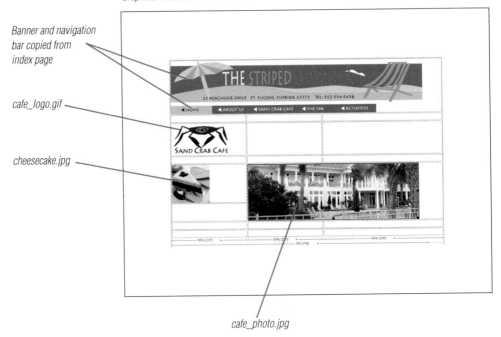

Banner and navigation bar copied from index page

cafe_logo.gif

cheesecake.jpg

cafe_photo.jpg

1. Click the **banner**, then click the **Align Center button** ≣ in the Property inspector.

   The banner and navigation bar move together to become centered in the cell. You may have copied the center alignment tag when you copied the banner and navigation bar from the index page. In that case, the banner and navigation bar will already be centered on the cafe page.

2. Center-align the logo and cheesecake images, then left-align the cafe photo, as shown in Figure 17.

   Notice the extra dotted lines surrounding the four images. Each one represents a div tag that was generated when the alignment button was applied to the graphic.

3. Save your work.

4. Preview the page in your browser, view the aligned images, then close your browser.

You center-aligned The Striped Umbrella banner and two other graphics within their respective cells. You left-aligned the fourth graphic.

FIGURE 17
Aligning images in cells

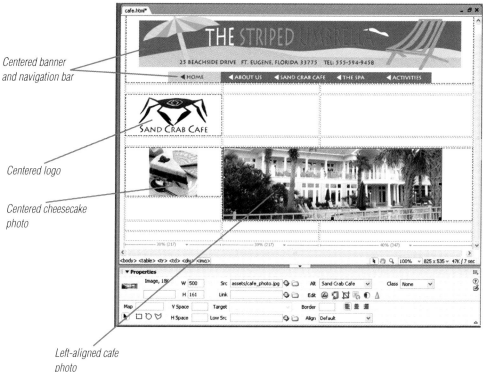

Centered banner and navigation bar

Centered logo

Centered cheesecake photo

Left-aligned cafe photo

INSERT TEXT AND FORMAT
CELL CONTENT

What You'll Do

In this lesson, you will insert text that describes the restaurant in a cell, type text in two cells, and then type the cafe hours in a nested table. You will also format the text to enhance its appearance on the page. Last, you will add formatting to some of the cells and cell content.

Inserting Text in a Table

You can enter text in a table either by typing it in a cell, copying it from another source and pasting it into a cell, or importing it from another program. Once you place text in a table cell, you can format it to make it more readable and more visually appealing on the page.

Formatting Cell Content

Making modifications and formatting changes to a table and its contents is easier to do in Standard mode than in Layout mode. To format the contents of a cell in Standard mode, select the contents in the cell, then apply formatting to it. If a cell contains multiple objects of the same type, such as text, you can either format each item individually or select the entire cell and apply formatting that will be applied identically to all items. You can tell whether you have selected the cell contents or the cell by looking to see what options are showing in the Property inspector. Figure 18 shows a selected graphic in a cell. Notice that the Property inspector displays options for formatting the object, rather than options for formatting the cell.

Formatting Cells

Formatting cells is different than formatting cell contents. Formatting a cell can include setting properties that visually enhance the cell appearance, such as setting a cell width, assigning a background color, or setting global alignment properties for the cell content. To format a cell, you need to either select the cell or place the insertion point inside the cell you want to format, then choose the cell formatting options you want in the Property inspector. For example, to choose a fill color for a selected cell, click the Background Color button in the Property inspector, then choose a color from the color picker. In order to format a cell, you must expand the Property inspector to display the cell formatting options. In Figure 19, notice that the insertion point is positioned in the cafe logo cell, but the logo graphic is not selected. The Property inspector displays the formatting options for cells.

FIGURE 18
Property inspector showing options for formatting cell contents

Property inspector shows properties for selected graphic

Graphic selected inside a cell

FIGURE 19
Property inspector showing options for formatting a cell

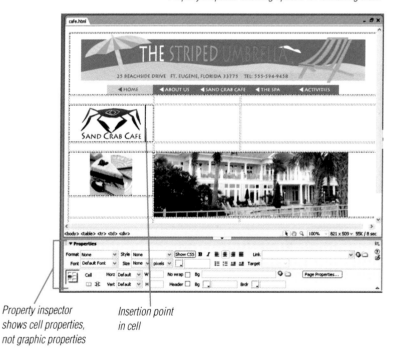

Property inspector shows cell properties, not graphic properties

Insertion point in cell

Insert text

1. Merge the two cells to the right of the cafe logo, click in the newly merged cell, then import the Word document, cafe.doc, from the chapter_5 assets folder.

2. Click in the cell under the cheesecake photo, then type **Banana Chocolate**, press **[Shift][Enter]** (Win) or **[Shift][return]** (Mac), type **Cheesecake**, press **[Shift][Enter]** (Win) or **[Shift][return]** (Mac), then type **Our signature dessert**.

3. Click in the next cell down and type **Reservations are recommended for The Dining Room during the peak summer season**, as shown in Figure 20.

You imported a Word document describing the restaurant into one cell and typed two descriptive paragraphs into two cells.

FIGURE 20
Importing and typing text into cells

Imported text describing the cafe

Text typed into cells

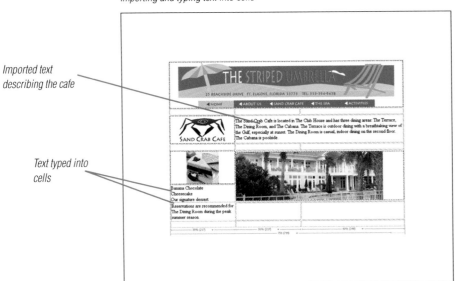

Importing and exporting data from tables

You can import and export tabular data into and out of Dreamweaver. Tabular data is data that is arranged in columns and rows and separated by a **delimiter**: a comma, tab, colon, semicolon, or similar character. **Importing** means to bring data created in another software program into Dreamweaver, and **exporting** means to save data created in Dreamweaver in a special file format that can be inserted into other programs. Files that are imported into Dreamweaver must be saved as delimited files. **Delimited files** are database or spreadsheet files that have been saved as text files with delimiters such as tabs or commas separating the data. Programs such as Microsoft Access and Microsoft Excel offer many file formats for saving files. To import a delimited file, click File on the menu bar, point to Import, then click Tabular Data. The Import Tabular Data dialog box opens, offering you formatting options for the imported table. To export a table that you created in Dreamweaver, click File on the menu bar, point to Export, then click Table. The Export Table dialog box opens, letting you choose the type of delimiter you want for the delimited file.

FIGURE 21
Table dialog box settings for nested table

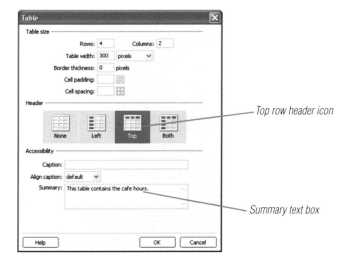

Top row header icon

Summary text box

FIGURE 22
Adding a nested table

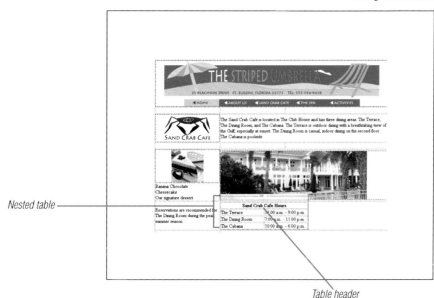

Nested table

Table header

Insert text using a nested table

1. Merge the two empty cells under the cafe photo.

2. Place the insertion point inside the newly merged cells, then click the **Table button**.

3. Type **4** in the Rows text box, type **2** in the Columns text box, type **300** in the Table width text box, click the **Table width list arrow**, click **pixels**, type **0** in the Border thickness text box, click the **Top row header icon** in the Header section, type **This table contains the cafe hours**. in the Summary text box, compare your Table dialog box to Figure 21, then click **OK**.

   The Top header option will automatically center and bold the text that is typed into the top cells of the table. The header will be read by screen readers, providing more accessibility for the table.

4. Merge the top row of cells in the nested table, then type **Sand Crab Cafe Hours**.

5. Enter the cafe dining area names and their hours, as shown in Figure 22.

You inserted a nested table and entered a schedule for the cafe hours.

Format cell content

1. Expand the CSS panel group (if necessary).

2. Click the **Attach Style Sheet button** to attach the su_styles.css file to the cafe page.

3. Select the paragraph next to the cafe logo, then use the Property inspector to apply the body_text style.

4. Select the text "Banana Chocolate Cheesecake", then apply the bullets style.

5. Select the text "Our Signature dessert" and the "Reservations information", then apply the body_text style.

6. Repeat Step 5 to apply the body_text style to the nested table text.

   Your screen should resemble Figure 23.

You formatted text in table cells using a Cascading Style Sheet.

FIGURE 23
Formatting text using a Cascading Style Sheet

body_text style

bullets style

body_text style

Click to select style

Attach Style Sheet button

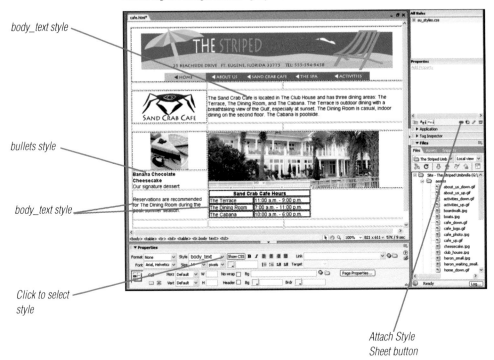

FIGURE 24

Formatting cells using horizontal alignment

Horz list arrow

Vert list arrow

Insertion point inside cell with no elements selected

1. Click to place the insertion point in the cell with the cheesecake name.

2. Click the **Horz list arrow**, then click **Center** to center the cell contents.

   You do not need to select the text because you are setting the alignment for all contents in the cell.

3. Repeat Steps 1 and 2 for the cell with the reservations paragraph as well as the cell with the nested table.

4. Click in the cell with the Reservations text, click the **Vert list arrow**, then click **Middle**, as shown in Figure 24.

5. Save your work.

You formatted table cells by adding horizontal and vertical alignment.

Modify cell content

1. Click **Modify** on the menu bar, then click **Navigation Bar** to open the Modify Navigation Bar dialog box.

2. Click the **Show "Down image" initially check box** to remove the check mark for the home button.

3. Click **cafe** in the Nav bar elements box, click the **Show "Down image" initially check box** to add a check mark, then click **OK**.

   The button now shows viewers that they are on the cafe page by displaying the down state when the page is open, as shown in Figure 25.

4. Save your work.

You edited the navigation bar to show the correct down state intially.

FIGURE 25
Edited navigation bar on the cafe page

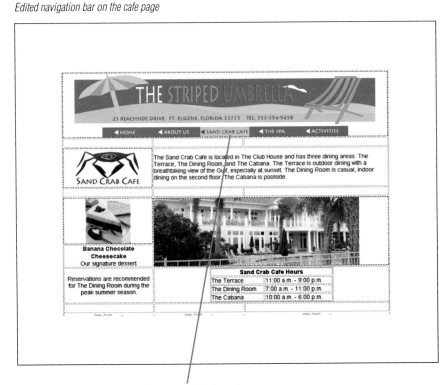

Correct button is shown in
the down state

FIGURE 26

Hiding visual aids

Visual Aids button

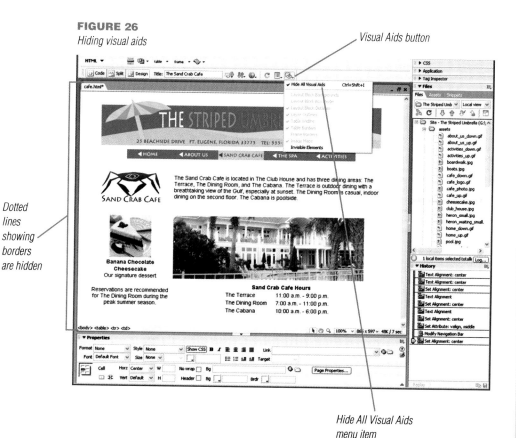

Dotted lines showing borders are hidden

Hide All Visual Aids menu item

Use visual aids to check layout

1. Click the **Visual Aids button** 🐾 on the Document toolbar, then click **Hide All Visual Aids**, as shown in Figure 26.

   The borders around the table, table cells, and div tags (where you used alignment options) are all hidden, allowing you to see more clearly how the page will look in the browser.

2. Repeat Step 1 to show the visual aids again.

3. Save your work, preview the cafe page in the browser, then close the browser.

You used the Hide All Visual Aids command to hide the table borders and layout block outlines, then showed them again.

PERFORM WEB SITE
MAINTENANCE

What You'll Do

In this lesson, you will use some of Dreamweaver's site maintenance tools to check for broken links, orphaned files, and missing alternate text. You will also verify that all colors are Websafe. You will then correct any problems that you find.

Maintaining a Web Site

As you add pages, links, and content to a Web site, it can quickly become difficult to manage. It's important to perform maintenance tasks frequently to make sure your Web site operates smoothly. To keep a Web site "clean," you should use Dreamweaver's site maintenance tools frequently. You have already learned about some of the tools described in the paragraphs below. Although it is important to use them as you create and modify your pages, it is also important to run them at periodic intervals after publishing your Web site to make sure your Web site is always error-free.

Checking Links Sitewide

Before and after you publish your Web site, you should use the Link Checker panel to make sure all internal links are working. If the Link Checker panel displays any broken links, you should repair them. If the Link Checker panel displays any orphaned files, you should evaluate whether to delete them or link them to existing pages.

Using the Assets Panel

You should also use the Assets panel to check the list of images and colors used in your Web site. If you see images listed that are not being used, you should move them to a storage folder outside the Web site until you need them. If you are concerned about using only Websafe colors, you should also check the Colors list to make sure that all colors in the site are Websafe. If there are non-Websafe colors in the list, locate the elements to which these colors are applied and apply Websafe colors to them.

Using Site Reports

You can use the Reports command in the Site menu to generate six different HTML reports that can help you maintain your Web site. You choose the type of report you want to run in the Reports dialog box, shown in Figure 27. You can specify whether to generate the report for the entire current local site, selected files in the site, or a selected folder. You can also generate Workflow reports to see files that have been checked out by others or recently modified or to view the Design Notes attached to files.

Using the Site Map

You can use the site map to check your navigation structure. Does the site map show that you have followed the file hierarchy in the storyboard and flow chart? Does the navigation structure shown in the site map reflect a logically organized flowchart? Is each page three or four clicks from the home page? If the answer is no to any of these questions, make adjustments to improve the navigation structure.

Testing Pages

Finally, you should test your Web site using many different types and versions of browsers, platforms, and screen resolutions. You should test all links to make sure they connect to valid, active Web sites. Pages that download slowly should be trimmed in size to improve performance. You should analyze all feedback on the Web site objectively, saving both positive and negative comments for future reference to help you make improvements to the site.

FIGURE 27
Reports dialog box

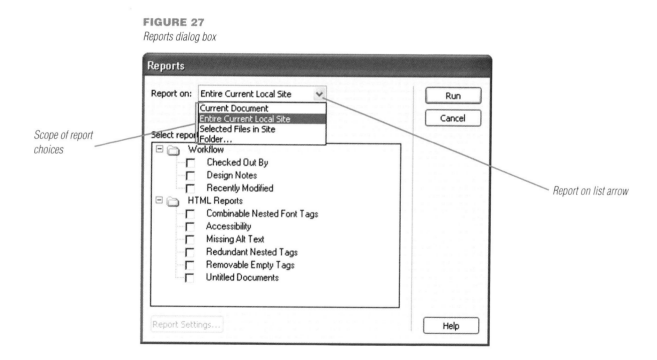

Check for broken links

1. Show the Files panel (if necessary).

2. Click **Site** on the menu bar, point to **Advanced**, then click **Recreate Site Cache**.

3. Click **Site** on the menu bar, then click **Check Links Sitewide**.

   No broken links are listed in the Link Checker, as shown in Figure 28.

You verified that there are no broken links in the Web site.

Check for orphaned files

1. Click the **Show list arrow**, then click **Orphaned Files**.

   As Figure 29 shows, there are no orphaned files.

2. Close the Results panel group.

You verified that there are no orphaned files in the Web site.

FIGURE 28
Link Checker panel displaying no broken links

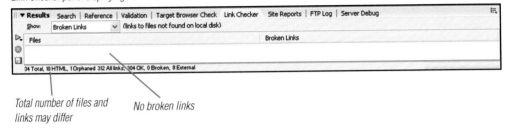

Total number of files and links may differ   *No broken links*

FIGURE 29
Link Checker panel displaying no orphaned files

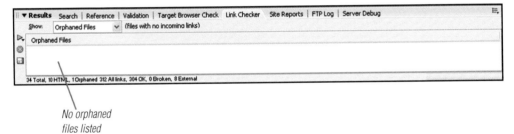

No orphaned files listed

1. Click the **Colors button** ▦ on the Assets panel to view the Web site colors, as shown in Figure 30.

   The Assets panel shows that all colors used in the Web site are Websafe.

You verified that the Web site contains all Websafe colors.

FIGURE 30

Assets panel displaying Websafe colors

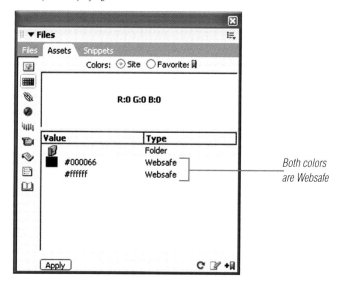

Both colors are Websafe

Check for untitled documents

1. Click **Site** on the menu bar, then click **Reports** to open the Reports dialog box.

2. Click the **Untitled Documents check box**, click the **Report on list arrow**, click **Entire Current Local Site**, as shown in Figure 31, then click **Run**.

   The Site Reports panel opens and shows no files, indicating that all documents in the Web site contain titles.

3. Close the Results panel group.

You verified that the Web site contains no untitled documents.

FIGURE 31

Reports dialog box with Untitled Documents option selected

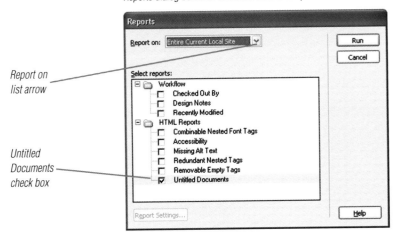

Report on list arrow

Untitled Documents check box

FIGURE 32

Reports dialog box with Missing Alt Text option selected

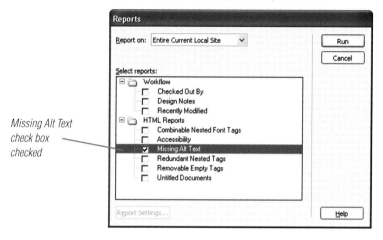

Missing Alt Text
check box
checked

FIGURE 33

Site Reports panel displaying missing "alt" tags

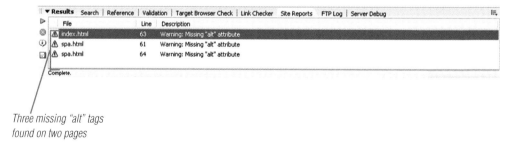

Three missing "alt" tags
found on two pages

Check for missing alternate text

1. Using Figure 32 as a guide, run another report that checks the entire current local site for missing alternate text.

    Two pages contain images that are missing alternate text, as shown in Figure 33.

2. Open the home page, then find the image that is missing alternate text.

    TIP The Reports panel documents the code line numbers where the missing alt tags occur. Sometimes it is faster to locate the errors in Code view, rather than in Design view.

3. Add appropriate alternate text to the image.

4. Repeat Steps 2 and 3 to locate the images on the spa page that are missing alternate text, then add alternate text to them.

5. Save your work, then run the report again to check the entire site for missing alternate text.

    No files should appear in the Site Reports panel.

6. Close the Results panel group, then close all open pages.

You ran a report to check for missing alternate text in the entire site. You then added alternate text to three images and ran the report again.

Create a table.

1. Open the blooms & bulbs Web site.
2. Open classes.html from the Web site.
3. Insert a table on the page with the following settings: Rows: 5, Columns: 3, Table width: 750 pixels, Border thickness: 0, Cell padding: 5, and Cell spacing: 5.
4. Enter the text **This table is used for page layout.** in the Summary text box.
5. Left-align the table on the page, then use Figure 34 as a guide for completing this exercise.
6. Title the page **Master Gardener classes begin soon!**, then save your work.

Resize, split, and merge cells.

1. Select the first cell in the first row, then set the cell width to 25%.
2. Select the second cell in the first row, then set the cell width to 40%.
3. Select the third cell in the first row, then set the cell width to 35%.
4. Merge the three cells in the first row.
5. Merge the first two cells in the second row.
6. Merge the third cell in the third row with the third cell in the fourth row.
7. Split the first cell in the fourth row into two columns.
8. Merge the three cells in the last row.
9. Save your work.

Insert and align graphics in table cells.

1. Copy the banner and the navigation bar together from the home page and paste them into the first row of the table.
2. Center the banner and the navigation bar.
3. Modify the navigation bar to show the classes element in the Down image state and the home element in the Up image state.
4. Use the Insert bar to insert flower_bed.jpg in the last row. You can find the flower_bed.jpg file in the chapter_5 assets folder where your Data Files are stored. Add the alternate text **Flower bed in downtown Alvin** to the flower_bed.jpg image when prompted, then center the image in the cell.
5. Use the tag selector to select the cell containing the flower_bed.jpg image, then set the vertical alignment to Top.
6. Save your work.

Insert text and format cell content.

1. Type **Master Gardener Classes Beginning Soon!** in the first cell in the second row.
2. Type **Who are Master Gardeners?** in the second cell in the second row.
3. Type **Schedule** in the first cell in the third row.
4. Type **Registration** in the second cell in the third row.
5. Type the dates and times for the classes from Figure 34 in the first and second cells in the fourth row.
6. Use Import Word Document command (File menu) to import the file registration.doc into the third cell in the fourth row, then use the Clean up Word HTML command (Commands menu) to remove any unnecessary code.
7. Repeat Step 6 to place the text from the gardeners.doc file into the next empty cell.
8. Attach the blooms_styles.css file, then apply the bodytext style to the dates, times, and two paragraphs of text describing the program.
9. Create a new style in the blooms_styles.css style sheet named **subheadings** with the following settings: Font: Arial, Helvetica, sans-serif; Size: 14; Style: normal; Weight: bold; Color: #003366.
10. Create another new style in the blooms_styles.css style sheet named **reverse_text** with the following settings: Font: Arial, Helvetica, sans-serif; Size: 14; Style: normal; Weight: bold; Color: #FFFFFF.
11. Select each cell that contains text and set the vertical alignment to Top.
12. Center-align the four headings (Master Gardener Classes Beginning Soon!, Who are Master Gardeners?, Schedule, and Registration).

13. Set the horizontal alignment for the cell with the dates to Center.

14. Set the horizontal alignment for the cell with the times and the cells describing registration and Master Gardeners to Left.

15. Select the cell with the word "Registration" in it, then change the cell background color to #000099.

16. Apply the subheadings style to the text "Schedule" and "Who are Master Gardeners".

17. Apply the reverse_text style to the heading "Registration," then apply the seasons style to the text "Master Gardener Classes Beginning Soon!"

18. Save your work, preview the page in your browser, then close your browser.

Perform Web site maintenance.

1. Use the Link Checker panel to check for broken links, then fix any broken links that appear.

2. Use the Link Checker panel to check for orphaned files. If any orphaned files appear in the report, take steps to link them to appropriate pages or remove them.

3. Use the Assets panel to check for Non-Websafe colors.

4. Run an Untitled Documents report for the entire local site. If the report lists any pages that have no titles, add page titles to the untitled pages. Run the report again to verify that all pages have page titles.

5. Run a report to look for missing alternate text. Add alternate text to any graphics that need it, then run the report again to verify that all images contain alternate text.

6. Save your work, then close all open pages.

FIGURE 34
Completed Skills Review

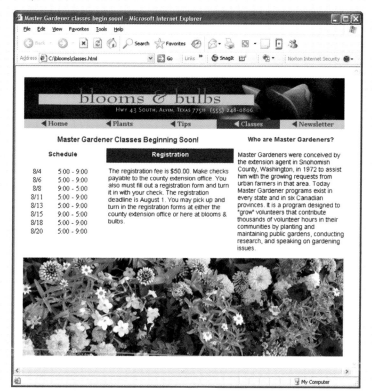

In this exercise you will continue your work on the TripSmart Web site that you began in Project Builder 1 in Chapter 1 and developed in Chapters 2 through 4. You are ready to begin work on a page that will feature catalog items. You plan to use a table for page layout.

1. Open the TripSmart Web site.
2. Open catalog.html from the Web site.
3. Insert a table with the following settings: Rows: 6, Columns: 3, Table width: 750 pixels, Border thickness: 0. Enter an appropriate table summary, then center-align the table.
4. Set the cell widths in the bottom row to 33%, 33%, and 34%.
5. Merge the cells in the top row, copy the TripSmart banner and navigation bar from the home page, paste them into the resulting merged cell, then center the banner if necessary. Add the following alternate text to the image: **TripSmart banner**, then center the banner.
6. Center the navigation bar, if necessary.
7. Merge the three cells in the second row, type **Our products are backed by a 100% guarantee**, then center the text.
8. Type **Protection from harmful UV rays, Cool, light-weight, versatile**, and **Pockets for everything** in the three cells in the third row.
9. Place the files hat.jpg, pants.jpg, and vest.jpg files from the chapter_5 assets folder in the three cells in the fourth row, add the following alternate text to the images: **Safari hat, Kenya convertible pants**, and **Photographer's vest**, then center the three images.
10. Type **Safari Hat, Kenya Convertible Pants**, and **Photographer's Vest** in the three cells in the fifth row, then center each label.
11. Type **Item number 50501** and **$29.00** with a line break between them in the first cell in the sixth row.
12. Repeat Step 11 to type **Item number 62495** and **$39.50** in the second cell in the sixth row.
13. Repeat Step 11 to type **Item number 52301** and **$54.95** in the third cell in the sixth row.
14. Attach the tripsmart_styles.css file to the page, apply the bodytext style to the three descriptions in the third row, then center each description.
15. Create a new style in the tripsmart_styles.css style sheet named **reverse_text** with the following settings: Font, Verdana, Arial, Helvetica, sans-serif; Size, 14 px; Style, normal; Weight, bold; Color, #FFFFFF.
16. Apply the reverse_text style to the text "Our products are backed by a 100% guarantee.", then change the cell background color to #666666.

17. Apply the reverse_text style to the three item names under the images, then change the background color to #999999 for the three cells containing the images.

18. Create a new style called **item_numbers** with the following settings: Font: Verdana, Arial, Helvetica, sans-serif; Size: 10 px; Style: normal; Weight: bold.

19. Apply the item_numbers style to the three items' numbers and prices.

20. Save your work, view the page in your browser, compare your screen with Figure 35, then close the browser.

21. Run reports for broken links, orphaned files, missing alternate text, and untitled documents. Make corrections as necessary.

22. Save your work, then close all open pages.

FIGURE 35
Completed Project Builder 1

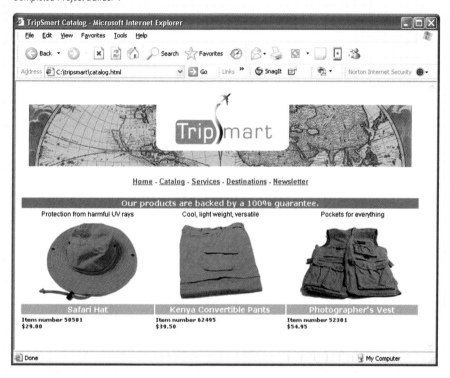

Use Figure 36 as a guide to continue your work on the emma's book bag Web site that you started in Project Builder 2 in Chapter 1 and developed in Chapters 2 through 4. You are now ready to begin work on a page that will showcase the small cafe in the bookstore. You decide to use a table to lay out the page.

1. Open the emma's book bag Web site, then open cafe.html.
2. Type **Cafe** for the page title, replacing the original title.
3. Create a table on the page with the following settings: Rows: 5, Columns: 3, Table width: 750 pixels, Border thickness: 0, adding an appropriate table summary.
4. Center-align the table and set the width of the three cells in the bottom row to 35%, 35%, and 30%.
5. Merge the cells in the first row, then insert the banner and navigation bar. (*Hint*: Copy the banner and navigation bar from the home page.) Enter appropriate alternate text for the banner, then center-align the banner and navigation bar, if necessary.
6. Merge the first two cells in the second row, then type **The Cafe is the perfect place to relax for a few minutes while you browse through a book or two or wait for a friend**.
7. Attach the book_bag_styles.css file to the page, then apply the bodytext style to the sentence you typed in Step 6.
8. Insert a horizontal rule in the first cell in the third row that is 200 pixels wide.
9. Type **Cafe hours:, Monday through Saturday, 10:30 - 2:00** in the second cell in the third row, using a line break between each line.
10. Import book club.doc in the first cell in the fourth row, then apply the bodytext style to the paragraph.
11. Type **Scones, cookies, and muffins are delivered fresh daily from an award winning local bakery. We proudly serve Starbucks Coffee and Republic of Tea tea**. in the second cell of the fourth row, then apply the bodytext style to the paragraph.

12. Create a new style in the book_bag_styles.css file called **subheading** with the following settings: Font: Verdana, Arial, Helvetica, sans-serif; Size: 12 px; Weight: bold; Color: #000066; apply it to the Cafe hours text, then center the text.

13. Merge the last cells in the second, third, fourth, and fifth rows, then insert muffins.jpg from the chapter_5 assets folder, adding appropriate alternate text.

14. Merge the first and second cells in the last row, then copy the two lines of text from the home page listing the name and hours of the bookstore into the newly merged cell.

15. Use horizontal and vertical cell alignment to balance the placement of the text in the cells.

16. Save your work, then preview the page in your browser.

17. Run reports for broken links, orphaned files, missing alternate text, and untitled documents. Make corrections as necessary, then close all open pages.

FIGURE 36
Completed Project Builder 2

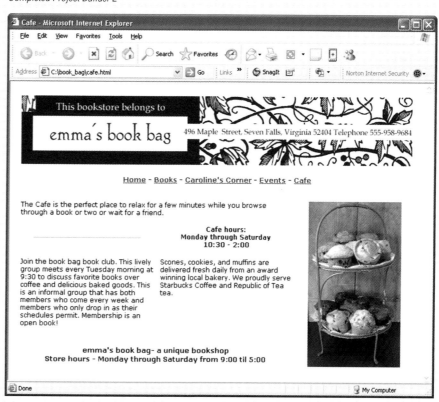

Vesta Everitt has opened a new shop called Needles and Thread that carries needlepoint, cross-stitching, and smocking supplies. She is considering creating a Web site to promote her services and products and would like to gather some ideas before she hires a Web designer. She decides to visit retail Web sites to look for design ideas, as shown in Figures 37 and 38.

1. Connect to the Internet, navigate to the Online Companion, then select a link for this chapter. The Web sites shown in the figures are Teva and L.L. Bean.
2. Click View on your browser's menu bar, then click the Source command to view the source code for the Web site you selected.
3. Search the code for table tags. Note the number that you find.
4. Select another link from the Online Companion, and repeat Steps 2 and 3.
5. Using a word processor or scrap paper, list five design ideas that you like from either of these pages. Be sure to specify which page was the source of each idea.

FIGURE 37
Design Project

FIGURE 38
Design Project

In this assignment, you will continue to work on the Web site that you started in Chapter 1 and developed in Chapters 2 through 4. There will be no data files supplied. You are building this Web site from chapter to chapter, so you must do each Portfolio Project assignment in each chapter to complete your Web site.

You will continue building your Web site by designing and completing a page that contains a table used for page layout. After completing your page, you will run several reports to test the Web site.

1. Take a few minutes to evaluate your story-board. Choose a page or pages to develop in which you will use a table for page layout.
2. Plan the content for the new page (or pages) by making a sketch of the table that shows where the content will be placed in the table cells. Split and merge cells and align each element as necessary to create a visually attractive layout.
3. Create the table and place the content in the cells using the sketch for guidance.

4. After you complete the pages, run a report that checks for broken links in the Web site. Correct any broken links that appear in the report.
5. Run a report on the Web site for orphaned files and correct any if found.
6. Run a report on pages that are missing alternate text. Add alternate text to elements that need it.
7. Run a report on any pages that do not have page titles and add titles to any pages, as needed.

8. Check for any Non-Websafe colors in the Web site. If any are found, replace them with Websafe colors.
9. Preview all the pages in your browser and test all links. Evaluate the pages for both content and layout, then use the check list in Figure 39 to make sure your Web site is completed.
10. Make any modifications necessary to improve the pages.

FIGURE 39
Portfolio Project check list

Web Site Check List

1. Title any pages that have no page titles.
2. Check to see that all pages have consistent navigation links.
3. Check to see that all links work correctly.
4. Check to see that all images have alternate text.
5. Remove any Non-Websafe colors.
6. Delete any unnecessary files.
7. Remove any orphaned files.
8. Use tables for layout when possible.
9. View all pages using at least two different browsers.
10. Verify that the home page has keywords, a description, and a point of contact.

1

GETTING STARTED WITH
MACROMEDIA FLASH

1. Understand the Macromedia Flash workspace.

2. Open a document and play a movie.

3. Create and save a movie.

4. Work with the timeline.

5. Plan a Web site.

6. Distribute a Macromedia Flash movie.

GETTING STARTED WITH
MACROMEDIA FLASH

Introduction

Macromedia Flash is a development tool that allows you to create compelling interactive experiences, often by using animation. While it is known as a tool for creating complex animations for the Web, Macromedia Flash also has excellent drawing tools and tools for creating interactive controls, such as navigation buttons and menus. In addition, Macromedia Flash provides the ability to incorporate sounds and video into an application. You can also use its publishing capabilities to create Web sites and Web-based applications, such as games.

In only a few short years, Macromedia Flash has become the standard for both professional and casual Web developers. The reason that Macromedia Flash has become so popular is that the program is optimized for the Web. Web developers need to provide high-impact experiences for the user, to make sites come alive and turn them from static text and pictures to dynamic, interactive experiences. The problem has been that incorporating high-quality graphics and motion into a Web site can dramatically increase the down-load time and frustrate viewers as they wait for an image to appear or for an animation to play. Macromedia Flash directly addresses this problem by allowing developers to use vector images, which reduce the size of graphic files. Vector images appeal to designers for two reasons. First, they are scalable, which means they can be resized and reshaped without distortion. For example, you could easily have an object, such as an airplane, become smaller as it moves across the screen without having to create the plane in different sizes. Second, Macromedia Flash provides for streaming content over the Internet. Instead of waiting for the entire contents of a Web page to load, the viewer sees a continuous display of images. For example, if your Web site has a Macromedia Flash movie that is played when the viewer first visits your Web site, the viewer does not have to wait for the entire movie to be downloaded before it starts. Streaming allows the movie to start playing when the Web site is opened, and it continues as frames of the movie are delivered to the viewer's computer.

Tools You'll Use

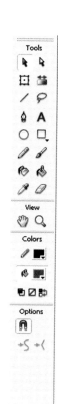

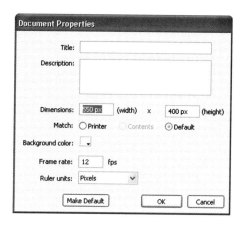

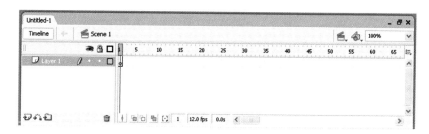

UNDERSTAND THE
MACROMEDIA FLASH
ENVIRONMENT

What You'll Do

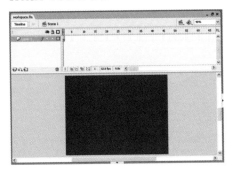

 In this lesson, you will learn about the development environment in Macromedia Flash and how to change Macromedia Flash settings to customize your workspace.

Organizing the Macromedia Flash Workspace

As a designer, one of the most important things to do is to organize your workspace—that is, to decide what to have displayed on the screen and how to arrange the various tools and windows. Because **Macromedia Flash** is such a powerful program with many tools, your workspace may become cluttered. Fortunately, it is easy to customize the workspace to display only the tools needed at any particular time.

The development environment in Macromedia Flash operates according to a movie metaphor: you create scenes on a stage; these scenes run in frames on a timeline. As you work in Macromedia Flash, you create a movie by arranging objects (such as graphics and text) on the stage, and animate the objects using the timeline. You can play the movie on the stage, as you are working on it, by using the movie controls (start, stop, rewind, and so on). In addition, you can test the movie in a browser. When the movie is ready for distribution, you can export it as a Macromedia Flash Player movie, which viewers can access using a Macromedia Flash Player. A **Macromedia Flash Player** is a program that is installed on the viewer's computer to allow Macromedia Flash movies to be played in Web browsers or as stand-alone applications. Virtually all computers that are connected to the Internet have the Macromedia Flash Player installed (a free download from the Macromedia Web site), allowing users to view and interact with Macromedia Flash movies and Web applications. Macromedia Flash movies can also be saved as executable files, called projectors, which can be viewed without the need for the Macromedia Flash Player.

When you start Macromedia Flash, three basic parts of the development environment (or workspace) are displayed: a main toolbar with menus and commands, a stage where objects are placed, and a timeline used to organize and control the objects on the stage. In addition, one or more panels may be displayed. Panels are used when working with objects and features of the movie.

Stage

The **stage** contains all of the objects (such as drawings) that are part of the movie that will be seen by your viewers. It shows how the objects behave within the movie and how they interact with each other. You can resize the stage and change the background color applied to it. You can draw objects directly on the stage or drag them from the Library panel to the stage. You can also import objects developed by another program directly to the stage. You can specify the size of the stage, which will be the size of the area within your browser window that displays the movie. The gray area surrounding the stage is the Pasteboard. You can place objects on the Pasteboard as you are creating a movie. However, neither the Pasteboard nor the objects on it will appear when the movie is played in a browser or the Flash Player.

Timeline

The **timeline** is used to organize and control the movie's contents by specifying when each object appears on the stage. The timeline is critical to the creation of movies, because a movie is merely a series of still images that appear over time. The images are contained within **frames**, which are segments of the timeline. Frames in a Macromedia Flash movie are similar to frames in a motion picture. When a Macromedia Flash movie is played, a playhead moves from frame to frame in the timeline, causing the contents of each frame to appear on the stage in a linear sequence.

The timeline indicates where you are at any time within the movie and allows you to insert, delete, select, and move frames. It shows the animation in your movie and the layers that contain objects. Layers help to organize the objects on the stage. You can draw and edit objects on one layer without affecting objects on other layers. Layers are a way to stack objects so they can overlap and give a 3-D appearance on the stage.

Panels

Panels are used to view, organize, and modify objects and features in a movie. The most commonly used panels are the Tools panel (also called the toolbox), the Properties panel (also called the Property inspector), and the Library panel. For example, the Property inspector is used to change the properties of an object, such as the fill color of a circle. The Property inspector is context sensitive so that if you are working with text it displays the appropriate options, such as font and font size.

You can control which panels are displayed individually or you can choose to display panel sets. Panel sets are groups of the most commonly used panels. In addition, you can control how a panel is displayed. That is, you can expand a panel to show all of its features or collapse it to show only the title bar.

Tools panel

The **Tools panel** contains a set of tools used to draw and edit graphics and text. It is divided into four sections.

Tools—Includes draw, paint, text, and selection tools, which are used to create lines, shapes, illustrations, and text. The selection tools are used to select objects so that they can be modified in a number of ways.

View—Includes the Zoom tool and the Hand tool, which are used to zoom in on and out of parts of the stage and to pan the stage window, respectively.

Colors—Includes tools and icons used to change the stroke (border of an object) and fill (area inside an object) colors.

Options—Includes options for selected tools, such as allowing you to choose the size of the brush when using the Brush tool.

Although several panels are available, you may choose to display them only when they are needed. This keeps your workspace from becoming too cluttered. Panels are floating windows, meaning that you can move them around the workspace. This allows you to dock (link) panels together as a way of organizing them in the workspace. You can also make room in the workspace by collapsing panels so only their title bars are displayed. You use the Window menu on the menu bar to display and hide panels.

Regardless of how you decide to customize your development environment, the stage and the menu bar are always displayed. Usually, you display the timeline, Tools panel, Library panel, Property inspector, and one or more other panels. Figure 1 shows the Macromedia Flash development environment with the stage, timeline, Tools panel, Library panel, and Property inspector displayed.

When you start a new Macromedia Flash document (movie), you can set the document properties, such as the size of the window (stage) the movie will play in, the background color, and the speed of the movie in frames per second. You can change these settings using the Document Properties dialog box, which can be displayed using the Document command on the Modify menu or by double-clicking the Frame Rate icon on the Timeline. You can also change the settings using the Property inspector. To increase the size of the stage so that the objects on the stage can be more easily edited, you can change the magnification setting using commands on the View menu.

FIGURE 1
Macromedia Flash default development environment

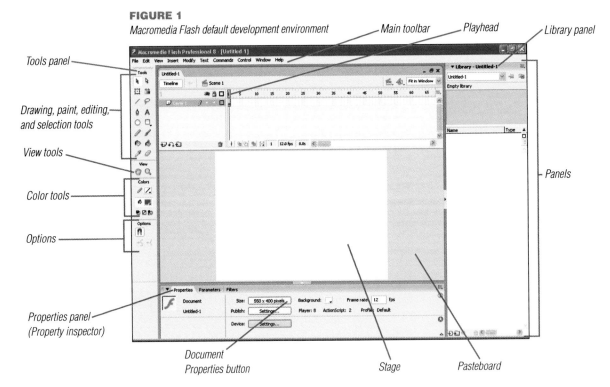

Tools panel

Drawing, paint, editing, and selection tools

View tools

Color tools

Options

Properties panel (Property inspector)

Main toolbar   Playhead   Library panel

Panels

Document Properties button   Stage   Pasteboard

FIGURE 2

The Open/Create screen

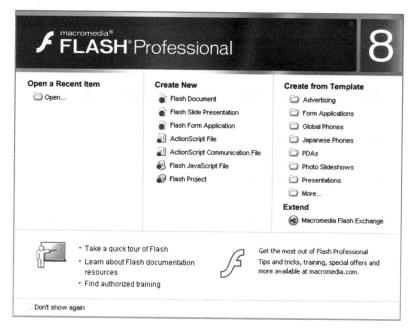

1. Click the **Start button** on the taskbar, point to **All Programs** or **Programs**, point to the **Macromedia** folder, then click the **Macromedia Flash 8 program icon** 🎯 (Win).

   TIP If you are starting Macromedia Flash 8 on a Macintosh, open the Finder, double-click the Applications folder, double-click the Macromedia Flash 8 folder, then double-click the Macromedia Flash 8 program icon.

   The Macromedia Flash Open/Create screen appears, as shown in Figure 2. This screen allows you to open a recent document or create a new Flash file. The File menu in the menu bar also allows you to open new or previously saved documents.

2. Click **File** on the menu bar, then click **New**.

3. Verify **Flash Document** is selected in the New Document dialog box, then click **OK**.

4. Click **Window** on the menu bar, then click **Hide Panels**.

5. Click **Window** on the menu bar, then click **Tools**.

6. Click **Window** on the menu bar, then click **Library**.

7. Click **Window** on the menu bar, point to **Properties**, then click **Properties**.

8. Click **File** on the menu bar, then click **Save**.

9. Navigate to the drive and folder where your data files are stored, type **workspace** for the file name, then click **OK**.

   The current workspace is typical of the development environment that you may want to start with when working with Macromedia Flash 8.

You started Flash, configured the workspace by opening and closing selected panels, and saved the document.

Working with Panels

1. Click the **Properties panel down arrow** in the title bar, as shown in Figure 3, to collapse the panel.

2. Click the **Properties panel arrow** in the title bar to expand the panel.

3. Right-click or **control-click** (Mac) the **Properties tab**, then click **Close panel group** to close the panel.

4. Click **Window** on the menu bar, point to **Properties**, then click **Properties**.

You opened and closed panels.

FIGURE 3
Property inspector panel

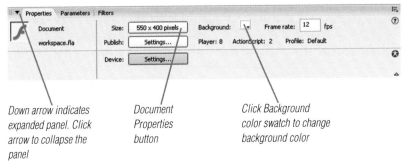

Down arrow indicates expanded panel. Click arrow to collapse the panel

Document Properties button

Click Background color swatch to change background color

FIGURE 4
Document Properties dialog box

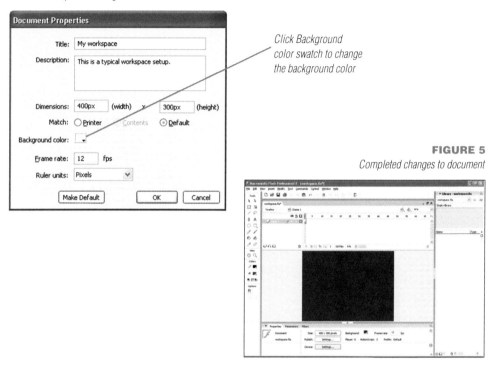

Click Background
color swatch to change
the background color

FIGURE 5
Completed changes to document

Understanding your workspace

Organizing the Macromedia Flash development environment is like organizing your desktop. You may work more efficiently if you have many of the most commonly used items in view and ready to use. Alternately, you may work better if your workspace is relatively uncluttered, giving you more free "desk space." Fortunately, Macromedia Flash makes it easy for you to decide which items to display and how they are arranged while you work. For example, to toggle the Main toolbar, click Window on the menu bar, point to Toolbars, then click Main. You should become familiar with quickly opening, collapsing, expanding, and closing the various windows, toolbars, and panels in Macromedia Flash, and experimenting with different layouts and screen resolutions to find the environment that works best for you.

1. Click the **Document properties button** `550 x 400 pixels` in the Property inspector to display the Document Properties dialog box.

2. Click inside the **Title text box**, then type **My workspace**.

3. Click inside the **Description text box**, then type **This is a typical workspace setup**.

   TIP Text entered into the Title and Description fields can be used by Web-based search engines to display files developed using Flash.

4. Double-click the number in the **width text box**, type **400**, double-click the number in the **height text box**, then type **300**.

5. Click the **Background color swatch**, shown in Figure 4, then click the **blue color swatch** on the left column of the color palette.

6. Accept the remaining default values, then click **OK** to close the Document Properties dialog box.

7. Drag the scroll bars at the bottom and the right of the screen to center the stage.

8. Click **View** on the menu bar, point to **Magnification**, then click **Fit in Window**. Your screen should resemble Figure 5.

9. Click **File** on the menu bar, then click **Close**.

10. Click **Yes** (Win) or **Save** (Mac) to save the movie (if necessary).

You set the document properties including the size of the stage and background color, then set the magnification.

OPEN A DOCUMENT
AND PLAY A MOVIE

What You'll Do

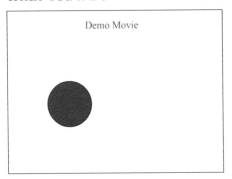

Demo Movie

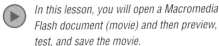

In this lesson, you will open a Macromedia Flash document (movie) and then preview, test, and save the movie.

Opening a Movie in Macromedia Flash

Macromedia Flash files are called documents and have a .fla file extension. If you have created a movie and saved it with the name mymovie, the file name will be mymovie.fla. Files with the .fla file extension can only be opened using Macromedia Flash. After they are opened, you can edit and resave them. Another file format for Macromedia Flash movies is the Macromedia Flash Player (.swf) format. These files are created from Macromedia Flash movies using the Publish command, which allows them to be played in a browser without the Macromedia Flash program. However, the viewer would need to have the Macromedia Flash Player installed on his or her computer. Because .swf files cannot be edited in the Macromedia Flash program, you should preview them on the stage and test them before you publish them. Be sure to keep the original .fla file so that you can make changes at a later date.

Previewing a Movie

After opening a Macromedia Flash movie, you can preview it within the development environment in several ways. When you preview a movie, you play the frames by directing the playhead to move through the timeline, and you watch the movement on the stage.

Control menu commands (and keyboard shortcuts)

Figure 6 shows the Control menu commands, which resemble common VCR-type options:

- Play ([Enter] (Win) or [return] (Mac)) begins playing the movie, frame by frame, from the location of the playhead and continuing until the end of the movie. For example, if the playhead is on Frame 5 and the last frame is Frame 40, choosing the Play command will play Frames 5–40 of the movie.

Getting Started with Macromedia Flash

When a movie starts, the Play command changes to a Stop command. You can also stop the movie by pressing [Enter] (Win) or [return] (Mac).

- Rewind ([Ctrl][Alt] [R] (Win)) or [option] $\mathcal{H}$ [R] (Mac) moves the playhead to Frame 1.
- Step Forward (.) moves the playhead forward one frame at a time.
- Step Backward (,) moves the playhead backward one frame at a time.

You can turn on the Loop Playback setting to allow the movie to continue playing repeatedly. A check mark next to the Loop Playback command on the Control menu indicates that the feature is turned on. To turn off this feature, click the Loop Playback command.

Controller

You can also preview a movie using the Controller. To display the Controller, click the Controller option on the Toolbar command of the Window menu.

The decision of which controls to use (the Control menu, keyboard shortcuts, or the Controller) is a matter of personal preference.

Testing a Movie

When you preview a movie, some interactive functions, such as buttons, that are used to jump from one part of the movie to another, do not work unless the movie is played using a Macromedia Flash Player. You can use the Test Movie command on the Control menu to test the movie using the Macromedia Flash Player.

You can drag the Playhead in the timeline to play the frames and display their contents on the stage. This process, called "scrubbing," provides a quick way to view parts of the movie.

FIGURE 6
Control menu commands

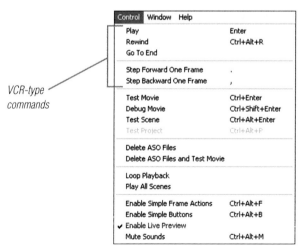

VCR-type
commands

Open and play a movie using the Control menu and the Controller

1. Open fl1_1.fla from the drive and folder where your Data Files are stored, then save it as **demomovie.fla**.

2. Click **View** on the menu bar, point to **Magnification**, then click **Fit in Window**.

3. Click **Control** on the menu bar, click **Play**. Notice how the playhead moves across the timeline as the blue circle moves from the left to the right, as shown in Figure 7.

4. Click **Control** on the menu bar, then click **Rewind**.

5. Press [**Enter**] (Win) or [**return**] (Mac) to play the movie, then press [**Enter**] (Win) or [**return**] (Mac) again to stop the movie before it ends.

6. Click **Window** on the menu bar, point to **Toolbars**, then click **Controller**.

7. Use all the buttons on the Controller to preview the movie, then close the Controller.

8. Point to the **Playhead** in the timeline, then click and drag the **Playhead** back and forth to view the contents of the frames and view the movie.

You opened a Macromedia Flash movie and previewed it, using various controls.

Playhead

FIGURE 7
Playhead moving across timeline

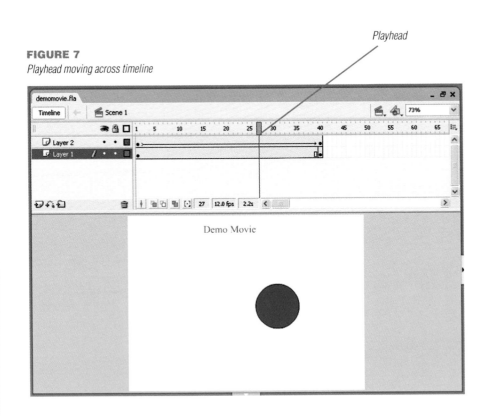

FIGURE 8

Macromedia Flash Player window

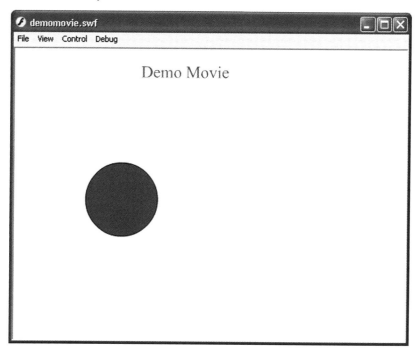

Test a movie

1. Click **Control** on the menu bar, then click **Test Movie** to view the movie in the Macromedia Flash Player window, as shown in Figure 8.

2. Click **Control** on the menu bar and review the available commands.

3. Click **File** on the menu bar, then click **Close** to close the Macromedia Flash Player window.

4. Navigate to the drive and folder where you saved the movie and notice the demomovie.swf file that has been created.

   TIP   When you test a movie, Macromedia Flash automatically runs the movie in Macromedia Flash Player, which creates a file that has a .swf extension in the folder where your movie is stored.

5. Close demomovie.fla, saving changes if prompted.

You tested a movie in the Macromedia Flash Player window.

Using the Macromedia Flash Player

In order to view a Macromedia Flash movie on the Web, your computer needs to have the Macromedia Flash Player installed. An important feature of multimedia players, such as Macromedia Flash Player, is that they can decompress a file that has been compressed to give it a small file size that can be more quickly delivered over the Internet. In addition to Macromedia, companies such as Apple, Microsoft, and RealNetworks create players that allow applications, developed with their and other company's products, to be viewed on the Web. The multimedia players are distributed free and can be downloaded from the company's Web site. The Macromedia Flash Player is created by Macromedia and is available at *www.macromedia.com/downloads*.

CREATE AND SAVE
A MOVIE

What You'll Do

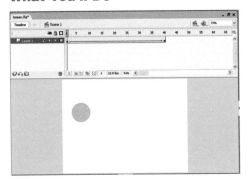

In this lesson, you will create a Macromedia Flash movie that will include a simple animation, then save the movie.

Creating a Macromedia Flash Movie

Macromedia Flash movies are created by placing objects (graphics, text, sounds, photos, and so on) on the stage, editing these objects (for example, changing their brightness), animating the objects, and adding interactivity with buttons and menus. You can create graphic objects in Macromedia Flash using the drawing tools, or you can develop them in another program, such as Macromedia Fireworks or Adobe Photoshop, and then import them into a Macromedia Flash movie. In addition, you can acquire clip art and stock photographs and import them into a movie. When objects are placed on the stage, they are automatically placed in a layer and in the currently selected frame of the timeline.

Figure 9 shows a movie that has an oval object created in Macromedia Flash. Notice that the playhead is on Frame 1 of the movie. The object placed on the stage appears in Frame 1 and appears on the stage when the playback head is on Frame

1. The dot in Frame 1 on the timeline indicates that this frame is a keyframe. The concept of keyframes is critical to understanding how Macromedia Flash works. A keyframe indicates that there is a change in the movie, such as the start or end of an animation, or the playing of a sound. A keyframe is automatically designated in frame 1 of every layer. In addition, you can designate any frame to be a keyframe.

The oval object in Figure 9 was created using the Oval tool. To create an oval or a rectangle, you select the desired tool and then drag the pointer over an area on the stage. If you want to draw a perfect circle or square, press and hold [Shift] when the tool is selected, and then drag the shape. If you make a mistake, you can click Edit on the menu bar, and then click Undo. In order to edit an object, you must first select it. You can use the Selection tool to select an entire object or group of objects. You drag the Selection tool pointer around the entire object to make a marquee selection. An object that has been selected displays a dot pattern or a blue border.

Creating an Animation

Figure 10 shows another movie that has 40 frames, as specified in the timeline. The arrow in the timeline indicates a motion animation. In this case, the object will move from left to right across the stage. The movement of the object is caused by having the object in different places on the stage in different frames of the movie. A basic motion animation requires two keyframes. The first keyframe sets the starting position of the object, and the second keyframe sets the ending position of the object. The number of frames between the two keyframes determines the length of the animation. For example, if the starting keyframe is Frame 1 and the ending keyframe is Frame 40, the object will be animated for 40 frames. Once the two keyframes are set, Macromedia Flash automatically fills in the frames between them, with a process called **motion tweening**.

Adding an Effect to an Object

In addition to animating the location of an object (or objects), you can also animate an object's appearance; for example, its shape, color, brightness, or transparency. The color of the circle on the left of the stage in Figure 10 has been lightened using the Brightness effect on the Property inspector. When the movie is played, the color of the circle will start out light and then become darker as it moves to the right.

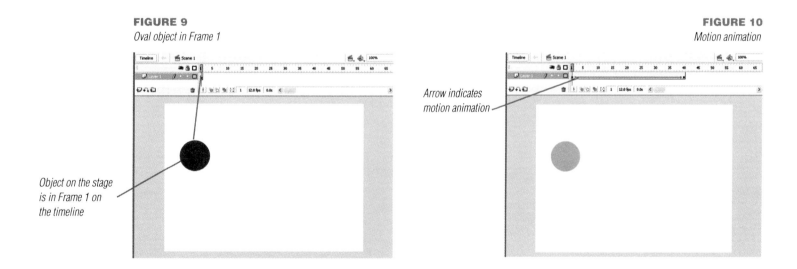

FIGURE 9
Oval object in Frame 1

Object on the stage is in Frame 1 on the timeline

FIGURE 10
Motion animation

Arrow indicates motion animation

Create objects using drawing tools

1. Click **File** on the menu bar, then click **New**.
2. Click **OK** in the New Document window to choose Flash Document as the new document to create, then save the movie as **tween**.
3. Click the **Oval tool** ○ on the Tools panel, then verify that the **Object Drawing option** in the Options panel is deselected, as shown in Figure 11.
4. Click the **Fill Color tool** on the Tools panel, then, if necessary, click the **red color swatch** in the left column of the color palette.
5. Press and hold **[Shift]**, then drag the **Oval tool** on the stage to draw the circle, as shown in Figure 12.

   Pressing and holding [Shift] creates a perfect circle. After releasing the mouse, the circle fills in red.
6. Click the **Selection tool** on the Tools panel, then drag a marquee selection around the object to select it, as shown in Figure 13.

   The object appears covered with a dot pattern.

You created an object using the Oval tool and then selected the object using the Selection tool.

Create basic animation

1. Click **Insert** on the menu bar, point to **Timeline**, then click **Create Motion Tween**.

   A blue border surrounds the object.
2. Click **Frame 40** on Layer 1 of the timeline.
3. Click **Insert** on the menu bar, point to **Timeline**, then click **Keyframe**.

(continued)

FIGURE 11
Object Drawing option

Object Drawing option is not selected

FIGURE 12
Drawing a circle

FIGURE 13
Creating a marquee selection

FIGURE 14
The circle on the right side of the stage

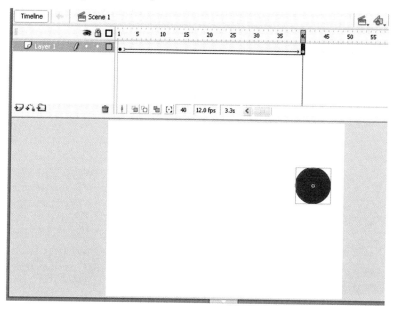

Using options and shortcuts

There is often more than one way to complete a particular function when using Macromedia Flash. For example, if you want to change the font for text you have typed, you can use Text menu options or the Property inspector. In addition, Macromedia Flash provides context menus that are relevant to the current selection. For example, if you point to a graphic and right-click (Win) or [control] click (Mac), a menu appears with graphic-related commands, such as distort and smooth. Shortcut keys are also available for many of the most common commands, such as [Ctrl] [Z] (Win) or [⌘] [Z] (Mac) for Undo.

A second keyframe is defined in Frame 40, and Frames 1–40 appear shaded.

4. Drag the circle to the right side of the stage, as shown in Figure 14.

   The movement of the circle on the stage corresponds to the new location of the circle as defined in the keyframe in Frame 40.

5. Press [Enter] to play the movie.

   The playhead moves through the timeline in Frames 1–40, and the circle moves across the stage.

You created a basic motion tween animation by inserting a keyframe and changing the location of an object.

Change the brightness of an object

1. Click **Window** on the menu bar, point to **properties**, then verify that Properties is checked.

2. Click **Frame 1** on Layer 1, then click the **circle**.

3. Click the **Color Styles list arrow** in the Property inspector, then click **Brightness**.

4. Click the **Brightness Amount list arrow**, then drag the slider up to 70%.

   TIP You can also double-click the Brightness Amount box and type a percentage.

5. Click anywhere on a blank area of the Property inspector to close the slider.

6. Play the movie, then save your work.

   The circle becomes brighter as it moves across the stage.

You used the Property inspector to change the brightness of the object in one of the keyframes.

WORK WITH THE TIMELINE

What You'll Do

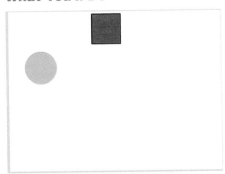

 In this lesson, you will add another layer, allowing you to create an additional animation, and you will use the timeline to help organize your movie.

Understanding the Timeline

The timeline organizes and controls a movie's contents over time. By learning how to read the information provided in the timeline, you can determine and change what will be happening in a movie, frame by frame. You can determine which objects are animated, what types of animations are being used, when the various objects will appear in a movie, which objects will appear on top of others, and how fast the movie will play. Features of the timeline are shown in Figure 15 and explained in this lesson.

Using Layers

Each new Macromedia Flash movie contains one layer, named Layer 1. **Layers** are like transparent sheets of acetate that are stacked on top of each other, as shown in Figure 16. Each layer can contain one or more objects. You can add layers using the Layer command on the Insert menu or by clicking the Insert Layer icon on the timeline. When you add a new layer, Macromedia Flash stacks it on top of the other layer(s) in the timeline. The stacking order of the layers in the timeline is important because objects on the stage will appear in the same stacking order. For example, if you had two overlapping objects, and the top layer had a drawing of a tree and the bottom layer had a drawing of a house, the tree would appear as though it were in front of the house. You can change the stacking order of layers simply by dragging them up or down in the list of layers. You can name layers, hide them so their contents do not appear on the stage, and lock them so that they cannot be edited.

Using Frames

The timeline is made up of individual segments called **frames**. The content of each layer is displayed in frames as the playhead moves over them while the movie plays. Frames are numbered in increments of five for easy reference, while colors and symbols are used to indicate the type of frame (for example, keyframe or motion animation). The upper-right corner of the timeline contains a Frame View icon. Clicking on this icon displays a menu that provides different views of the timeline, showing more frames or showing thumbnails of the objects on a layer, for example. The status bar at the bottom of the timeline indicates the current frame (the frame that the playhead is currently on), the frame rate (frames per second), and the elapsed time from Frame 1 to the current frame.

Using the Playhead

The **playhead** indicates which frame is playing. You can manually move the play-head by dragging it left or right. This makes it easier to locate a frame that you may want to edit. Dragging the playhead also allows you to do a quick check of the movie without having to play it.

Understanding Scenes

When you create a movie, Scene 1 appears in the timeline. You can add scenes to a movie at any time. Scenes are a way to organize long movies. For example, a movie created for a Web site could be divided into anumber of scenes: an introduction, a home page, and content pages. Without them, scrolling through the timeline to work on different parts of the movie could become a very frustrating and inefficient way to work. Scenes have their own timeline. You can insert new scenes by using the Insert menu. Scenes can be given descriptive names, which will help you find them easily if you need to edit a particular scene. The number of scenes is limited only by the computer's memory.

FIGURE 15
Elements of the timeline

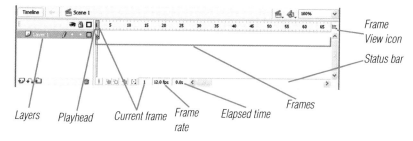

Frame
View icon

Status bar

Frames

Layers   Playhead   Current frame   Frame
rate   Elapsed time

FIGURE 16
The concept of layers

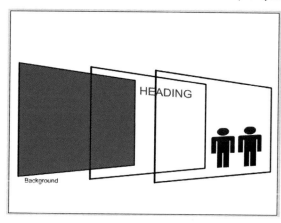

Working with the Timeline

Figure 17 shows the timeline of a movie created in Lesson 2 with a second object, a square at the top of the stage. By studying the timeline, you can learn several things about this movie. First, the second object is placed on its own layer, Layer 2. Second, the layer has a motion animation (indicated by the arrow and blue background in the frames). Third, the animation runs from Frame 1 to Frame 40. Fourth, if the objects intersect during the animation, the square will be on top of the circle, because the layer it is placed on is above the layer that the circle is placed on. Fifth, the frame rate is set to 12, which means that the movie will play 12 frames per second. Sixth, the playhead is at Frame 1, which causes the contents for both layers of Frame 1 to be displayed on the stage.

QUICKTIP

You can adjust the height of the timeline by positioning the mouse over the bottom edge, then dragging the border up or down.

FIGURE 17

The timeline of a movie with a second object

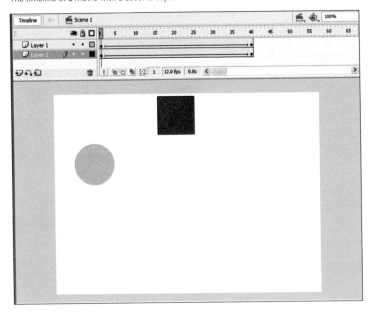

FIGURE 18
Drawing a square

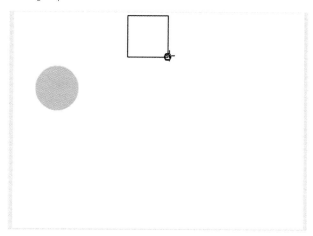

FIGURE 19
Positioning the square at the bottom of the stage

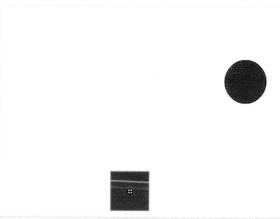

Add a layer

1. Save tween.fla as **layers.fla**.
2. Click **Frame 1** on Layer 1.
3. Click **View** on the menu bar, point to **Magnification**, then click **Fit in Window**.
4. Click **Insert** on the menu bar, point to **Timeline**, then click **Layer**.

   A new layer—Layer 2—appears at the top of the timeline.

You added a layer to the timeline.

Create a second animation

1. Click **Frame 1** of Layer 2 on the timeline.
2. Click the **Rectangle tool** on the Tools panel, press and hold [**Shift**], then draw a square resembling the dimensions, as shown in Figure 18.
3. Click the **Selection tool** on the Tools panel, then drag a marquee around the square.
4. Click **Insert** on the menu bar, point to **Timeline**, then click **Create Motion Tween**.
5. Click **Frame 40** on Layer 2, click **Insert** on the menu bar, point to **Timeline**, then click **Keyframe**.
6. Drag the square to the bottom of the stage, as shown in Figure 19, then play the movie.

   The square appears on top when the two objects intersect.

You drew an object and used it to create a second animation.

Work with layers and view features in the timeline

1. Click **Layer 2** on the timeline, then drag it below Layer 1.

   Layer 2 is now the bottom layer.

2. Play the movie and notice how the square appears beneath the circle when they intersect.

3. Click the **Frame View icon** ≡ on the end of the timeline to display the menu, as shown in Figure 20.

4. Click **Tiny** to display more frames.

5. Click the **Frame View icon** ≡ , click **Preview**, then note the object thumbnails that appear on the timeline.

6. Click the **Frame View icon** ≡ , then click **Normal**.

You changed the order of the layers and changed the display of frames on the timeline.

FIGURE 20
Changing the view of the timeline

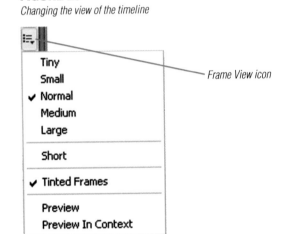

Frame View icon

FIGURE 21

Changing the frame rate

New frame rate

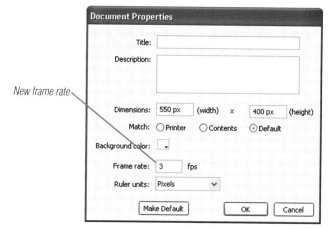

Modify the frame rate

1. Double-click the **Frame Rate icon** `12.0 fps` on the bottom of the timeline to open the Document Properties dialog box.

2. Double-click **12**, type **3** in the Frame rate text box, then compare your Document Properties dialog box to Figure 21.

3. Click **OK**.

4. Play the movie and notice that the speed of the movie changes.

   TIP fps stands for frames per second. Frames per second is the unit of measurement for movies.

5. Repeat Steps 1 through 4, but change the frame rate to 18 and then to 12.

6. Click **Frame 1** on the timeline.

7. Drag the **playhead** left and right to display specific frames.

8. Save your work, then close layers.fla.

You changed the frame rate of the movie and used the playhead to display the contents of frames.

Getting Help

Macromedia Flash provides a comprehensive Help feature that can be very useful when first learning the program. You can access Help by clicking commands on the Help menu. The Help feature includes the Macromedia Flash manual, which is organized by topic and can be accessed through the index or by using a keyword search. In addition, the Help menu contains samples and tutorials that cover basic Macromedia Flash features.

PLAN A
WEB SITE

What You'll Do

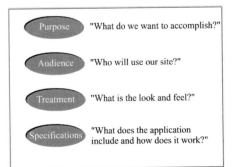

Purpose — "What do we want to accomplish?"

Audience — "Who will use our site?"

Treatment — "What is the look and feel?"

Specifications — "What does the application include and how does it work?"

In this lesson, you will learn how to plan a Macromedia Flash application. You will also learn about the guidelines for screen design and the interactive design of Web pages.

Planning an Application

Macromedia Flash can be used to develop animations (movies) that are part of a product, such as a game or educational tutorial, delivered on CD-ROM or DVD. You can use Macromedia Flash to create enhancements to Web pages, such as animated logos and interactive navigation buttons. You can also use Macromedia Flash to create entire Web sites. No matter what the application, the first step is planning. Often, the temptation is to jump right into the program and start developing movies. The problem is that this invariably results in a more time-consuming process at best; and wasted effort, resources, and money at worst. The larger in scope and the more complex the project

is, the more critical the planning process becomes. Planning an entire Web site should involve the following steps:

Step 1: Stating the Purpose (Goals). "What, specifically, do we want to accomplish?"

Determining the goals of a site is a critical step in planning, because goals guide the development process, keep the team members on track, and provide a way to evaluate the site both during and after its development.

Step 2: Identifying the Target Audience. "Who will use the Web site?"

Understanding the potential viewers helps in developing a site that can address their needs. For example, children respond to exploration and surprise, so having a dog wag its tail when the mouse pointer rolls over it might appeal to this audience.

Step 3: Determining the Treatment. "What is the look and feel?"

The treatment is how the Web site will be presented to the user, including the tone, approach, and emphasis.

Tone. Will the site be humorous, serious, light, heavy, formal, or informal? The tone of a site can often be used to make a statement projecting a progressive, high-tech, well-funded corporate image, for instance.

Approach. How much direction will be provided to the user? An interactive game site might focus on exploration, while an informational site might provide lots of direction, such as menus.

Emphasis. How much emphasis will be placed on the various multimedia elements? For example, a company may want to develop an informational site that shows the features of their new product line, including animated demonstrations of how each product works. The budget might not allow for the expense of creating the animations, so the emphasis would shift to still pictures with text descriptions.

Step 4: Developing the Specifications and Storyboard. "What precisely does the application include and how does it work?"

The specifications state what will be included in each screen, including the arrangement of each element and the functionality of each object (for example, what happens when you click the button

labeled Skip Intro). Specifications should include the following:

Playback System. The choice of what configuration to target for playback is critical, especially Internet connection speed, browser versions, screen resolution, and plug-ins.

Elements to Include. The specifications should include details about the various elements that are to be included in the site. What are the dimensions for the animations, and what is the frame rate? What are the sizes of the various objects such as photos, buttons, and so on? What fonts, font sizes, and type styles will be used?

Functionality. The specifications should include the way the program reacts to an action by the user, such as a mouse click. For example, clicking on a door (object) might cause the door to open

Rich Media Content and Accessibility

Macromedia Flash provides the tools that allow you to create compelling Web sites by incorporating rich media content, such as animations, sound, and video. Generally, incorporating rich media enhances the user's experience. However, accessibility becomes an issue for those that are visually, hearing, or mobility impaired, or have a cognitive disability. Designers need to utilize techniques that help ensure accessibility, such as providing consistency throughout the Web site in navigation and layout, labeling graphics, captioning audio content, and providing keyboard access.

(an animation), a doorbell to ring (sound), an "exit the program" message to appear (text), or an entirely new screen to be displayed.

User Interface. The user interface involves designing the appearance of objects (how each object is arranged on the screen) and the interactivity (how the user navigates through the site).

A flowchart is a visual representation of how the contents in an application or Web site are organized and how various screens are linked. It provides a guide for the developer and helps to identify problems with the navigation scheme before work begins. Figure 22 shows a simple flowchart illustrating the site organization and links. A storyboard shows the layout of the various screens. It describes the contents and illustrates how text, graphics, animation, and other screen elements will be positioned. It also indicates the navigation process, such as menus and buttons. Figure 23 shows a storyboard. The exact content (such as a specific photo) does not have to be decided upon, but it is important to show where text, graphics, photos, buttons, and other elements, will be placed. Thus, the storyboard includes placeholders for the various elements.

Using Screen Design Guidelines

The following screen design guidelines are used by Web developers. The implementation of these guidelines is affected by the goals of the site, the intended audience, and the content.

Balance—Balance in screen design refers to the distribution of optical weight in the layout. Optical weight is the ability of an object to attract the viewer's eye, as determined by the object's size, shape, color, and so on. In general, a balanced design is more appealing to a viewer.

FIGURE 22
Sample Flowchart

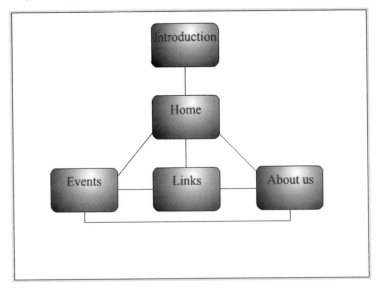

FIGURE 23
Sample Storyboard

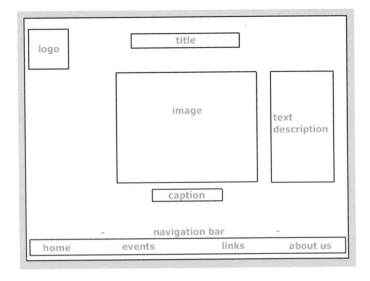

Getting Started with Macromedia Flash

Unity—Intra-screen unity has to do with how the various screen objects relate and how they all fit in. Unity helps them reinforce each other. Inter-screen unity refers to the design that viewers encounter as they navigate from one screen to another, and it provides consistency throughout the site.

Movement—Movement refers to the way the viewer's eye moves through the objects on the screen. Techniques in an animation, such as movement, can be used to draw the viewer to a location on the screen.

Using Interactive Design Guidelines

In addition to screen design guidelines, interactive guidelines determine the interactivity of the site. The following guidelines are not absolute rules but are affected by the goals of the site, the intended audience, and the content:

- Make it simple, easy to understand, and easy to use. Make the site intuitive so that viewers do not have to spend time learning what the site is all about and what they need to do.
- Build in consistency in the navigation scheme. Help the users know where they are in the site and help them avoid getting lost.
- Provide feedback. Users need to know when an action, such as clicking a button, has been completed. Changing its color or shape, or adding a sound can indicate this.
- Give the user control. Allow the user to skip long introductions; provide controls for starting, stopping, and rewinding animations, video, and audio; and provide controls for adjusting audio.

Project Management

Developing Web sites or any extensive application, such as a game, involves project management. A project plan needs to be developed that provides the project scope and identifies the milestones including analyzing, designing, building, testing, and launching. Personnel and resource needs are identified, budgets built, tasks assigned, and schedules developed. Successful projects are a team effort relying on the close collaboration of designers, developers, project managers, graphic artists, programmers, testers, and others.

DISTRIBUTE A MACROMEDIA
FLASH MOVIE

What You'll Do

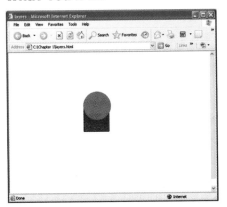

In this lesson you will prepare a movie for distribution in various formats.

Distributing Movies

When you develop Macromedia Flash movies, the application saves them in a file format (.fla) that only users who have the Macromedia Flash program installed on their computers can view. Usually, Macromedia Flash movies are viewed on the Web as part of a Web site or directly from a viewer's computer using the Macromedia Flash Player. In order to view your Macromedia Flash movies on the Web, you must change the movie to a Macromedia Flash Player (.swf) file format and generate the HTML code that references the Macromedia Flash Player file. You can accomplish both of these tasks by using the publish feature of Macromedia Flash.

The process for publishing a Macromedia Flash movie is to create and save a movie and then click the Publish command on the File menu. You can also specify various settings such as dimensions for the window that the movie plays within in the browser, before publishing the movie. Publishing a movie creates two files: an HTML file and a Macromedia Flash file. Both of these files retain the same name as the Flash movie file, but with different file extensions:

- .html—the HTML document
- .swf—the Macromedia Flash Player file

For example, publishing a movie named layers.fla would generate layers.html and layers.swf. The HTML document contains the code that the browser interprets to display the movie on the Web. The code also specifies the Macromedia Flash Player movie that the browser will play. Sample HTML code referencing a Macromedia Flash Player movie is shown in Figure 24.

Macromedia Flash provides several other ways to distribute your movies that may or may not involve delivery on the Web. You can create a stand-alone movie called a **projector**. Projector files, such as Windows .exe files, maintain the movie's interactivity. Alternately, you can create self-running movies, such as QuickTime .mov files, that are not interactive.

You can play projector and non-interactive files directly from a computer, or you can incorporate them into an application, such as a game, that is downloaded or delivered on a CD or DVD.

FIGURE 24

Sample HTML code

```
<!-- saved from url=(0013)about:internet -->
<!DOCTYPE html PUBLIC "-//W3C//DTD XHTML 1.0 Transitional//EN"
"http://www.w3.org/TR/xhtml1/DTD/xhtml1-transitional.dtd">
<html xmlns="http://www.w3.org/1999/xhtml" xml:lang="en" lang="en">
<head>
<meta http-equiv="Content-Type" content="text/html; charset=iso-8859-1" />
<title>layers</title>
</head>
<body bgcolor="#ffffff">
<!--url's used in the movie-->
<!--text used in the movie-->
<!-- saved from url=(0013)about:internet -->
<object classid="clsid:d27cdb6e-ae6d-11cf-96b8-444553540000"
codebase="http://fpdownload.macromedia.com/pub/shockwave/cabs/flash/swflash.cab#version=8,0,0,0"
width="550" height="400" id="layers" align="middle">
<param name="allowScriptAccess" value="sameDomain" />
<param name="movie" value="layers.swf" /><param name="quality" value="high" /><param name="bgcolor"
value="#ffffff" /><embed src="layers.swf" quality="high" bgcolor="#ffffff" width="550" height="400"
name="layers" align="middle" allowScriptAccess="sameDomain" type="application/x-shockwave-flash"
pluginspage="http://www.macromedia.com/go/getflashplayer" />
</object>
</body>
</html>
```

Code specifying the Macromedia Flash Player movie that the browser will play

.swf extension indicates a Macromedia Flash Player file

Publish a movie for distribution on the Web

1. Open layers.fla.

2. Click **File** on the menu bar, then click **Publish**.

3. Navigate to the drive and folder where you save your work.

4. Notice the three files that begin with "layers", as shown in Figure 25.

   Layers.fla, the Flash movie; layers.swf, the Macromedia Flash Player file; and layers.htm, the HTML document, appear in the window.

5. Double-click **layers.html**, then notice that the movie plays in the browser.

6. Close the browser.

You used the Publish command to create an HTML document and a Macromedia Flash Player file, then displayed the HTML document in a Web browser.

FIGURE 25
The three layers files after publishing the movie

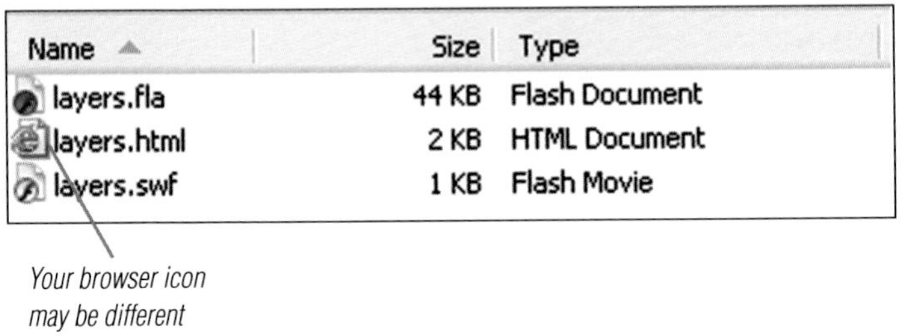

Name ▲	Size	Type
layers.fla	44 KB	Flash Document
layers.html	2 KB	HTML Document
layers.swf	1 KB	Flash Movie

Your browser icon may be different

FIGURE 26

The Flash Player window playing the Macromedia Flash Player movie

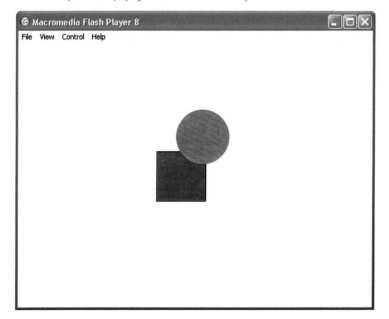

Create a projector file

1. Return to Flash, click **File** on the menu bar, then click **Publish Settings** to open the Publish Settings dialog box.

2. Click the **Windows Projector (.exe)** (Win) or **Macintosh Projector** (Mac) **check box**, then deselect other file formats (if necessary).

3. Click **Publish**, then click **OK**.

4. Navigate to the drive and folder where you save your work.

5. Double-click **layers.exe** (Win), or **layers Projector** (Mac), then notice that the application plays in the Macromedia Flash Player window, as shown in Figure 26.

6. Close the Macromedia Flash Player window.

7. Close layers.fla in Macromedia Flash, saving your changes if prompted.

8. Exit the Macromedia Flash program.

You created and displayed a stand-alone projector file.

Start Macromedia Flash, open a movie, and set the movie properties and magnification.

1. Start Macromedia Flash, open fl1_2.fla, and then save it as **skillsdemo1**.
2. Display the Document Properties dialog box, add a title, **Animated Objects**, then add a description, **A review of skills learned in Chapter 1**.
3. Change the movie window dimensions to width: 550 px and height: 450 px.
4. Change the background color to blue. (*Hint*: Select the blue color swatch in the left column of the color palette.)
5. Close the Document Properties dialog box.
6. Change the magnification to 50% using the View menu.
7. Change the magnification to Fit in Window.

Display, close, and collapse panels.

1. Hide all panels.
2. Display the Tools panel, Property inspector, and the Library panel.
3. Collapse the Property inspector and Library panels.

4. Close the Library panel to remove it from the screen.
5. Expand the Property inspector.

Play and test a movie.

1. Drag the playhead to view the contents of each frame. Use the commands in the Control menu to play and rewind the movie.
2. Press [Enter] (Win) or [return] (Mac) to play and stop the movie.
3. Use the Controller to rewind, play, stop, and start the movie.
4. Test the movie in the Macromedia Flash Player window, then close the test movie window.

Create an object, create a basic animation, and apply an effect.

1. Insert a new layer above layer 2, then select Frame 1 of the new layer.
2. Draw a red circle in the lower-left corner of the stage, approximately the same size as the green ball. (*Hint*: Use the scroll bar on the timeline to view the new layer.)

3. Select the circle, then create a Motion Tween to animate the circle so that it moves across the screen from left to right, beginning in Frame 1 and ending in Frame 60. (*Hint*: Add a keyframe in the ending frame.)
4. Use the Selection Tool to select the circle (if necessary), then change the brightness from 0% to -100%, in the last frame of the animation.
5. Play the movie, then rewind it.

Add a layer, change the frame rate, and change the view of the timeline.

1. Add a new layer above layer 3, select Frame 1, then create a second circle in the lower-right corner of the stage that's approximately the same size as the circle you created in the lower-left corner of the stage.
2. Animate the circle so that it moves across the screen from right to left beginning in Frame 1 and ending in Frame 60.
3. Use the Selection Tool to select the circle, then change the brightness from 0% to 100%.
4. Play the movie.
5. Change the frame rate to 8 frames per second.

6. Change the view of the timeline to display more frames.
7. Change the view of the timeline to display a preview of the object thumbnails.
8. Change the view of the timeline to display the Normal view.
9. Use the playhead to display each frame, then compare your screens to Figure 27.
10. Save the movie.

Publish a movie.

1. Click File on the menu bar, then click Publish.
2. Open your browser, then open skillsdemo1.html.
3. View the movie, then close your browser.

Create a projector file.

1. Display the Publish Settings dialog box.
2. Select the appropriate projector setting for your operating systems and remove all of the other settings.
3. Publish the movie.
4. Navigate to the drive and folder where you save your work, then open skillsdemo1 projector file.
5. View the movie, then close the Macromedia Flash Player window.
6. Save and close the Macromedia Flash document.
7. Exit Flash.

FIGURE 27
Completed Skills Review

A friend cannot decide whether to sign up for a class in Macromedia Flash or Macromedia Dreamweaver. You help her decide by showing her what you already know about Macromedia Flash. Since you think she'd love a class in Macromedia Flash, you decide to show her how easy it is to create a simple animation involving two objects that move diagonally across the screen.

1. Open a Flash document, then save it as **demonstration**.
2. Use the tools on the Tools panel to create a simple shape or design, and place it off the left side of the stage, halfway down the stage.
3. Select the object and insert a motion tween.
4. Insert a keyframe in Frame 20, then move the object to the middle of the stage.
5. Insert a new layer, then select Frame 1 of the layer.
6. Create another object that covers the first object, then insert a motion tween for the object.
7. Insert a keyframe in Frame 40, then move the object to the right side off the stage.
8. Insert a new layer, then select Frame 1 of the layer.
9. Draw an object off the top of the stage, about midway across the stage.
10. Animate the object to move straight down and off the bottom of the stage for 40 frames.
11. Change the brightness of the object to 80% in Frame 40.

12. Add a background color.
13. Preview the movie and test it.
14. Save the movie, then compare it to the example shown in Figure 28.

FIGURE 28
Sample completed Project Builder 1

You've been asked to develop a simple movie about recycling for a day care center. For this project, you will add two animations to an existing movie. You will show three objects that appear on the screen at different times, and then move each object to a recycle bin at different times. You can use any objects using the Tools on the Tools panel.

1. Open fl1_3.fla, then save it as **recycle**.
2. Play the movie and study the timeline to familiarize yourself with the movie's current settings.
3. Insert a new layer above Layer 2, insert a keyframe in Frame 10 of the new layer, then draw a small object in the upper-left corner of the stage.
4. Create a motion animation that moves the object to the recycle bin.
5. Insert a new layer above the top layer, insert a keyframe in Frame 20, draw a small object in the upper center of the stage, then create a motion animation that moves the object to the recycle bin.
6. Insert a new layer above the top layer, insert a keyframe in Frame 30, draw a small object in the upper-right corner of the stage, then create a motion animation that moves the object to the recycle bin.
7. Move Layer 1 to the top of all the layers.
8. Play the movie and compare it to Figure 29.
9. Save the movie.

FIGURE 29
Sample completed Project Builder 2

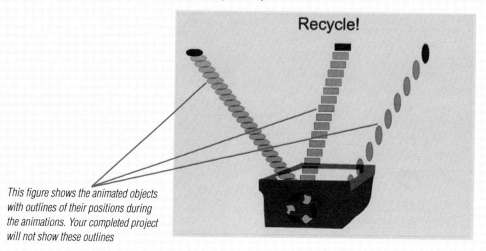

This figure shows the animated objects with outlines of their positions during the animations. Your completed project will not show these outlines

Figure 30 shows the home page of a Web site. Study the figure and answer the following questions. For each question, indicate how you determined your answer.

1. Connect to the Internet, go to *www.course. com*, navigate to the page for this book, click the Online Companion link, then click the link for this chapter.

2. Open a document in a word processor or open a new Macromedia Flash document, save the file as **dpc1**, then answer the following questions. (*Hint*: Use the Text tool in Macromedia Flash.)

   - Whose Web site is this?
   - What is the goal(s) of the site?
   - Who is the target audience?
   - What treatment (look and feel) is used?
   - What are the design layout guidelines being used (balance, movement, etc.)?
   - How can animation enhance this page?
   - Do you think this is an effective design for the company, its products, and its target audience? Why, or why not?
   - What suggestions would you make to improve on the design, and why?

FIGURE 30
Design Project

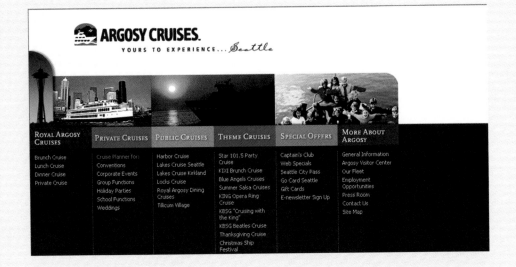

Getting Started with Macromedia Flash

There are numerous companies in the business of developing Web sites for others. Many of these companies use Macromedia Flash as one of their primary development tools. These companies promote themselves through their own Web sites and usually provide online portfolios with samples of their work. Log onto the Internet, then use your favorite search engine (use keywords such as Macromedia Flash developers and Macromedia Flash animators) to locate three of these companies, and generate the following information for each one. A sample is shown in Figure 31.

1. Company name:
2. Contact information (address, phone, and so on):
3. Web site URL:
4. Company mission:
5. Services provided:
6. Sample list of clients:
7. Describe three ways they seem to have used Macromedia Flash in their own sites. Were these effective? Why, or why not?
8. Describe three applications of Macromedia Flash that they include in their portfolios (or showcases or samples). Were these effective? Why, or why not?

9. Would you want to work for this company? Why, or why not?
10. Would you recommend this company to another company that was looking to enhance its Web site? Why, or why not?

FIGURE 31
Portfolio Project

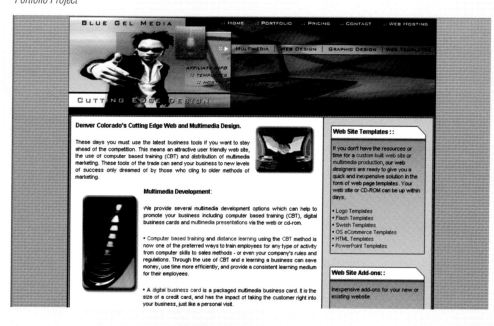

2

DRAWING OBJECTS IN
MACROMEDIA FLASH

1. Use the Macromedia Flash drawing tools.

2. Select Objects and Apply Colors.

3. Work with objects.

4. Work with text and text objects.

5. Work with layers and objects.

2 DRAWING OBJECTS IN
MACROMEDIA FLASH

Introduction

One of the most compelling features of Macromedia Flash is the ability to create and manipulate vector graphics. Computers can display graphics in either a bitmap or a vector format. The difference between these formats is in how they describe an image. Bitmap graphics represent the image as an array of dots, called **pixels**, which are arranged within a grid. Each pixel in an image has an exact position on the screen and a precise color. To make a change in a bitmap, you modify the pixels. When you enlarge a bitmap graphic, the number of pixels remains the same, resulting in jagged edges that decrease the quality of the image. Vector graphics represent the image using lines and curves, which you can resize without losing image quality. Also, because vector images are generally smaller than bitmap images, they are particularly useful for a Web site. However, vector graphics are not as effective as bitmap graphics for representing photo-realistic images.

Images (objects) created using Macromedia Flash drawing tools have a stroke, a fill, or both. In addition, the stroke of an object can be segmented into smaller lines. You can modify the size, shape, rotation, and color of each stroke, fill, and segment.

Macromedia Flash provides two drawing modes, called models. In the Merge Drawing Model, when you draw two shapes and one overlaps the other, a change in the top object may affect the object beneath it. For example, if you draw a circle on top of a rectangle and then move the circle off the rectangle, the portion of the rectangle overlapped by the circle is removed. The Object Drawing Model allows you to overlap shapes which are then kept separate, so that changes in one object do not affect another object. Another way to avoid having changes in one object affect another is to place them on separate layers in the timeline.

Tools You'll Use

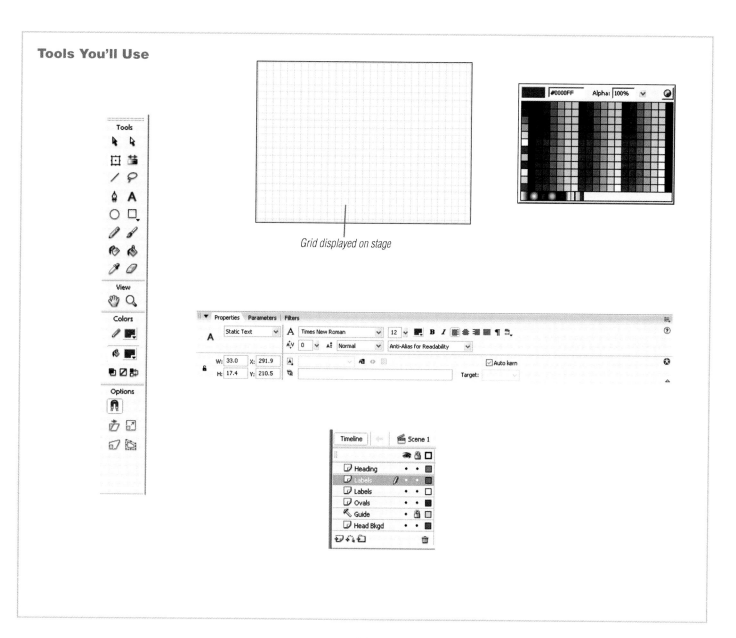

Grid displayed on stage

USE THE MACROMEDIA FLASH DRAWING TOOLS

What You'll Do

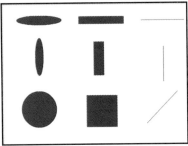

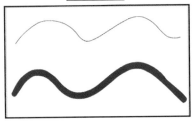

 In this lesson, you will use several drawing tools to create various vector graphics.

Using Macromedia Flash Drawing and Editing Tools

When you point to a tool on the Tools panel, its name appears next to the tool. Figure 1 identifies the tools described below. Several of the tools have options that modify their use.

Selection—Used to select an object or parts of an object, such as the stroke or fill; and to reshape objects. The options available for the Selection tool are Snap to Objects (aligns objects), Smooth (smoothes lines), and Straighten (straightens lines).

Subselection—Used to select, drag, and reshape an object. Vector graphics are composed of lines and curves (each of which is a segment) connected by **anchor points**. Selecting an object with this tool displays the anchor points and allows you to use them to edit the object.

Free Transform—Used to transform objects by rotating, scaling, skewing, and distorting them.

Gradient Transform—Used to transform a gradient fill by adjusting the size, direction, or center of the fill.

Line—Used to draw straight lines. You can draw vertical, horizontal, and 45° diagonal lines by pressing and holding [Shift] while drawing the line.

Lasso—Used to select objects or parts of objects. The Polygon Mode option allows you to draw straight lines when selecting an object.

Pen—Used to draw lines and curves by creating a series of dots, known as anchor points, that are automatically connected.

Text—Used to create and edit text.

Oval—Used to draw oval shapes. Press and hold [Shift] to draw a perfect circle.

Rectangle—Used to draw rectangular shapes. Press and hold [Shift] to draw a perfect square. The Round Rectangle Radius option allows you to round the corners of a rectangle.

Pencil—Used to draw freehand lines and shapes. The options available for the Pencil tool are Straighten (draws straight lines), Smooth (draws smooth curved lines), and Ink (draws freehand with no modification).

Brush—Used to draw (paint) with brush-like strokes. Options allow you to set the size and shape of the brush, and to determine the area to be painted, such as inside or behind an object.

Ink Bottle—Used to apply line colors and thickness to the stroke of an object.

Paint Bucket—Used to fill enclosed areas of a drawing with color. Options allow you to fill areas that have gaps and to make adjustments in a gradient fill.

Eyedropper—Used to select stroke, fill, and text attributes so they can be copied from one object to another.

Eraser—Used to erase lines and fills. Options allow you to choose what part of the object to erase, as well as the size and shape of the eraser.

The Oval, Rectangle, Pencil, Brush, Line, and Pen tools are used to create vector objects.

Displaying Gridlines, Guides, and Rulers

Gridlines, guides, and rulers can be used to position objects on the stage. The Grid, Guides, and Rulers commands, found on the View menu, are used to turn on and off these features. You can modify the grid size and color, and you can specify the unit of measure for the rulers. In addition, Guide layers can be used to position objects on the stage.

FIGURE 1
Macromedia Flash tools

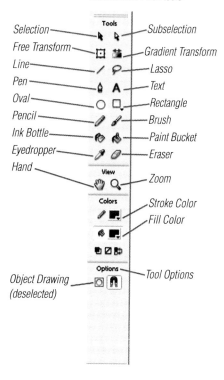

Show gridlines and check settings

1. Start Macromedia Flash, create a new Flash Document, then save it as **tools**.

2. Click **Window** on the menu bar, then click **Hide Panels**.

3. Click **Window** on the menu bar, then click **Tools**.

4. Click **Window** on the menu bar, point to **Properties**, then click **Properties**.

5. Click **View** on the menu bar, point to **Magnification**, then click **Fit in Window**.

6. Click the **Stroke Color tool** on the Tools panel, then click the **red color swatch** in the left column of the color palette (if necessary).

7. Click the **Fill Color tool** on the Tools panel, then click the **blue color swatch** in the left column of the color palette (if necessary).

8. Click **View** on the menu bar, point to **Grid**, then click **Show Grid** to display the gridlines.

   A gray grid appears on the stage.

9. Point to several tools on the Tools panel, then read their names, as shown in Figure 2.

You started a new document, saved it, set up the workspace, changed the stroke and fill colors, then displayed the grid and viewed tool names on the Tools panel.

FIGURE 2
Tool name on the Tools panel

Point to a tool to display its name

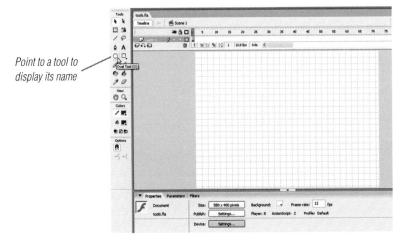

FIGURE 3

Objects created with drawing tools

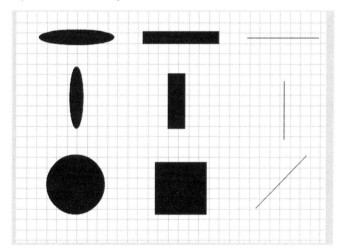

Use the Oval, Rectangle, and Line Tools

1. Click the **Oval tool** ○ on the Tools panel.

2. Verify that the **Object Drawing option** ◎ in the Options section of the Tools panel is deselected.

3. Using Figure 3 as a guide, draw the three oval shapes.

   TIP   Use the grid to approximate shape sizes and Hold down [Shift] to draw a circle, square and diagonal line. To undo an action, click the Undo command on the Edit menu.

4. Click the **Rectangle tool** ▢▾, then using Figure 3 as a guide, draw the three rectangle shapes.

5. Click the **Line tool** ╱, then, using Figure 3 as a guide, draw the three lines.

   Notice that the ovals and rectangles display both the stroke and fill colors, while the line tool displays only the stroke color.

You used the Oval, Rectangle, and Line tools to draw objects on the stage.

Use the Pen, Pencil, and Brush Tools

1. Click **Insert** on the menu bar, point to **Timeline**, then click **Layer**.

   A new layer—Layer 2—appears above Layer 1.

2. Click **Frame 5** on Layer 2.

3. Click **Insert** on the menu bar, point to **Timeline**, then click **Keyframe**.

   Since the objects were drawn in Frame 1, they are no longer visible when you insert a keyframe in Frame 5.

4. Click the **Zoom tool** 🔍 on the Tools panel, point near the upper-left quadrant of the stage, then click to zoom in.

5. Click the **Pen tool** ♠ on the Tools panel, position it in the upper-left quadrant of the stage, as shown in Figure 4, then click to set an anchor point.

6. Using Figure 5 as a guide, click the remaining anchor points to complete drawing an arrow.

   TIP   To close an object, be sure to re-click the first anchor point as your last action.

7. Click **View** on the menu bar, point to **Magnification**, then click **100%**.

8. Insert a new layer, Layer 3, then insert a keyframe in Frame 10.

9. Click the **Pencil tool** ✏ on the Tools panel.

10. Click the **Pencil Mode tool** ⤵ in the Options section of the Tools panel, then click the **Smooth option** ⟨, as shown in Figure 6.

11. Draw the top image, as shown in Figure 7.

   (continued)

FIGURE 4
Positioning the Pen Tool on the stage

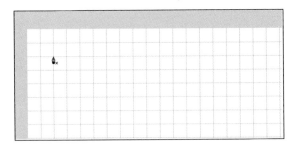

FIGURE 5
Setting anchor points to draw an arrow

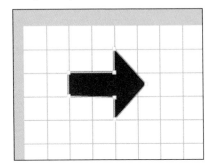

FIGURE 6
Pencil Tool options

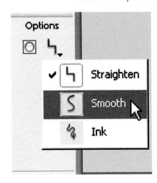

FIGURE 7
Images drawn using drawing tools

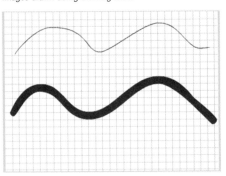

Drawing Objects in Macromedia Flash

12. Click the **Brush tool** on the Tools panel.

13. Click the **Brush Size list arrow** in the Options section of the Tools panel, then click the 5th option from the top.

14. Repeat Step 11, drawing the bottom image. Notice the pencil tool displays the stroke color and the brush tool displays the fill color.

You added a layer, inserted a keyframe, then used the Pen Tool to draw an arrow; you selected the Smooth option for the Pencil tool and drew an object; you selected a brush size for the Brush tool and drew an object.

Modify an object using tool options

1. Click the **Selection tool** on the Tools panel, then drag a marquee around the top object to select it.

2. Click the **Smooth option** S. in the Options section of the Tools panel.

   The line becomes smoother.

3. Select the bottom object, then click the **Smooth option** S. in the Options section of the Tools panel.

   Your object should look similar to Figure 8. The object becomes smoother.

4. Save your work.

You smoothed objects using the tool options.

FIGURE 8

The dot pattern indicating the object is selected

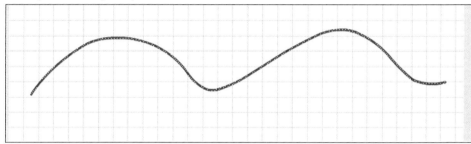

SELECT OBJECTS
AND APPLY COLORS

What You'll Do

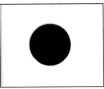

 In this lesson, you will use several techniques to select objects, change the color of strokes and fills, and create a gradient fill.

Selecting Objects

Before you can edit a drawing, you must first select the object, or part of the object, on which you want to work. Objects are made up of a stroke(s) and a fill. Strokes can have several segments. For example, a rectangle will have four stroke segments, one for each side of the object. These can be selected separately or as a whole. Macromedia Flash highlights objects that have been selected, as shown in Figure 9. When the stroke of an object is selected, a colored line appears. When the fill of an object is selected, a dot pattern appears; and when objects are grouped, a bounding box appears.

Using the Selection Tool

You can use the Selection tool to select part or all of an object, and to select multiple objects. To select only the fill, click just the fill; to select only the stroke, click just the stroke. To select both the fill and the stroke, double-click the object or draw a marquee around it. To select part of an object, drag a marquee that defines the area you wish to

select, as shown in Figure 9. To select multiple objects or combinations of strokes and fills, press and hold [Shift], then click each item. To deselect an item(s), click a blank area of the stage.

Using the Lasso Tool

The Lasso tool provides more flexibility when selecting an area on the stage. You can use the tool in a freehand manner to select any size and shape of area. Alternately, you can use the Polygon Mode option to draw straight lines and connect them.

Object Drawing Model

Macromedia Flash provides two drawing modes, called models. In the Merge Drawing Model mode, the stroke and fill of an object are separate. Thus, as you draw an object such as a circle, the stroke and fill can be selected individually as described above. When using the Object Drawing Model mode, the stroke and fill are combined and cannot be selected individually. However, you can use the Break Apart option from the Modify menu to separate the stroke and fill so that they can be selected individually. In addition, you can turn off either the stroke or fill when drawing an object in either mode. You can toggle between the two modes using the Object Drawing icon in the options section of the Tools panel.

Working with Colors

Macromedia Flash allows you to change the color of the stroke and fill of an object. Figure 10 shows the Colors section of the Tools panel. To change a color, you click the Stroke Color tool or the Fill Color tool, and then select a color swatch on the color palette. The color palette, as shown in Figure 11, allows you to type in a six character code that represents the values of three colors (red, green, blue), referred to as RGB. When these characters are combined in various ways they can represent virtually any color. The values are in a hexadecimal format (base 16), so they include letters and digits (A-F + 0-9 = 16 options), and they are preceded by a pound sign (#). The first two characters represent the value for red, the next two for green, and the last two for blue. For example, #000000 represents black (lack of color); #FFFFFF represents white; #00FF00 represents green; and FFCC33 represents a shade of gold. You do not have to memorize the code for all colors. There are reference manuals available for looking up the codes, and many programs allow you to set the values visually by selecting a color from a palette.

You can set the desired colors before drawing an object, or you can change a color of a previously drawn object. You can use the Ink Bottle tool to change the stroke color, and you can use the Paint Bucket tool to change the fill color. You can also use the Property inspector to change the stroke and fill colors.

Working with Gradients

A gradient is a color fill that makes a gradual transition from one color to another. Gradients can be very useful for creating a 3-D effect, drawing attention to an object, and generally enhancing the appearance of an object. You can apply a gradient fill by using the Paint Bucket tool. The position of the Paint Bucket tool over the object is important because it determines the direction of the gradient fill.

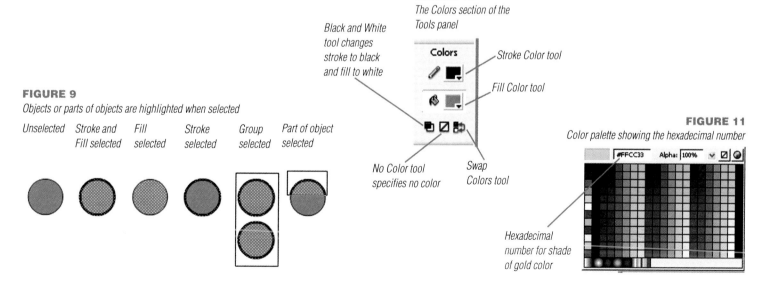

FIGURE 10
The Colors section of the Tools panel

Black and White tool changes stroke to black and fill to white

Stroke Color tool

Fill Color tool

FIGURE 9
Objects or parts of objects are highlighted when selected

Unselected   *Stroke and Fill selected*   *Fill selected*   *Stroke selected*   *Group selected*   *Part of object selected*

No Color tool specifies no color

Swap Colors tool

FIGURE 11
Color palette showing the hexadecimal number

Hexadecimal number for shade of gold color

Select a drawing using the mouse and the Lasso Tool

1. Click **Frame 1** on the timeline.

   TIP The actions you perform on the stage will produce very different results depending on whether you click a frame on the timeline or on a layer.

2. Click the **Selection tool** 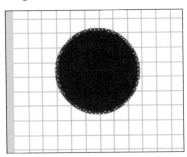 on the Tools panel (if necessary), then drag the marquee around the circle to select the entire object (both the stroke and the fill).

3. Click anywhere on the stage to deselect the object.

4. Click inside the circle to select the fill only, then click outside the circle to deselect it.

5. Click the stroke of the circle to select it, as shown in Figure 12, then deselect it.

6. Double-click the **circle** to select it, press and hold **[Shift]**, double-click the **square** to select both objects, then deselect both objects.

7. Click the right border of the square to select it, as shown in Figure 13, then deselect it.

You used the Selection tool to select the stroke and fill of an object, and to select multiple objects.

FIGURE 12

Using the Selection tool to select the stroke of the circle

FIGURE 13

Using the Selection tool to select a segment of the stroke of the square

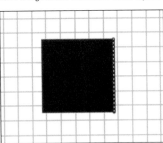

Drawing Objects in Macromedia Flash

FIGURE 14
Circles drawn with the Oval tool

FIGURE 15
Changing the stroke color

Change fill and stroke colors

1. Click **Layer 3**, click **Insert** on the menu bar, point to **Timeline**, then click **Layer**.

2. Click **Frame 15** of the new layer, click **Insert** on the menu bar, point to **Timeline**, then click **Keyframe**.

3. Click **View** on the menu bar, point to **Grid**, then click **Show Grid** to remove the gridlines.

4. Click the **Oval tool** ⭕ on the Tools panel, then draw two circles similar to those shown in Figure 14.

5. Click the **Fill Color tool** 🪣▢ on the Tools panel, then click the **yellow color swatch** in the left column of the color palette.

6. Click the **Paint Bucket tool** 🪣 on the Tools panel, then click the fill of the right circle.

7. Click the **Stroke Color tool** ✏️▢ on the Tools panel, then click the **yellow color swatch** in the left column of the color palette.

8. Click the **Ink Bottle tool** 🍶 on the Tools panel, then click the stroke of the left circle, as shown in Figure 15.

You used the Ink Bottle and Paint Bucket tools to change the fill and stroke colors of an object.

Create a gradient

1. Click the **Fill Color tool** on the Tools panel, then click the **red gradient color swatch** in the bottom row of the color palette, as shown in Figure 16.

2. Click the **Paint Bucket tool** 🖌 on the Tools panel, then click the yellow circle.

3. Click different parts of the right circle, then click the right side, as shown in Figure 17.

4. Click the **Gradient Transform tool** 🔲 on the Tools panel, then click the gradient-filled circle.

5. Drag each of the four handles, as shown in Figure 18, to determine their effects on the gradient, then click the stage to deselect the circle.

6. Click the **Fill Color tool** 🖌, click the **Hex Edit text box**, type **#0000FF**, then press **[Enter]** (Win) or **[return]** (Mac).

7. Save your work.

You applied a gradient fill and you used the Gradient Transform tool to alter the gradient.

FIGURE 16
Selecting the red gradient

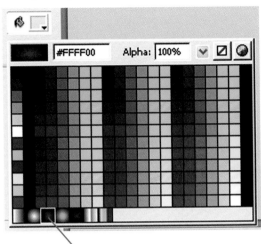

Click red gradient
color swatch to
select it

FIGURE 18
Gradient Transform handles

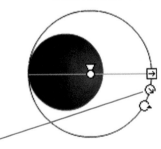

Handles are
used to adjust
the gradient
effect

FIGURE 17
Clicking the right side of the circle

Drawing Objects in Macromedia Flash

FIGURE 19

Circle drawn using the Object Drawing Model mode

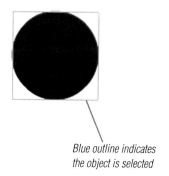

Blue outline indicates
the object is selected

1. Insert a new layer, then insert a keyframe on Frame 20.

2. Click the **Oval tool** ○ .

3. Click the **Stroke Color tool** 🖍▾ , then click the red swatch.

4. Click the **Fill Color tool** 🖌▾ , then click the black swatch.

5. Click the **Object Drawing option** ◎ in the Options section of the Tools panel to change the mode to the Object Drawing Model.

6. Draw a circle on the stage, as shown in Figure 19.

   Notice that when you use the Object Drawing Model mode, objects are automatically selected, and the stroke and fill areas are combined.

7. Click the **Selection tool** ▸ in the Tools panel, then click on a blank area of the stage to deselect the object.

8. Click once on the circle.

   The entire object is selected, including the stroke and fill areas.

9. Click **Modify** on the menu bar, then click **Break Apart**.

   Breaking apart an object drawn using the Object Drawing Model mode allows you to select the strokes and fills.

10. Click a blank area on the stage, then save your work.

You used the Object Drawing Model mode to draw an object, deselect it, and then break it apart to display the stroke and fill.

WORK WITH OBJECTS

What You'll Do

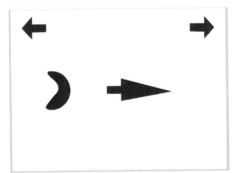

 In this lesson, you will copy, move, and transform (resize, rotate, and reshape) objects.

Copying and Moving Objects

To copy one or more objects, select them, then click the Copy command on the Edit menu. To paste the object, click the Paste command on the Edit menu. You can copy an object to another layer by selecting the frame and layer prior to pasting the object.

You can move an object by selecting it and dragging it to a new location. You can precisely position an object by selecting it and then pressing the arrow keys, which move the selection up, down, left, and right in small increments.

Transforming Objects

You can use the Free Transform tool to resize, rotate, skew, and reshape objects. After selecting an object, you can click the Free Transform tool to display eight square-shaped handles used to transform the object, and a circle-shaped transformation point located at the center of the object. The transformation point is the point around which the object can be

rotated. You can also change its location. The Free Transform tool has four options: Rotate and Skew, Scale, Distort, and Envelope. These tool options restrict the transformations that can be completed; you can select only one option at a time.

Resizing an Object

You can enlarge or reduce the size of an object using the Scale option of the Free Transform tool. The process is to select the object and click the Free Transform tool, then click the Scale option in the Options section of the Tools panel. Eight handles appear around the selected object. You can drag the corner handles to resize the object without changing its proportions. That is, if the object starts out as a square, dragging a corner handle will change the size of the object, but it will still be a square. On the other hand, if you drag one of the middle handles, the object will be reshaped as taller, shorter, wider, or narrower.

Rotating and Skewing an Object

You can use the Rotate and Skew option of the Free Transform tool to rotate an object and to skew it. Select the object, click the Free Transform tool, then click the Rotate and Skew option in the Options section of the Tools panel. Eight square-shaped handles appear around the object. You can drag the corner handles to rotate the object, or you can drag the middle handles to skew the object, as shown in Figure 20. The Transform panel can be used to rotate and skew an object in a more precise way; select the object, display the Transform panel, enter the desired rotation of skew in degrees, then press [Enter] (Win) or [return] (Mac).

Distorting an Object

You can use the Distort and Envelope options to reshape an object by dragging its handles. The Envelope option provides more than eight handles to allow for more precise distortions.

Reshaping a Segment of an Object

You can use the Subselection tool to reshape a segment of an object. Click an edge of the object to display handles that can be dragged to reshape the object.

You can use the Selection tool to reshape objects. When you point to the edge of an object, the pointer displays an arc symbol. Using the Arc pointer, you can drag the edge of the object you want to reshape, as shown in Figure 21. If the Selection tool points to a corner of an object, the pointer displays an L-shaped symbol—dragging the pointer reshapes the corner of the object.

Flipping an Object

You can use an option under the Transform command to flip an object either horizontally or vertically. Select the object, click the Transform command on the Modify menu, and then choose Flip Vertical or Flip Horizontal. Other Transform options allow you to rotate and scale the selected object, and the Remove Transform command allows you to restore an object to its original state.

FIGURE 20
Using handles to manipulate an object

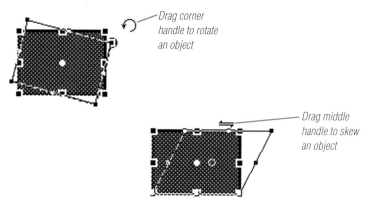

Drag corner handle to rotate an object

Drag middle handle to skew an object

FIGURE 21
Using the Selection tool to distort an object

Copy and move an object

1. Click **Frame 5** on the timeline.
2. Click the **Selection tool** on the Tools panel, then draw a marquee around the arrow object to select it.
3. Click **Edit** on the menu bar, click **Copy**, click **Edit** on the menu bar, click **Paste in Center**, then compare your image to Figure 22.

   A copy of the arrow is pasted on the center of the stage.
4. Drag and align the newly copied arrow under the original arrow, as shown in Figure 23.

You used the Selection tool to select an object, then you copied and moved the object.

FIGURE 22
A copy of the arrow on the stage

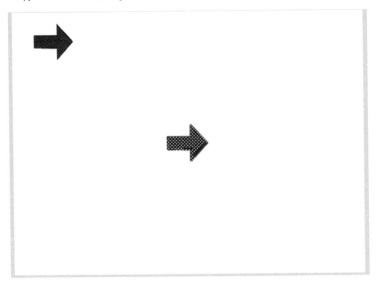

FIGURE 23
Aligning the arrows

Drawing Objects in Macromedia Flash

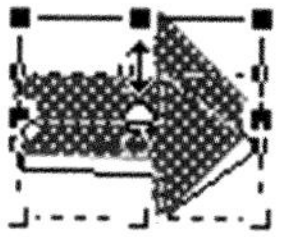

Resize and reshape an object

1. Verify that the bottom arrow is selected, then click the **Free Transform tool** ⊡ on the Tools panel.

2. Click the **Scale option** ⬔ in the Options section of the Tools panel.

3. Drag each corner handle towards and then away from the center of the object, as shown in Figure 24.

   As you drag the corner handles, the object's size is changed, but its proportions remain the same.

4. Click **Edit** on the menu bar, then click **Undo Scale**.

5. Repeat step 4 until the arrow returns to its original size.

6. Click the **Selection tool** ⬉ (if necessary), then draw a marquee around the arrow to select it.

7. Drag each middle handle away and then toward the center of the object, as shown in Figure 25. As you drag the middle handles, the object's size and proportions are changed.

8. Click **Edit** on the menu bar, then click **Undo** to return the arrow to its original size.

You used the Free Transform tool and the Scale option to display an object's handles, and you used the handles to resize and reshape the object.

FIGURE 24

Resizing an object using the corner handles

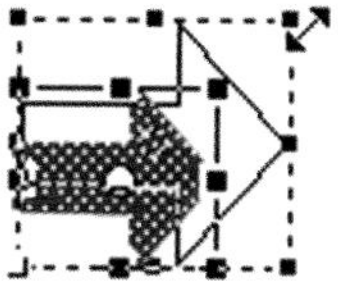

FIGURE 25

Reshaping an object using the middle handles

Rotate, skew, and flip an object

1. Verify that the arrow is selected (dot pattern displayed), click the **Free Transform tool** ⊞, then click the **Rotate and Skew option** ⟳ in the Options section of the Tools panel.

2. Click the upper-right corner handle, then rotate the object clockwise.

3. Click the upper-middle handle, then drag it to the right.

   The arrow slants to the right.

4. Click **Edit** on the menu bar, click the **Undo** command, then repeat until the arrow is in its original shape and orientation.

5. Click the **Selection tool** ▶ on the Tools panel, verify that the bottom arrow is selected, click **Window** on the menu bar, then click **Transform**.

6. Double-click the **Rotate text box**, type **45**, then press **[Enter]** (Win) or **[return]** (Mac).

7. Click **Edit** on the menu bar, then click **Undo**.

8. Close the Transform panel.

9. Verify that the arrow is selected, click **Modify** on the menu bar, point to **Transform**, then click **Flip Horizontal**.

10. Move the arrows to the positions shown in Figure 26.

    TIP   Drag a marquee around them to select the fill and the stroke.

11. Save your work.

You used Tools panel options, the Transform panel, and Modify menu commands to rotate, skew, and flip an object.

FIGURE 26
Moving objects on the stage

FIGURE 27

Using the Subselection tool to select an object

FIGURE 28

Using the Subselection tool to drag a handle to reshape the object

FIGURE 29

Using the Selection tool to drag an edge to reshape the object

Change view and reshape an object using the Subselection Tool

1. Select the arrow in the upper-right corner of the stage, click **Edit** on the menu bar, click **Copy**, click **Edit** on the menu bar, then click **Paste in Center**.

2. Click the **Zoom tool** on the Tools panel, then click the middle of the copied object to enlarge the view.

3. Click the **Subselection tool** on the Tools panel, then click the tip of the arrow to display the handles, as shown in Figure 27.

   TIP   The handles allow you to change any segment of the object.

4. Click the handle at the tip of the arrow, then drag it, as shown in Figure 28.

5. Click the **Zoom tool** on the Tools panel, click the **Reduce option button** in the Options section of the Tools panel, then click the middle of the arrow.

6. Click the **Fill Color tool** , click the **blue color swatch**, click the **Oval tool** on the Tools panel, verify that the **Object Drawing option** in the Options section of the Tools panel is deselected, then draw a circle to the left of the middle arrow.

7. Click the **Selection tool** on the Tools panel, then point to the left edge of the circle until the Arc pointer is displayed.

8. Drag the pointer to the position shown in Figure 29.

9. Save your work.

You used the Zoom tool to change the view, and you used the Subselection and Selection tools to reshape objects.

WORK WITH TEXT
AND TEXT OBJECTS

What You'll Do

Classic Car Club

Join Us Now

**We have great events
each year including a
Car Rally!**

In this lesson, you will enter text using text blocks. You will also resize text blocks, change text attributes, and transform text.

Learning About Text

Macromedia Flash provides a great deal of flexibility when using text. Among other settings, you can select the typeface (font), size, style (bold, italic), and color (including gradients) of text. You can transform the text by rotating, scaling, skewing, and flipping it. You can even break apart a letter and reshape its segments.

Entering Text and Changing the Text Block

It is important to understand that text is entered into a text block, as shown in Figure 30. You use the Text tool to place a text block on the stage and to enter and edit text. A text block expands as more text is entered and may even extend beyond the edge of the stage. You can adjust the size of the text block so that it is a fixed width by dragging the handle in the upper- right corner of the block. Figure 31 shows the process of using the Text tool to enter text and resize the text block. Once you select the tool, you click the pointer on the stage where you want the text to appear. An

insertion point indicates where in the text block the next character will appear when typed. You can reshape the text block by pressing [Enter] (Win) or [return] (Mac) or by dragging the circle handle. After reshaping the text block, the circle handle changes to a square, indicating that the text block now has a fixed horizontal width. Then, when you enter more text, it automatically wraps within the text block. You can resize or move the text block at any time by selecting it with the Selection tool and dragging the section.

Changing Text Attributes

You can use the Properties panel to change the font, size, and style of a single character or an entire text block. Figure 32 shows the Properties panel when a text object is selected. You select text, display the Properties panel, and make the desired changes. You can use the Selection tool to select the entire text block by drawing a box around it. You can use the Text tool to select a single character or string of characters by dragging the

I-beam pointer over them, as shown in Figure 33.

Working with Paragraphs

When working on large bodies of text, such as paragraphs, Macromedia Flash provides many of the features found in a word processor. You can align paragraphs (left, right, center, justified) within a text block. You can use the Properties panel to set margins (space between the border of a text block and the paragraph text), indents for the first line of a paragraph, and line spacing (distance between paragraphs).

Transforming Text

It is important to understand that a text block is an object. Therefore, you can transform (reshape, rotate, skew, and so on) a text block as you would other objects. If you want to transform individual characters within a text block, you must first break it apart. Use the Selection tool to select the text block, and then click the Break Apart command on the Modify menu. Each character (or a group of characters) in the text block can now be selected and transformed.

FIGURE 30
A text block

This is a text block used to enter text

FIGURE 31
Using the Text tool

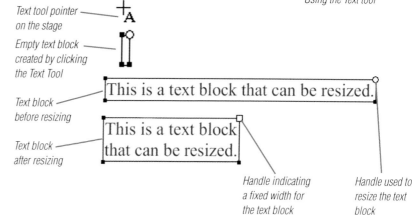

Text tool pointer on the stage

Empty text block created by clicking the Text Tool

This is a text block that can be resized.

Text block before resizing

This is a text block that can be resized.

Text block after resizing

Handle indicating a fixed width for the text block

Handle used to resize the text block

FIGURE 32
The Properties panel when a text object is selected

FIGURE 33
Dragging the I-Beam pointer to select text

This is a text block that can be resized.

I-Beam pointer

Enter text and change text attributes

1. Click **Layer 5**, insert a new layer, then insert a keyframe in Frame 25 of the new layer.

2. Click the **Text tool** **A** on the Tools panel, click the center of the stage, click in the **text box**, then type **We have great events each year including a Rally**!

3. Click the **I-Beam pointer** ⌶ before the word "Rally," as shown in Figure 34, then type **Car**.

4. Verify that the Property inspector panel is displayed, then drag the I-Beam pointer ⌶ across the text to select all the text.

5. Click the **Font list arrow**, click **Arial Black**, click the **Font Size list arrow**, then drag the slider to **16**.

6. Click the **Text (fill) color swatch** ▉, click the **Hex Edit text box**, type **#990000**, then press **[Enter]** (Win) or **[return]** (Mac).

7. Position the **text pointer** +ₐ over the circle handle until the pointer changes to a double arrow ↔, then drag the handle to the left, as shown in Figure 35.

8. Highlight the text using the text pointer +ₐ, then click the **Align Center button** ≣ in the Property inspector.

9. Click the **Selection tool** ◥ on the Tools panel, click the text object, then drag the object to the lower middle of the stage.

> TIP The Selection tool is used to select the text block, and the Text tool is used to select and edit the text within the text block.

You entered text, and also resized the text block and changed the font, type size, text color and text alignment.

FIGURE 34
Using the Text tool to enter text

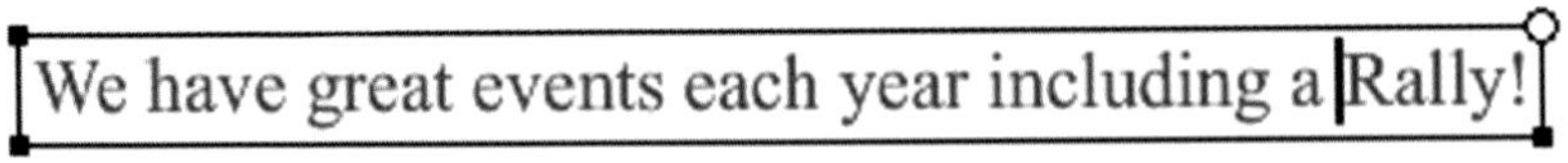

We have great events each year including a |Rally!|

FIGURE 35
Resizing the text block

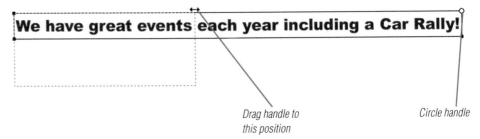

We have great events each year including a Car Rally!

Drag handle to this position

Circle handle

Using Filters

You can apply special effects, such as drop shadows, to text using the Filters option in the Property inspector. The process is to select the desired text, click the Filters tab in the Property inspector panel, choose the desired effect, and make any adjustments, such as changing the color of a gradient glow.

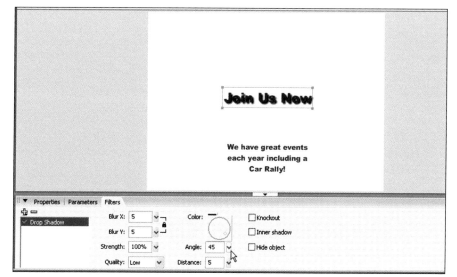

FIGURE 36

The Filters options in the Property inspector panel

1. Click the **Text tool** **A** on the Tools panel, click the center of the stage, click in the **text box**, then type **Join Us Now**.

2. Drag the **Text pointer** $+_A$ across the text to select it, then use the Property inspector to change the Font size to **30** and the Fill color to **#003399**.

3. Click **Filters** on the title bar of the Property inspector.

4. Click the **Add filter icon** ⊕, then click **Drop Shadow**.

5. Click the **Selection tool** **▶** in the Tools panel, then verify that the **text block** is selected.

6. Click the **Angle option list arrow** in the Filters section of the Property inspector, as shown in Figure 36.

7. Click and rotate the small circle within the larger circle and notice the changes in the drop shadow.

8. Set the angle to **50**.

9. Click the **Distance list arrow**, then move the slider and notice the changes in the drop shadow.

10. Set the Distance to **5**.

11. Save your work.

You used the Filter feature to create a drop shadow and then made changes to it.

Skew text

1. Verify that **Text tool** **A** is selected, click the pointer near the top middle of the stage, click in the **text box**, then type **Classic Car Club**.

   The attributes of the new text reflect the most recent settings changed in the Properties panel.

2. Drag the **I-Beam pointer** $\mathbb{I}$ across the text to select it, then using the Property inspector change the font size to **40** and the fill color to **#990000**.

3. Click the **Selection tool** on the Tools panel, click the **Free Transform tool** on the Tools panel, then click the **Rotate and Skew option** in the Options section of the Tools panel.

4. Drag the top middle handle to the right to skew the text, as shown in Figure 37.

You entered a heading, changed the type size, and skewed text using the Free Transform tool.

FIGURE 37
Skewing the text

FIGURE 38
Reshaping a letter

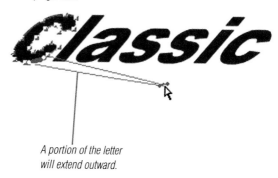

A portion of the letter
will extend outward.

FIGURE 39
Applying a gradient fill to each letter

Reshape and apply a gradient to text

1. Click the **Selection tool** on the Tools panel, click the Classic Car Club text block to select it, click **Modify** on the menu bar, then click **Break Apart**.

   The words are now individual text blocks.

2. Click **Modify** on the menu bar, then click **Break Apart**.

   The letters are filled with a dot pattern, indicating that they can now be edited.

3. Click the **Zoom tool** on the Tools panel, click the **Enlarge option** in the Options section of the Tools panel, then click the **"C"** in Classic.

4. Click the **Subselection tool** on the Tools panel, then click the edge of the letter **"C"** to display the object's segment handles.

5. Drag a lower handle on the "C" in Classic, as shown in Figure 38.

6. Click the **Selection tool**, click the **Fill Color tool** on the Tools panel, then click the **red gradient color swatch** in the bottom row of the color palette.

7. Click the **Paint Bucket tool** on the Tools panel, then click the top of each letter to change the fill to a red gradient, as shown in Figure 39.

8. Click the **Selection tool** on the Tools panel, click **View** on the menu bar, point to **Magnification**, then click **Fit in Window**.

9. Click **Control** on the menu bar, click **Test Movie**, watch the movie, then close the Flash Player window.

10. Save your work, then close the movie.

You broke apart a text block, reshaped text, and added a gradient to the text.

WORK WITH LAYERS
AND OBJECTS

What You'll Do

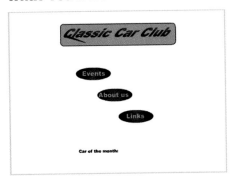

 In this lesson, you will create, rename, reorder, delete, hide, and lock layers. You will also display outline layers, use a Guide layer, distribute text to layers, and create a folder layer.

Learning About Layers

Macromedia Flash uses two types of spatial organization. First, there is the position of objects on the stage, and then there is the stacking order of objects that overlap. An example of overlapping objects is text placed on a banner. Layers are used on the timeline as a way to organize objects. Placing objects on their own layer makes them easier to work with, especially when reshaping them, repositioning them on the stage, or rearranging their order in relation to other objects. In addition, layers are useful for organizing other elements such as sounds, animations, and ActionScript.

There are six types of layers:

Normal—The default layer type. All objects on these layers appear in the movie.

Guide (Standard and Motion)— Standard Guide layers serve as a reference point for positioning objects on the stage. Motion Guide layers are used to create a path for animated objects to follow.

Guided—A layer that contains an animated object, linked to a Motion Guide layer.

Mask—A layer that hides and reveals portions of another layer.

Masked—A layer that contains the objects that are hidden and revealed by a Mask layer.

Folder—A layer that can contain other layers.

Motion Guide and Mask layer types will be covered in a later chapter.

Drawing Objects in Macromedia Flash

Working with Layers

The Layer Properties dialog box allows you to specify the type of layer. It also allows you to name, show (and hide), and lock them. Naming a layer provides a clue to the objects on the layer. For example, naming a layer Logo might indicate that the object on the layer is the company's logo. Hiding a layer(s) may reduce the clutter on the stage and make it easier to work with selected objects from the layer(s) that are not hidden. Locking a layer(s) prevents the objects from being accidentally edited. Other options in the Layer Properties dialog box allow you to view layers as outlines and change the outline color. Outlines can be used to help you determine which objects are on a layer. When you turn on this feature, each layer has a colored box that corresponds with the color of the objects on its layer, as shown in Figure 40. Icons on the Layers section of the timeline correspond to features in the Layer Properties dialog box, as shown in Figure 41.

FIGURE 40

Displaying outlines

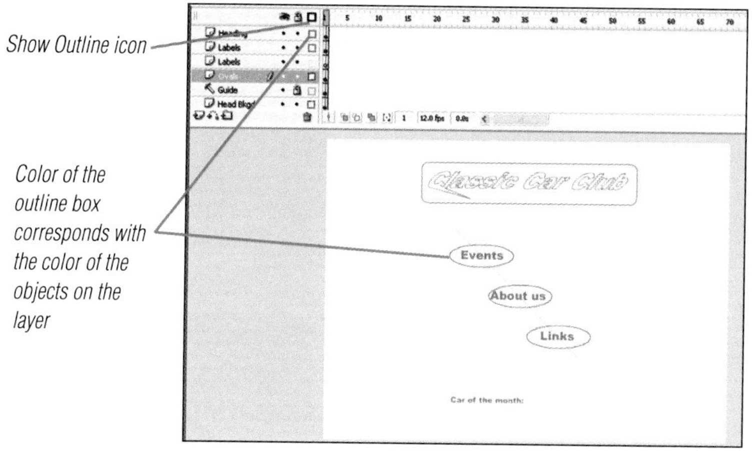

Show Outline icon

Color of the outline box corresponds with the color of the objects on the layer

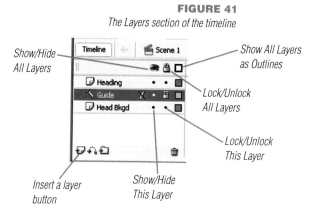

FIGURE 41

The Layers section of the timeline

Show/Hide All Layers

Show All Layers as Outlines

Lock/Unlock All Layers

Lock/Unlock This Layer

Insert a layer button

Show/Hide This Layer

Using a Guide Layer

Guide layers are useful in aligning objects on the stage. Figure 42 shows a Guide layer that has been used to align three buttons along a diagonal path. The process is to insert a new layer, click the Layer command on the Modify menu to display the Layer Properties dialog box, select Guides as the layer type, then draw a path that will be used as the guide to align objects. You then display the Guides options from the View menu, turn on Snap to Guides, and drag the desired objects to the Guide line. Objects have a registration point that is used to snap when snapping to a guide. By default, this point is at the center of the object. Figure 43 shows the process.

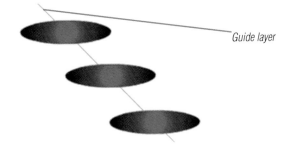

FIGURE 42
A Guide layer used to align objects on the stage

Guide layer

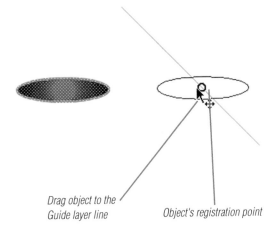

FIGURE 43
The registration point of an object

Drag object to the
Guide layer line

Object's registration point

Drawing Objects in Macromedia Flash

Distributing Text to Layers

Text blocks are made up of one or more characters. When you break apart a text block, each character becomes an object that can be edited independent of the other characters. You can use the Distribute to Layers command to cause each character to automatically be placed on its own layer. Figure 44 shows the seven layers created after the text block containing 55 Chevy has been broken apart and distributed to layers.

Using Folder Layers

As movies become larger and more complex, the number of layers increases. Macromedia Flash allows you to organize layers by creating folders and grouping other layers in them. Figure 45 shows a layers folder—Layer 6—with seven layers in it. You can click the Folder layer triangle next to Layer 6 to open and close the folder.

FIGURE 44
Distributing text to layers

FIGURE 45
A folder layer

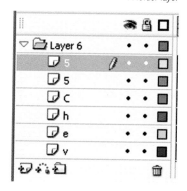

Create and reorder layers

1. Open fl2_1.fla from the drive and folder where your Data Files are stored, then save it as **layers2.fla**.

2. Click **View** on the menu bar, point to **Magnification**, then click **Fit in Window**.

3. Click the **Insert Layer icon** ☞ on the bottom of the timeline (below the layer names) to insert a new layer, Layer 2.

4. Click the **Rectangle tool** ▢ on the Tools panel, then click the **Set Corner Radius option** ⌐ in the Options section of the Tools panel.

5. Type **10**, then click **OK**.

6. Click the **Fill Color tool** on the Tools panel, click the **Hex Edit text box**, type **#999999**, then press **[Enter]** (Win) or **[return]** (Mac).

7. Click the **Stroke Color tool** on the Tools panel, click the **Hex Edit text box**, type **#000000**, then press **[Enter]** (Win) or **[return]** (Mac).

8. Draw the rectangle shown in Figure 46 so it masks the text heading.

9. Drag Layer 1 above Layer 2 on the timeline, as shown in Figure 47.

You added a layer, drew an object on the layer, and reordered layers.

FIGURE 46
Drawing a rectangle with a rounded corner

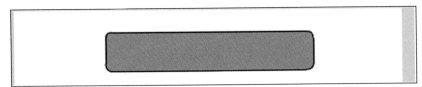

FIGURE 47
Dragging Layer 1 above Layer 2

Drag Layer 1 above Layer 2

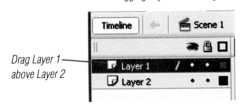

Drawing Objects in Macromedia Flash

Rename and delete layers on the timeline

1. Double-click **Layer 1** on the timeline, type **Heading** in the Layer Name text box, then press **[Enter]** (Win) or **[return]** (Mac).

2. Rename Layer 2 as **Head Bkgd**. Compare your timeline to Figure 48.

3. Click the **Heading layer**, then click the **Delete Layer icon** 🗑 on the bottom of the timeline.

4. Click **Edit** on the menu bar, then click **Undo Delete Layer**.

You renamed layers to associate them with objects on the layers, then deleted and restored a layer.

FIGURE 48
Renaming layers

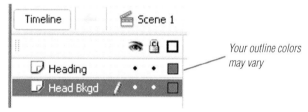

Your outline colors
may vary

Hide, lock, and display layer outlines

1. Click the **Show/Hide All Layers icon** 👁 to hide all layers, then compare your image to Figure 49.

2. Click the **Show/Hide All Layers icon** 👁 to show all the layers.

3. Click the **Heading layer**, then click the **Show/Hide icon** • twice to hide and show the layer.

4. Click the **Lock/Unlock All Layers icon** 🔒 to lock all layers.

5. With the layers locked, try to select and edit an object.

6. Click the **Lock/Unlock All Layers icon** 🔒 again to unlock the layers.

7. Click the **Show All Layers as Outlines icon** ☐ twice to display and turn off the outlines of all objects.

You hid and locked layers and displayed the outlines of objects in a layer.

FIGURE 49
Hiding all the layers

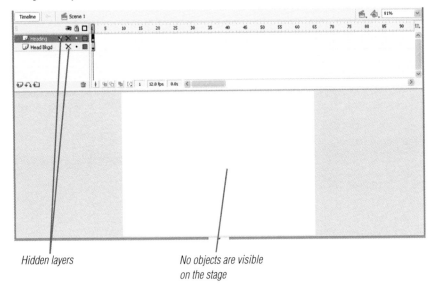

Hidden layers

No objects are visible on the stage

FIGURE 50

A diagonal line

Car of the month:

FIGURE 51

Layer 3 locked

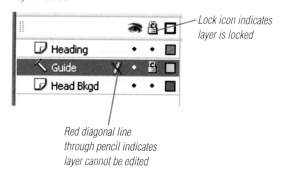

Lock icon indicates
layer is locked

Red diagonal line
through pencil indicates
layer cannot be edited

Create a guide for a Guide layer

1. Click the **Head Bkgd layer**, then click the **Insert Layer icon** on the timeline to add a new layer, Layer 3.

2. Rename the layer **Guide**.

3. Click **Modify** on the menu bar, point to **Timeline**, click **Layer Properties** to display the Layer Properties dialog box, click the **Guide option button**, then click **OK**.

4. Click the **Line tool** on the Tools panel, press and hold **[Shift]**, then draw the diagonal line, as shown in Figure 50.

5. Click the **Lock/Unlock This Layer icon** in Layer 3 to lock it, then compare your layers to Figure 51.

You created a guide for a Guide layer and drew a guide line.

Add objects to a Guide layer

1. Add a new layer on the timeline. Name it **Ovals**, then click **Frame 1** of the Ovals layer.

2. Click the **Fill Color tool** on the Tools panel, then click the **red gradient color swatch** in the bottom row of the color palette, if necessary.

3. Click the **Oval tool** on the Tools panel, then verify that the **Object Drawing option** in the Options section of the Tools panel is deselected.

4. Draw the oval, as shown in Figure 52.

5. Click the **Selection tool** on the Tools panel, then draw a marquee around the oval object to select it.

   TIP Make sure the entire object (stroke and fill) is selected and slowly drag the object so that its center is on the line.

6. Point to the center of the oval, click, then slowly drag it to the Guide layer line, as shown in Figure 53.

7. With the oval object selected, click **Edit** on the menu bar, then click **Copy**.

8. Click **Edit** on the menu bar, click **Paste in Center**, then, if necessary, align the copied object to the Guide layer line beneath the first oval.

9. Click **Edit** on the menu bar, click **Paste in Center**, then align the copied object to the bottom of the Guide layer line.

   TIP Objects are pasted in the center of the stage, and one object may cover up another object.

You created a Guide Layer and used it to align objects on the stage.

FIGURE 52
An oval object

FIGURE 53
Dragging an object to the Guide layer line

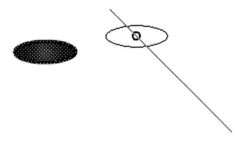

FIGURE 54

Adding text to the oval objects

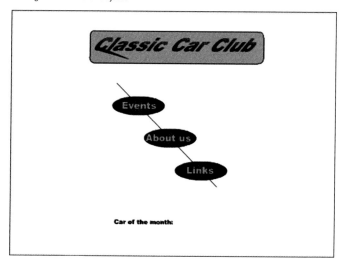

Adding text on Top of an Object

1. Insert a new layer on the timeline, then name it **Labels**.

2. Click Frame 1 of the Labels layer.

3. Click the **Text tool A** on the Tools panel, click the top oval, then type **Events**.

4. Drag the **I-Beam pointer** ⊺ across Events to select the text, then using the Property inspector, set the font to **Arial Black**, the font size to **16**, and the fill color to **#999999**, if necessary.

5. Click the **Selection tool** ▸ on the Tools panel, click the text box to select it, then drag the text box to center it on the oval, as shown in Figure 54.

   | TIP   Use the arrow keys on the keyboard to nudge the text in place, if necessary.

6. Repeat Steps 3 through 5, typing **About us** and **Links** text blocks.

7. Test the movie, then save and close the document.

8. Exit Flash.

You used the Text tool to create text blocks that were placed above objects.

Draw objects with the drawing tools.

1. Start Macromedia Flash, create a new Flash document, then save it as **skillsdemo2**.
2. Display the Grid.
3. Set the stroke color to black (Hex: 000000) and the fill color to blue (Hex: 0000FF).
4. Use the Oval tool to draw an oval on the left side of the stage, then draw a circle beneath the oval.
5. Use the Rectangle tool to draw a rectangle in the middle of the stage, then draw a square beneath the rectangle. If necessary, change the Round Rectangle Radius to 0.
6. Use the Line tool to draw a horizontal line on the right side of the stage, then draw a vertical line beneath the horizontal line and a diagonal line beneath the vertical line.
7. Use the Pen tool to draw an arrow-shaped object above the rectangle.
8. Use the Pencil tool to draw a freehand line above the oval, then use the Smooth option to smooth out the line.
9. Save your work.

Select and edit objects.

1. Use the Selection tool to select the stroke of the circle, then deselect the stroke.
2. Use the Selection tool to select the fill of the circle, then deselect the fill.
3. Use the Lasso tool to select several of the objects, then deselect them.
4. Use the Ink Bottle tool to change the stroke color of the circle to red (Hex #FF0000).
5. Use the Paint Bucket tool to change the fill color of the square to a red gradient.
6. Change the fill color of the oval to a blue gradient.
7. Save your work.

Work with objects.

1. Copy and paste the arrow object.
2. Move the copied arrow to another location on the stage.
3. Rescale both arrows to approximately half their original size.
4. Flip the copied arrow horizontally.
5. Rotate the rectangle to a 45° angle.
6. Skew the square to the right.
7. Copy one of the arrows and use the Subselection tool to reshape it, then delete it.
8. Use the Selection tool to reshape the circle to a crescent shape.
9. Save your work.

Enter and edit text.

1. Enter the following text in a text block at the top of the stage: **Gateway to the Pacific**.
2. Change the text to font: Tahoma, size: 24, color: red.
3. Use the gridlines to help align the text block to the top center of the stage.
4. Skew the text block to the right.
5. Save your work.

Work with layers.

1. Insert a layer into the document.
2. Change the name on the new layer to **Heading Bkgnd**.
3. Draw a rounded corner rectangle that covers the words Gateway to the Pacific.
4. Switch the order of the layers.
5. Lock all layers.
6. Unlock all layers.
7. Hide the Heading Bkgnd layer.
8. Show the Heading Bkgnd layer.
9. Show all layers as outlines.
10. Turn off the view of the outlines.
11. Create a Guide layer and move the arrows to it.
12. Add a layer and use the Text tool to type **SEATTLE** below the heading.
13. Break the text block apart and distribute the text to layers.
14. Create a Folder layer and add each of the SEATTLE text layers to it.
15. Save your work.

Use the Merge Drawing Model mode.

1. Insert a new layer and name it **MergeDraw**.
2. Click the Rectangle tool and verify that the Object Drawing option is deselected.
3. Draw a square, then use the Oval tool to draw a circle with a different color that covers approximately half of the square.
4. Use the Selection tool to drag the circle off of the square.

Use the Object Drawing Model mode.

1. Insert a new layer and name it **ObjectDraw**.
2. Click the Rectangle tool and click the Object Drawing option to select it.
3. Draw a square, then use the Oval tool to draw a circle with a different color that covers approximately half of the square.
4. Use the Selection tool to drag the circle off of the square.

5. Save your work, then compare your image to the example shown in Figure 55.
6. Test the movie, then save and close the document.
7. Exit Flash.

FIGURE 55
Completed Skills Review

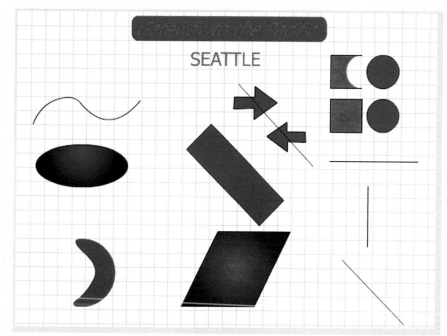

A local travel company, Ultimate Tours, has asked you to design several sample homepages for their new Web site. The goal of the Web site is to inform potential customers of their services. The company specializes in exotic treks, tours, and cruises. Thus, while their target audience spans a wide age range, they are all looking for something out of the ordinary.

1. Open a new Flash Document and save it as **ultimatetours2**.
2. Set the document properties, including the size and background color.
3. Create the following on separate layers and name the layers:
   ■ A text heading; select a font size and font color. Skew the heading, break it apart, then reshape one or more of the characters.
   ■ A subheading with a different font size and color.
   ■ A guide path.
   ■ At least three objects.
4. Snap the objects to the guide path.
5. On another layer, add text to the objects and place them on the guide path.
6. Lock all layers.
7. Compare your image to the example shown in Figure 56.
8. Save your work.
9. Test the movie, then close the movie.

FIGURE 56
Sample completed Project Builder 1

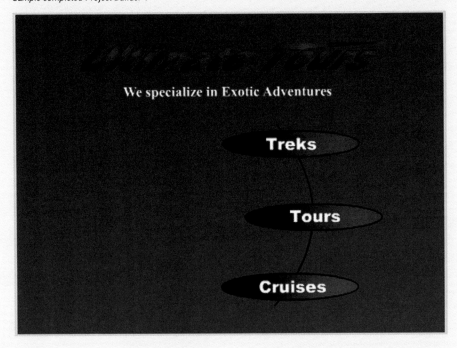

Drawing in Macromedia Flash

You have been asked to create several sample designs for the homepage of a new organization called The Jazz Club. The club is being organized to bring together music enthusiasts for social events and charitable fund-raising activities. They plan to sponsor weekly jam sessions and a show once a month. Because the club is just getting started, the organizers are looking to you for help in developing a Web site.

1. Plan the site by specifying the goal, target audience, treatment ("look and feel"), and elements you want to include (text, graphics, sound, and so on).
2. Sketch out a storyboard that shows the layout of the objects on the various screens and how they are linked together. Be creative in your design.
3. Open a new movie and save it as **thejazzclub2**.
4. Set the document properties, including the size and background color, if desired.
5. Display the gridlines and rulers and use them to help align objects on the stage.
6. Create a heading with a background, text objects, and drawings to be used as links to the categories of information provided on the Web site.
7. Hide the gridlines and rulers.
8. Save your work, then compare your image to the example shown in Figure 57.

FIGURE 57
Sample completed Project Builder 2

Figure 58 shows the homepage of a Web site. Study the figure and complete the following. For each question indicate how you determined your answer.

1. Connect to the Internet, go to *www.course.com*, navigate to the page for this book, click the Online Companion link, then click the link for this chapter.

2. Open a document in a word processor or open a new Macromedia Flash document, save the file as **dpc2**, then answer the following questions. (*Hint*: Use the Text tool in Macromedia Flash.)

   ■ Whose Web site is this?
   ■ What is the goal(s) of the site?
   ■ Who is the target audience?
   ■ What is the treatment ("look and feel") that is used?
   ■ What are the design layout guidelines being used (balance, movement, and so on)?
   ■ What may be animated on this homepage?
   ■ Do you think this is an effective design for the company, its products, and its target audience? Why or why not?
   ■ What suggestions would you make to improve on the design and why?

FIGURE 58
Design Project

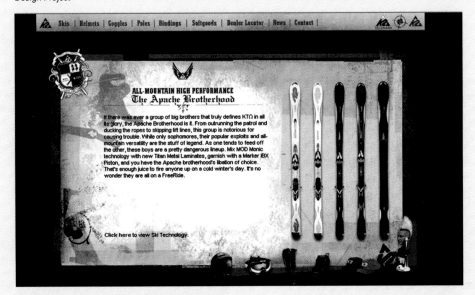

After weeks of unsuccessful job hunting, you have decided to create a personal portfolio of your work. The portfolio will be a Web site done completely in Macromedia Flash.

1. Research what should be included in a portfolio.
2. Plan the site by specifying the goal, target audience, treatment ("look and feel"), and elements you want to include (text, graphics, sound, and so on).
3. Sketch out a storyboard that shows the layout of the objects on the various screens and how they are linked together. Be creative in your design.
4. Design the homepage to include personal data, contact information, previous employment, education, and samples of your work.
5. Open a new Flash document and save it as **portfolio2**.
6. Set the document properties, including the size and background color, if desired.
7. Display the gridlines and rulers and use them to help align objects on the stage.
8. Add a border the size of the stage. (*Hint*: Use the Rectangle tool and set the fill color to none.)

9. Create a heading with its own background, then create other text objects and drawings to be used as links to the categories of information provided on the Web site. (*Hint*: In this file, the Tahoma font is used. You can replace this font with Impact or any other appropriate font on your computer.)
10. Hide the gridlines and rulers.
11. Save your work, then compare your image to the example shown in Figure 59.

FIGURE 59
Sample completed Portfolio Project

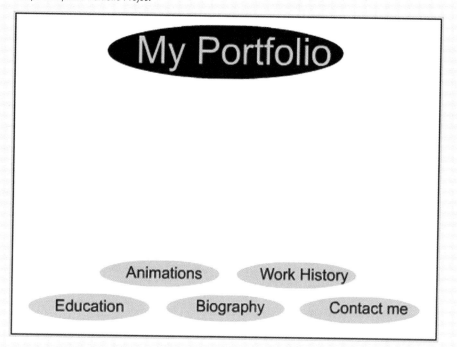

WORKING WITH SYMBOLS
AND INTERACTIVITY

1. Create symbols and instances.

2. Work with Libraries.

3. Create buttons.

4. Assign actions to buttons.

MACROMEDIA FLASH 8

Introduction

An important benefit of Macromedia Flash is its ability to create movies with small file sizes. This allows the movies to be delivered from the Web more quickly. One way to keep the file sizes small is to create reusable graphics, buttons, and movie clips. Macromedia Flash allows you to create a graphic (drawing) and then make unlimited copies, which you can use in other movies. Macromedia Flash calls the original drawing a **symbol** and the copied drawings **instances**. Using instances reduces the movie file size because Macromedia Flash needs to store only the symbol's information (size, shape, color). When you want to use a symbol in a movie, Macromedia Flash creates an instance (copy), but does not save the instance in the Macromedia Flash movie; this keeps down the movie's file size. What is especially valuable about this process is that you can change the attributes (such

as color and shape) for each instance. For example, if your Web site contains drawings of cars, you have to create just one drawing, insert as many instances of the car as you like, and then change the instances accordingly. Macromedia Flash stores symbols in the Library panel—each time you need a copy of the symbol, you can open the Library panel and drag the symbol to the stage, creating an instance of the symbol.

There are three categories of symbols: graphic, button, and movie clip. A graphic symbol is useful because you can reuse a single image and make changes in each instance of the image. A button symbol is useful because you can create buttons for interactivity, such as starting or stopping a movie. A movie clip symbol is useful for creating complex animations because you can create a movie within a movie. Movie clips will be covered in a later chapter.

Tools You'll Use

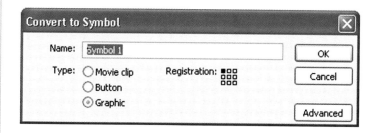

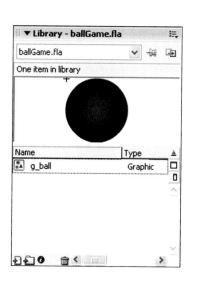

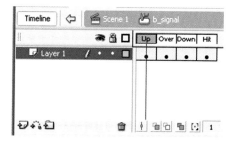

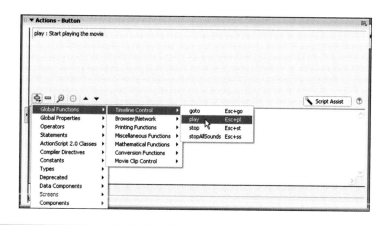

CREATE SYMBOLS
AND INSTANCES

What You'll Do

▶ *In this lesson, you will create graphic symbols, turn them into instances, and then edit the instances.*

Creating a Graphic Symbol

You can use the New Symbol command on the Insert menu to create and then draw a symbol. You can also draw an object and then use the Convert to Symbol command on the Modify menu to convert the object to a symbol. The Convert to Symbol dialog box, shown in Figure 1, allows you to name the symbol and specify the type of symbol you want to create (Movie Clip, Button, or Graphic). When naming a symbol, it's a good idea to use a naming convention that allows you to quickly identify the type of symbol and to group like symbols together. For example, you could identify all graphic symbols by naming them g_*name* and all buttons as b_*name*.

After you complete the Convert to Symbol dialog box, Macromedia Flash places the symbol in the Library panel, as shown in Figure 2. To create an instance of the symbol, you simply drag a symbol from the Library panel to the stage. To edit a symbol, you select it from the Library panel or use the Edit Symbol command on the Edit menu. When you edit a

symbol, the changes are reflected in all instances of that symbol in your movie. For example, you can draw a car, convert the car to a symbol, and then create several instances of the car. You can uniformly change the size of all the cars by selecting the car symbol from the Library panel and then rescaling it to the desired size.

Working with Instances

You can have as many instances as needed in your movie, and you can edit each one to make it somewhat different than the others. You can rotate, skew (slant), and resize graphic and button instances. In addition, you can change the color, brightness, and transparency. However, there are some limitations. An instance is a single object with no segments or parts, such as a stroke and a fill—you cannot select a part of an instance. Therefore, any changes to the color of the instance are made to the entire object. Of course, you can use layers to stack other objects on top of an instance to change its appearance. In addition, you can use the Break Apart command on the Modify menu to break the link between an instance and a symbol. Once the link is broken, you can make any changes to the object, such as changing its stroke and fill color. However, because the link is broken, the object is no longer an instance, and any changes you make to the original symbol would not affect the object.

The process for creating an instance is to open the Library panel and drag the desired symbol to the stage. You select an instance by using the Selection tool to draw a box around it. A blue border indicates that the object has been selected. Then, you can use the Free Transform tool options (such as Rotate and Skew, or Scale) to modify the entire image, or you can break apart the instance and edit individual lines and fills.

QUICKTIP

You need to be careful when editing an instance. Use the Selection tool to draw a box around the instance, or click the object once to select it. Do not double-click the instance; otherwise, you will open an edit window that is used to edit the symbol, not the instance.

FIGURE 1

Using the Convert to Symbol dialog box to convert a symbol

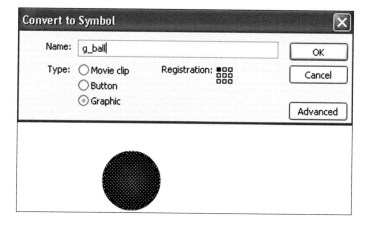

FIGURE 2

A graphic symbol in the Library panel

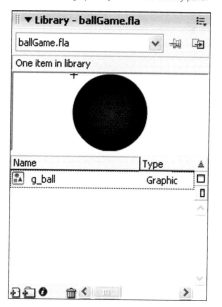

Create a symbol

1. Open fl3_1.fla from the drive and folder where your Data Files are stored, then save it as **coolcar**.

2. Hide all panels, display the Property inspector, the Library panel, and the Tools panel, then set the magnification to **Fit in Window**.

3. Click the **Selection tool** ▸ on the Tools panel, then drag the marquee around the car to select it.

4. Click **Modify** on the menu bar, then click **Convert to Symbol**.

5. Type **g_car** in the Name text box.

6. Click the **Graphic option button**, as shown in Figure 3, then click **OK**.

7. Click the **g_car symbol** in the Library panel to display the car, as shown in Figure 4.

You opened a file with an object, converted the object to a symbol, and displayed the symbol in the Library panel.

FIGURE 3
Options in the Convert to Symbol dialog box

FIGURE 4
Newly created symbol in the Library panel

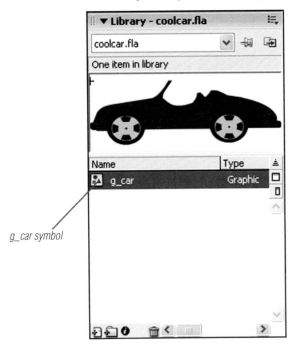

g_car symbol

Working with Symbols and Interactivity

FIGURE 5
Creating an instance

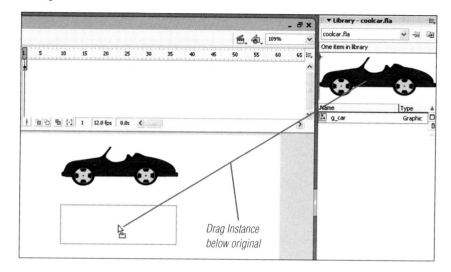

Drag Instance
below original

FIGURE 6
The alpha set to 50%

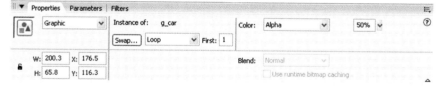

Create and edit an instance

1. Point to the car image in the Item Preview window, then drag the image to the stage beneath the first car, as shown in Figure 5.

   TIP You can also drag the name of the symbol from the Library panel to the stage.

2. Click the **Selection tool** ▸ on the Tools panel (if necessary), verify that the bottom car is selected, click **Modify** on the menu bar, point to **Transform**, then click **Flip Horizontal**.

3. Expand the Property inspector, if necessary.

4. Click the **Color list arrow** on the Property inspector, then click **Alpha**.

5. Click the **Alpha Amount list arrow** ▾, then drag the slider to **50%**, and notice how the transparency changes.

   Figure 6 shows the transparency set to 50%.

6. Click a blank area of the stage.

   Changing the alpha setting gives the car a more transparent look.

You created an instance of a symbol and edited the instance on the stage.

Edit a symbol in symbol-editing mode

1. Double-click the **g_car symbol icon** [icon] in the Library panel to enter symbol-editing mode, then compare your screen to Figure 7.

   The g_car symbol appears on the stage above the timeline, indicating that you are editing the g_car symbol.

   > TIP You can also edit a symbol by clicking Edit on the menu bar, then clicking Edit Symbols.

2. Click a blank area of the stage to deselect the car.

3. Verify that the **Selection tool** [icon] is selected, then click the **light gray hubcap** inside the front wheel to select it.

4. Press and hold **[Shift]**, then click the **hubcap** inside the back wheel to select the fills of both hubcaps.

5. Click the **Fill Color tool** [icon] on the Tools panel, click the **blue color swatch** in the left column of the color palette, then compare your image to Figure 8.

   Changes you make to the symbol affect every instance of the symbol on the stage. The hubcap color becomes blue in the Library panel and on the stage.

6. Click **Scene 1** above the Timeline layers to return to the main timeline.

   The hubcap color of the instances on the stage reflects the color changes you made to the symbol.

You edited a symbol in symbol-editing mode that affected all instances of the symbol.

FIGURE 7
Symbol-editing mode

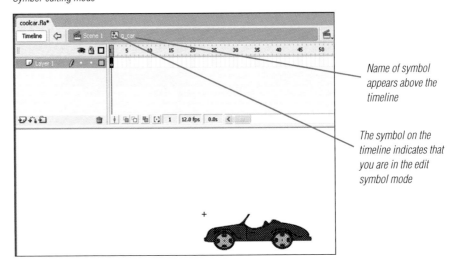

Name of symbol appears above the timeline

The symbol on the timeline indicates that you are in the edit symbol mode

FIGURE 8
Edited symbol

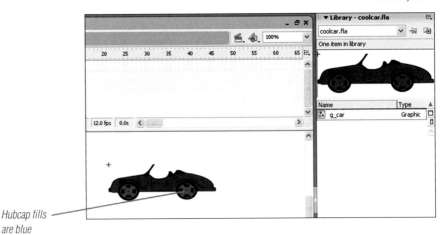

Hubcap fills are blue

Working with Symbols and Interactivity

FIGURE 9

The car with the maroon body selected

Break apart an instance

1. Click the **Selection tool** ![cursor] on the Tools panel, then drag the marquee around the bottom car to select it.

2. Click **Modify** on the menu bar, then click **Break Apart**.

   The object is no longer linked to the symbol, and its parts (strokes and fills) can now be edited.

3. Click a blank area of the stage to deselect the object.

4. Click the **blue front hubcap**, press and hold **[Shift]**, then click the **blue back hubcap** to select both hubcaps.

5. Click the **Fill Color tool** ![icon] on the Tools panel, then click the **green color swatch** in the left column of the color palette.

6. Double-click the **g_car symbol icon** ![icon] in the Library window to enter symbol-editing mode.

7. Click the **maroon front body** of the car to select it, press and hold **[Shift]**, then click the **maroon back body** of the car, as shown in Figure 9.

8. Click the **Fill Color tool** ![icon], then click the **yellow color swatch** in the left column of the color palette.

9. Click **Scene 1** above the timeline layers, then compare your image to Figure 10.

   The body color of the car in the original instance is a different color, but the one to which you applied the Break Apart command remains unchanged.

10. Save your work.

You used the Break Apart command to break the link of the instance to its symbol, then you edited the object and the symbol.

FIGURE 10

Changing the symbol affects only the one instance of the symbol

Instance of the symbol ———

Object that is no longer an ———
instance of the symbol

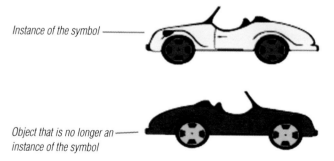

WORK WITH
LIBRARIES

What You'll Do

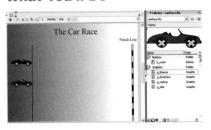

In this lesson, you will use the Library panel to organize the symbols in a movie.

Understanding the Library

The Library in a Macromedia Flash movie contains the movie symbols. The Library provides a way to view and organize the symbols, and allows you to change the symbol name, display symbol properties, and add and delete symbols. Figure 11 shows the Library panel for a movie. Refer to this figure as you read the following description of the parts of the Library.

Title bar—Names the movie with which the Library is associated. The list box below the title bar can be used to display the Library panel of any open document. This allows you to use the objects from other movies in the current movie by simply

dragging them to the stage from any Library panel. In addition to the movie libraries, you can create permanent libraries that are available whenever you start Macromedia Flash. Macromedia Flash also has sample libraries that contain buttons and other objects. The permanent and sample libraries are accessed through the Common Libraries command on the Windows menu. All of the assets in all of the libraries are available for use in any movie.

Options menu—Shown in Figure 12; provides access to several features used to edit symbols (such as renaming symbols) and organize symbols (such as creating a new folder).

Item Preview window—Displays the selected symbol. If the symbol is a movie clip, a control button appears allowing you to preview the movie.

Toggle Sorting Order icon—Allows you to reorder the list of folders and symbols within folders.

Wide Library View and Narrow Library View icons—Used to expand and collapse the Library window to display more or less of the symbol properties.

Name text box—Lists the folder and symbol names. Each symbol type has a different icon associated with it. Clicking a symbol name or icon displays the symbol in the Item Preview window.

New Symbol icon—Displays the Create New Symbol dialog box, allowing you to create a new symbol.

New Folder icon—Allows you to create a new folder.

Properties icon—Displays the Symbol Properties dialog box for the selected symbol.

Delete Item icon—Deletes the selected symbol or folder.

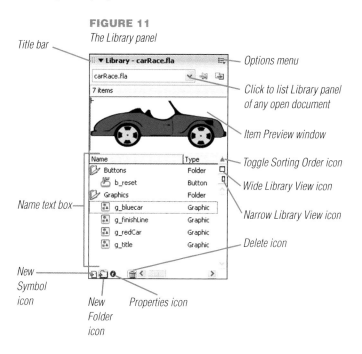

FIGURE 11
The Library panel

Title bar

▼ Library - carRace.fla — Options menu

carRace.fla — Click to list Library panel of any open document

7 items

Item Preview window

Name | Type — Toggle Sorting Order icon

Buttons | Folder — Wide Library View icon

b_reset | Button — Narrow Library View icon

Name text box — Graphics | Folder

g_bluecar | Graphic

g_finishLine | Graphic

g_redCar | Graphic

g_title | Graphic — Delete icon

New Symbol icon

New Folder icon

Properties icon

FIGURE 12
The Options menu

New Symbol...
New Folder
New Font...
New Video...
Rename
Move to New Folder...
Duplicate...
Delete
Edit
Edit with...
Properties...
Linkage...
Component Definition...

Select Unused Items
Update...
Play

Expand Folder
Collapse Folder

Expand All Folders
Collapse All Folders

Shared Library Properties...

Keep Use Counts Updated
Update Use Counts Now

Help

Group Library with ▶
Close Library

Rename panel group...
Maximize panel group
Close panel group

Create folders in the Library panel

1. Open fl3_2.fla, then save it as **carRace**.

2. Hide all panels, display the Property inspector and the Tools panel, then set the magnification to **Fit in Window**.

3. Click **Window** on the menu bar, then click **Library** to open the Library panel, as shown in Figure 13.

4. Click the **New Folder icon** 🗀 in the Library panel.

5. Type **Graphics** in the Name text box, then press **[Enter]** (Win) or **[return]** (Mac).

6. Click the **New Folder icon** 🗀 in the Library panel.

7. Type **Buttons** in the Name text box, then press **[Enter]** (Win) or **[return]** (Mac).

   Your Library panel should resemble Figure 14.

You opened a Macromedia Flash movie and created folders in the Library panel.

FIGURE 13
The open Library panel

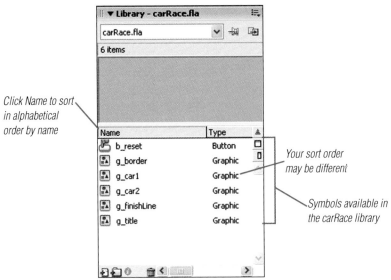

Click Name to sort in alphabetical order by name

Your sort order may be different

Symbols available in the carRace library

FIGURE 14
The Library panel with the folders added

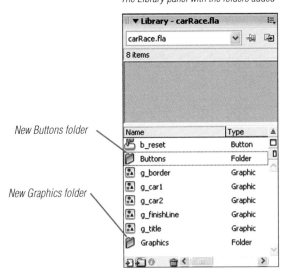

New Buttons folder

New Graphics folder

Working with Symbols and Interactivity

FIGURE 15

The Library panel after moving the symbols to the folders

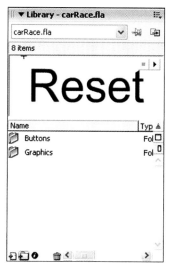

1. Drag the **g_title symbol** in the Library panel to the Graphics folder.

2. Drag the other graphic symbols to the Graphics folder.

3. Drag the **b_reset symbol** to the Buttons folder, then compare your Library panel to Figure 15.

4. Double-click the **Graphics folder** to open it and display the symbols.

5. Double-click the **Graphics folder** to close the folder.

You organized the symbols within the folders and opened and closed the folders.

Display the properties of a symbol, rename and delete symbols

1. Double-click the **Graphics folder icon** to display the symbols.

2. Click the **g_car1 symbol**, then click the **Properties icon** ⊙ to display the Symbol Properties dialog box.

3. Type **g_redCar** in the Name text box, as shown in Figure 16, then click **OK**.

4. Repeat steps 2 and 3 renaming the g_car2 symbol to **g_blueCar**.

   TIP Double-click the name to rename it without opening the Symbol Properties dialog box.

5. Click **g_border** in the Library panel to select it.

6. Click the **Delete icon** 🗑 at the bottom of the Library panel.

7. If necessary, click **Yes** to complete the delete process.

   TIP You can also select an item and press [Delete], or use the Options menu in the Library panel to remove an item from the library.

You used the Library panel to display the properties of a symbol and rename and delete symbols.

FIGURE 16
Renaming a symbol

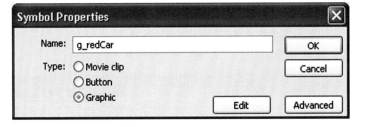

FIGURE 17

The carRace.fla document and the coolcar.fla Library panel

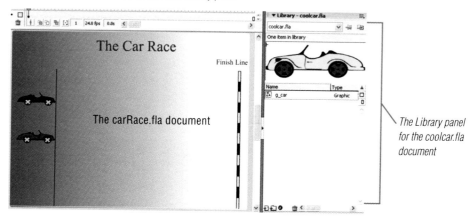

The Library panel
for the coolcar.fla
document

Use multiple Library panels

1. Click the **Library panel text box list arrow** ⌄ near the top of the Library panel to display the open documents.

2. Click **coolcar.fla**.

   The Library panel for the coolcar document is displayed. However, the carRace document remains open, as shown in Figure 17.

3. Drag the **car** from the Library panel to the center of the stage.

4. Click the **Library panel text box list arrow** ⌄ to display the open documents.

5. Click **carRace.fla** to view the carRace document's Library panel.

   Notice the g_car symbol is automatically added to the Library panel of the carRace document.

6. Click the **g_car symbol** in the Library panel.

7. Click the **Delete icon** 🗑 at the bottom of the Library panel, then (if necessary) click **Yes** to delete the symbol.

   You deleted the g_car symbol from the carRace Library but it still exists in the coolcar library.

8. Save your work.

9. Click **coolcar.fla** above the timeline to display the document.

10. Close the coolcar document.

You used the Library panel to display the contents of a Library and added an object from the Library to the current document.

CREATE
BUTTONS

What You'll Do

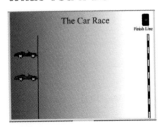

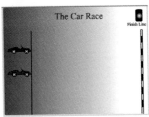

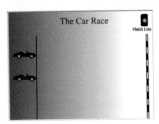

 In this lesson, you will create buttons, edit the four button states, and test a button.

Understanding Buttons

Button symbols are used to provide inter-activity. When you click a button, an action occurs, such as starting an animation or jumping to another frame on the timeline. Any object, including Macromedia Flash drawings, text blocks, and imported graphic images, can be made into buttons. Unlike graphic symbols, buttons have four states: Up, Over, Down, and Hit. These states correspond to the use of the mouse and recognize that the user requires feed-back when the mouse is pointing to a but-ton and when the button has been clicked. This is often shown by a change in the but-ton (such as a different color or different shape). These four states are explained below and shown in Figure 18.

Up—Represents how the button appears when the mouse pointer is not over it.

Over—Represents how the button appears when the mouse pointer is over it.

Down—Represents how the button appears after the user clicks the mouse.

Hit—Defines the area of the screen that will respond to the click. In most cases, you will want the Hit state to be the same or similar to the Up state in location and size.

When you create a button symbol, Macromedia Flash automatically creates a new timeline. The timeline has only four frames, one for each state. The timeline does not play; it merely reacts to the mouse pointer by displaying the appropri-ate button state and performing an action, such as jumping to a specific frame on the main timeline.

The process for creating and previewing buttons is as follows:

Create a button symbol—Draw an object or select an object that has already been created and placed on the stage. Use the Convert to Symbol command on the Modify menu to convert the object to a but-ton symbol and to enter a name for the but-ton.

Working with Symbols and Interactivity

Edit the button symbol—Select the button and choose the Edit Symbols command on the Edit menu or double-click the button symbol in the Library panel. This displays the button timeline, shown in Figure 19, which allows you to work with the four button states. The Up state is the original button symbol that Macromedia Flash automatically places in Frame 1. You need to determine how the original object will change for the other states. To change the button for the Over state, click Frame 2 and insert a keyframe. This automatically places a copy of the button in Frame 1 into Frame 2. Then, alter the button's appearance for the Over state. Use the same process for the Down state. For the Hit state, you insert a keyframe on Frame 4 and then specify the area on the screen that will respond to the pointer.

Return to the main timeline—Once you've finished editing a button, choose the Edit Document command on the Edit menu, or click Scene 1 above the timeline layers, to return to the main timeline.

Preview the button—By default, Macromedia Flash disables buttons so that you can manipulate them on the stage. You can preview a button by choosing the Enable Simple Buttons command on the Control menu. You can also choose the Test Movie command on the Control menu to play the movie and test the buttons.

FIGURE 18
The four button states

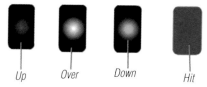

Up   Over   Down   Hit

FIGURE 19
The button timeline

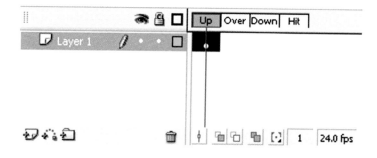

Create a button

1. Insert a layer above the top layer in the carRace document timeline, then name the layer **signal**.

2. Click the **Rectangle tool** ⬜ on the Tools panel, click the **Stroke Color tool** ✏⬜ on the Tools panel, then click the **black color swatch** in the left column of the color palette.

3. Click the **Fill Color tool** ⬤⬜ on the Tools panel, then click the **red gradient color swatch** in the bottom row of the color palette.

4. Click the **Set Corner Radius icon** 🔲 in the Options section of the Tools panel, type **5**, then click **OK**.

5. Draw the rectangle shown in Figure 20.

6. Click the **Zoom tool** 🔍 on the Tools panel, then click the **rectangle** to enlarge it.

7. Click the **Gradient Transform tool** 🔲 in the Tools panel, then click the **rectangle**.

8. Drag the diagonal arrow towards the center of the rectangle, as shown in Figure 21.

9. Click the **Selection tool** ⬆ on the Tools panel, then drag the marquee around the rectangle to select it.

10. Click **Modify** on the menu bar, then click **Convert to Symbol**.

11. Type **b_signal** in the Name text box, click the **Type Button option button**, then click **OK**.

12. Drag the **b_signal symbol** to the Buttons folder in the Library panel.

You created a button symbol on the stage and dragged it to the Buttons folder in the Library panel.

FIGURE 20
The rectangle object

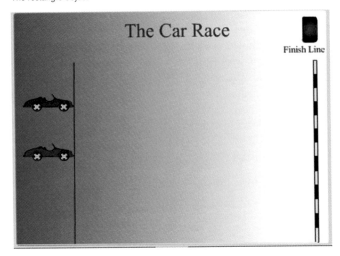

FIGURE 21
Adjusting the gradient

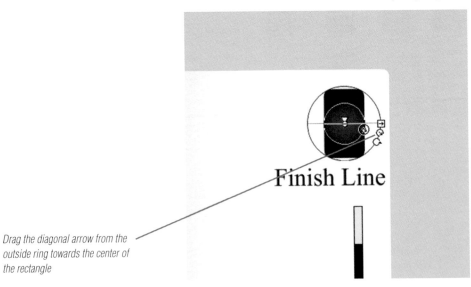

Drag the diagonal arrow from the outside ring towards the center of the rectangle

Working with Symbols and Interactivity

FIGURE 22
Specifying the hit area

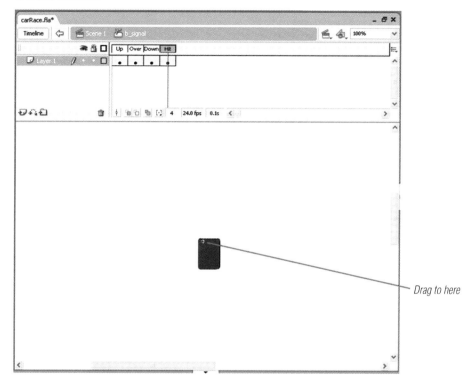

Drag to here

Edit a button and specify a Hit area

1. Open the Buttons folder, right-click (Win) or control-click (Mac) **b_signal** in the Library panel, then click **Edit**.

   Macromedia Flash switches to symbol-editing mode, and the timeline contains four button states.

2. Click the blank **Over frame** on Layer 1, then insert a keyframe.

   TIP The [F6] key inserts a keyframe in the selected frame.

3. Click the **Fill Color tool** on the Tools panel, then click the **grey gradient color swatch** on the bottom of the color palette.

4. Insert a keyframe in the Down frame on Layer 1.

5. Click the **Fill Color tool**, then click the **green gradient color swatch** on the bottom of the color palette.

6. Insert a keyframe in the Hit frame on Layer 1.

7. Click the **Rectangle tool** on the Tools panel, click the **Fill Color tool**, then click the **blue color swatch** in the left column of the color palette.

8. Draw a rectangle that covers the button.

   Your screen should resemble Figure 22.

   TIP The Hit area is not visible on the stage.

9. Click **Scene 1** above the Timeline layers to return to the main timeline.

You edited a button by changing the color of its Over and Down states, and you specified the Hit area.

Test a button

1. Click the **Selection tool** , then click a blank area of the stage.

2. Click **Control** on the menu bar, then click **Enable Simple Buttons**.

3. Point to the signal button on the stage; the pointer changes to 🖐, and the button changes to a grey gradient, the color you selected for the Over state. Compare your image to Figure 23.

4. Press and hold the mouse button, then notice that the button changes to a green gradient, the color you selected for the Down state, as shown in Figure 24.

(continued)

FIGURE 23
The button's Over state

FIGURE 24
The button's Down state

Working with Symbols and Interactivity

FIGURE 25

The button's Up state

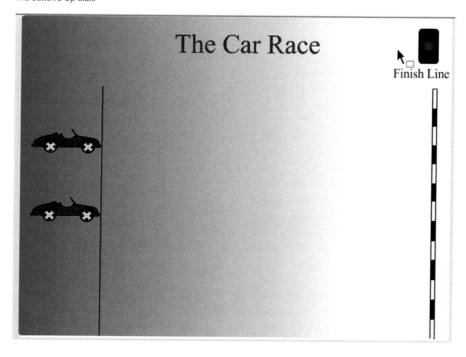

5. Release the mouse and notice that the button changes to the Over state color.

6. Move the mouse away from the signal button, and notice that the button returns to a red gradient, the Up state color, as shown in Figure 25.

7. Click **Control** on the menu bar, then click **Enable Simple Buttons** to turn it off.

8. Click **Window** on the menu bar, then click **Library** to close the Library panel.

9. Click **View** in the menu bar, point to **Magnification**, then click **Fit in Window**.

10. Save your work.

You used the mouse to test a button and view the button states.

ASSIGN ACTIONS
TO BUTTONS

What You'll Do

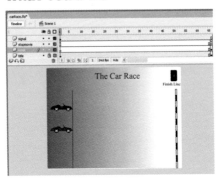

In this lesson, you will use ActionScripts to assign actions to frames and buttons.

Understanding Actions

In a basic movie, Macromedia Flash plays the frames sequentially, repeating the movie without stopping for user input. However, you may often want to provide users with the ability to interact with the movie by allowing them to perform actions such as starting and stopping the movie or jumping to a specific frame in the movie. One way to provide user interaction is to assign an action to the Down state of a button or preferably to the instance of a button. Then, whenever the user clicks the button, the action occurs. Macromedia Flash provides a scripting language, called ActionScript, that allows you to add actions to buttons and frames within a movie. For example, you can place a stop action in a frame that pauses the movie and then assign a play action to a button that starts the movie when the user clicks the button.

Analyzing ActionScript

ActionScript is a powerful scripting language that allows those with even limited programming experience to create complex actions. For example, you can create order forms that capture user input, or volume controls that display when sounds are played. A basic ActionScript involves an event (such as a mouse click) that causes some action to occur by triggering the script. The following is an example of a basic ActionScript:

```
on (release) {
        gotoAndPlay(10);
}
```

In this example, the event is a mouse click (indicated by the word release) that causes the movie's playback head to go to Frame 10 and play the frame. This is a simple ActionScript and is easy to follow. Other ActionScripts can be quite complex and may require programming expertise to understand. Fortunately, Macromedia Flash provides an easy way to use ActionScripts without having to learn the scripting language. The Script Assist feature within the Actions panel allows you to assign basic actions to frames and objects, such as buttons. Figure 26 shows the Actions panel displaying an ActionScript indicating that when the user clicks on the selected object (a button), the movie plays.

The process for assigning actions to buttons, shown in Figure 27, is as follows.

- Select the desired button on the stage.
- Display the Actions panel.
- Select the Script Assist button to display the Script Assist panel within the ActionScript panel.
- Click the Add a new item to the script icon to display a list of Action categories.
- Select the appropriate category from a drop-down list. Macromedia Flash provides several Action categories. The Timeline Control category within the Global Functions allows you to create scripts for controlling movies and navigating within movies. You can use these actions to start and stop movies, jump to specific frames, and respond to user mouse movements and keystrokes.
- Select the desired action, such as play.
- Specify the event that triggers the action.

Button actions respond to one or more mouse events, including:

Release—With the pointer inside the button Hit area, the user presses and releases (clicks) the mouse button. This is the default event.

Key Press—With the Macromedia Flash button displayed, the user presses a predetermined key on the keyboard.

Roll Over—The user moves the pointer into the button Hit area.

Drag Over—The user holds down the mouse button, moves the pointer out of the button Hit area and then back into the Hit area.

Using Frame Actions—In addition to assigning actions to buttons which require some user interaction, you can assign actions to frames. Actions that are assigned to frames are executed when the playhead reaches the frame. A common frame action is stop, which is often assigned to the first and last frame in the timeline.

FIGURE 26

The Actions panel displaying an ActionScript

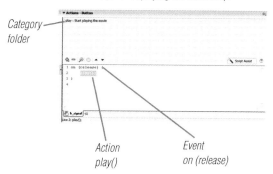

Category folder

Action
play()

Event
on (release)

FIGURE 27

The process for assigning actions to buttons

4. Click the Add a new item to the script icon

2. Hide the left Window. (The hide/display arrow used to hide and display the windows in the Actions panel)

1. Select the button

3. Select the Script Assist button

5. Select the Actions category and the action

Assign a stop action to frames

1. Click **Control** on the menu bar, then click **Test Movie**.

   The movie plays and continues to loop.

2. Close the test movie window.

3. Hide all panels, then display the Tools panel.

4. Insert a new layer, name it **stopmovie**, then click **Frame 1** of the layer.

5. Click **Window** on the menu bar, then click **Actions** to display the Actions panel, as shown in Figure 28.

6. Drag the **Actions panel top border** down to display the stage, click the **hide/display arrow** ⫶ to close the left window of the Actions panel, then click the **Script Assist button** to turn on this feature.

7. Click the **Add a new item to the script button** ⊹ to display the Script categories, point to **Global Functions**, point to **Timeline Control**, then click **stop**, as shown in Figure 29.

8. Insert a keyframe in Frame 66 on the stopmovie layer, then repeat step 7. Compare your screen to Figure 30.

9. Test the movie.

   The movie does not play because there is a stop action assigned to Frame 1.

10. Close the test movie window.

You inserted a layer and assigned a stop action to the first and last frames on the layer.

FIGURE 28

The Actions panel with both windows displayed

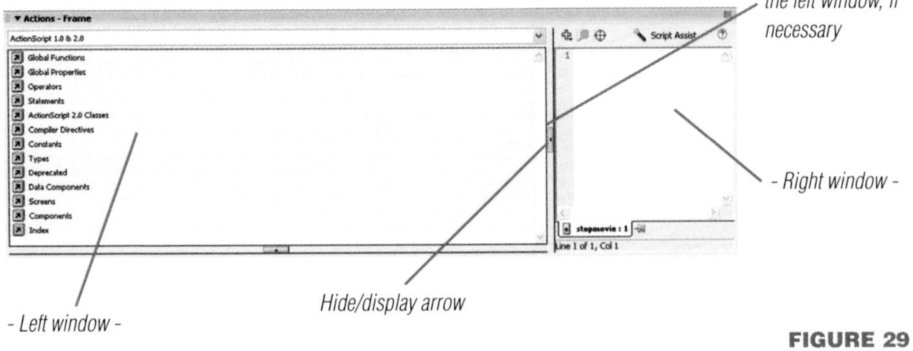

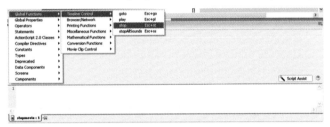

Click here to hide the left window, if necessary

- Right window -

Hide/display arrow

- Left window -

FIGURE 29

Assigning an action to Frame 1 on the stopmovie layer

FIGURE 30

Script for the stopmovie layer

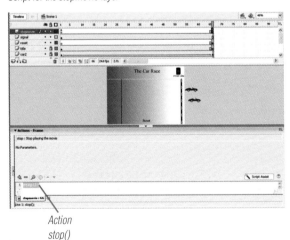

Action stop()

FIGURE 31
Assigning a play action to a button

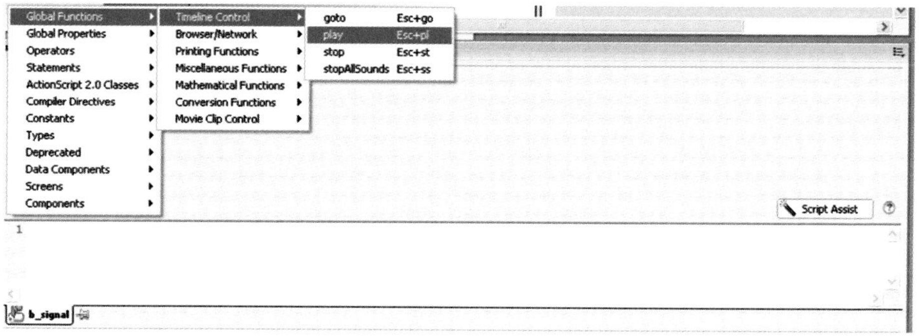

Understanding the Actions panel

The Actions panel has two windows. The left window uses folders to display the Action categories. The right window uses lists to display the categories. The right window, called the Script pane, is used with the Script Assist feature and it displays the ActionScript code as the code is being generated. When using the Script Assist feature, it is best to close the left window. This is done by clicking the hide/display arrow.

1. Click **View** on the menu bar, point to **Magnification**, then click **Fit in Window**.

   TIP If you want a larger view of the stage, you can use the Selection tool to drag the bottom border of the timeline up to hide more layers.

2. Click **Frame 1** of the Signal layer.

3. Click the **button** on the stage. Verify that b_signal is displayed in the lower left of the Actions panel.

   TIP To select the button, click it with the Selection tool.

4. Click ⚛ to display the Script categories, point to **Global Functions**, point to **Timeline Control**, then click **play**, as shown in Figure 31.

5. Click **Control** on the menu bar, then click **Test Movie**.

6. Click the **signal button**.

   The movie plays and stops. The reset button appears but it does not have an action assigned to it.

7. Close the test movie window.

You used the Actions panel to assign a play action to a button.

Assign a goto frame action to a button

1. Click **Frame 66** of the reset layer to display the Reset button.

2. Click the **Reset button** on the stage to select it.

3. Click ⚒ to display the Script categories, point to **Global Functions**, point to **Timeline Control**, then click **goto**.

   The Script Assist window displays options that allow you to specify the frame number to go to and play, as shown in Figure 32. Frame 1 is the default frame number.

4. Click **Control** on the menu bar, then click **Test Movie**.

5. Click the **signal button** to start the movie, then when the movie stops, click the **Reset button**.

6. Close the test movie window.

You used the Actions panel to assign an action to a button.

FIGURE 32

Assigning a goto action to a button

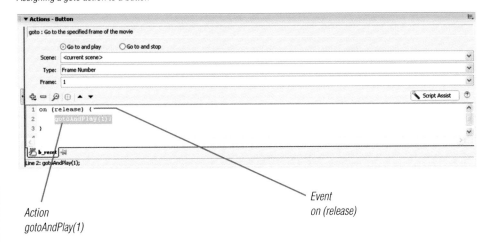

Action
gotoAndPlay(1)

Event
on (release)

FIGURE 33

Assigning a keypress action to a button

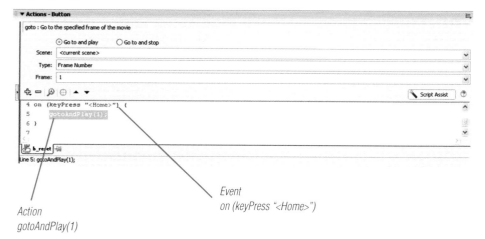

Action
gotoAndPlay(1)

Event
on (keyPress "<Home>")

1. Click after the **right curly bracket** (}) in the Actions panel to highlight the bracket in step 3 of the ActionScript.

2. Click ⊕ in the Script Assist window, point to **Global Functions**, point to **Movie Clip Control**, then click **on**.

   The Script Assist window displays several event options. Release is selected.

3. Click the **Release check box** to deselect the option.

4. Click the **Key Press check box** to select it, then press [**Home**].

5. Click ⊕ in the Script Assist window, point to **Global Functions**, point to **Timeline Control**, then click **goto**.

   The ActionScript now indicates that pressing the [Home] key will cause the playhead to go to Frame 1, as shown in Figure 33.

6. Click **File** on the menu bar, point to **Publish Preview**, then click **Default – (HTML)**.

   The movie opens in your default browser.

7. Click the **signal button** to start the movie, then when the movie stops, press the [**Home**] key.

8. Close the browser window, then save and close the movie.

9. Exit Flash.

You added an event that triggers a goto frame action.

Create a symbol.

1. Start Flash, open fl3_3.fla, then save it as **skillsdemo3**.
2. Change the background color of the document to **#CCCCCC**.
3. Change the title, Color Spin, to font size **30**.
4. Insert a new layer above the ballspin layer and name it **titlebkgnd**.
5. Draw a black rectangle behind the Color Spin title text using the Set Corner Radius option, and set the Corner radius points to **10**.
6. Select the rectangle, convert it to a graphic symbol, then name it **g_bkgnd**.
7. Save your work.

Create and edit an instance.

1. Insert a new layer above the title layer and name it **vballs-sm**.
2. Display the Library panel, if necessary.
3. Drag the g_vball-sm symbol to the upper-left corner of the stage.
4. Drag the g_vball-sm symbol three more times to each of the remaining corners of the stage.
5. Double-click the g_vball-sm symbol icon in the Library panel to switch to symbol-editing mode.
6. Change the color of the ball to red.
7. Return to the document and notice how all instances have been changed to red.
8. Select the ball in the upper-right corner of the stage and break apart the object.

9. Change the color to a blue gradient.
10. Select, break apart, and change the bottom-left ball to a green gradient and the bottom-right ball to white.
11. Save your work.

Create a folder in the Library panel.

1. Use the Options menu in the Library panel to create a new folder.
2. Name the folder **Graphics**.
3. Move the three graphic symbols to the Graphics folder.
4. Expand the Graphics folder.
5. Save your work.

Work with the Library window.

1. Rename the g_bkgnd symbol to **g_title-bkgnd** in the Library panel.
2. Collapse and expand the folder.
3. Save your work.

Create a button.

1. Insert a new layer above the vballs-sm layer and name it **start**.
2. Drag the g_title-bkgnd symbol from the Library panel to the bottom center of the stage.
3. Create a white, bold, 30-pt Arial text block on top of the g_title-bkgnd object, then type **Start**. (*Hint*: Center the text block in the background object.)

4. Select the rectangle and the text. (*Hint*: Click the Selection tool, then press and hold [Shift].)
5. Convert the selected objects to a button symbol and name it **b_start**.
6. Create a new folder named **Buttons** in the Library panel and move the b_start button symbol to the folder.
7. Display the b_start button timeline.
8. Insert a keyframe in the Over frame.
9. Select the text and change the color to gray.
10. Insert a keyframe in the Down frame.
11. Select the text and change the color to blue.
12. Insert a keyframe in the Hit frame.
13. Draw a rectangular object that covers the area for the Hit state.
14. Return to movie-editing mode.
15. Save your work.

Test a button.

1. Turn on Enable Simple Buttons.
2. Point to the button and notice the color change.
3. Click the button and notice the other color change.

Stop a movie.

1. Insert a new layer and name it **stopmovie**.
2. Insert a keyframe in Frame 40 on the new layer.
3. With Frame 40 selected, display the Actions panel.
4. Assign a stop action to the frame.
5. Click Frame 1 on the new layer.
6. Assign a stop action to Frame 1.
7. Save your work.

Assign an action to a button.

1. Click Control on the menu bar, then click Enable Simple Buttons to turn off this feature.
2. Use the Selection tool to select the button on the stage.
3. Use Script Assist in the Actions panel to assign an event and a play action to the button.
4. Test the movie.
5. Save your work, then compare your image to Figure 34.
6. Exit Flash.

FIGURE 34
Completed Skills Review

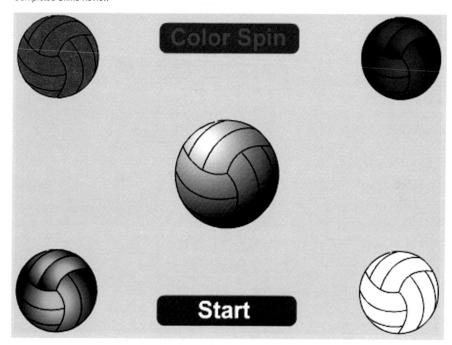

The Ultimate Tours travel company has asked you to design a sample navigation scheme for its Web site. The company wants to see how its homepage will link with one of its main categories (Treks). Figure 35 shows a sample homepage and Treks screen. Using these or the homepage you created in Chapter 2 as a guide, you will add a Treks screen and link it to the homepage. (*Hint*: Assume that all of the drawings on the homepage are on Frame 1, unless noted.)

1. Open ultimatetours2.fla (the file you created in Chapter 2 Project Builder 1), then save it as **ultimatetours3**.

2. Insert a layer above the Subheading layer, name it **logo**, then type logo as a placeholder in the upper-left corner of the stage.

3. Select the layer that the Ultimate Tours text block is on, then insert a keyframe on a frame at least five frames further along the timeline.

4. Insert a new layer, name it **treks headings**, insert a keyframe on the last frame of the movie, then create the Treks screen, except for the home graphic.

5. Convert the Treks graphic on the homepage to a button symbol, then edit the symbol so that different colors appear for the different states.

6. Assign a goto action that jumps the playhead to the Treks screen when the Treks button is clicked.

7. Insert a new layer and name it **stopmovie**. Add stop actions that cause the movie to stop after displaying the homepage and after displaying the Treks page.

8. Insert a new layer and name it **homeButton**, insert a keyframe on the appropriate frame, then draw the home button image with the Home text.

9. Convert the image to a button symbol, then edit the symbol so that different colors appear for the different states. Assign a goto action for the button that jumps the movie to Frame 1.

10. Test the movie.

11. Save your work, then compare your Web page to the sample shown in Figure 35.

FIGURE 35
Sample completed Project Builder 1

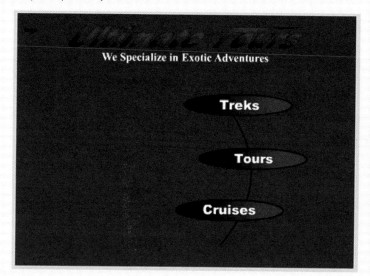
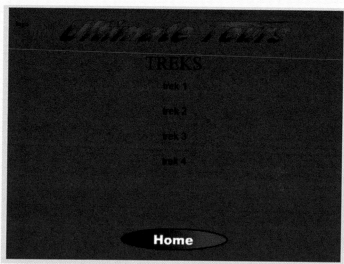

You have been asked to assist the International Student Association (ISA). The association sponsors a series of monthly events, each focusing on a different culture from around the world. The events are led by a guest speaker who makes a presentation, followed by a discussion. The events are free and they are open to everyone. ISA would like you to design a Macromedia Flash movie that will be used with its Web site. The movie starts by providing information about the series, and then provides a link to the upcoming event.

1. Open a new Flash document and save it as **isa3**.
2. Create an initial Information screen with general information about the association's series.
3. Assign an action that stops the movie.
4. Add a button on the general information screen that jumps the movie to a screen that presents information about the next event.
5. Add a button on the information screen that jumps the movie to a screen that lists the series (all nine events for the school year-September through May).

6. On the next event and series screens, add a Return button that jumps the movie back to the general information screen.
7. Specify different colors for each state of each button.
8. Test the movie.
9. Save your work, then compare your movie to the sample shown in Figure 36.

FIGURE 36
Sample completed Project Builder 2

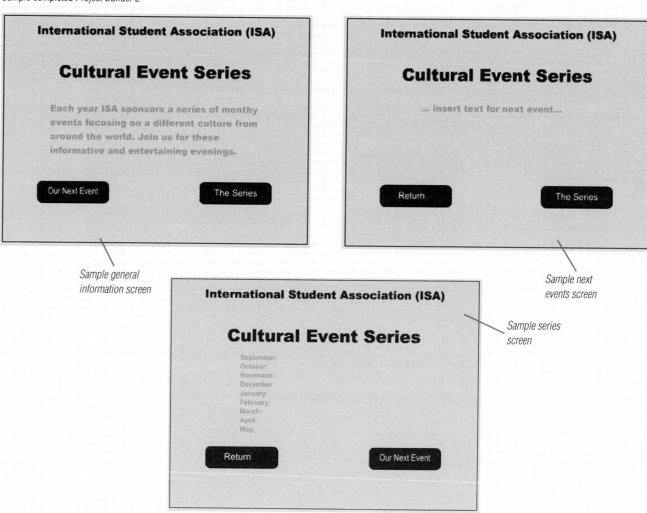

Sample general
information screen

Sample next
events screen

Sample series
screen

Figure 37 shows the homepage of a Web site. Study the figure and complete the following questions. For each question, indicate how you determined your answer.

1. Connect to the Internet, go to *www.course.com*, navigate to the page for this book, click the Online Companion link, then click the link for this chapter.

2. Open a document in a word processor or open a new Macromedia Flash document, save the file as **dpc3**, then answer the following questions. (*Hint*: Use the Text tool in Macromedia Flash.)

   ■ Whose Web site is this?

   ■ What is the goal(s) of the site?

   ■ Who is the target audience?

   ■ What is the treatment ("look and feel") that is used?

   ■ What are the design layout guidelines being used (balance, movement, and so on)?

   ■ What may be animated in this home page?

   ■ Do you think this is an effective design for the company, its products, and its target audience? Why or why not?

   ■ What suggestions would you make to improve on the design, and why?

FIGURE 37
Design Project

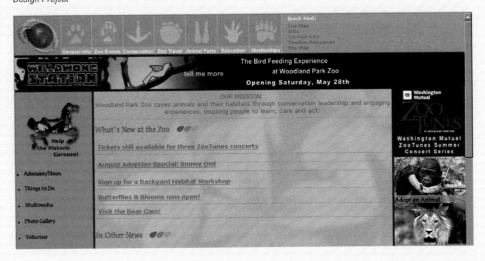

This is a continuation of Portfolio Project in Chapter 2, which is the development of a personal portfolio. The homepage has several categories, including the following:

- Personal data
- Contact information
- Previous employment
- Education
- Samples of your work

In this project, you will create a button that will be used to link the homepage of your portfolio to the animations page. Next, you will create another button to start the animation.

1. Open portfolio2.fla (the file you created in Portfolio Project, Chapter 2), then save it as **portfolio3**. (*Hint*: When you open the file, you may receive a warning message that the font is missing. You can replace this font with the default, or with any other appropriate font on your computer.)
2. Unlock the layers as needed.
3. Change the My Portfolio text to **#003366** and the oval background to **#CCCCCC**.
4. Insert a new layer, insert a keyframe on Frame 3 (or one frame past the last frame of the movie), then create an animation using objects that you create.
5. Insert a new layer, insert a keyframe on Frame 2 (or one frame before the

animation frame), then create a Sample Animation screen.
6. Convert the title into a button symbol, then edit the symbol so that different colors appear for the different states. Assign an action that jumps to the frame that plays an animation.
7. Change the Animations graphic on the homepage to a button, then edit the symbol

so that different colors appear for the different states. Assign an action that jumps to the Sample Animation screen.
8. Insert a new layer, then name it **stopmovie**. Insert keyframes and assign stop actions to the appropriate frames.
9. Test the movie.
10. Save your work, then compare your movie to the sample shown in Figure 38.

FIGURE 38
Sample completed Portfolio Project

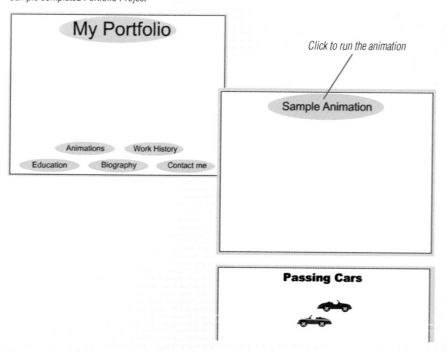

chapter

4

CREATING
ANIMATIONS

1. Create frame-by-frame animations.

2. Create motion-tweened animation.

3. Work with motion guides.

4. Create animation effects.

5. Animate text.

4 CREATING ANIMATIONS

Introduction

Animation can be an important part of your Web site, whether the site focuses on e-commerce (attracts attention and provides product demonstrations), education (simulates complex processes such as DNA replication), or entertainment (provides interactive games).

How Does Animation Work?

The perception of motion in an animation is actually an illusion. Animation is like a motion picture in that it is made up of a series of still images. Research has found that our eye captures and holds an image for one-tenth of a second before processing another image. By retaining each impression for one-tenth of a second, we perceive a series of rapidly displayed still images as a single, moving image. This phenomenon is known as persistence of vision and provides the basis for the frame rate in animations. Frame rates of 10–12 frames-per-second (fps) generally provide

an acceptably smooth computer-based animation. Lower frame rates result in a jerky image, while higher frame rates may result in a blurred image. Macromedia Flash uses a default frame rate of 12 fps.

Macromedia Flash Animation

Creating animation is one of the most powerful features of Macromedia Flash, yet developing basic animations is a simple process. Macromedia Flash allows you to create animations that can move and rotate an object around the stage, and change its size, shape, or color. You can also use the animation features in Macromedia Flash to create special effects, such as an object zooming or fading in and out. You can combine animation effects so that an object changes shape and color as it moves across the stage. Animations are created by changing the content of successive frames. Macromedia Flash provides two animation methods: frame-by-frame animation and tweened animation.

Tools You'll Use

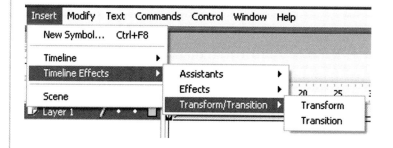

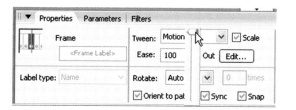

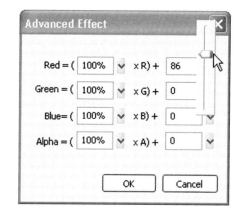

CREATE FRAME-BY-FRAME ANIMATIONS

What You'll Do

In this lesson you will create frame-by-frame animations.

Understanding Frame-by-Frame Animations

A frame-by-frame animation (also called a frame animation) is created by specifying the object that is to appear in each frame of a sequence of frames. Figure 1 shows three images that are variations of a cartoon character. In this example the head and body remain the same, but the arms and legs change to represent a walking motion. If these individual images are placed into succeeding frames (with keyframes), an animation is created.

Frame-by-frame animations are useful when you want to change individual parts of an image. The images in Figure 1 are simple—only three images are needed for the animation. However, depending on the complexity of the image and the desired movements, the time needed to display each change can be substantial. When creating a frame-by-frame animation, you need to consider the following points:

- The number of different images. The more images there are, the more effort is needed to create them. However, the greater the number of images, the less change you need to make in each image. Therefore, the movement in the animation may seem more realistic.
- The number of frames in which each image will appear. If each image appears in only one frame, the animation may appear rather jerky, since the changes are made very rapidly. In some instances, you may want to give the impression of a rapid change in an object, such as rapidly blinking colors. The number of frames creates varied results.
- The movie frame rate. Frame rates below 10 may appear jerky, while those above 30 may appear blurred. The frame rate is easy to change, and you should experiment with different rates until you get the desired effect.

Keyframes are critical to the development of frame animations because they signify a change in the object. Because frame animations are created by changing the

Creating Animations

object, all frames in a frame animation may need to be keyframes. The exception is when you want an object displayed in several frames before it changes.

Creating a Frame-by-Frame Animation

To create a frame animation, select the frame on the layer where you want the animation to begin, insert a keyframe, and then place the object on the stage. Next, select the frame where you want the change to occur, insert a keyframe, then change the object. You can also add a new object in place of the original one. Figure 2 shows the first six frames of an animation in which the front end of a car raises up and down in place. The movement of the animation is visible because the Onion Skin feature is turned on; this feature will be discussed later in this chapter. In this case, the car stays in place during the animation. A frame animation can also involve movement of the object around the stage.

FIGURE 1
Three images used in an animation

FIGURE 2
The first six frames of an animation

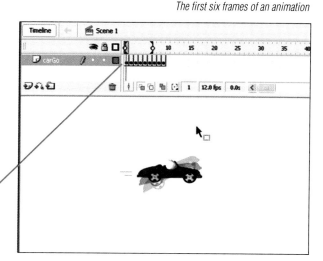

In each frame, the car is in a different position

Create an in-place frame-by-frame animation

1. Open fl4_1.fla from the drive and folder where your Data Files are stored, then save it as **frameAn**.

2. Hide all panels, then open the Tools panel, Property inspector and Library panel.

3. Click **View** on the menu bar, point to **Magnification**, then click **Fit in Window**.

4. Click Frame 2 on the carGo layer, then press [**F6**] to insert a keyframe.

5. Verify that the car is selected, click the **Free Transform tool** 🔲 on the Tools panel, then click the **Rotate and Skew option** 🔁 in the Options section of the Tools panel.

6. Drag the top-right handle 🔄 up one position, as shown in Figure 3.

7. Insert a keyframe in Frame 3 on the carGo layer.

8. Drag the top-right handle 🔄 up one more position.

9. Insert a keyframe in Frame 4 on the carGo layer, then drag the top-right handle 🔄 down one position.

10. Insert a keyframe in Frame 5 on the carGo layer, then drag the top-right handle 🔄 down to position the car to its original horizontal position.

11. Insert a keyframe in Frame 6 on the carGo layer, then compare your timeline to Figure 4.

You created an in-place frame animation by inserting several keyframes and adjusting an object in each of the frames.

FIGURE 3
Rotating the car

— Click handle and drag up

FIGURE 4
The timeline with keyframes

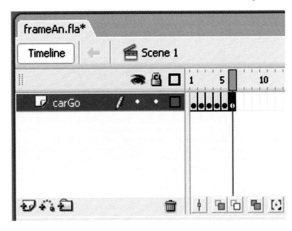

Creating Animations

Add detail to the animation

1. Click the **Pencil tool** on the Tools panel.
2. Click the **Stroke Color tool** on the Tools panel, then click the **black color swatch** in the left column of the color palette (if necessary).

   TIP Adjust the Zoom settings as needed using the View menu or Zoom tool.

3. Verify Frame 6 is selected, then draw the two lines shown in Figure 5.

   TIP Press and hold [Shift] to draw straight lines.

4. Click **Control** on the menu bar, then click **Play**.

You added lines to the animation that indicate motion.

FIGURE 5
Adding lines to the object

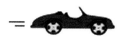

Create a moving frame animation

1. Insert a keyframe in Frame 7 on the carGo layer.

2. Click the **Selection tool** ▶ on the Tools panel, drag a marquee around the car and the lines to select them.

3. Drag the car and the two lines to the right approximately half the distance to the right edge of the stage, as shown in Figure 6.

4. Insert a keyframe in Frame 8 on the carGo layer.

5. Click the **Pencil tool** 🖉 on the Tools panel, then draw a third line, as shown in Figure 7.

6. Click the **Selection tool** ▶ , drag a marquee around the car and lines, then drag the car and the three lines to the right edge of the stage.

7. Insert a keyframe in Frame 9 on the carGo layer, then drag the car and the three lines completely off the right side of the stage, as shown in Figure 8.

8. Play the movie.

You created a moving frame animation by dragging the object across the stage.

FIGURE 6
Positioning the car

FIGURE 7
The car with a third line

FIGURE 8
Positioning the car off the stage

Change the frame rate

1. Double-click the **Frame Rate icon** 12.0 fps on the timeline to display the Document Properties dialog box.

2. Type **6** in the Frame Rate text box, as shown in Figure 9, then click **OK**.

3. Click **Control** on the menu bar, then click **Play** to play the movie.

4. Repeat Steps 1 through 3, typing **18** in the Frame Rate text box.

5. Change the frame rate to 12.

6. Save your work.

7. Play the movie, then close the movie.

You changed the frame rate for the movie to see its effect on the movement of the object.

FIGURE 9

Changing the frame rate

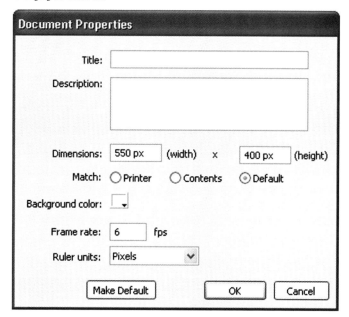

CREATE MOTION-TWEENED ANIMATION

What You'll Do

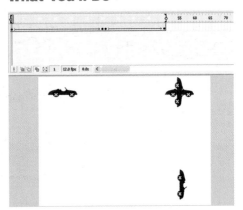

In this lesson, you will create motion-tweened animations.

Understanding Motion Tweening

Frame-by-frame animation can be a tedious process, especially if you have to alter an object's position an infinitesimal amount in every frame. Fortunately, once you create start and end frames, Macromedia Flash can fill in the in-between frames, a process called **tweening**. In tweened animation, Macromedia Flash stores only the attributes that change from frame to frame. For example, if you have an object that moves across the stage, Macromedia Flash stores the location of the object in each frame, but not the other attributes of the object, such as its dimensions and color. In contrast, for frame-by-frame animation, all of the attributes for the object need to be stored in each frame. Frame animations have larger file sizes than tweened animations.

There are two types of tweened animation: shape and motion. Shape animations are similar to the process of image morphing in which one object slowly turns into another—often unrelated—object, such as a robot that turns into a man. Shape-tweened animations will be covered in the next chapter. You can use **motion tweening** to create animations in which objects move and in which they are resized, rotated, and recolored. Figure 10 shows a motion-tweened animation of a car moving diagonally across the screen. There are only two keyframes needed for this animation: a keyframe in Frame 1 where the car starts, and a keyframe in Frame 30 where the car ends. Macromedia Flash automatically fills in the other frames. In Figure 10 the Onion Skin feature is enabled so that outlines of the car are displayed for each frame of the animation.

To create a motion-tweened animation, select the starting frame and, if necessary, insert a keyframe. Position the object on the stage and verify that it is selected. Next, choose the Create Motion Tween command from the Timeline option on the Insert menu, then insert a keyframe in the ending frame of the animation. Figure 10 shows the timeline after creating a Motion Tween and specifying an ending keyframe. Motion tweening is represented by black dots displayed in the keyframes and a black arrow linking the keyframes against a light blue background. The final step is to move the object and/or make changes to the object, such as changing its size or rotating it. Keep in mind the following points as you create motion-tweened animations.

- If you change the position of the object, it will move in a direct line from the starting position to the ending position. To move the object on a predetermined path, you can create several motion-tweened animations in succeeding frames, or you can use a motion guide as explained in the next lesson.

- If you reshape an object in the ending keyframe, the object will slowly change from the starting to the ending keyframes. If this is not the effect you want, you can add a keyframe immediately after the tweened animation and reshape the object at that point.

- When you select an object and create a motion tween, Macromedia Flash automatically creates a symbol, names it Tween 1, and places it in the Library panel.

- You can remove a motion tween animation by selecting a frame within the tween and using the Remove Tween command from the Timeline option in the Insert menu.

QUICK TIP

Make sure that you add a keyframe at the beginning and at the end of each animation. By default, the first frame in a layer is a keyframe.

FIGURE 10
Sample motion-tweened animation

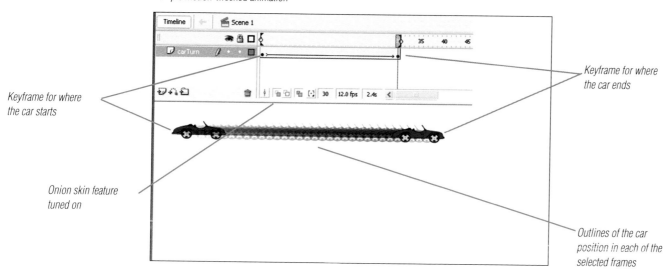

Keyframe for where the car starts

Keyframe for where the car ends

Onion skin feature tuned on

Outlines of the car position in each of the selected frames

Create a motion-tweened animation

1. Open fl4_2.fla, then save it as **carAn**.

2. Click **Frame 1** on the carTurn layer, click **Insert** on the menu bar, point to **Timeline**, then click **Create Motion Tween**.

3. Insert a keyframe in Frame 30 on the carTurn layer.

4. Click the **Selection tool** on the Tools panel (if necessary), select the car, then drag the car to the position on the stage shown in Figure 11.

5. Play the movie.

You created a motion-tweened animation, causing an object to move across the stage.

FIGURE 11
Final position of the first motion tween

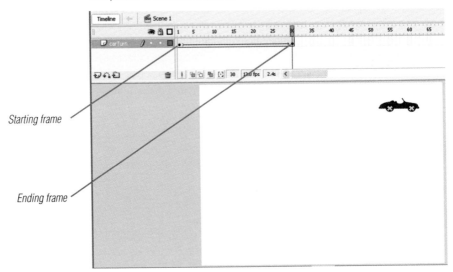

Starting frame

Ending frame

FIGURE 12

Final position of the combined motion tweens

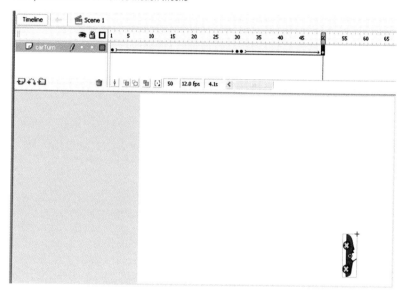

1. Click **View** on the menu bar, point to **Magnification**, then click **Fit in Window**.

2. Insert a keyframe in Frame 31 on the carTurn layer.

3. Verify that the car is selected, click **Modify** on the menu bar, point to **Transform**, then click **Rotate 90° CW**.

    | TIP   CW means clockwise.

4. Insert a keyframe in Frame 50 on the carTurn layer.

    A motion-tween is automatically inserted in the timeline because of the previous motion-tween that was created for the object.

    TIP   If you did not want another motion tween to be automatically inserted, you could add a Blank Keyframe to the frame following the animation. You use the Timeline option from the Insert menu.

5. Click the **Selection tool** ▶ on the Tools panel (if necessary), then drag the car to the location shown in Figure 12.

6. Play the movie.

7. Save your work, then close the movie.

You combined two motion-tweened animations with a rotation between the animations.

WORK WITH
MOTION GUIDES

What You'll Do

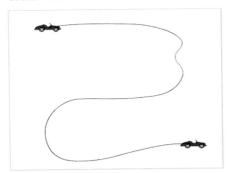

In this lesson, you will create a motion guide and attach an animation to it.

Understanding Motion Guides

In the previous lesson, you combined two animations to cause an object to change directions. Macromedia Flash provides a way for you to create a path that will guide moving objects around the stage in any direction, as shown in Figure 13 (Note: the onion skin feature is turned on to show how the car follows the path). **Motion guide layers** allow you to draw a motion guide path and attach motion-tweened animations to the path. The animations are placed on their own layer beneath the motion guide layer. There are two ways to work with motion guides. One way is to insert a guide layer, draw a path, then create an animation and attach the animated object to the path. The second way is to create an animation, insert a motion guide layer and draw a path, then attach the animated object to the path. The process for using the second method is as follows:

- Create a motion-tweened animation.
- Select the layer the animation is on and insert a motion guide layer. The selected layer is indented below the motion guide layer, as shown in Figure 14. This indicates that the selected layer is associated with the motion guide layer.
- Draw a path using the Pen, Pencil, Line, Circle, Rectangle, or Brush tools.
- Attach the object to the path by dragging the object by its registration point to the beginning of the path in the first frame, and to the end of the path in the last frame.

Depending on the type of object you are animating and the path, you may need to orient the object to the path. This means that the object will rotate in response to the direction of the path. The Property inspector is used to specify that the object will be oriented to the path. The advantages of using a motion guide are that you can have an object move along any path, including a path that intersects itself, and you can easily change the shape of the path, allowing you to experiment with different motions. A consideration when using a motion guide is that, in some instances, orienting the object along the path may result in an unnatural-looking animation. You can fix this by stepping through the animation one frame at a time until you reach the frame where the object is positioned poorly. You can then insert a keyframe and adjust the object as desired.

Working with the Property Inspector When Creating Motion-Tweened Animations

The Property inspector provides the following options when creating motion-tweened animations:

- Tween—specifies Motion, Shape, or None.
- Scale—tweens the size of an object. Select this option when you want an object to grow smaller or larger.
- Ease—specifies the rate of change between tweened frames. For

example, you may want to have an object—such as a car—start out slowly and accelerate gradually. Ease values are between –100 (slow) to 100 (fast).

- Rotate—specifies the number of times an object rotates clockwise (CW) or counterclockwise (CCW).
- Orient to path—orients the baseline of the object to the path.
- Sync—ensures that the object loops properly.
- Snap—attaches the object to the path by its transformation point.

Transformation Point and Registration Point

Each symbol has a transformation point (O) that is used to orient the object when it is being animated. For example,

when you rotate a symbol, the transformation point is the pivot point around which the object rotates. The transformation point is also the point that snaps to a motion guide, as shown in Figure 13. When attaching an object to a path you can drag the transformation point to the path. The default position for a transformation point is the center of the object. You can reposition the transformation point while in the symbol edit mode by dragging the transformation point to a different location in the object. Objects also have a registration point (+) that is used to position the object on the stage using ActionScript code. The transformation and registration points can overlap—this is displayed as a plus sign within a circle.

FIGURE 13

A motion guide with an object (car) attached

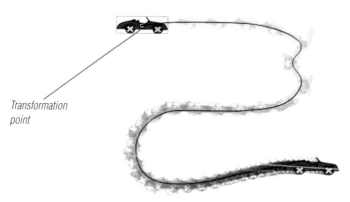

Transformation point

FIGURE 14

A motion guide layer

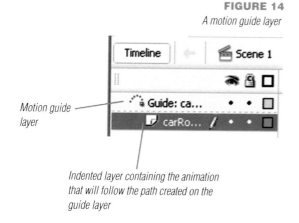

Motion guide layer

Indented layer containing the animation that will follow the path created on the guide layer

Create an animation without a motion guide

1. Open fl4_3.fla, then save it as **carPath**.

2. Set the View to Fit in Window.

3. Click **Frame 1** of the carRoute layer.

4. Make sure that the car is selected, click **Insert** on the menu bar, point to **Timeline**, then click **Create Motion Tween**.

5. Insert a keyframe in Frame 40 on the carRoute layer.

6. Drag the **car** to the lower-right corner of the stage, as shown in Figure 15.

7. Play the movie.

   The car moves diagonally down to the corner of the stage.

You created a motion animation that moves an object in a diagonal line across the stage.

FIGURE 15
Positioning the car

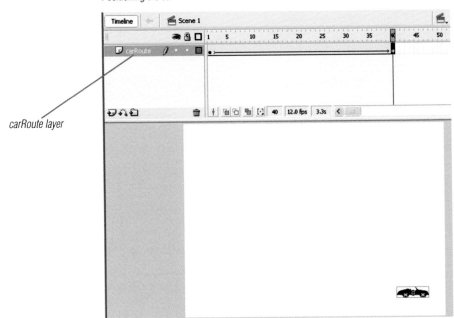

carRoute layer

FIGURE 16

The completed motion path

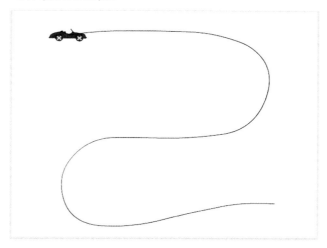

FIGURE 17

Snapping an object to the path

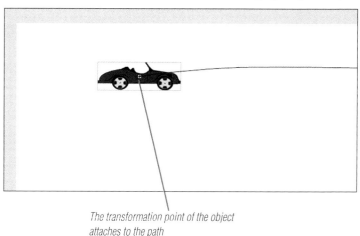

The transformation point of the object
attaches to the path

Add a motion guide to an animation

1. Click **Frame 1** on the carRoute layer.

2. Click **Insert** on the menu bar, point to **Timeline**, then click **Motion Guide**.

   The carRoute layer is indented beneath the guide layer on the timeline.

3. Click **Frame 1** of the Guide layer, click the **Pencil tool** 🖉 on the Tools panel, click the **Smooth option** S in the Options section of the Tools panel, then draw a path starting at the transformation point inside the car similar to the one shown in Figure 16.

4. Click the **Selection tool** ↖ on the Tools panel.

5. Click **Frame 1** of the carRoute layer. If the transformation point is not on the path, click the transformation point ⊕ of the car, then drag it to the beginning of the path, as shown in Figure 17.

   TIP An object is snapped to the beginning or end of a motion path when the start or end point of the motion path intersects the car's transformation point.

6. Click **Frame 40** on the carRoute layer.

7. If the car does not snap to the end of the path, click the **Selection tool** ↖ , click the transformation point ⊕ of the car, then drag it to the end of the path.

8. Play the movie.

You created a motion guide on a path and attached an animation to it.

Orient an object to the path

1. Play the movie again and notice how the car does not turn front-first in response to the turns in the path.

2. Make sure the Property inspector is displayed, then click **Frame 1** on the carRoute layer.

3. Make sure the car is selected, then click the **Orient to path check box**.

4. Play the movie.

   Notice the car is oriented front-first to the turns in the path.

You used the Property inspector to specify that the object is oriented to the path.

Alter the path

1. Click **Frame 1** on the carRoute layer.

2. Click the **Selection tool**, if necessary.

3. Point to the middle of the right curve line of the path.

4. When the pointer changes to the arc pointer , drag the line up, as shown in Figure 18.

   Your path may be different.

5. Play the movie.

You altered the motion guide path.

FIGURE 18
Dragging the line to alter the path

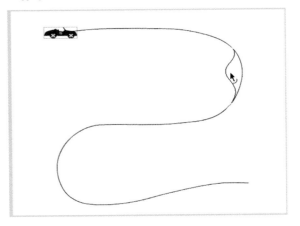

FIGURE 19

Setting the Ease value

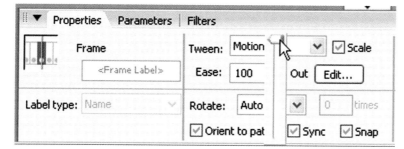

1. Play the movie and notice the speed of the car is constant.

2. Click **Frame 1** on the carRoute layer.

3. Click the **Ease list arrow** ⌄ in the Property inspector, then drag the slider up to **100**, as shown in Figure 19.

4. Play the movie and notice how the car starts out fast and decelerates as it moves toward the end of the path.

5. Click **Frame 1** on the carRoute layer.

6. Click the **Ease list arrow** ⌄ in the Property inspector, drag the slider down to **–100**, then click a blank area outside the stage.

7. Play the movie and notice how the car starts out slow and accelerates as it moves toward the end of the path.

8. Click **Control** on the menu bar, then click **Test Movie.**

9. View the movie, then close the test movie window.

10. Save your work.

You set Ease values to alter the starting and ending speed of the car.

CREATE ANIMATION EFFECTS

What You'll Do

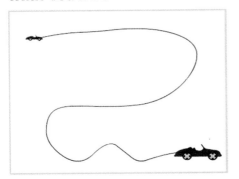

 In this lesson, you will use motion tween-ing to resize, rotate, and change the color of animated objects.

Creating Motion Animation Effects

Up to this point, you have created motion-tweened animations that cause an object to move around the stage. There are several other effects that you can create using motion tweening, including resizing, rotating, and changing the color of an object as it is in motion.

Resizing an Object Using a Motion Tween

The simplest process for resizing an object during a motion tween is to select a frame as the starting frame, draw or place an object on the stage, then create a motion tween. You can select an ending frame and resize the object using the resize handles that are displayed when you select the Free Transform tool and the Scale option on the Tools panel. The results of this process are shown in Figure 20. By moving and resizing an object, you can create the effect that it is moving away from you or toward you. If you have the object remain stationary while it is being resized, the effect is similar to zooming in or out.

Rotating an Object Using a Motion Tween

You have several options when rotating an object using a motion tween. You can cause the object to rotate clockwise or counterclockwise any number of degrees and any number of times. You can also stipulate an Ease value to cause the rotation to accelerate or decelerate. These effects can be specified using the Free Transform tool and the Rotate option on the Tools panel, adjusting settings in the Property inspector, or clicking a Transform option on the Modify menu. The Transform options include Flip Vertical and Flip Horizontal. Choosing these options causes the object to slowly flip throughout the length of the anima-tion. You can combine effects so that they occur simultaneously during the anima-tion. For example, you can have a car rotate and get smaller as it moves across the stage. The Scale and Rotate dialog box allows you to specify a percentage for scaling and a number of degrees for rotating.

Changing an Object's Color Using a Motion Tween

Macromedia Flash provides several ways in which you can alter the color of objects using a motion tween. The most basic change involves starting with one color for the object and ending with another color. The tweening process slowly changes the color across the specified frames. When the movie is played, the colors are blended as the object moves across the stage. If you start with a red color and end with a blue color, at the middle of the animation the object's color is purple with equal portions of the blue and red colors mixed together.

More sophisticated color changes can be made using the Property inspector. You can adjust the brightness; tint the colors; adjust the transparency (Alpha option); and change the red, green, and blue values of an object. One of the most popular animation effects is to cause an object to slowly fade in. You can accomplish this by motion tweening the object, setting the Alpha value to 0 (transparent) in the starting frame, and then setting it to 100 in the ending frame. To make the object fade out, just reverse the values.

Using the Onion Skin Feature

Figure 21 displays the animation using the Onion Skin feature. Normally, Macromedia Flash displays one frame of an animation sequence at a time on the stage. Turning on the Onion Skin feature allows you to view an outline of the object(s) in any number of frames. This can help in positioning animated objects on the stage. The Edit Multiple Frames feature is also turned on allowing you to view the objects in the Keyframes in a non-outline form.

FIGURE 20
Resizing an object during a motion tween

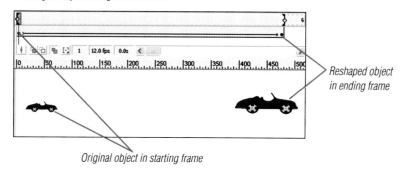

Reshaped object in ending frame

Original object in starting frame

FIGURE 21
Onion skin feature turned on

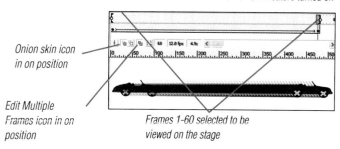

Onion skin icon in on position

Edit Multiple Frames icon in on position

Frames 1-60 selected to be viewed on the stage

Combining Various Animation Effects

Macromedia Flash allows you to combine the various motion-tween effects so that you can rotate an object as it moves across the stage, changes color, and changes size. Macromedia Flash allows you to combine motion-tweened animations to create various effects. For example, if you create an airplane object, you can apply the following aerial effects:

- enter from off stage and perform a loop;
- rotate the plane horizontally to create a barrel roll effect;
- grow smaller as it moves across the screen to simulate the effect of the plane speeding away;
- change colors on the fuselage to simulate the reflection of the sun.

Creating Timeline Effects

Macromedia Flash provides several pre-built Timeline effects, such as having an object fade-in, that allow you to create complex animations with only a few steps. You simply select an object, select an effect, then specify the settings. You can apply Timeline effects to the following objects:

- Text
- Graphics, including shapes, groups, and graphic symbols
- Bitmap images
- Button symbols

When you apply a Timeline effect to an object, Macromedia Flash creates a layer and transfers the object to the new layer. The object is placed inside the effect graphic, and all tweens and transformations required for the effect reside in the graphic on the new layer. The new layer automatically receives the same name as the effect, with a number appended that represents the order in which the effect is applied. An effect symbol is created and placed in an Effects Folder that is added to the Library panel. Also, the effect graphic is added to the Library panel.

Adding an Effect to an Object

To add an effect to an object, you select the object, then choose Timeline Effects from

FIGURE 22

The Timeline Effects options on the Insert menu

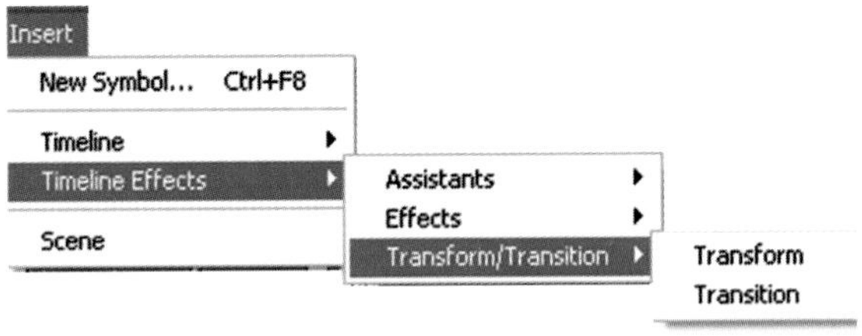

Creating Animations

the Insert menu. Three options appear that are used to display categories of effects available for the type of object you've selected, as shown in Figure 22. When you choose an effect a dialog box appears, illustrating the effect and allowing you to modify the default settings. Figure 23 shows the default settings for the Fade effect. These settings allow you to:

- Specify the duration of the effect in number of frames
- Specify the direction (In or Out)
- Specify a motion ease

When you select the object on the stage, you can view properties for the effect in the Property inspector.

Editing a Timeline Effect

To edit a Timeline effect you select the object associated with the effect on the Stage and click Edit in the Property inspector. This displays the appropriate Effects Setting dialog box.

Deleting a Timeline Effect

The context menu is used to delete Timeline effects. On the Stage, right-click (Win) or control click (Mac) the object and select Timeline Effects from the context menu, then select Remove Effect.

FIGURE 23
Default settings for the Fade In effect

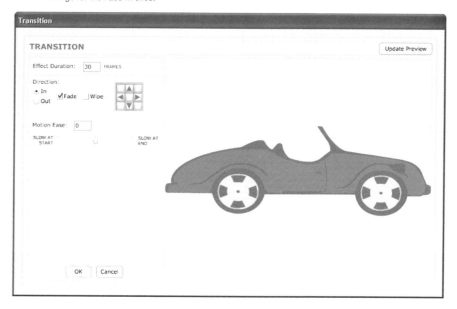

Use motion tweening to resize an object

1. Make sure that the carPath.fla movie is open.

2. Click **Frame 1** on the carRoute layer.

3. Make sure the car is selected, click the **Free Transform tool**  on the Tools panel, then click the **Scale option** in the Options section of the Tools panel.

4. Drag the upper-left corner handle inward until the car is approximately half the original size, as shown in Figure 24.

   TIP   Use the Zoom tool to enlarge the view of the car, if desired.

5. Click **Frame 40** on the carRoute layer.

6. Make sure the car is selected, then click the **Scale option** .

7. Drag the upper-right corner handle outward until the car is approximately twice the original size, as shown in Figure 25.

8. Play the movie and notice how the car is resized.

9. Save your work, then close the movie.

You used the Scale option to resize an object in a motion animation.

FIGURE 24
Using the handles to reduce the size of the car

Click and drag the handle toward the car

FIGURE 25
Using the handles to increase the size of the car

Click and drag the handle away from the car

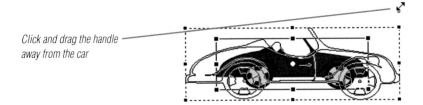

FIGURE 26

Specifying the rotate settings

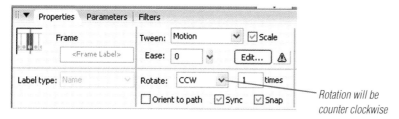

Rotation will be counter clockwise

FIGURE 27

Repositioning the motorbike

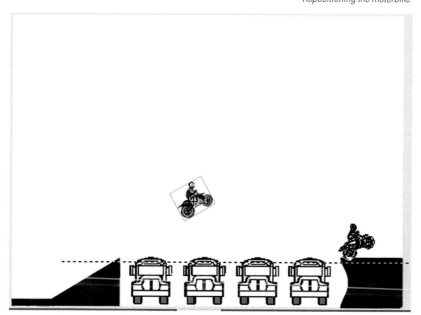

Use motion tweening to rotate an object

1. Open fl4_4.fla, then save it as **mBikeRotate**, then play the movie.

2. Click **Frame 10** on the motorBike layer.

3. Make sure the motorbike is selected, click **Insert** on the menu bar, point to **Timeline**, then click **Create Motion Tween**.

4. Click the **Rotate list arrow** on the Property inspector, click **CCW**, then verify 1 is entered into the times box, as shown in Figure 26.

5. Insert a keyframe in Frame 20 on the motorbike layer.

6. Play the movie; notice the motorbike moves forward, then rotates in place in the middle of the buses.

7. Click **Frame 20** on the motorBike layer, then drag the motorbike across the stage to the edge of the landing area, as shown in Figure 27.

8. Insert a Keyframe in Frame 21 on the motorbike layer.

9. Verify the motorbike is selected, click **Modify** on the menu bar, point to **Transform**, then click **Scale and Rotate**.

10. Type **30** for the Rotate value, then click **OK**.

11. Insert a keyframe in Frame 22, then drag the motorbike to the edge of the stage.

12. Play the movie; notice that the motorbike rotates as it moves over the buses to the landing area in the new location.

13. Save your work.

You created a motion animation and used the Property inspector to rotate the object.

Use motion tweening to change the color of an object

1. Click **Frame 20** on the motorBike layer.

2. Click the **Selection tool** ⬦ on the Tools panel, then click the motorbike to select it.

3. Click the **Color list arrow** in the Property inspector, click **Advanced**, then click the **Settings button** [Settings...].

4. Click the **xR)+ list arrow**, then drag the slider to **86**, as shown in Figure 28.

5. Click **OK**.

6. Click **Frame 1** on the timeline, then play the movie. You can see how the color slowly changes to a red shade.

> TIP Because motion tweening is performed on instances of symbols and text blocks, changing the color of a motion-tweened object affects the entire object. To make changes in individual areas of an object, you must first select the object and choose the Break Apart command from the Modify menu.

You used the Property inspector to change the color of an object as it was being animated.

FIGURE 28
Changing the color settings

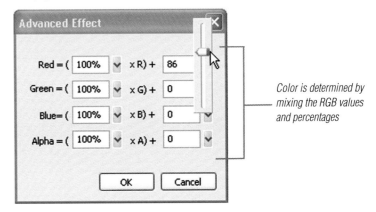

Color is determined by mixing the RGB values and percentages

FIGURE 29
Using the Onion Skin feature

Start Onion
Skin slider

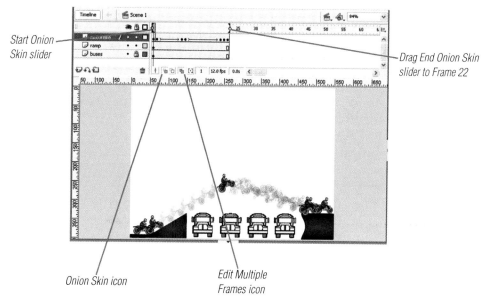

Drag End Onion Skin
slider to Frame 22

Onion Skin icon

Edit Multiple
Frames icon

1. Click **Frame 1** on the motorBike layer, then click the **Onion Skin icon** on the timeline.

2. Click the **Edit Multiple Frames icon** on the timeline.

3. Drag the **End Onion Skin slider** in the timeline to Frame 22, then compare your timeline to Figure 29.

   Each frame of the animation is visible on the stage.

4. Play the movie and notice that the animation is not affected by the onion skin feature being turned on.

5. Click the **Onion Skin icon** and the **Edit Multiple Frames icon** on the timeline to turn off these features.

6. Save and close the movie.

You displayed the animation using the Onion Skin feature, allowing you to view the object as it appears in each frame of the animation.

Create a Timeline Effect

1. Open fl4_5.fla, then save it as **carEffects**.

2. Click **Window** on the menu bar, then click **Library** to display the Library panel.

   Notice that there is only one item, a graphic named g_car, in the Library.

3. Click the **Selection tool** ⬚ on the Tools panel (if necessary), then drag the car from the Library panel to the upper-left corner of the stage, as shown in Figure 30.

4. Click **Modify** on the menu bar, then click **Break Apart**.

5. Click **Insert** on the menu bar, point to **Timeline Effects**, point to **Transform/ Transition**, then click **Transition**.

   The Transition dialog box opens allowing you to change the settings for Fade and Wipe effects. The preview shows how the default settings will affect the object on the stage, including a fade, a wipe and a duration of 30 frames.

6. Click the **Wipe check box** to turn off this effect, then click **Update Preview**. Notice that fade is the only effect.

7. Click **OK** to close the dialog box.

   A new layer was created and given the same name (Transition 1) as the effect, as shown in Figure 31. Note: the number after the word Transition may vary.

8. Play the movie.

You created a Fade in Timeline Effect.

FIGURE 30
Positioning the car on the stage

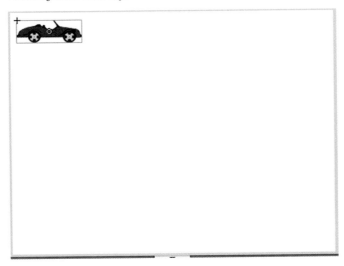

FIGURE 31
The layer name displays the effect name

Car is not visible because the fade in transition effect starts in Frame 1

FIGURE 32

The Library panel displaying the Transition Effect

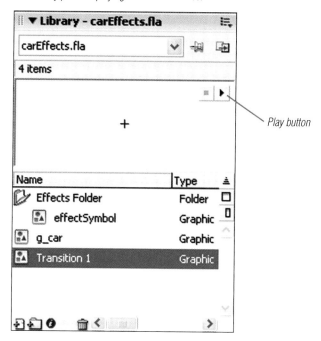

Play button

1. Double click the **Effects Folder icon** in the Library panel, then click **effectSymbol** to display the graphic symbol in the Item preview window of the Library panel.

   The effectSymbol was created and added to an Effects Folder in the Library panel when the Timeline effect was specified.

2. Click the **Transition symbol1** in the Library panel.

   The Transition graphic was created and added to the Library panel when the Timeline effect was specified. This graphic holds the effect which can be viewed in the Library panel.

3. Click the **Play button** in the Item preview window of the Library panel, as shown in Figure 32.

You viewed the effectSymbol and played the transition using the graphic within the Library panel.

Edit and remove a
Timeline Effect

1. Display the Property inspector panel, if necessary.

2. Click **Frame 30** on the timeline, click the **Selection tool** , then click the **car**.

3. Click the **Edit button** Edit... on the Properties panel to open the Transition dialog box.

4. Click the **Out option button** to change the direction.

5. Drag the **Motion Ease slider** to the right to set the Motion Ease to **100**, then compare your screen to Figure 33.

6. Click **Update Preview**, then click **OK**.

7. Play the movie.

8. Click **Frame 1** on the Timeline.

9. Right-click (Win) or control click (Mac) the car, point to **Timeline Effects**, then click **Remove Effect**.

10. Play the movie.

You edited a timeline effect using an Effect Settings dialog box, then removed the effect.

FIGURE 33
The completed Transition dialog box

Fade

Direction

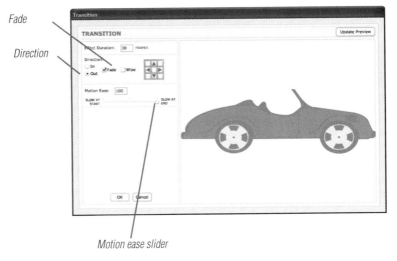

Motion ease slider

FIGURE 34
The completed Transform dialog box

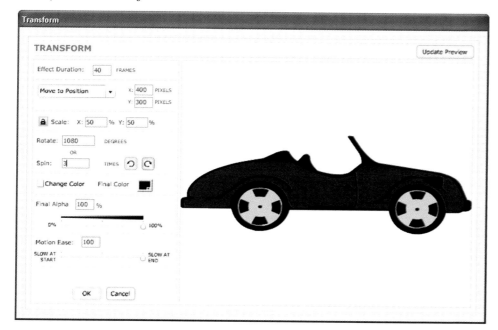

1. Click the **Selection tool** ![Selection tool] on the Tools panel, then drag a marquee around the car to select it.

2. Click **Insert** on the menu bar, point to **Timeline Effects**, point to **Transform/Transition**, then click **Transform**.

3. Change the effect duration to **40** frames.

4. Click the **Change Position by list arrow**, then click **Move to Position**.

5. Double-click **0** in the X Position text box, then type **400**.

6. Double-click **0** in the Y Position text box, then type **300**. X and Y are the coordinates (in pixels) for the position of the object on the stage. If the stage dimensions are 800x600, then 400(X-width) and 300(Y-height) would position the object in the middle of the stage.

7. Click the **Scale Lock icon** ![lock] to unlock it.

8. Double-click **100** in the X Scale text box, then type **50**.

9. Double-click **100** in the Y Scale text box, then type **50**.

10. Change the spin times to **3**.

11. Change the Motion Ease value to **100**, then compare your screen to Figure 34.

12. Click **Update Preview**, then click **OK**.

13. Play the movie, then save and close the movie.

You used the Effect Settings dialog box to apply several effects to a single object.

ANIMATE TEXT

What You'll Do

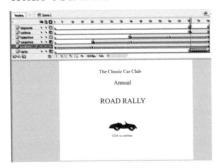

In this lesson, you will animate text by scrolling, rotating, zooming, and resizing it.

Animating Text

You can motion tween text block objects just as you do graphic objects. You can resize, rotate, reposition, and change their colors. Figure 35 shows three examples of animated text with the Onion Skin feature turned on. When the movie starts, each of the following can occur one after the other:

- The Classic Car Club text block scrolls in from the left side to the top center of the stage. This is done by positioning the text block off the stage and creating a motion-tweened animation that moves it to the stage.
- The Annual text block appears and rotates five times. This occurs after you create the Annual text block, position it in the middle of the stage under the heading, and use the Property inspector to specify a clockwise rotation that repeats five times.

- The ROAD RALLY text block slowly zooms out and appears in the middle of the stage. This occurs after you create the text block and use the Free Transform tool handles to resize it to a small block. You use the Property inspector to specify a transparent value. Finally, the text block is resized to a larger size at the end of the animation.

Once you create a motion animation using a text block, the text block becomes a symbol and you are unable to edit individual characters within the text block. You can, however, edit the symbol as a whole.

FIGURE 35
Three examples of animated text

Text scrolls from off the stage to the stage

The Classic Car Club

The Classic Car Club

Text rotates

Annual

ROAD RALLY

Text zooms

Select, copy, and paste frames

1. Open frameAn.fla (the file you created earlier in this chapter), then save the movie as **textAn**.

2. Click **Frame 10** on the carGo layer, press and hold **[Shift]**, then click **Frame 1** to select all the frames, as shown in Figure 36.

3. Click **Edit** on the menu bar, point to **Timeline**, then click **Cut Frames**.

4. Click **Frame 71** on the carGo layer.

5. Click **Edit** on the menu bar, point to **Timeline**, then click **Paste Frames**.

6. Play the movie, then save your work.

7. Click **Frame 1** of the carGo layer.

You selected frames, and moved them from one location on the timeline to another location on the timeline.

FIGURE 36
Selecting frames

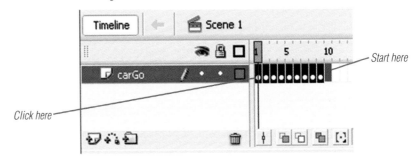

Creating Animations

FIGURE 37

Positioning the Text tool pointer outside the stage

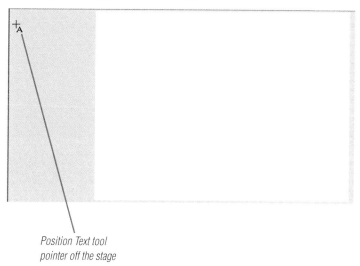

Position Text tool pointer off the stage

FIGURE 38

Positioning the text block

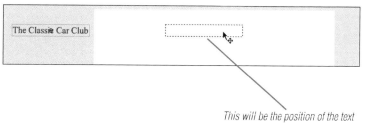

This will be the position of the text block at the end of the animation

Create animated text

1. Insert a new layer, then name it **scrollText**.

2. Click **Frame 1** on the scrollText layer, then verify that the Property inspector is displayed.

3. Click the **Text tool A** on the Tools panel, click the ⁺ₐ pointer outside the stage in the upper-left corner of the workspace, as shown in Figure 37, then click to display a text box.

4. Click the **Font list arrow** in the Property inspector, then click **Times New Roman**, if necessary.

5. Click the **Font Size list arrow** in the Property inspector, then drag the slider to **20**.

6. Click the **Text (fill) color swatch** ▉, click the **blue color swatch** on the left column of the color palette, then click the **Left Align button** ≡ in the Property inspector.

7. Type **The Classic Car Club**.

8. Click the **Selection tool** ▶ on the Tools panel, click the **text block**, click **Insert** on the menu bar, point to **Timeline**, then click **Create Motion Tween**.

9. Insert a keyframe in Frame 20 on the scrollText layer.

10. Drag the text block horizontally to the top center of the stage, as shown in Figure 38.

11. Insert a keyframe in Frame 80 on the scrollText layer.

12. Play the movie.

    The text moves to center stage from offstage left.

You created a text block object and applied a motion tween animation to it.

Create rotating text

1. Insert a new layer, then name it **rotateText**.

2. Insert a keyframe in Frame 21 on the rotateText layer.

3. Click the **Text tool A** on the Tools panel, position the pointer beneath the "a" in "Classic," then click to display a blank text box.

4. Click the **Font Size list arrow** on the Property inspector, drag the slider to **24**, click in the new text box, type **Annual**, then compare your image to Figure 39.

5. Click the **Selection tool** ⬉ on the Tools panel, click **Insert** on the menu bar, point to **Timeline**, then click **Create Motion Tween**.

6. Click **Frame 21** on the rotateText layer, click the **Rotate list arrow** in the Property inspector, click **CW**, then type **2** in the times text box.

7. Insert keyframes in Frames 40 and 80 on the rotateText layer.

8. Play the movie.

   The Annual text rotates clockwise two times.

You inserted a new layer, created a rotating text block, and used the Property inspector to rotate the text box.

FIGURE 39
Positioning the Annual text block

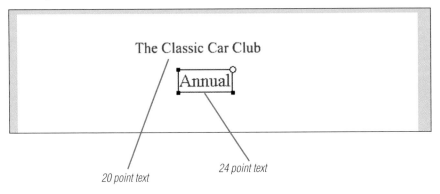

The Classic Car Club

Annual

20 point text

24 point text

FIGURE 40
Using the Text Tool to type ROAD RALLY

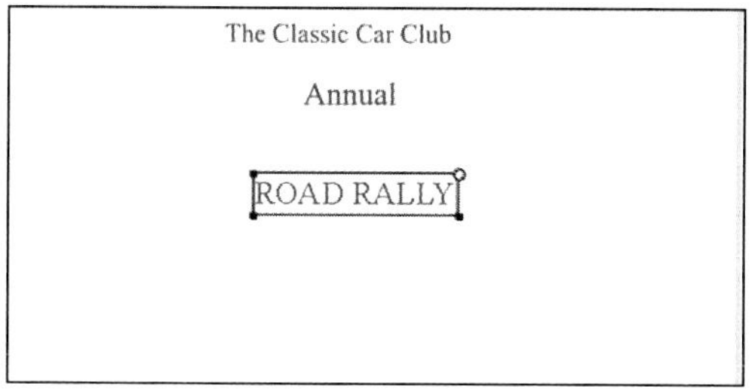

The Classic Car Club

Annual

ROAD RALLY

FIGURE 41
Resizing and repositioning the text block

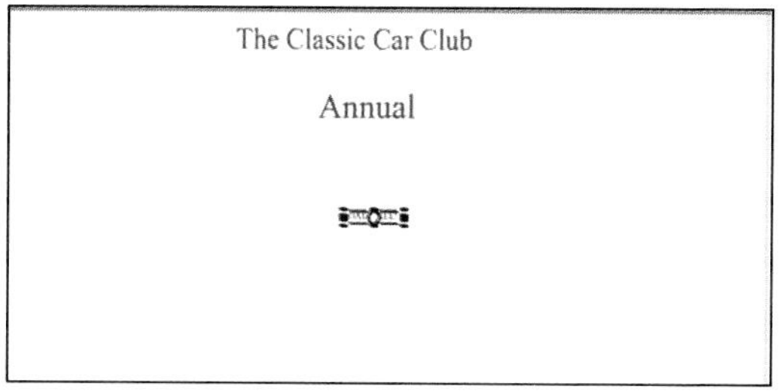

The Classic Car Club

Annual

FIGURE 42
The enlarged text block

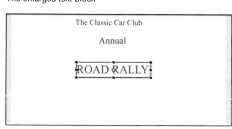

The Classic Car Club

Annual

ROAD RALLY

1. Insert a new layer, name it **fadeinText**, then insert a keyframe in Frame 40 on the fadeinText layer.

2. Click the **Text tool** **A** on the Tools panel, position the pointer beneath the Annual text box aligning with the "T" in "The", then type **ROAD RALLY**, as shown in Figure 40.

3. Click the **Free Transform tool** ⊡ on the Tools panel, then click the **Scale option** ⊡ in the Options section.

4. Drag the upper-left corner handle ⌐ inward to resize the text block, then position the text block, as shown in Figure 41.

5. Click **Insert** on the menu bar, point to **Timeline**, then click **Create Motion Tween**.

6. Click the **Color list arrow** on the Property inspector, click **Alpha**, click the **Alpha Amount list arrow**, then drag the slider to **0**.

7. Insert a keyframe in Frame 60 on the fadeinText layer, then click the object.

8. Click the **Alpha Amount list arrow** in the Property inspector, then drag the slider to **100**.

9. Click the **ROAD RALLY** text block, click the **Free Transform tool** ⊡, click the **Scale option** ⊡, drag the upper-left corner handle ⌐ outward to resize the text block, then position it, as shown in Figure 42.

10. Insert a keyframe in Frame 80 on the fadeinText layer.

11. Play the movie.

You created a motion animation that caused a text block to fade in and zoom out.

Make a text block into a button

1. Insert a new layer, then name it **continue**.

   TIP Scroll up the timeline to view the new layer.

2. Insert a keyframe in Frame 71 on the continue layer.

3. Click the **Text tool A** on the Tools panel, position the **Text Tool pointer** ⁺A beneath the back wheel of the car, then type **Click to continue**.

4. Drag the pointer over the text to select it, click the **Font Size list arrow** in the Property inspector, drag the slider to **12**, click the **Selection tool** ▶ on the Tools panel, then compare your image to Figure 43.

5. Verify that the text box is selected, click **Modify** on the menu bar, click **Convert to Symbol**, type **b_continue** in the Name text box, click the **Type Button option button** (if necessary), then click **OK**.

6. Click the **Selection tool** ▶ (if necessary), then double-click the **text block** to edit the button.

7. Insert a keyframe in the Over frame, click the **Fill Color tool** ◆⬚ on the Tools panel, then click the **black color swatch** in the left column of the color palette.

8. Insert a keyframe in the Down frame, click the **Fill Color tool** ◆⬚, then click the **bright green color swatch** in the left column of the color palette.

9. Insert a keyframe in the Hit frame, click the **Rectangle tool** ⬚ on the Tools panel, then draw a rectangle that covers the text block and the car, as shown in Figure 44.

10. Click **Scene 1** above the Timeline layers to return to the main timeline.

You made the text block into a button.

FIGURE 43
Adding a button

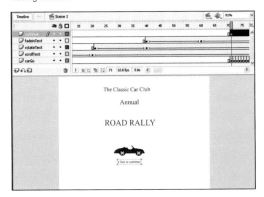

FIGURE 44
The rectangle that defines the hit area

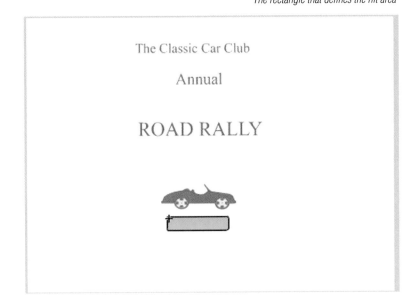

FIGURE 45

Add a play action

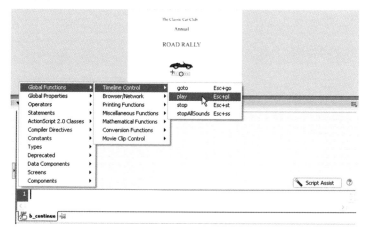

1. Display the Actions panel.

2. Click the **Selection tool** on the Tools panel, then click the **continue button** on the stage.

3. Click the **ScriptAssist button** to turn it on, then verify the b_continue button symbol is displayed in the lower left corner of the Actions panel.

4. Click the **Add a new item to the script button** in the Script Assist window, point to **Global Functions**, point to **Timeline Control**, then click **play**, as shown in Figure 45.

5. Insert a new layer, name it **stopmovie**, then insert a keyframe in Frame 71.

6. Click the **Add a new item to the script button** in the Script Assist window, point to **Global Functions**, point to **Timeline Control**, then click **stop**.

7. Click **Control** on the menu bar, then click **Test Movie**.

   The movie plays the animated text blocks, then plays the animated car when you click the ActionScript text.

8. Close the test movie window, then save and close the movie.

9. Exit Flash.

You inserted a play button and added a stop action to it.

Create a frame animation.

1. Start Flash, openfl4_6.fla, then save it as **skillsdemo4**.
2. Add a background color of **#006666**.
3. Insert a keyframe in Frame 22 on the v-ball layer.
4. Resize the object to approximately one-fourth its original size.
5. Insert a keyframe in Frame 23 on the v-ball layer.
6. Resize the object back to approximately its original size.
7. Insert a keyframe in Frame 24 on the v-ball layer, then drag the object to the upper-left corner of the stage.
8. Insert a keyframe in Frame 25 on the v-ball layer, then drag the object to the lower-left corner of the stage.
9. Insert a keyframe in Frame 26 on the v-ball layer, then drag the object to the upper-right corner of the stage.
10. Insert a keyframe in Frame 27 on the v-ball layer, then drag the object to the lower-right corner of the stage.
11. Change the movie frame rate to 3 frames per second, then play the movie.
12. Change the movie frame rate to 12 frames per second, play the movie, then save your work.

Create a motion-tweened animation.

1. Insert a new layer and name it **ballAn**.
2. Insert a keyframe in Frame 28 on the ballAn layer.
3. Display the Library panel, then drag the g_vball graphic symbol to the lower-left corner of the stage.
4. Make sure the object is selected, then create a Motion Tween.
5. Insert a keyframe in Frame 60 on the ballAn layer.
6. Drag the object to the lower-right corner of the stage.
7. Play the movie, then save your work.

Create a motion guide.

1. Click Frame 28 on the ballAn layer.
2. Insert a Motion Guide layer.
3. Use the Pencil tool to draw a motion path in the shape of an arc, then alter the path to resemble Figure 46.
4. Attach the object to the left side of the path in Frame 28 on the ballAn layer.
5. Attach the object to the right side of the path in Frame 60 on the ballAn layer.
6. Use the Property inspector to orient the object to the path.
7. Play the movie, then save your work.

Accelerate the animated object.

1. Click Frame 28 on the ballAn layer.
2. Use the Property inspector to change the Ease value to **–100**.
3. Play the movie, then save your work.

Create motion animation effects.

1. Click Frame 60 on the ballAn layer, and use the Free Transform tool and the Scale tool option handles to resize the object to approximately one-fourth its original size.
2. Click Frame 28 on the ballAn layer, and use the Property inspector to specify a clockwise rotation that plays five times.
3. Play the movie.
4. Select Frame 60 on the ballAn layer, then select the ball.
5. Use the Advanced Color option in the Property inspector to change the color of the object to green by specifying **143** as the green value.
6. Play the movie, then save your work.

Animate text.

1. Click the Guide: ballAn layer, then insert a new layer and name it **heading**.
2. Click Frame 1 on the heading layer.
3. Use the Text tool to type **Having fun with a** in a location off the top-left of the stage.
4. Change the text to Arial, 20 point, gray, and boldface.
5. Insert a motion tween.
6. Insert a keyframe in Frame 10 on the heading layer.
7. Drag the text to the top center of the stage.
8. Insert a keyframe in Frame 60 on the heading layer.
9. Play the movie and save your work.
10. Insert a new layer and name it **zoom**.
11. Insert a keyframe in Frame 11 on the zoom layer.
12. Use the Text Tool to type **Volleyball** below the heading, then center it as needed.

13. Create a motion tween.
14. Insert a keyframe in Frame 20 on the zoom layer.
15. Click Frame 11 on the zoom layer and select the text block.
16. Use the Property inspector to set the Alpha color option to **0**.

17. Resize the text block to **7** pixels in height in Frame 11 on the zoom layer.
18. Select Frame 20 on the zoom layer, and resize the text block to approximate the size shown in Figure 46.

19. Insert a keyframe in Frame 60 of the zoom layer.
20. Test the movie, then save your work.
21. Exit Flash.

FIGURE 46
Completed Skills Review

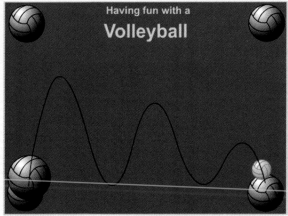

The Ultimate Tours travel company has asked you to design several sample animations for their Web site. Figure 47 shows a sample homepage and the Cruises screen. Using these (or one of the homepages you created in Chapter 3) as a guide, complete the following:

For the Ultimate Tours homepage:

1. Open ultimatetours3.fla (the file you created in Chapter 3 Project Builder 1) and save it as **ultimatetours4**.
2. Animate the heading **Ultimate Tours** so that it zooms out from a transparent text block.
3. After the heading appears, make the subheading **We Specialize in Exotic Adventures** appear.
4. Make each of the buttons (Treks, Tours, Cruises) scroll from the bottom of the stage to their positions on the stage. Stagger the buttons so that each one scrolls after the other.
5. Make the logo text appear.

6. Assign a stop action after the homepage appears.
7. Assign a go-to action to the Cruises button to jump to the frame that has the Cruises screen.
8. Add a Cruises screen, then display the heading, subheading, and logo.
9. To the Library panel, import the graphic file ship.gif from the drive and folder where your Data Files are stored, then rename the graphic file **g_ship**.
10. Create a motion-tweened animation that moves the ship across the screen.
11. Add a motion path that has a dip in it.
12. Attach the boat to the motion path, and orient it to the path.

13. Add a new layer, name it **cruise placeholder**, then add three placeholders (Cruise 1, Cruise 2, Cruise 3) to the last frame of the timeline.
14. Add the Home button.
15. Test the movie, then compare your movie to the example shown in Figure 47.

FIGURE 47
Sample completed Project Builder 1

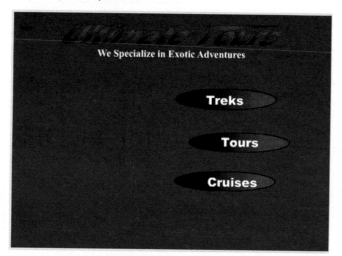

You have been asked to develop a Web site for the school's summer basketball camp. The camp caters to kids aged 6 to 12 years old. Participants are grouped by ability and given instruction on the fundamentals of basketball such as dribbling, passing, and shooting; the rules of the game; teamwork; and sportsmanship. A tournament is played at the end of the two-week camp.

Include the following on the Web site:

1. An initial screen with information about the camp (you provide the camp name, dates, and so on).

2. A black border around the stage, and add a colored background.

3. A frame-by-frame animation.

4. A motion-tweened animation.

5. One or more animations that has an object(s) change location on the stage, rotate, change size, and change color.

6. One or more animations that has a text block(s) change location on the stage, rotate, change size, change color, zoom in or out, and fade in or out.

7. An animation that uses a motion guide.

8. An animation that changes the Ease setting.

9. Save the movie as **summerBB4**, then compare your image to the example shown in Figure 48.

FIGURE 48
Sample completed Project Builder 2

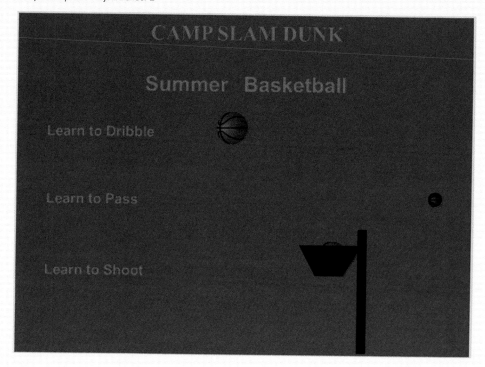

Figure 49 shows a Web site for kids. Study the figure and complete the following. For each question, indicate how you determined your answer.

1. Connect to the Internet, go to *www.course.com*, navigate to the page for this book, click the Online Companion link, then click the link for this chapter.
2. Open a document in a word processor or open a new Macromedia Flash document, save the file as **dpc4**, then answer the following questions. (*Hint*: Use the Text tool in Macromedia Flash.)
   - What seems to be the purpose of this site?
   - Who would be the target audience?
   - How might a frame animation be used in this site?
   - How might a motion-tweened animation be used?
   - How might a motion guide be used?
   - How might motion animation effects be used?
   - How might the text be animated?

FIGURE 49
Design Project

Creating Animations

This is a continuation of the Portfolio Project in Chapter 3, which is the development of a personal portfolio. The homepage has several categories, including the following:

- Personal data
- Contact information
- Previous employment
- Education
- Samples of your work

In this project, you will create several buttons for the sample animations screen and link them to the animations.

1. Open portfolio3.fla (the file you created in Portfolio Project, Chapter 3) and save it as **portfolio4**.
2. Display the Sample Animation screen and change the heading to Sample Animations.
3. Add layers and create buttons for the tweened animation, frame-by-frame animation, motion path animation, and animated text.
4. Create a tweened animation or use the passing cars animation from Chapter 3, and link it to the appropriate button on the Sample Animations screen.

5. Create a frame-by-frame animation, and link it to the appropriate button on the Sample Animations screen.
6. Create a motion path animation, and link it to the appropriate button on the Sample Animations screen.
7. Create several text animations, using scrolling, rotating, and zooming; link them to the appropriate button on the Sample Animations screen.

8. Add a layer and create a Home button that links the Sample Animations screen to the Home screen.
9. Create frame actions that cause the movie to return to the Sample Animations screen after each animation has been played.
10. Test the movie.
11. Save your work, then compare sample pages from your movie to the example shown for two of the screens in Figure 50.

FIGURE 50
Sample completed Portfolio Project

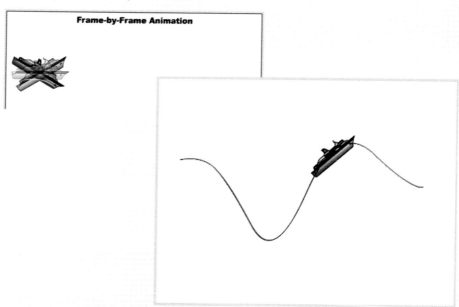

5

CREATING SPECIAL EFFECTS

chapter

1. Create shape-tweened animations.

2. Create a mask effect.

3. Add sound.

4. Add scenes.

5. Create an animated navigation bar.

5 CREATING SPECIAL EFFECTS

Introduction

Now that you are familiar with the basics of Macromedia Flash, you can begin to apply some of the special features that can enhance a movie. Special effects can provide variety and add interest to a movie, as well as draw the viewer's attention to a location or event in the movie. One type of special effect is an animation that changes the shape of an object. This can be done using the shape tween feature of Flash. Another, related, type of special effect is morphing. The process of morphing makes one shape appear to change into another shape over time, such as an airplane changing into a hot air balloon as it flies across the sky. Another special effect is a spotlight that highlights an area(s) of the movie or reveals selected contents on the stage. You can use sound effects to enhance a movie by creating moods and dramatizing events. Another type of special effect is an animated navigation bar. For example, one that causes a drop down menu when the user rolls over a button. This effect can be created using masks and invisible buttons.

In addition to working with special effects, you now have experience in developing several movies around one theme, Classic Car Club, and are ready to incorporate these individual movies into a single movie with several scenes. Scenes provide a way to organize a large movie that has several parts, such as a Web site.

Tools You'll Use

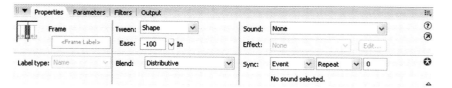

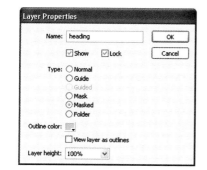

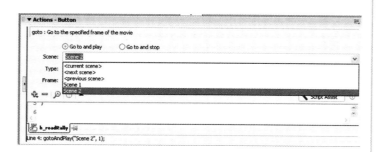

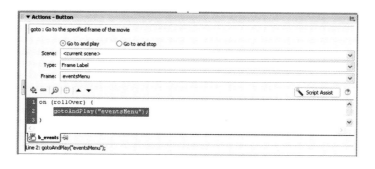

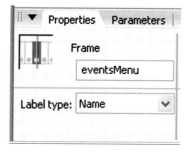

CREATE SHAPE TWEEN
ANIMATIONS

What You'll Do

 In this lesson, you will create a shape-tweened animation and specify shape hints.

Shape Tweening

In Chapter 4, you learned that you can use motion tweening to change the shape of an object. You accomplish this by selecting the Free Transform tool and then dragging the handles. This process allows you to resize and skew the object. While this is easy and allows you to include motion along with the change in shape, there are two drawbacks. First, you are limited in the type of changes (resizing and skewing) that can be made to the shape of an object. Second, you must work with the same object throughout the animation. When you use **shape tweening**, however, you can have an animation change the shape of an object to any form you desire, and you can include two objects in the animation with two different shapes. As with motion tweening, you can use shape tweening to change other properties of an object, such as the color, location, and size.

Using Shape Tweening to Create a Morphing Effect

Morphing involves changing one object into another, sometimes unrelated, object.

For example, you could turn a robot into a man, or turn a football into a basketball. The viewer sees the transformation as a series of incremental changes. In Macromedia Flash, the first object appears on the stage and changes into the second object as the movie plays. The number of frames included from the beginning to the end of this shape-tweened animation determines how quickly the morphing effect takes place. The first frame in the animation displays the first object and the last frame displays the second object. The in-between frames display the different shapes that are created as the first object changes into the second object.

When working with shape tweening you need to keep the following points in mind:

- Shape tweening can be applied only to editable graphics. To apply shape tweening to instances, groups, symbols, text blocks, or bitmaps, you can use the Break Apart command on the Modify menu to break apart an object and make it editable. When you break apart an instance of a symbol, it is no longer linked to the original symbol.

- You can shape tween more than one object at a time as long as all the objects are on the same layer. However, if the shapes are complex and/or if they involve movement in which the objects cross paths, the results may be unpredictable.
- You can use shape tweening to move an object in a straight line, but other options, such as rotating an object, are not available.
- You can use the settings in the Property inspector to set options (such as acceleration or deceleration) for a shape tween.
- Shape hints can be used to control more complex shape changes.

Properties Panel Options

Figure 1 shows the Property inspector options for a shape tween. The options allow you to adjust several aspects of the animation, as described below.

- Adjust the rate of change between frames to create a more natural appearance during the transition by setting an ease value. Setting the value between -1 and -100 will begin the shape tween gradually and accelerate it toward the end of the animation. Setting the value between 1 and 100 will begin the shape tween rapidly and decelerate it toward the end of the animation. By default, the rate of change is set to 0, which causes a constant rate of change between frames.
- Choose a blend option. The Distributive option creates an animation in which the in-between shapes are smoother and more irregular. The Angular option preserves the corners and straight lines and works only with objects that have these features. If the objects do not have corners, Macromedia Flash will default to the Distributive option.

Shape Hints

You can use shape hints to control the shape's transition appearance during animation. Shape hints allow you to specify a location on the beginning object that corresponds to a location on the ending object. Figure 2 shows two shape animations of the same objects, one using shape hints and the other not using shape hints. The figure also shows how the object being reshaped appears in one of the in-between frames. Notice that with the shape hints the object in the in-between frame is more recognizable.

FIGURE 1
The Property inspector options for a shape tween

FIGURE 2
Two shape animations: with and without shape hints

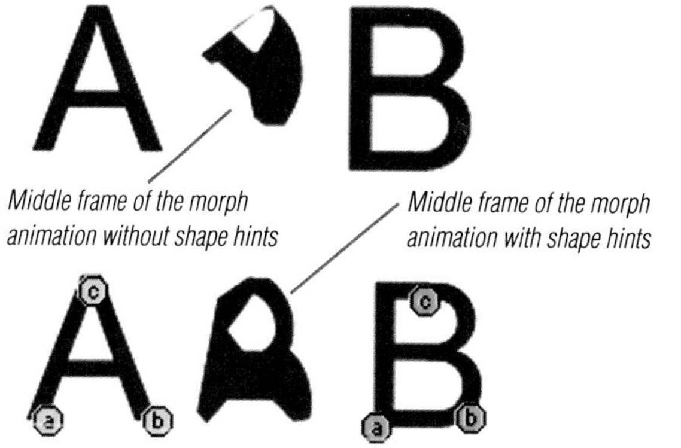

Middle frame of the morph animation without shape hints

Middle frame of the morph animation with shape hints

Create a shape tween animation

1. Open fl5_1.fla from the drive and folder where your Data Files are stored, then save it as **antiqueCar**.

2. Hide all panels, open the Tools and Property inspector panels, then change the view to Fit in Window.

3. Click **Frame 30** on the shape layer, then press **[F6]** to insert a keyframe.

4. Click a blank area outside the stage to deselect the car.

5. Point to the right side of the top of the car, then use the arc pointer to drag the car top to the shape, as shown in Figure 3.

6. Click anywhere on the shape layer between Frames 1 and 30.

7. Make sure the Property inspector is displayed, click the **Tween list arrow**, then click **Shape**.

8. Click **Frame 1** on the shape layer, then play the movie.

9. Click **Frame 30** on the shape layer.

10. Click the **Selection tool** (if necessary) on the Tools panel, then drag a marquee around the car to select it.

11. Drag the car to the right side of the stage.

12. Play the movie, then save and close it.

You created a shape-tweened animation, causing an object to change shape as it moves over several frames.

FIGURE 3
The reshaped object

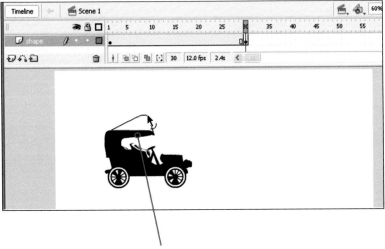

Drag up from here

Creating Special Effects

FIGURE 4

Positioning the car instance on the stage

Line up both cars so it
appears that there is
only one car

1. Open fl5_2.fla from the drive and folder where your Data Files are stored, then save it as **morphCar**.
2. Click **Frame 40** on the morph layer.
3. Click **Insert** on the menu bar, point to **Timeline**, then click **Blank Keyframe**.

    TIP Inserting a blank keyframe prevents the object in the preceding keyframe from automatically being inserted into the blank frame.

4. Click the **Edit Multiple Frames icon** 🖼 on the timeline.

    Turning on the Edit Multiple Frames feature will allow you to align the two objects to be morphed.

5. Open the Library panel.
6. Drag the **g_antiqueCarTopDown graphic** symbol from the Library panel directly on top of the car on the stage, as shown in Figure 4.

    TIP Use the arrow keys to move the object in small increments.

7. Make sure that the **g_antiqueCarTopDown** object is selected, click **Modify** on the menu bar, then click **Break Apart**.
8. Click the **Edit Multiple Frames icon** 🖼 to turn off the feature.
9. Click anywhere between Frames 1 and 40 on the morph layer, click the **Tween list arrow** ⌄ on the Property inspector, then click **Shape**.
10. Click **Frame 1** on the timeline, then play the movie.

    The first car morphs into the second car.

11. Save the movie.

You created a morphing effect, causing one object to change into another.

Adjust the rate of change in a shape-tweened animation

1. Click **Frame 40** on the morph layer.

2. Click the **Selection tool** ▸ (if necessary) on the Tools panel, then drag a marquee around the car to select it.

3. Drag the **car** to the right side of the stage.

4. Click **Frame 1** on the morph layer.

5. Click the **Ease list arrow** on the Property inspector, then drag the slider down to **–100**, as shown in Figure 5.

6. Play the movie.

   The car starts out slow and speeds up as the morphing process is completed.

7. Repeat Steps 4 and 5, but change the Ease value to **100**.

8. Click **Frame 1** on the timeline, then play the movie.

   The car starts out fast and slows down as the morphing process is completed.

9. Save your work, then close the movie.

You added motion to a shape-tweened animation and changed the Ease values.

FIGURE 5
Changing the Ease value for the morph

FIGURE 6
Positioning a shape hint

FIGURE 7
Adding shape hints

FIGURE 8
Matching shape hints

1. Open fl5_3.fla from the drive and folder where your Data Files are stored, then save it as **shapeHints**.

2. Play the movie and notice how the L morphs into a Z.

3. Click **Frame 15** on the timeline, the midpoint of the animation, then notice the shape.

4. Click **Frame 1** on the hints layer to display the first object.

5. Make sure the object is selected, click **Modify** on the menu bar, point to **Shape**, then click **Add Shape Hint**.

6. Drag the **Shape Hint icon** to the location shown in Figure 6.

7. Repeat Steps 5 and 6 to set a second and third Shape Hint icon, as shown in Figure 7.

8. Click **Frame 30** on the hints layer. The shape hints are stacked on top of each other.

9. Drag the **Shape Hint icons**  to match Figure 8.

10. Click **Frame 15** on the hints layer, then notice how the object is more recognizable now that the shape hints have been added.

11. Click **Frame 1** on the timeline, then play the movie.

12. Save your work, then close the movie.

You added shape hints to a morph animation.

CREATE A
MASK EFFECT

What You'll Do

Cla ssi Car lub

 In this lesson, you will apply a mask effect.

Understanding Mask Layers

A **mask layer** allows you to cover up the objects on one or more layers and, at the same time, create a window through which you can view various objects on the other layer. You can determine the size and shape of the window and specify whether it moves around the stage. Moving the window around the stage can create effects such as a spotlight that highlights certain contents on the stage, drawing the viewer's attention to a specific location. Because the window can move around the stage, you can use a mask layer to reveal only the area of the stage and the objects you want the viewer to see.

You need at least two layers on the timeline when you are working with a mask layer. One layer, called the mask layer, contains the window object through which you view the objects on the second layer below. The second layer, called the masked layer, contains the object(s) that are viewed through the window. Figure 9 shows how a mask layer works: The top part of the figure shows the mask

layer with the window in the shape of a circle. The next part of the figure shows the layer to be masked. The last part of the figure shows the results of applying the mask. Figure 9 illustrates the simplest use of a mask layer. In most cases, you want to have other objects appear on the stage and have the mask layer affect only a certain portion of the stage.

Following is the process for using a mask layer:

- Select an original layer that will become the masked layer—it contains the objects that you want to display through the mask layer window.
- Insert a new layer above the masked layer that will become the mask layer. A mask layer always masks the layer(s) immediately below it.
- Draw a filled shape, such as a circle, or create an instance of a symbol that will become the window on the mask layer. Macromedia Flash will ignore bitmaps, gradients, transparency colors, and line styles on a mask layer. On a mask layer, filled areas become

transparent and non-filled areas become opaque.

- Select the new layer and open the Layer Properties dialog box using the Timeline option from the Modify menu. Then select Mask. Macromedia Flash converts the layer to become the mask layer.

- Select the original layer and open the Layer Properties dialog box after selecting the Layer command on the Modify menu, then choose Masked. Macromedia Flash converts the layer to become the masked layer.
- Lock both the mask and masked layers.
- To mask additional layers: Drag an existing layer beneath the mask layer,

or create a new layer beneath the mask layer and use the Layer Properties dialog box to convert it to a masked layer.

- To unlink a masked layer: Drag it above the mask layer, or select it and select Normal from the Layer Properties dialog box.

FIGURE 9
A mask layer with a window

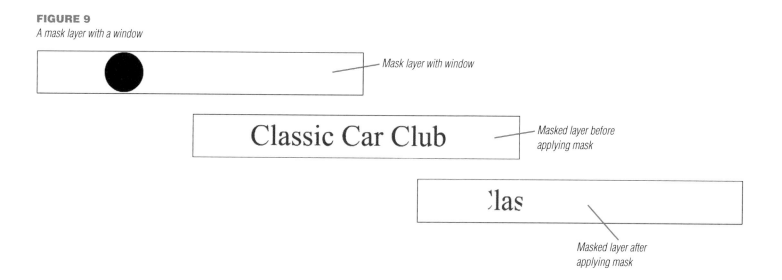

Mask layer with window

Classic Car Club

Masked layer before applying mask

'las

Masked layer after applying mask

Create a mask layer

1. Open fl5_4.fla, then save it as **classicCC**.

2. Insert a new layer, name it **mask**, then click **Frame 1** of the mask layer.

3. Click the **Oval tool** ○ on the Tools panel, click the **Stroke Color tool** ✐ ☐ on the Tools panel, then click the **No Stroke icon** ☑ on the top row of the color palette.

4. Click the **Fill Color tool** 🖌 ☐ on the Tools panel, then click the black color swatch in the left column of the color palette.

5. Draw the circle shown in Figure 10, click the **Selection tool** ▶ on the Tools panel, draw a marquee around the circle to select it, click **Insert** on the menu bar, point to **Timeline**, then click **Create Motion Tween**.

6. Insert a keyframe in Frame 40 on the mask layer, then drag the circle to the position shown in Figure 11.

7. Click the **mask layer** on the timeline to select it, click **Modify** on the menu bar, point to **Timeline**, then click **Layer Properties**.

8. Verify that the **Show check box** is selected in the Name section, click the **Lock check box** to select it, click the **Mask option button** in the Type section, then click **OK**.

   The mask layer has a shaded mask icon next to it on the timeline.

9. Play the movie from Frame 1 and notice how the circle object covers the text in the heading layer as it moves across the stage.

You created a mask layer containing an oval object that moves across the stage.

FIGURE 10
Object to be used as the window on a mask layer

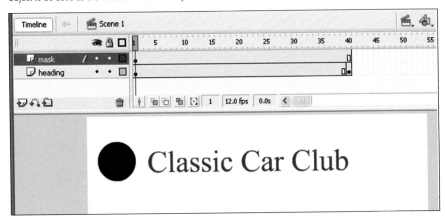

FIGURE 11
Repositioning the circle

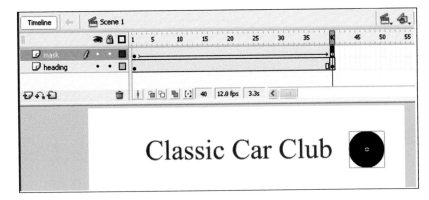

Creating Special Effects

FIGURE 12

The completed Layer Properties dialog box

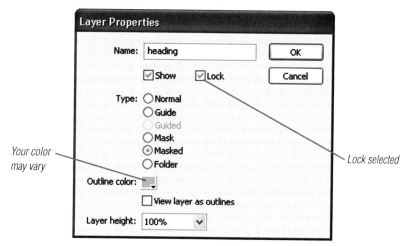

*Your color
may vary*

Lock selected

Create a masked layer

1. Click the **heading layer** to select it, click **Modify** on the menu bar, point to **Timeline**, then click **Layer Properties** to open the Layer Properties dialog box.

2. Verify that the **Show check box** is selected in the Name section, click the **Lock check box** to select it, click the **Masked option button** in the Type section, compare your dialog box to Figure 12, then click **OK**.

   The heading layer appears indented and has a shaded masked icon next to it on the timeline.

3. Play the movie and notice how the circle object acts as a window to display the text on the heading layer.

4. Save your work, then close the movie.

You used the Layer Properties dialog box to create a masked layer.

ADD
SOUND

What You'll Do

 In this lesson, you will add sound to an animation.

Incorporating Animation and Sound

Sound can be extremely useful in a Macromedia Flash movie. Sounds are often the only effective way to convey an idea, elicit an emotion, dramatize a point, and provide feedback to a user's action, such as clicking a button. How would you describe in words or show in an animation the sound a whale makes? Think about how chilling it is to hear the footsteps on the stairway of a haunted house. Consider how useful it is to hear the pronunciation of "Buenos Dias" as you are studying Spanish. All types of sounds can be incorporated into a Macromedia Flash movie: for example, CD-quality music that might be used as background for a movie; narrations that help explain what the user is seeing; various sound effects, such as a car horn beeping; and recordings of special events, such as a presidential speech or a rock concert.

Following is the process for adding a sound to a movie:

- Import a sound file into the movie; Macromedia Flash places the sound into the movie's Library.
- Create a new layer.
- Select the desired frame in the new layer and drag the sound symbol to the stage.

You can place more than one sound file on a layer, and you can place sounds on layers with other objects. However, it is recommended that you place each sound on a separate layer as though it were a sound channel. In Figure 13, the sound layer shows a wave pattern that extends from Frame 1 to Frame 14. The wave pattern gives some indication of the volume of the sound at any particular frame. The higher spikes in the pattern indicate a louder sound. The wave pattern also gives some indication of the pitch. The denser the wave pattern, the lower the pitch. You can alter the sound by adding or removing frames.

However, removing frames may create undesired effects. It is best to make changes to a sound file using a sound-editing program.

You can use options in the Property inspector, as shown in Figure 14, to synchronize a sound to an event—such as clicking a button—and to specify special effects—such as fade in and fade out. You can import the following sound file formats into Macromedia Flash:

- WAV (Windows only)
- AIFF (Macintosh only)
- MP3 (Windows or Macintosh)

If you have QuickTime 4 or later installed on your computer, you can import these additional sound file formats:

- AIFF (Windows or Macintosh)
- Sound Designer II (Macintosh only)
- Sound Only QuickTime Movies (Windows or Macintosh)
- Sun AU (Windows or Macintosh)
- System 7 Sounds (Macintosh only)
- WAV (Windows or Macintosh)

FIGURE 13
A sound symbol displayed on the timeline

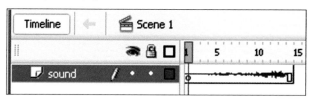

FIGURE 14
The sound options in the Property inspector

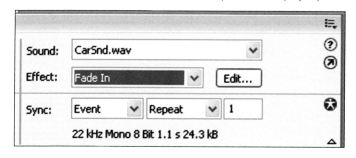

Add sound to a movie

1. Open fl5_5.fla, then save it as **rallySnd**.

2. Play the movie and notice that there is no sound.

3. Click the **stopmovie layer**, insert a new layer, then name it **carSnd**.

4. Insert a keyframe in Frame 72 on the carSnd layer.

5. Click **File** on the menu bar, point to **Import**, then click **Import to Library**.

6. Use the Import to Library dialog box to navigate to the drive and folder where your Data Files are stored, click the **CarSnd.wav file**, then click **Open** (Win) or **Import to Library** (Mac).

7. Open the Library Panel, if necessary.

8. Click **Frame 72** of the CarSnd layer.

9. Drag the **CarSnd sound symbol** 🔊 to the stage, as shown in Figure 15.

10. Click **Control** on the menu bar, then click **Test Movie**.

11. Click the **Click to continue text button** to test the sound, then close the test movie window.

You imported a sound and added it to a movie.

FIGURE 15
Dragging the CarSnd symbol to the stage

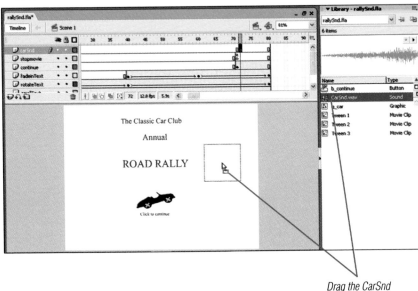

Drag the CarSnd
symbol to the stage

Creating Special Effects

FIGURE 16
The button timeline with the sound layer

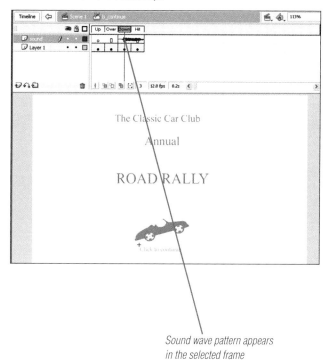

*Sound wave pattern appears
in the selected frame*

1. Click **Frame 71** on the carSnd layer.

2. Click the **Selection tool** ▸ on the Tools panel, drag a marquee around "Click to continue" to select the button, then double-click the selection to display the button's timeline.

3. Insert a new layer above Layer 1, then name it **sound**.

4. Click the **Down frame** on the sound layer, click **Insert** on the menu bar, point to **Timeline**, then click **Blank Keyframe**.

5. Click **File** on the menu bar, point to **Import**, then click **Import to Library**.

6. Use the Import to Library dialog box to navigate to the drive and folder where your Data Files are stored, click the **beep.wav file,** then click **Open** (Win) or **Import to Library** (Mac).

7. Drag the **beep.wav sound symbol** to the stage, then compare your timeline to Figure 16. Dragging the sound symbol to the stage causes the sound to be inserted into the selected frame.

8. Click **Scene 1** above the Timeline layers to display the main Timeline.

9. Click **Control** on the menu bar, click **Test Movie** to test the movie, then close the test movie window.

10. Save your work, then close the movie.

You added a sound layer to a button, imported a sound, then attached the sound to the button.

ADD SCENES

What You'll Do

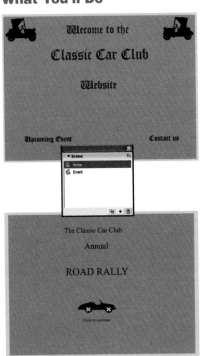

 In this lesson, you will add scenes to a movie and combine scenes from multiple movies into one movie.

Understanding Scenes

Until now you have been working with relatively short movies that have only a few layers and less than 100 frames. However, movies can be quite complex and extremely large. One way to help organize large movies is to use scenes. Just as with their celluloid equivalent, Macromedia Flash scenes are discrete parts of a movie. They have their own timeline and they can be played in any order you specify, or they can be linked through an interactive process that lets the user navigate to a desired scene.

QUICKTIP

There are no guidelines for the length or number of scenes appropriate for any size movie. The key is to determine how best to break down a large movie so that the individual parts are easier to develop, edit, and combine.

Working with Scenes

To add a scene to a movie, you choose Scene from the Insert menu or use the Scene panel. The Scene panel option is found in the Windows menu. The Scene panel can be used to accomplish the following:

- Rename a scene by double-clicking the scene name, then typing in the new name.
- Duplicate a scene by selecting it, then clicking the Duplicate Scene icon.
- Add a scene by clicking the Add Scene icon.
- Delete a scene by selecting it, then clicking the Delete scene icon.
- Reorder the scenes by dragging them up or down the list of scenes.

Creating Special Effects

When a movie is played, the scenes are played in the order they are listed in the Scene panel. You can use the interactive features of Flash, such as a stop action and buttons with goto actions to allow the user to jump to various scenes.

Following is the process for combining scenes from several movies into one movie:

- Open the movie that will be used as Scene 1.
- Insert a new scene into the movie.
- Open the movie that will be used as Scene 2.

- Copy the frames from the second movie into Scene 2 of the first movie.
- Continue the process until the scenes for all the movies have been copied into one movie.

The home page for the Classic Car Club Web site, shown in Figure 17, will become the first scene of a multi-scene movie.

FIGURE 17
The Classic Car Club home page

Add and name a scene

1. Open fl5_6.fla, then save it as **cccHome**.

2. Click **Window** on the menu bar, point to **Other Panels**, then click **Scene** to open the Scene panel.

3. Double-click **Scene 1** in the Scene panel, type **Home**, then press **[Enter]** (Win) or **[return]** (Mac).

4. Click the **Add scene icon** ＋ , double-click **Scene 2**, type **Event**, press **[Enter]** (Win) or **[return]** (Mac), then compare your Scene panel with Figure 18.

   When the new scene, Event, is created, the stage and timeline are blank.

5. Click **Home** in the Scene panel and notice that the timeline changes to the Home scene.

6. Click **Event** in the Scene panel and notice that the timeline changes to the Event scene, which is blank.

7. Click **Control** on the menu bar, then click **Test Movie** to test the movie and notice how the movie moves from Scene 1 to the blank Scene 2.

   There is no content or stop action scripts in the Events scene, so the movie just jumps from one scene to another.

8. Close the test movie window.

You added a scene and used the Scene panel to rename the scenes.

FIGURE 18
Changes to the Scene panel

FIGURE 19

Selecting all the frames

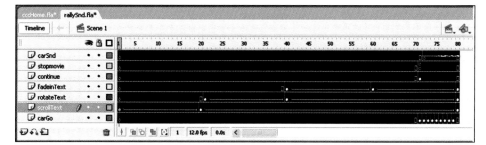

1. Open rallySnd.fla.

   TIP: rallySnd.fla is the file you created in Lesson 3.

2. Click **Edit** on the menu bar, point to **Timeline**, then click **Select All Frames** to select all the frames in all the layers, as shown in Figure 19.

3. Click **Edit** on the menu bar, point to **Timeline**, then click **Copy Frames**.

4. Close rallySnd.fla without saving the changes.

5. Click **Window** on the menu bar, then click **cccHome.fla**, if necessary.

6. Make sure that the Event scene is selected.

7. Click **Frame 1** on Layer 1 of the Event scene.

8. Click **Edit** on the menu bar, point to **Timeline**, then click **Paste Frames**.

   The layers and frames from rallySnd.fla appear in the timeline of the Event scene.

9. Click **Home** in the Scene panel.

10. Test the movie and notice how the Home scene is played, followed by the Event scene.

11. Click the **Click to continue button** to complete the Events scene.

12. Close the test movie window.

You copied frames from one movie into a scene of another movie.

Add interactivity to scenes

1. Make sure that the Home scene is displayed.

2. Drag the **Scene panel** to display the entire stage, if necessary.

3. Click the **Selection tool** ⬉ on the Tools panel, then click the **Upcoming Event text button** on the stage.

4. Open the Actions panel, if necessary.

5. Verify the **Script Assist button** is selected and the script window is in view.

6. Verify the b_event button symbol is displayed in the lower left corner of the Actions panel.

7. Click the **Add a new item to the script icon** ⚛, point to **Global Functions**, point to **Movie Clip Control**, then click **on**.

8. Verify **Release** is selected, click the **Add a new item to the script icon** ⚛, point to **Global Functions**, point to **Timeline Control**, then click **goto**.

9. Click the **Scene list arrow** ⌄, then click **Event**.

10. Compare your Actions panel with Figure 20.

You used the Actions panel to assign a goto action to a button that caused the movie to jump to another scene.

FIGURE 20
The completed Actions panel

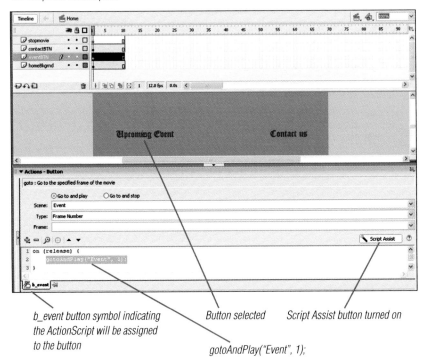

b_event button symbol indicating the ActionScript will be assigned to the button

Button selected

Script Assist button turned on

gotoAndPlay("Event", 1);

Add a Stop Action to a Frame

1. Click **Frame 1** of the stopmovie layer.

2. Click the **Add a new item to the script icon** ⊕ , point to **Global Functions**, point to **Timeline Control**, then click **stop**.

3. Compare your Actions panel to Figure 21.

4. Test the movie, click the **Upcoming Event button**, then notice how the Event scene plays.

5. Close the Scene panel.

6. Close the test movie window.

7. Save your work, then close the movie.

You added a stop action to a frame to cause the movie to stop playing.

FIGURE 21
Adding a stop action

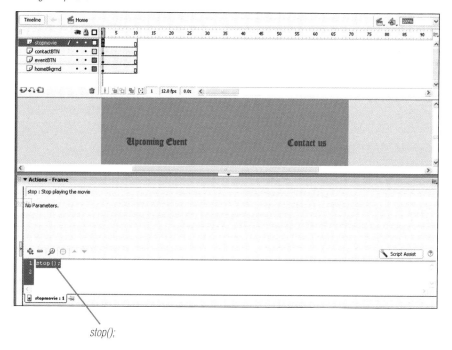

stop();

CREATE AN ANIMATED
NAVIGATION BAR

What You'll Do

 In this lesson you will work through this process to create one drop down menu. The Web site is similar to the one in the previous lesson, however a navigation bar has been provided as well as the necessary buttons.

Understanding Animated Navigation Bars

A common navigation scheme for a Web site is a navigation bar with drop down menus such as the one shown in Figure 22. This scheme has several advantages. First, it allows the developer to provide several menu options to the user without cluttering the screen, thereby, providing more screen space for the Web site content. Second, it allows the user to go quickly to a location on the site without having to navigate through several screens to find the desired content. Third, it provides consistency in function and appearance making it easy for users to learn and work with the navigation scheme.

There are several ways to create drop down menus using the animation capabilities of Macromedia Flash. One common technique allows you to give the illusion of a drop down menu by using masks that reveal the menu. When the user points to (rolls over) an option in the navigation bar, a list or "menu" of buttons is displayed ("drops down"). Then the user can click a button to go to another location in the Web site or trigger some other action. The dropping down of the list is actually an illusion created by using a mask to "uncover" the menu options.

The process is:
- Create a navigation bar. This could be as basic as a background graphic in the shape of a rectangle with navigation bar buttons.
- Position the drop down buttons. Add a layer beneath the navigation bar layer. Then place the buttons below the navigation bar beneath their respective menu items on the stage. If the navigation bar has an Events button with two choices, Road Rally and Auction, that you want to have appear on a drop down menu, you would position these two buttons below the Events button on this drop down buttons layer.
- Add the animated mask. Add a mask layer above the drop down buttons layer and create an animation

Creating Special Effects

of an object that starts above the drop down buttons and moves down to reveal them. Then change the layer to a mask layer and the button layers to masked layers.

- Assign actions to the drop down buttons. Select each drop down button and assign an action, such as "on release go to a Frame".
- Assign a roll over action to the navigation bar button.
  The desired effect is to have the drop down buttons appear when the user points to a navigation bar button. Therefore, you need to assign a "on rollOver" action to the navigation bar button that causes the playhead to go to the frame that plays the animation on the mask layer. This can be done using the Script Assist feature.

- Create an invisible button.
  When the user points to a navigation bar button, the drop down menu appears showing the drop down buttons. There needs to be a way to have the menu disappear when the user points away from the navigation bar button. This can be done by creating a button on a layer below the masked layers. This button would be slightly larger than the drop down buttons and their navigation bar button as shown in Figure 23. A rollOver action would be assigned to this button so that when the user rolls off the drop down or navigation bar buttons, they will roll on to this button and the action would be carried out. This button should be made transparent so the user does not see it.

Using Frame Labels

Until now you have been working with frame numbers in ActionScript code when creating a go to action. Frame labels can also be used in the code. You can assign a label to a frame as an identifier. For example, you could assign the label home to frame 10 and then create a goto home action that will cause the playhead to jump to frame 10. One advantage of using frame labels is that if you insert frames in the timeline the label adjusts for the added frames. So, you do not have to change the ActionScript that uses the frame label. Another advantage is that the descriptive labels help you identify parts of the movie as you work with the timeline. You assign a frame label by selecting the desired frame and typing a label in the Frame text box in the Property inspector.

FIGURE 22

A Web site with a navigation bar with drop down menus

FIGURE 23

A button that will be assigned a rollOver action

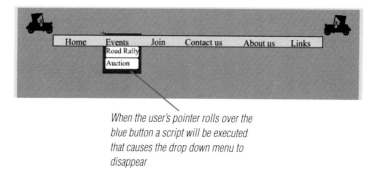

When the user's pointer rolls over the blue button a script will be executed that causes the drop down menu to disappear

Position the Drop Down Buttons

1. Open fl5_7.fla from the drive and folder where your Data Files are stored, then save it as **navBar**.

2. Hide all panels, then open the Tools, Library, and Property inspector panels.

3. Set the view to **Fit in Window**.

4. Click the **homeBkgrnd layer**, insert a new layer, then name it roadRally.

5. Click **Frame 2** of the roadRally layer, then press **[F6]** to insert a Keyframe.

6. Expand the Library panel, double-click the **Buttons folder**, then drag the **b_roadRally button** to the position just below the Events button on the Navigation bar, as shown in Figure 24.

7. Insert a layer above the homeBkgrnd layer, then name it **auction**.

(continued)

FIGURE 24
Positioning the b_roadRally button

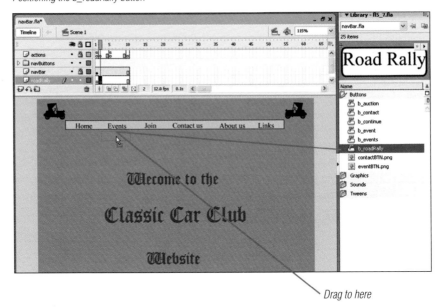

Drag to here

Creating Special Effects

FIGURE 25
Positioning the buttons

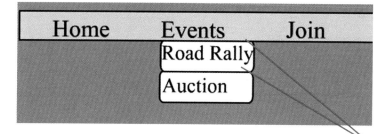

Make sure the button borders overlap

8. Click **Frame 2** of the auction layer, then press **[F6]** to insert a Keyframe.

9. Drag the **b_auction button** from the Library panel and position it below the b_roadRally button.

10. Click the **Zoom tool** Q on the Tools panel, then click the **Events button** on the stage to enlarge the view.

11. Click the **Selection tool** ▸ on the Tools panel, then click each button and use the arrow keys to position them, as shown in Figure 25.

The top line of the Road Rally button must overlap with the bottom border of the navigation bar. And the bottom border of the Road Rally button must overlap with the top border of the Auction button.

You placed the drop down button on the stage and repositioned them.

Add a Mask Layer

1. Click the **roadRally layer**, insert a new layer above the roadRally layer, then name it **mask**.

2. Click **Frame 2** of the mask layer, then press **[F6]** to insert a Keyframe.

3. Click the **Rectangle tool** ▢ on the Tools panel, set the Stroke Color to none ⬚ , then set the Fill Color to black.

4. Draw a rectangle that covers the buttons, as shown in Figure 26.

5. Click the **Selection tool** ↖ on the Tools panel, then drag the **rectangle** to above the buttons, as shown in Figure 27.

6. Verify the rectangle is selected, click **Insert** on the menu bar, point to **Timeline**, then click **Create Motion Tween**.

7. Click **Frame 5** on the mask layer, then press **[F6]** to insert a Keyframe.

(continued)

FIGURE 26
The drawn rectangle that covers the buttons

FIGURE 27
Dragging the rectangle above the buttons

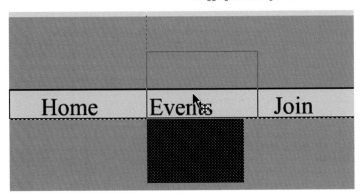

FIGURE 28
The rectangle positioned over the buttons

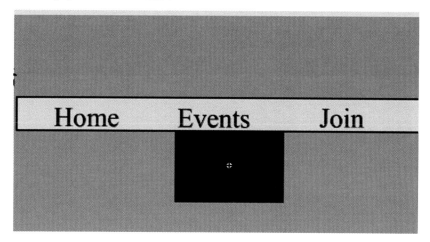

8. Click the **Selection tool** on the Tools panel, then drag the **rectangle** down to cover the buttons, as shown in Figure 28.

9. Click **mask** on the Timeline, click **Modify** on the menu bar, point to **Timeline**, click **Layer Properties**, click the **Mask option button**, then click **OK**.

10. Click **roadRally** on the Timeline, click **Modify** on the menu bar, point to **Timeline**, then click **Layer Properties**, click the **Masked option button**, then click **OK**.

11. Click **auction** on the Timeline, click **Modify** on the menu bar, point to **Timeline**, then click **Layer Properties**, click the **Masked option button**, then click **OK**.

12. Drag the **playhead** in the Timeline and notice how the mask hides and reveals the buttons.

13. Save your work.

You added a mask that animates to hide and reveal the menu buttons.

Assign an Action to a Drop Down Button

1. Click **Frame 2** of the roadRally layer, then click the **Road Rally button** to select it.

2. Open the Actions panel and verify the Script Assist window is visible and the b_roadRally button symbol is displayed, as shown in Figure 29.

3. Click the **Add a new item to the script icon** 🖫, point to **Global Functions**, point to **Timeline Control**, then click **goto**.

4. Click the **Scene list arrow** ⌄, then click **Scene 2**, as shown in Figure 30.

5. Set the Type to **Frame Number** and the Number to **1**.

You used the Script Assist window to assigned a goto action to a menu button.

FIGURE 29
The Actions panel with the b_roadRally button selected

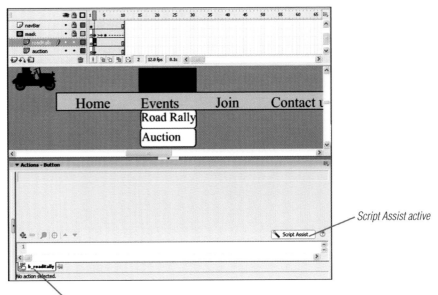

Script Assist active

b_roadRally button symbol indicating the action to be created will be assigned to the button

FIGURE 30
Selecting the scene to go to

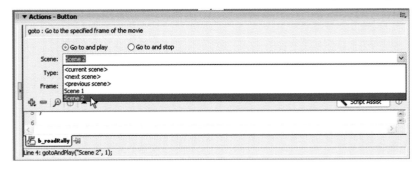

Creating Special Effects

FIGURE 31

Specifying a frame label

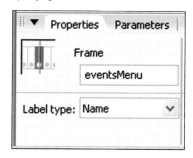

FIGURE 32

The completed Actions panel

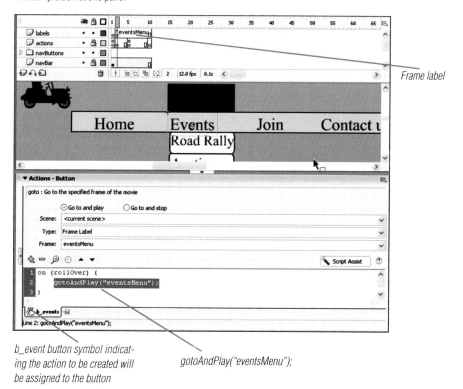

Frame label

b_event button symbol indicating the action to be created will be assigned to the button

gotoAndPlay("eventsMenu");

Add a Frame Label and Assign a Rollover Action

1. Insert a layer at the top of the Timeline, name it **labels**, then insert a Keyframe in Frame 2 of the labels layer.

2. Verify that the Property inspector panel is open, click inside the **Frame text box**, then type **eventsMenu**, as shown in Figure 31.

3. Collapse the Property inspector panel, then click the **Events button** on the stage to select it.

4. Verify the b_events button symbol is displayed in the lower left corner of the Actions panel.

5. Click the **Add a new item to the script icon** ⚑, point to **Global Functions**, point to **Movie Clip Control**, then click **on**.

6. Click the **Release check box** to deselect it, then click the **Roll Over check box** to select it.

7. Click the **Add a new item to the script icon** ⚑, point to **Global Functions**, point to **Timeline Control**, then click **goto**.

8. Click the **Type list arrow** ⌄, then click **Frame Label**.

9. Click the **Frame list arrow** ⌄, then click **eventsMenu**. Your screen should resemble Figure 32.

10. Click **Control** on the menu bar, then click **Test Movie**.

11. Point to **Events**, then click **Road Rally**.

12. Close the test window, then save your work.

You added a frame label and assigned a rollOver action using the frame label.

Add an Invisible Button

1. Click **Control** on the menu bar, click **Test Movie**, move the pointer over Events on the navigation bar, then move the pointer away from Events.

   Notice that when you point to Events the drop down menu appears, however, when you move the pointer away from the menu it does not disappear.

2. Close the test window.

3. Insert a layer above the homeBkgrnd layer, then name it **rollOver**.

4. Click the **Rectangle tool** on the Tools panel, verify that the Stroke Color is set to none, then set the Fill Color to blue.

5. Insert a Keyframe in Frame 2 of the rollover layer.

6. Draw a rectangle, as shown in Figure 33.

7. Click the **Selection tool** on the Tools panel, then click the blue rectangle to select it.

8. Click **Modify** on the menu bar, then click **Convert to Symbol**.

9. Type **b_rollOver** for the name, click the **Button option button**, then click **OK**.

(continued)

FIGURE 33
Drawing the rectangle

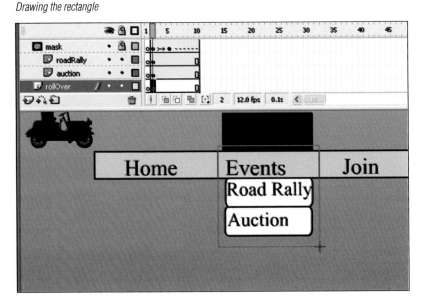

Creating Special Effects

FIGURE 34

The Actions panel displaying the b_rollOver button symbol

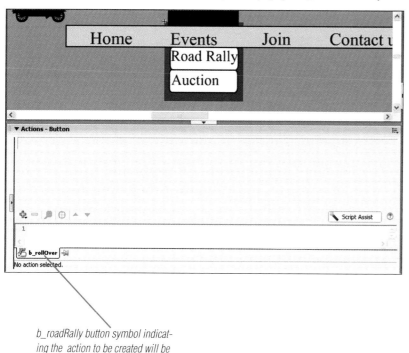

b_roadRally button symbol indicating the action to be created will be
assigned to the button

10. Verify the button is selected and the b_rollOver button symbol is displayed in the Actions panel, as shown in Figure 34.

11. Click the **Add a new item to the script icon** ⊕, point to **Global Functions**, point to **Movie Clip Control**, then click **on**.

12. Click the **Release check box** to deselect it, then click the **Roll Over check box** to select it.

13. Click the **Add a new item to the script icon** ⊕, point to **Global Functions**, point to **Timeline Control**, then click **goto**.

14. Verify Frame 1 is specified.

15. Display the Property inspector, click the **Color list arrow**, click **Alpha**, then set the percentage to 0.

16. Click **Control** on the menu bar, then click **Test Movie**.

17. Point to **Events** to display the drop down menu, then move the pointer away from Events and notice the drop down menu disappears.

18. Close the test window, then save and close the movie.

19. Exit Flash.

You added a button and assigned a rollOver action to it, then made the button transparent.

Create a shape-tweened animation.

1. Start Flash, open f15_8.fla, save it as **skillsdemo5**.
2. Insert keyframes in Frames 45 and 65 on the face2 layer.
3. In frame 65, use the Selection tool to drag and reshape the mouth of face2 into a smile.
4. Display the Properties panel.
5. Click anywhere between Frames 45 and 65.
6. Use the Properties panel to specify a Shape Tween.
7. Play the movie.
8. Save your work.

Create a morphing effect.

1. Insert a keyframe in Frame 65 on the number1 layer.
2. Use the Selection Tool to select 1, then break it apart twice.
3. Insert a blank keyframe in Frame 85 on the number1 layer.
4. Display the Library panel.
5. Click the Edit Multiple Frames icon on the timeline to turn on this feature.
6. Drag the g_number2 symbol and place it directly over the 1 so that both graphics are visible.
7. Break apart the 2 symbol twice.
8. Turn off the Edit Multiple Frames feature.
9. Click anywhere between Frames 65 and 85 on the number1 layer.

10. Use the Properties panel to specify a Shape tween.
11. Play the movie, then save your work.

Use shape hints.

1. Click Frame 65 of the number1 layer.
2. With the 1 selected, add two shape hints, one at the top and one at the bottom of the 1.
3. Click Frame 85 of the number1 layer, then position the shape hints accordingly.
4. Play the movie, then save your work.

Create and apply a mask layer.

1. Insert a new layer above the heading layer, then name it **mask**.
2. Click Frame 1 on the mask layer.
3. Drag the g_face graphic from the Library panel to the left side of the word "How".
4. Insert a Motion tween.
5. Insert a keyframe in Frame 45 on the mask layer.
6. Drag the face to the right side of the word "faces?".
7. Click the mask layer on the timeline, click Modify on the menu bar, point to Timeline, then click Layer Properties.
8. Use the Layer Properties dialog box to specify a Mask layer that is locked.
9. Click heading in the timeline, then use the Layer Properties dialog box to specify a Masked layer that is locked.
10. Play the movie, then save your work.

Add and name a scene.

1. Display the Scene panel.
2. Rename Scene 1 **faces**.
3. Add a new scene, then name it **correct**.
4. Type a heading, **That's correct**, with a red, Arial, 72 pt font, and center it near the top of the stage.
5. Change the name of Layer 1 to **heading**.
6. Insert a keyframe in Frame 30 on the heading layer.
7. Test the movie.
8. Save your work.

Add interactivity to a scene.

1. Display the faces scene, insert a new layer above the face2 layer, and name it **stopmovie**.
2. Insert a keyframe in Frame 85 on the stopmovie layer and add a stop action to it.
3. Use the Selection Tool to select the Continue button on the stage.
4. Use the Actions panel to assign a goto action to the Continue button that jumps the movie to the scene named correct.
5. Test the movie.
6. Save your work.

Add sound to a movie.

1. Use the Scene panel to display the correct scene.
2. Insert a new layer and name it **applause**.
3. Click Frame 1 on the applause layer.
4. Display the Library panel and drag the applause sound symbol to the stage.
5. Test the movie.
6. Save your work.

Add a transition effect.

1. Display the correct scene, if necessary.
2. Insert a new layer above the heading layer, name it **mask,** then specify it as a mask layer.
3. Draw a rectangle, then create a motion tween that causes the rectangle to move from above the stage to covering the stage.
4. Verify that the heading layer is a masked layer.
5. Test the movie.
6. Save your work, then compare your images to Figure 35.
7. Exit Flash.

FIGURE 35
Completed Skills Review

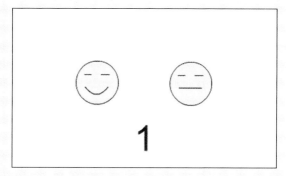

That's correct

The Ultimate Tours travel company has asked you to design several sample animations for their Web site. Figure 36 shows a sample Cruises screen with morphed and shape-tweened animations, as well as a mask effect. Using these or one of the sites you created in Chapter 4 as a guide, complete the following for the Cruises screen of the Ultimate Tours Web site:

1. Open ultimatetours4.fla (the file you created in Chapter 4 Project Builder 1) and save it as **ultimateTours5**.
2. Create a morph animation.
3. Create a shape-tweened animation.
4. Create a button that goes to another scene.

For the new scene:

5. Create a scene and give it an appropriate name.

6. Rename Scene 1.
7. Create an animation using a mask effect in the new scene.
8. Add a sound to the scene (foghorn.wav is provided for you).
9. Add an action to go to the Cruises screen when the animation is done and the viewer clicks a button.
10. Test the movie, then compare your image to the example shown in Figure 36.

FIGURE 36

Sample completed Project Builder 1

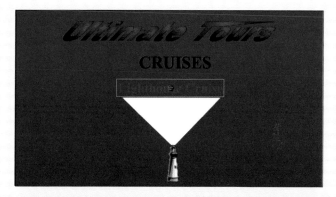

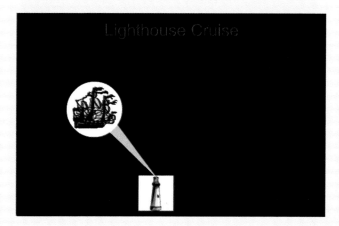

You have been asked to develop a Web site illustrating the signs of the zodiac. The introductory screen will have a heading with a mask effect and links to the 12 zodiac signs. Clicking a sign will display another screen with a different graphic to represent the sign and information about the sign, as well as special effects such as sound, shape animation, and morphing. Each information screen will be linked to the introductory screen.

1. Open a new Flash document, then save it as **zodiac5**.
2. Create an introductory screen for the Web site with the following:
   - A heading
   - A mask layer that creates a spotlight effect
   - Several graphics
   - Two graphics that are buttons that jump to another scene when clicked
3. Create a second scene that has
   - A morph animation using two graphics
   - A sound
   - A Home button with a sound when clicked
4. Create a third scene that has
   - A shape animation using shape hints
   - A Home button with a sound when clicked
5. Rename all of the scenes.
6. Test the movie.
7. Save the movie, then compare your image to the example shown in Figure 37.

FIGURE 37
Sample completed Project Builder 2

Figure 38 shows the homepage of a Web site. Study the figure and complete the following questions. For each question, indicate how you determined your answer.

1. Connect to the Internet, go to *www.course.com*, navigate to the page for this book, click the Online Companion link, then click the link for this chapter.
2. Open a document in a word processor or open a new Macromedia Flash document, save the file as **dpc5**, then answer the following questions. (*Hint*: Use the Text tool in Macromedia Flash.)
   - What seems to be the purpose of this site?
   - Who would be the target audience?
   - How might a shape-tweened animation be used in this site?
   - How might a morph animation be used?
   - How might a mask effect be used?
   - How might sound be used?
   - What suggestions would you make to improve the design and why?

FIGURE 38
Design Project

This is a continuation of Portfolio Project in Chapter 4, which is the development of a personal portfolio. The homepage has several categories, including the following:

- Personal data
- Contact information
- Previous employment
- Education
- Samples of your work

In this project, you will create several buttons for the Sample Animations screen and link them to the animations.

1. Open portfolio4.fla (the file you created in Portfolio Project, Chapter 4) and save it as **portfolio5**.
2. Display the Sample Animations screen.
3. Add layers and create buttons for a shape-tweened animation, morph animation, and an animation using shape hints.
4. Add a new scene and create the morph animation in this scene.
5. Rename the new scene and Scene 1 using appropriate names.
6. Add a sound to the scene.
7. Add a new scene with a navigation bar animation and name the scene appropriately. Add a button on the Sample Animations screen that links to this scene.

8. Create frame actions that cause the movie to return to the Sample Animations screen after each animation has been played.
9. Test the movie.

FIGURE 39
Sample completed Portfolio Project

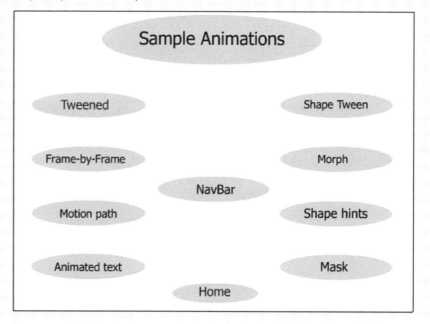

10. Save your work, then compare your image to the example shown in Figure 39.

GETTING STARTED
WITH MACROMEDIA FIREWORKS

1. Understand the Fireworks work environment.

2. Work with new and existing documents.

3. Work with bitmap images.

4. Create shapes.

5. Create and modify text.

1 GETTING STARTED
WITH MACROMEDIA FIREWORKS

Understanding Fireworks

Fireworks is a graphics program intended specifically for the Web. Both Web enthusiasts and professionals can create, edit, and optimize files, and then add animation and JavaScript-enabled interactivity to those optimized files. Many Fireworks tasks are compartmentalized so that graphic artists can enhance or create designs without disturbing the programming added by developers, and vice versa.

In Fireworks, you can also work with files created by other graphic design programs, and save and export files you create in Fireworks to other programs. Fireworks is an integral component of Macromedia Studio 8, and integrates seamlessly with other Macromedia applications, including Macromedia Flash, Dreamweaver, FreeHand, ColdFusion, and Director. In addition, you can use other applications, such as Flash or Dreamweaver, to edit Fireworks images using the Fireworks interface from within the host application. Fireworks also allows file sharing with other applications, such as Adobe Photoshop.

In this book, you will learn to use the tools and apply the concepts that make Fireworks a comprehensive Web graphics program. In addition to creating files that can be used in other programs, you will create sample Web pages and animated graphics.

Tools You'll Use

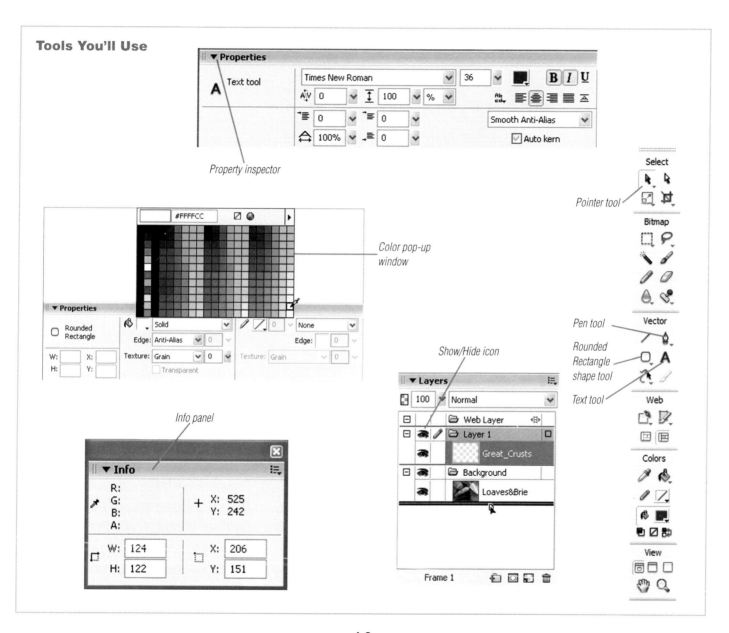

Property inspector

Color pop-up window

Info panel

Show/Hide icon

Select

Pointer tool

Bitmap

Pen tool

Vector

Rounded Rectangle shape tool

Text tool

Web

Colors

View

UNDERSTAND THE FIREWORKS WORK ENVIRONMENT

What You'll Do

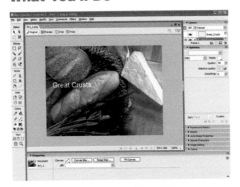

 In this lesson, you will start Fireworks, open a file, and adjust panels, including undocking and collapsing them.

Viewing the Fireworks Window

The Fireworks window, shown in Figures 1 and 2, contains the space where you work with documents, tools, and panels. The overall Fireworks environment emulates the familiar interface in other Macromedia applications. When you open or create a document, the Document window contains four display buttons: Original, Preview, 2-Up, and 4-Up. You can work in your document when you click the Original button; the other three are document preview buttons. You can view the current settings in your document using the Preview button. The 2-Up and 4-Up buttons allow you to select different optimization settings and evaluate them side by side. The main area of the Document window contains the **canvas**.

When you open multiple documents and the Document window is maximized, each open document's title appears on a separate tab.

QUICKTIP

The bottom of each Document window also contains frame control buttons for playing animation.

Tools are housed in the **Tools panel**; other functions are contained in panels such as the Optimize panel, Layers panels, and Assets panel. The Tools panel is organized into **tool groups**: Select, Bitmap, Vector, Web, Colors, and View, so you can easily locate the tool you need. You can modify selected objects and set tool properties and other options using the **Property inspector**. Depending on the

---

Opening Windows-specific toolbars

If you are using Windows, you can open the Main and Modify toolbars from the Toolbars command on the Window menu. The Main toolbar includes buttons for common tasks, whereas the Modify toolbar contains buttons for modifying objects.

action you are performing, information on the Property inspector changes. For example, when you select a tool, an object, or the canvas, properties specific to the selection appear on the Property inspector.

You can rearrange panels in the Fireworks window based on your work preferences. Fireworks allows you to dock, undock, regroup, collapse, expand, and close panels or panel groups. To open or close a panel, click the panel name on the Window menu. To expand or collapse a panel, click the panel title or arrow in the title bar. To move a panel to a new panel docking area, drag the **gripper**, the textured area on the left side of the title bar, to the left until a placement preview rectangle appears. To undock a panel, drag the gripper and move the translucent panel copy into the work area. You can resize a panel by placing the mouse pointer at the bottom of the panel, and then dragging the double-sided arrow pointer. Note that displaying all of the panels at one time can obscure your view of the Document window.

QUICK TIP
You can quickly hide or show all open panels by pressing [Tab] or [F4].

FIGURE 1
Fireworks window (Windows)

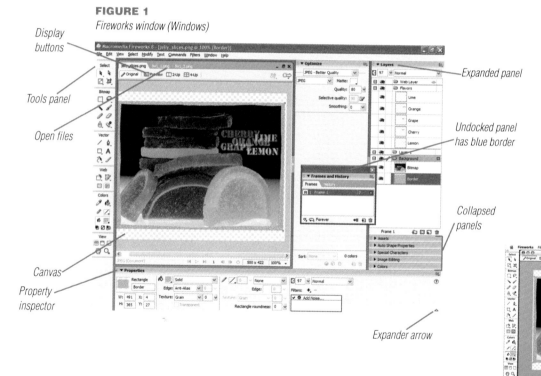

Display buttons

Tools panel

Open files

Canvas

Property inspector

Expanded panel

Undocked panel has blue border

Collapsed panels

Expander arrow

FIGURE 2
Fireworks window (Macintosh)

Start Fireworks and open a Fireworks document

1. Windows users, click the **Start button** 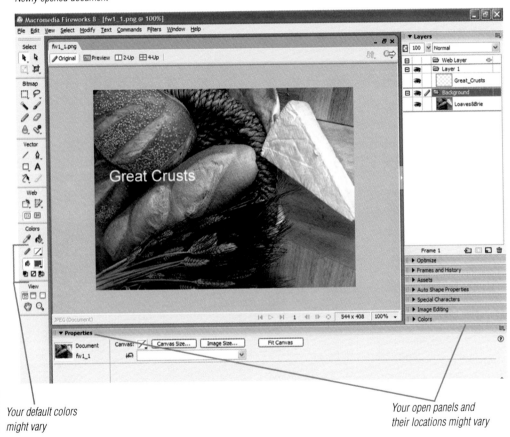 on the taskbar, point to **All Programs**, point to the **Macromedia folder**, then click the **Macromedia Fireworks 8 program icon** (Win) .

   Mac users, click **Finder** on the Dock, click **Applications** on the sidebar in the window that appears, click or double-click the **Macromedia Fireworks 8 folder**, then double-click the **Fireworks 8 program icon** . After Fireworks is running, control-click in the Dock, then click **Keep In Dock** (if necessary).

   The application opens with the Start page displayed.

2. Click **File** on the menu bar, then click **Open**.

   TIP You can also press [Ctrl][O] (Win) or ⌘[O] (Mac) to open a file, or you can click options on the Start page. To disable the Start page, click the Don't show again check box.

3. Navigate to the drive and folder where your Data Files are stored, click **fw1_1.png**, then click **Open**.

   TIP If the drive containing your Data Files is not displayed, click the Look in list arrow (Win).

4. Compare your default Fireworks window to Figure 3.

You started Fireworks and opened a file.

FIGURE 3
Newly opened document

Your default colors might vary

Your open panels and their locations might vary

FIGURE 4

Opening panels from the Window menu (Win)

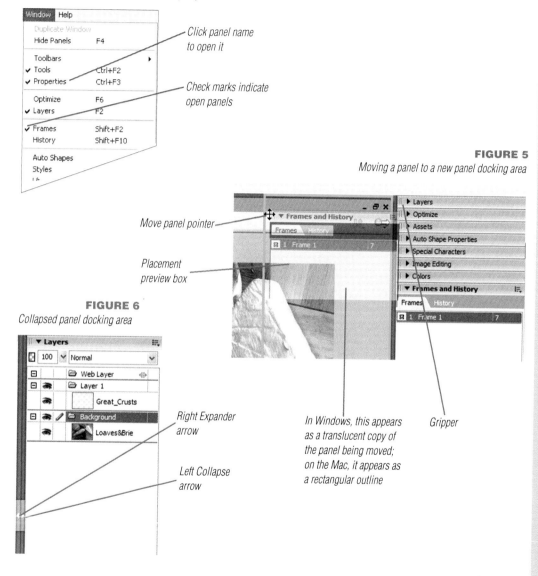

Click panel name to open it

Check marks indicate open panels

FIGURE 5

Moving a panel to a new panel docking area

Move panel pointer

Placement preview box

FIGURE 6

Collapsed panel docking area

Right Expander arrow

In Windows, this appears as a translucent copy of the panel being moved; on the Mac, it appears as a rectangular outline

Gripper

Left Collapse arrow

1. Click **Window** on the menu bar, then click to open or close each **panel** until your menu resembles Figure 4.

   TIP   Each time you click to open or close a panel, the Window menu closes, so you may need to open the menu more than once.

2. Position the mouse pointer on the top of the **Frames and History panel**, drag the **gripper** ⁝⁝ to the left until you see the placement preview rectangle shown in Figure 5 (Mac users will see a plain rectangle), then release the mouse button.

3. Click the **Frames and History panel title** to collapse the panel, then click the **panel title** again to expand the panel.

   The panel docking area remains open.

4. Click the **Layers panel title** (if necessary) to expand the panel.

5. Click the **Left Collapse arrow** ▮ (Win) in the left side of the Frames and History panel docking area to collapse the area, then compare your image to Figure 6.

6. Click the **Right Expander arrow** ▮ (Win) to expand the panel area.

7. Click the **Options menu button** ≣▾ in the Frames and History panel, then click **Close Panel Group**.

8. Click **File** on the menu bar, then click **Close**.

   TIP   You can also press [Ctrl][W] (Win) or ⌘[W] (Mac) to close a file.

You adjusted panels in the Fireworks window, and opened and closed a document.

WORK WITH NEW AND
EXISTING DOCUMENTS

EXISTING DOCUMENTS

What You'll Do

In this lesson, you will set document properties, use the Index and Search tabs of Help, add a layer, and copy an object between documents.

Working with Files

Fireworks files are known as **documents**. When you create a new document, you can set properties such as the document's size, resolution, and canvas color. Fireworks will retain the changes you make to document properties as the default settings for new documents. A Fireworks document consists of many **layers**, which you can use to organize the elements of your document. A layer can contain multiple objects, all of which are managed on the Layers panel.

Although you can open or import a wide range of file formats, the files you create in Macromedia Fireworks are PNG files and have a .png extension. PNG files have unique characteristics that afford you considerable flexibility in working with images. Different file formats support images differently. You can divide a document or image into parts and then individually optimize and export them in the format that best supports the image. For example, you can save a photograph in your document as a JPEG and a cartoon

---

Duplicating options in Fireworks

You can duplicate an object within a document by selecting the object on the canvas, pressing and holding [Alt] (Win) or [option] (Mac), and then dragging the object to a new location. However, if you open a document immediately after copying an object to the Clipboard, Fireworks automatically sets the size of a new document to those dimensions.

illustration as a GIF. JPEG format compresses color well, and is thus best suited for photographs, whereas GIF format is suitable for line art.

You can also open an existing file or import a file into a Fireworks document. You can copy and paste or drag and drop images or text into a Fireworks document from other documents or applications, or from a

scanner or digital camera. Figure 7 shows an object copied from a source document to a target document.

Accessing Help

In Windows, the Fireworks Help system consists of tabs that you can use to access Help topics: Contents, Index, and Search. On the Mac, Help is configured slightly differently but contains similar functionality. In Windows, the Contents tab lists various topics by subject matter. You can type a keyword on the Index tab and access all the topics that begin with that keyword. You can also enter a word or phrase on the Search tab and retrieve a listing of the topics that contain the word or phrase. On the

Mac, instead of multiple tabs, Help appears as a single page with an Ask a Question text box and links to additional pages.

In Help, commands on the menu bar help you navigate and print topics. Other commands on the Help menu link you to online support, such as the Fireworks Support Center and Macromedia Online Forums. You can also obtain updates and tips and search for information on the Fireworks page of the Macromedia Web site.

FIGURE 7
Object copied between documents

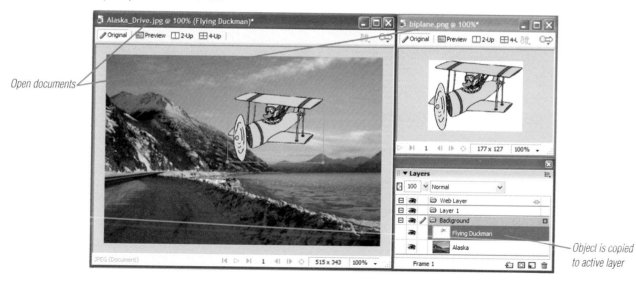

Open documents

Object is copied to active layer

Create and save a new document

1. Click **File** on the menu bar, then click **New**.

   TIP You can also press [Ctrl][N] (Win) or ⌘ [N] (Mac) to open a new file, or you can click an option on the Start page.

2. Type **325** in the Width text box, double-click the value in the Height text box, type **275**, then verify that the resolution is **72**.

3. Click the **Custom option** in the Canvas color section of the New Document dialog box, then click the **Canvas Color box** 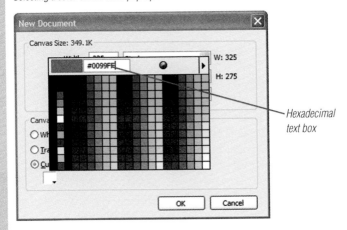.

4. Select the value in the hexadecimal text box, type **#0099FF**, as shown in Figure 8, press **[Enter]** (Win) or **[return]** (Mac), then click **OK**.

   A new Document window appears in the Fireworks window.

   TIP You can also select a canvas color by clicking a color swatch in the color pop-up window.

5. Click **File** on the menu bar, click **Save As**, type **my_blue_heaven** in the File name text box (Win) or Save As text box (Mac), click the **Save in list arrow** (Win) or **Where box list arrow** (Mac) to choose your destination drive and folder, then click **Save**.

6. Compare your document to Figure 9.

You created a new document, set properties for the new document, and saved it.

FIGURE 8
Selecting a color on the color pop-up window

Hexadecimal text box

FIGURE 9
Newly created document

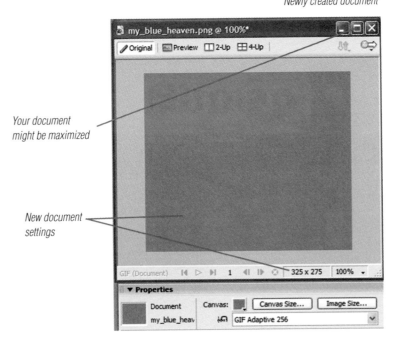

Your document might be maximized

New document settings

FIGURE 10

Getting help on a topic

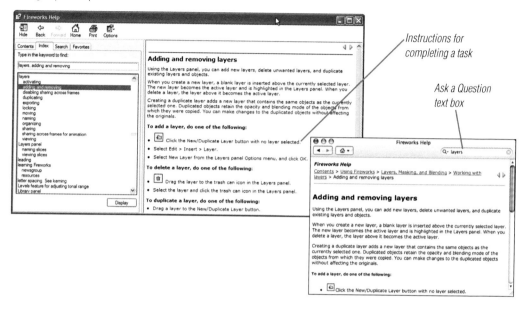

Instructions for completing a task

Ask a Question text box

FIGURE 11

Layer added to Layers panel

Your Layers panel might be docked

New layer is added above previously selected layer

Get Help and add a layer

1. Click **Help** on the menu bar, click **Fireworks Help**, then click the **Index tab** (Win) (if necessary).

   TIP You can also open the Help system by pressing [F1] (Win).

2. Type **layers** in the Type in the keyword to find text box (Win) or Ask a Question text box (Mac) at the top of the Help window, press **[return]** (Mac), then double-click **adding and removing** (Win) or **Adding and removing layers** (Mac) in the topic list.

3. Read the instructions on adding a layer, compare your Help window to Figure 10, then click the **Help window Close button**.

4. Click **Window** on the menu bar, click **Layers** to select it (if necessary), click the **New/Duplicate Layer button** on the Layers panel, then compare your Layers panel to Figure 11.

   A new layer, Layer 2, appears on the Layers panel above the active layer.

   TIP Expand the Layers panel (if necessary) to see all the layers.

You used Help to get instructions for adding a layer in Fireworks, and then used that information to add a layer in the Layers panel.

Use Help to search for a term

1. Open **pool.png**, then resize the Document windows as necessary so that you can see the contents of both open documents.

   TIP If the .png extension is not visible, Windows users can open the file management tool on their operating system, then adjust the settings to display extensions.

2. Drag the **pool.png document** to a blank part of the Fireworks window, then make sure that your view of the documents is unobstructed, as shown in Figure 12.

   TIP Depending on the size and resolution of your monitor, adjust panels and the size of both Document windows as needed.

3. Click **Help** on the menu bar, click **Using Fireworks**, then click the **Search tab** (Win).

4. Click **Options** on the tool bar, then verify that **Search Highlight Off** appears in the menu (Win), indicating that the Search Highlight feature is currently turned on.

5. Windows users, type **Inserting objects into** in the Type in the keyword to find text box, then click **List Topics**.

   Mac users, type **Inserting objects into** in the Ask a Question text box at the top of the Help window, then press [**return**].

6. Double-click the topic that begins **Inserting objects**, then compare your Help window (Win) to Figure 13.

7. Read the instructions for inserting objects, then close the Help window.

You searched for a term in Help and learned more about inserting objects into a Fireworks document.

FIGURE 12
Open documents in the Fireworks window

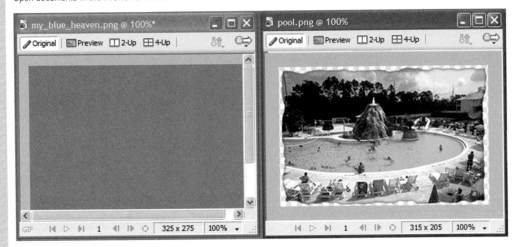

FIGURE 13
Searching for a term in Help

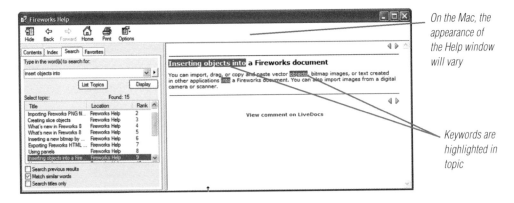

On the Mac, the appearance of the Help window will vary

Keywords are highlighted in topic

FIGURE 14
Object being copied

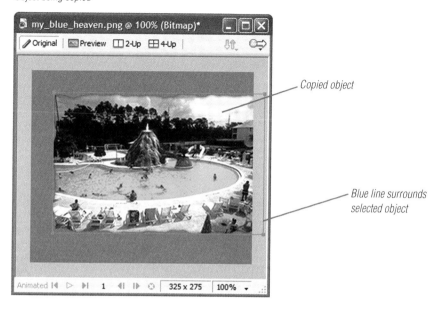

Copied object

Blue line surrounds selected object

FIGURE 15
Object centered in document

Drag and drop an image

1. Make sure that the **Pointer tool** is selected on the Tools panel.

2. Click the mouse anywhere on the pool image, drag it to the my_blue_heaven document, then compare your image to Figure 14.

   TIP You can also select the object, click Edit on the menu bar, click Copy, position the pointer in the target document, click Edit on the menu bar, then click Paste.

3. Use the arrow keys to center the image on the canvas.

   TIP The arrow keys move an object in 1-pixel increments; press and hold [Shift] to move in 10-pixel increments.

4. Click **Window** on the menu bar, click **Pool.png**, click **File** on the menu bar, then click **Close**.

   TIP If you are prompted to save changes, click No (Win) or Don't Save (Mac).

5. Click the **blank area** around the canvas to deselect the object, then compare your document to Figure 15.

6. Click **File** on the menu bar, click **Close**, then click **Yes** (Win) or **Save** (Mac) to save changes.

You dragged an image from one file to another.

WORK WITH
BITMAP IMAGES

What You'll Do

In this lesson, you will modify a bitmap image and create and lock a layer.

Understanding the Layers Panel

Although *layer* is a common term in graphic design applications, a layer's function varies depending on the program. In other applications, such as Adobe Photoshop, you use layers to manipulate **pixels**, discrete squares of color values that can be drawn in a document. In Fireworks, you use layers to position **objects**, which are the individual elements in your document. One function of the Layers panel is to arrange the elements in your document in a logical design order. For example, you can place related elements on the same layer, such as the design elements of a logo, or all the buttons for a Web page. The position of objects/layers in the Layers panel affects their appearance in your document. Each object is akin to an image on a clear piece of acetate—you can stack them on top of each other and view them from the top. The artwork on the bottom may be obscured by the layers above it, but you can adjust visibility by making some pieces more transparent.

You can place as many objects as you want on a layer, arrange them in any order, and select one or more of them at a time. A document can easily accumulate numerous layers and objects, which can make it difficult to quickly find the ones with which you want to work. You can collapse or expand layers to show all or none of the objects. Figure 16 shows components of the Layers panel.

Customizing your view of the Layers panel
You can select the size of the thumbnails that are displayed in the Layers panel or choose not to display them at all. To change thumbnail size, click the Options menu button on the Layers panel, click Thumbnail Options, and then select the option you want.

Understanding Bitmap Images and Vector Objects

Fireworks allows you to work with both bitmap and vector graphic images in your document. A **bitmap graphic** represents a picture image as a matrix of dots, or pixels, on a grid. Bitmaps allow your computer screen to realistically depict the pixel colors in a photographic image. In con-trast, **vector graphics** are mathematically calculated objects composed of anchor points and straight or curved line segments, which you can fill with color or a pattern and outline with a stroke.

Because a bitmap image is defined pixel by pixel, when you scale a bitmap graphic, you lose the sharpness of the original image. **Resolution** refers to the number of pixels in an image. Resolution also refers to an image's clarity and fineness of detail. On-screen resolution is usually 72 or 96 pixels per inch (ppi). (Print graphics require greater resolution.) Bitmap images are, therefore, resolution-dependent—resizing results in a loss of image quality. The most visible evidence is the all-too-familiar jagged appearance in the edges of a resized image.

Because they retain their appearance regardless of how you resize or skew them, vector graphics offer far more flexibility than bitmap images. They are resolution-independent—enlarging retains a crisp edge. Figure 17 compares the image quality of enlarged vector and bitmap images.

FIGURE 16
Layers panel

Pencil icon
Collapsed layer
Expanded layer
Show/Hide Layer icon
Lock/Unlock Layer icon

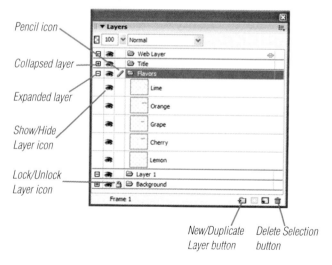

New/Duplicate Layer button
Delete Selection button

FIGURE 17
Comparing vector and bitmap graphics

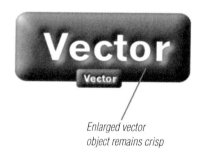

Enlarged vector object remains crisp

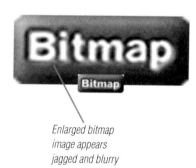

Enlarged bitmap image appears jagged and blurry

Open a document and display the Layers panel

1. Open fw1_1.png, then save it as **breads**.

2. Make sure that the Layers panel is displayed and expanded to show all the layers.

3. Click the **Show/Hide Layer icon** 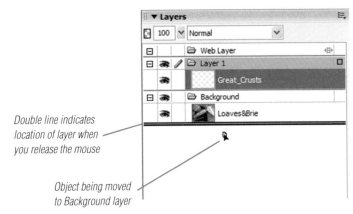 next to the Great_Crusts object in Layer 1 on the Layers panel to hide the layer.

   Notice that the Show/Hide Layer icon toggles between an eye icon and a blank box, depending on whether the layer is hidden or visible.

   | TIP If you do not see an object in a layer, click the Expand Layer icon.

4. Compare your image to Figure 18, then click the **Show/Hide Layer icon** next to the Great_Crusts object in Layer 1.

5. Click the **Great_Crusts object** in Layer 1 on the Layers panel, then drag it beneath the Loaves&Brie object in the Background layer until a flashing double line (Win) or dark black line (Mac) appears beneath the Loaves&Brie object, as shown in Figure 19.

   The Great_Crusts object is now beneath or behind the Loaves&Brie object in the Background layer, so it is no longer visible, although you can still see its blue selection line.

6. Verify that the Great_Crusts object is still selected, then click the **Delete Selection button** on the Layers panel.

You hid and displayed an object in a layer on the Layers panel and moved and deleted an object. Moving an object on the Layers panel affects its visibility in the document.

FIGURE 18
Object hidden on the Layers panel

Text is no longer visible

Show/Hide Layer icon (blank box) indicates this layer is hidden

Show/Hide Layer icon (eye icon) indicates this layer is not hidden

FIGURE 19
Object moved between layers

Double line indicates location of layer when you release the mouse

Object being moved to Background layer

FIGURE 20

Brightness/Contrast dialog box

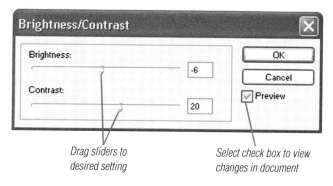

Drag sliders to
desired setting

Select check box to view
changes in document

Edit a bitmap image and lock a layer

1. Click the **Loaves&Brie object** on the Background layer to select it (if necessary).

2. Click **Filters** on the menu bar, point to **Adjust Color**, then click **Brightness/Contrast**.

3. Drag the Brightness slider to **–6**, then drag the Contrast slider to **20**.

   TIP You can also enter values in the text boxes.

4. Compare your Brightness/Contrast dialog box to Figure 20, then click **OK**.

   The colors in the image appear richer.

5. Click the **pencil icon** in the column next to the Background folder icon to lock the layer.

   The padlock icon replaces in the column.

   TIP While it is locked, you cannot edit a layer or its objects.

6. Compare your Layers panel to Figure 21.

7. Click **File** on the menu bar, then click **Save**.

You adjusted the brightness and contrast of the Loaves&Brie object, locked the layer, and saved the file.

FIGURE 21

Layer locked on Layers panel

Click pencil icon or
blank box in column
to lock layer

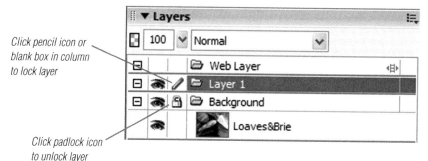

Click padlock icon
to unlock layer

CREATE
SHAPES

What You'll Do

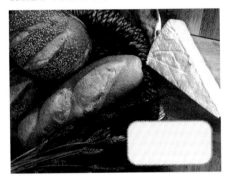

In this lesson, you will display rulers and guides, and create and modify a vector object.

Using Rulers, Guides, and the Grid

Rulers, guides, and the grid are design aides that help you precisely align and position objects in your document. Because Fireworks graphics are Web-oriented, where the rule of measurement is in pixels, ruler units are always in pixels. You insert guides from the rulers by dragging them onto your canvas. Guides do not print or export, although you can save them in the original .png document. If you want to specify an exact location, you can double-click a guide and then enter a coordinate. For each open document, you can adjust the grid size to create squares or rectangles and snap objects directly to guides and the grid at any time.

> QUICKTIP
>
> To change guide and grid line colors, point to the Grid command or Guides command on the View menu, then click Edit Grid or Edit Guides, respectively.

Sizing and Repositioning Objects

You can use the Info panel and the Property inspector to view information about the position of the pointer on the canvas and selected objects. When an object is selected, the lower half of the Info panel contains the same settings that are in the left corner of the Property inspector. The W and H values show the object's size, while the X and Y values show the object's position on the canvas. You can use the coordinate values to create, resize, or move an object to a precise location. You can also resize and move objects by dragging their sizing handles and moving them on the canvas. The upper half of the Info panel contains the R, G, B, and A (Red, Green, Blue, and Alpha) color values, and the X and Y coordinate values correspond to the area of the canvas where the pointer is currently positioned.

Using the Tools Panel

The Tools panel contains selection, drawing, and editing tools. Although you can use many tools on both bitmap and vector graphics, graphic mode-specific tools are housed in separate sections of the Tools panel.

Some tools have multiple tools associated with them. A small arrow in the lower right corner of a tool button indicates that more tools are available in that tool group. To select additional tools, press and hold the tool, then click the tool you want from the list, as shown in Figure 22. The properties associated with a selected tool are displayed on the Property inspector, although not all tools have properties associated with them. For example, when you select any of the basic tools or Auto Shapes, such as the Ellipse tool or the Arrow Auto Shape, you

can adjust the object's fill and stroke settings on the Property inspector.

Based on the object, layer, or tool, Fireworks automatically determines whether you are editing a bitmap or a vector graphic, and activates or nullifies the tool appropriately. Figure 23 shows the Blur tool (a bitmap tool) actively blurring the floral bitmap image, but the tool can't blur the text because text is a vector object. Bitmap selection tools modify the pixels in a bitmap image, which makes them useful for retouching photographic images.

You can create vector shapes using the tools in the Vector portion of the Tools panel. The shape tool group is divided

into two groups: basic shape tools (Ellipse, Rectangle, and Polygon tools) and Auto Shapes. You can adjust the height, width, and overall size of basic shapes by dragging their sizing handles.

Understanding Auto Shapes

You can create basic or Auto Shapes by selecting the shape and then dragging the mouse pointer on the canvas. For Auto Shapes, you can also click the canvas to create a presized Auto Shape. Auto Shapes are complex vector shapes that you can manipulate by dragging control points. A **control point** is the yellow diamond that appears when you select an Auto Shape on the canvas. When you roll the mouse

FIGURE 22
Selecting tools on the Tools panel

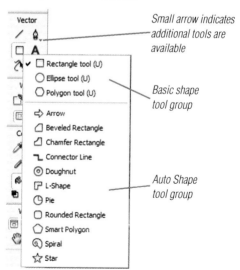

Small arrow indicates additional tools are available

Basic shape tool group

Auto Shape tool group

FIGURE 23
Using a tool on different graphic types

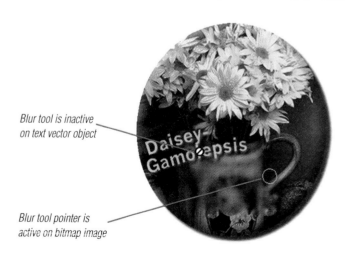

Blur tool is inactive on text vector object

Blur tool pointer is active on bitmap image

pointer over a control point, a tool tip appears, giving you information on how to adjust the Auto Shape. You can adjust individual aspects specific to each shape, such as tips, corners, roundness, the number of points or sectors, and so on. Figure 24 shows the control points for an Auto Chamfer Rectangle and for an Auto Polygon. You can modify an Auto Shape by dragging the control point or by pressing a keyboard shortcut key, such as [Shift], [Alt], and [Ctrl] (Win) or [Shift], [option], and ⌘ (Mac), and then dragging a control point. Figure 25 shows how you can radically alter the appearance of an Auto Shape by dragging control points.

QUICKTIP

To access additional Auto Shapes in Fireworks, open the Auto Shapes panel on the Window menu, and then drag one of the displayed Auto Shapes to the canvas. To download Auto Shapes from the Macromedia Web site, click the Options menu button on the Shapes panel, and then click Get More Auto Shapes.

Applying Fills and Strokes

You can fill an object with a solid color, texture, or pattern. When you apply a **fill**, you can adjust the following attributes: its color and category (such as solid, gradient, or pattern), and the type and amount of edge of the fill. You can apply a border, known as a **stroke**, to an object's edge. You can set several stroke attributes, including color, tip size (the size of the stroke), softness, and texture.

Anti-aliasing blends the edges of a stroke or text with surrounding pixels so that the edges appear to smooth into the background. Anti-aliasing reduces the contrast between the edge and the background by adding pixels of intermediate color. When editing a vector shape other than text, you can select one of four anti-alias settings: No, Crisp, Strong, or Smooth, which make the edges look smoother or crisper. When you select a text object, you can also select a System or Custom anti-alias setting. When you select Custom anti-alias, a dialog box appears in which you can set the oversampling rate, sharpness, and strength of the anti-alias.

QUICKTIP

Aliasing can occur when an analog image is represented in a digital mode, such as a graphic image viewed on a computer. The edges of the graphic are discrete rectangles and squares, which do not always illustrate a curve very well.

FIGURE 24

Control points for smart shapes

FIGURE 25

Auto Shape variants

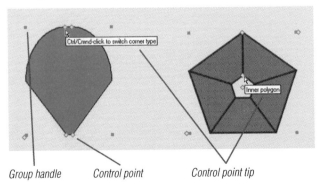

Ctrl/Cmnd-click to switch corner type

Inner polygon

Group handle   Control point   Control point tip

Doughnut shape

Spiral shape

Arrow shape

Star shape

FIGURE 26

Guides displayed

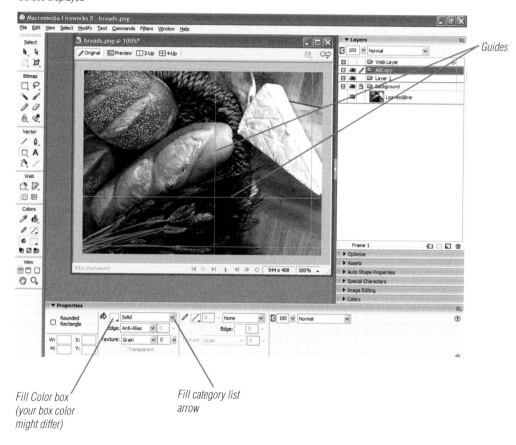

Fill Color box
(your box color
might differ)

Fill category list
arrow

Display the guides

1. Verify that Layer 1 is active, then click the
New/Duplicate Layer button on the
Layers panel to create a new layer, Layer 2.

2. Double-click **Layer 2**, type **AdCopy** in
the Layer name text box, then press
[Enter] (Win) or **[return]** (Mac).

3. Click **View** on the menu bar, point to **Guides**,
then click **Show Guides** (if necessary).

Horizontal and vertical guides appear in the
Document window, as shown in Figure 26.

*You created and named a layer, and displayed
guides in the Document window.*

Create a vector object

1. Press and hold the **Rectangle tool** on
the Tools panel, then click the **Rounded
Rectangle Shape tool** (if necessary).

2. Click the **Fill category list arrow** on the
Property inspector, click **Solid** (if necessary),
then click the **Fill Color box** to open
the color pop-up window.

(continued)

3. Click the **rightmost swatch** in the second row from the bottom (#FFFFCC) ✐, as shown in Figure 27.

4. Click the **Edge of fills list arrow**, click **Anti-Alias** (if necessary), click the **Texture name list arrow**, click **Grain** (if necessary), click the **Amount of texture list arrow**, drag the slider to **10**, then click the **Transparent check box** to select it.

> TIP Fireworks automatically applies the last selected stroke and fill to an object.

5. Click **Window** on the menu bar, click **Info** to open the Info panel, expand the panel, so you can see all the information it contains, then move it out of the way (if necessary).

6. Use the guides to position the pointer ✛ at approximately **300 X/280 Y**, click, then drag the pointer to **520 X/390 Y**, noticing the changing coordinates in the Info panel.

7. Click **Edit** on the menu bar, then click the **Undo Shape Tool** (Win) or **Undo AutoShape Tool (Mac)**.

The rectangle disappears.

> TIP You can also press [Ctrl][Z] (Win) or ⌘ [Z] (Mac) to undo a command.

8. Click **Edit** on the menu bar, click **Redo Shape Tool** (Win) or **Redo AutoShape Tool** (Mac), then compare your image to Figure 28.

> TIP You can also press [Ctrl][Y] (Win) or ⌘ [Y] (Mac) to redo a command.

You set properties for the Rounded Rectangle tool, opened the Info panel, and created a rounded rectangle shape.

FIGURE 27
Selecting the fill color

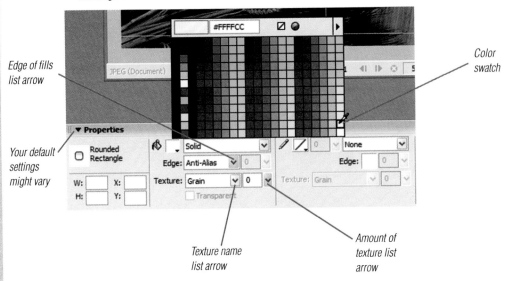

Edge of fills list arrow

Your default settings might vary

Texture name list arrow

Color swatch

Amount of texture list arrow

FIGURE 28
Creating a rounded rectangle

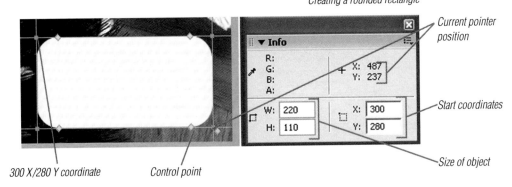

Current pointer position

Start coordinates

Size of object

300 X/280 Y coordinate

Control point

Getting Started with Macromedia Fireworks Chapter 1

FIGURE 29
Stroke properties

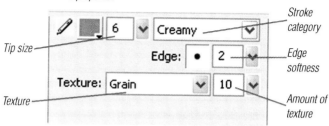

Tip size —

Texture —

Stroke category

Edge softness

Amount of texture

FIGURE 30
Stroke applied to rectangle

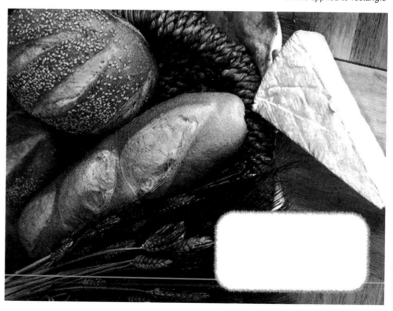

1. Click the **Stroke Color box** 🖉 ▇ on the Property inspector, type **#FF9900** in the hexadecimal text box, then press **[Enter]** (Win) or **[return]** (Mac).

2. Click the **Stroke category list arrow**, point to **Charcoal**, then click **Creamy**.

3. Click the **Tip size list arrow**, then drag the slider to **6**.

4. Enter the remaining stroke values shown in Figure 29.

   TIP To create an ellipse, drag the control points toward the center.

5. Click **View** on the menu bar, point to **Guides**, then click **Show Guides** to turn off guides.

6. Click **Select** on the menu bar, click **Deselect** (if necessary), then compare your image to Figure 30.

7. Save your work.

You fine-tuned stroke properties to add a border to an object that suits the style and mood you want to create. You selected stroke properties, applied a stroke to the rectangle, and turned off the guides. You used the Deselect command so that you could see the results of your work without seeing the selection line.

CREATE AND
MODIFY TEXT

What You'll Do

Upper Crust Shoppe

▶ *In this lesson, you will create text and a path, attach the text to the path, save your document, and then exit the program.*

Using Text in a Document

The text features in Macromedia Fireworks are typical of most desktop publishing programs—after you select the Text tool, you can preview the font family and modify properties, including size, color, style, kerning, leading, alignment, text flow, offset, and anti-alias properties. **Kerning** adjusts the spacing between adjacent letters or a range of letters, whereas **leading** adjusts the amount of space between lines of text. You can set other text attributes, such as indent, alignment, the space before and after a paragraph, and baseline shift, on the Property inspector. Figure 31 shows Text tool properties on the Property inspector. You can automatically preview in your document the changes you make to Text tool properties.

After you create text, you can edit the text block as a whole, or edit just a range of text. When you create text, you can create auto-sizing or fixed-width text blocks. **Auto-sizing** means that the text block expands to accommodate the text you enter. If you delete text, the text block contracts. You can spell check text at any time, including selecting multiple text blocks to check their spelling.

QUICKTIP

You can change the orientation of any selected text block by clicking the Text orientation button on the Property inspector, and then selecting an option from the pop-up menu. You can choose a vertical or horizontal text orientation and display the characters left to right or right to left.

Using the Text Editor

You can use the Text Editor to preview fonts and view and modify text that may be difficult to see in your document. To open the Text Editor, select a text block or a range of text, click Text on the menu bar, then click Editor. You can also copy text from the Text Editor and paste it as text into other applications.

Attaching Text to a Path

You can manipulate text by creating a path, and then attaching text to it. A **path** is an open or closed vector consisting of a series of anchor points. **Anchor points** join path segments—they delineate changes in direction, whether a corner or a curve. To create a path, you use the Pen tool to define points in your document, then attach the text to it. You can edit text after you've attached it to a path. You can also edit the path, but only if it is not attached to text. Figure 32 shows text attached to paths.

QUICKTIP

You can also attach text to paths created with a basic shape tool or to paths of Auto Shapes that you've modified with the Freeform tool or the Reshape Area tool.

To edit a path, you adjust the anchor points. To adjust the anchor points, select the path, select the Subselection tool on the Tools panel, and then drag points to new locations on the path as desired. You can also modify the appearance of text on a path by changing its alignment, orientation, and direction. By combining the shape of the path with the text alignment, orientation, and direction, you can create unique-looking text objects that convey the exact message you want.

FIGURE 31

Text properties on the Property inspector

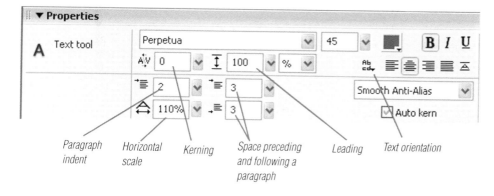

Paragraph indent

Horizontal scale

Kerning

Space preceding and following a paragraph

Leading

Text orientation

FIGURE 32

Text on paths

Image with text attached to paths

Paths visible with text attached

Create text using the Text tool

1. Verify that the AdCopy layer is selected on the Layers panel, then click the **Text tool** A on the Tools panel.

2. Click the **Font list arrow** on the Property inspector, click **Times New Roman**, double-click the **Size text box**, then type **36**.

3. Click the **Fill Color box** ▦, type **#663300** in the hexadecimal text box, then press **[Enter]** (Win) or **[return]** (Mac).

4. Click the **Bold button** B to select it.

5. Click the **Italic button** I to select it.

6. Verify that the Center alignment button ▤ and Smooth Anti-Alias option are selected, then compare your Property inspector to Figure 33.

(continued)

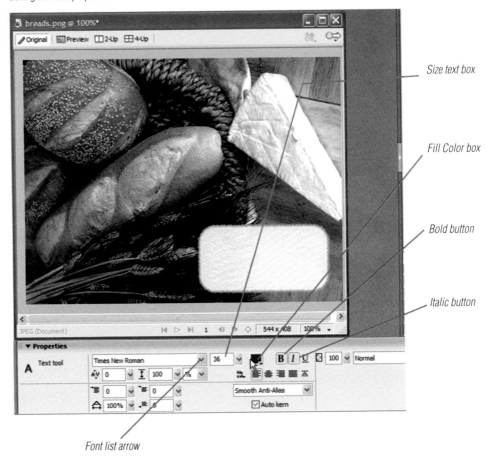

FIGURE 33
Setting Text tool properties

Size text box

Fill Color box

Bold button

Italic button

Font list arrow

FIGURE 34
Newly created text

7. Click the middle of the rectangle, type **Upper Crust**, press **[Enter]** (Win) or **[return]** (Mac), then type **Shoppe**.

8. Click the **Pointer tool** on the Tools panel, then center the text by dragging it in the rectangle (if necessary).

9. Click **Select** on the menu bar, then click **Deselect**.

TIP You can also press [Ctrl][D] (Win) or ⌘ [A] (Mac) to deselect an object.

10. Compare your image to Figure 34.

Lesson 5   Create and Modify Text

Spell check text

1. Click the **Text tool** A on the Tools panel, double-click the **Size text box** on the Property inspector, type **24**, then verify that the Bold **B** and Italic *I* buttons are selected.

2. Click the top of the cheese wedge, type **Frehs Daily**, then compare your image to Figure 35.

3. Click **Text** on the menu bar, click **Check Spelling**, then click **Change**.

   The word "Fresh" is now spelled correctly.

   TIP If prompted to continue checking the current document, click Cancel. If prompted to select a dictionary, choose an appropriate language. If you have not used the spell checker in Fireworks before now, perform Spelling Setup.

You added text and then checked the spelling of the new text.

FIGURE 35
Misspelled text

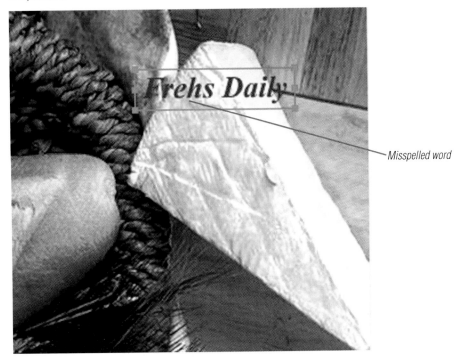

—*Misspelled word*

FIGURE 36
Path created in document

Last/selected
path point
created is solid

FIGURE 37
Text on path

Text follows
points on path

Create a path, attach text to it, then exit Fireworks

1. Click the **Pen tool** ✍ on the Tools panel.

2. Click the **Fill category list arrow** on the Property Inspector, click **None** (if necessary), click the **canvas** in the locations shown in Figure 36, then double-click when you reach the last point.

   A path appears in the document and the path is complete.

3. Click the **Pointer tool** ✎ on the Tools panel, press and hold **[Shift]**, then click the **Fresh Daily** text to select both the path and the text.

   > TIP To select multiple objects on the canvas at once, press and hold [Shift] while selecting each object.

4. Click **Text** on the menu bar, then click **Attach to Path**.

5. Click **Text** on the menu bar, point to **Align**, then click **Stretched**.

6. Click a blank part of the Document window, then compare your image to Figure 37.

7. Save your work.

8. Click **File** on the menu bar, click **Exit** (Win) or click **Fireworks**, then click **Quit Fireworks** (Mac).

You created a path using the Pen tool, attached text to it, then saved the document and exited the program.

Start Fireworks and open a document.

1. Start Fireworks.
2. Open fw1_2.png.
3. Undock the Layers panel (Win).
4. Collapse and expand the Layers panel.
5. Close fw1_2.png without saving changes.

Create a new document and use Help.

1. Create a new document and set the Width to 200, the Height to 150, and the Canvas Color to #DB7839.
2. Save the document as **pasta_1.png**.
3. Access the Search tab of Help (Win) and search for layers. (*Hint*: Click the Adding and removing layers topic in the Topics found dialog box.)
4. Read the topic on duplicating a layer, then close the Help window.
5. Add a layer to the Layers panel.
6. Access the Search tab of Help (Win) and search for "creating bitmap objects."
7. Read the topic on creating bitmap objects, then close the Help window.
8. Open elbow.gif.
9. Drag the object to pasta_1.png. (*Hint*: You might need to resize the elbow.gif Document window to see the pasta_1.png Document window.)

10. Center the object on the canvas.
11. Close elbow.gif without saving changes.
12. Compare your image to Figure 1-38.
13. Save and close pasta_1.png.

Work with the Layers panel and edit a bitmap image.

1. Open fw1_2.png.
2. Save the file as **pasta_2.png**.
3. Select the Varieties object on the Background layer of the Layers panel.
4. Hide and display the Varieties object on the Layers panel.
5. Move the Ingredients object from Layer 1 above the Varieties object so that it is now in the Background layer.
6. Delete the Ingredients object.
7. Select the Varieties object.
8. Open the Brightness/Contrast dialog box, and set the Brightness to 5 and the Contrast to 25. (*Hint*: Use the Adjust Color command on the Filters menu.)
9. Lock the Background layer.
10. Save your work.

Create a vector object.

1. Display the guides.
2. Create a new layer above Layer 1.
3. Rename the newly created layer **Proper_Names**. (*Hint*: Double-click the layer name.)
4. Select the Rounded Rectangle tool.
5. Enter the following fill color properties on the Property inspector: Color: #66CC00, Fill category: Solid, Edge: Feather, Feather amount: 4, Texture: Burlap, and Texture amount: 20%.
6. Open the Info panel.
7. Drag the pointer from approximately 10 X/250 Y to 90 X/300 Y.
8. Apply a stroke with the following properties: Color: #339900, Tip size: 2, Category: Air Brush Basic, Edge: 100, and Texture amount: 0.
9. Save your work.

Create and modify text.

1. Select the Text tool.
2. Enter the following properties in the Property inspector: Font: Times New Roman, Size: 22 pt, Color: #000000, Bold, and Left alignment.

3. Click the pointer at 20 H/280 V, then type **Rotelie**.

4. Center the text in the rectangle, if necessary, then deselect it.

5. Make sure that the Text tool is selected, then enter the following properties: Font: Impact, Size: 65 pt, Color: #990000, Bold, and Center alignment.

6. Click the pointer above the jars, then type **Pasta Figura**.

7. Deselect the Pasta Figura text.

8. Select the Pen tool, then create a path at approximately 250 X/80 Y, 300 X/65 Y, 350 X/60 Y, 400 X/50 Y, 460 X/60 Y, 500 X/80 Y. (*Hint*: Use the Info panel.)

9. Attach the Pasta Figura text to the path.

10. Change the alignment setting of the text on the path to Stretched.

11. Deselect the text on the path.

12. Turn off the guides.

13. Save your work, then compare your document to Figure 38.

FIGURE 38
Completed Skills Review

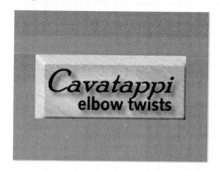

You are in charge of new services at Crystal Clear Consulting. You're preparing to roll out a new Crisis Solutions division, designed to help companies that are experiencing management or financial difficulties. You plan to brief your coworkers on the services at an upcoming company lunch. Each department head—including you—is going to submit a sample introductory Web ad announcing the division. You'll use your Fireworks skills to design a simple ad.

1. Obtain images that symbolize the new consulting service. You will import and copy these images to a layer in the document. You can obtain an image from your computer, from the Internet, from a digital camera, or from scanned media. You can use images from the Web that are free for both personal and commercial use (check the copyright information for any such file before downloading it).

2. Create a new document and save it as **crystal.png**.

3. Access Help, select the Search titles only check box at the bottom of the window (Win), then search for "import an image."

4. Import one of the images you obtained in Step 1 so that it serves as the background.

5. Rename Layer 1 **Background**.

6. Create a new layer and give it an appropriate name.

7. Open another image that you obtained in Step 1 and copy it to the document.

8. Create a new layer and name it **Text Objects**.

9. Create at least one vector object and apply a fill to it.

10. Create at least two text objects. (*Hint*: The font in the sample is Matisse ITC and Eras Demi ITC. You can substitute these fonts with other fonts on your computer.)

11. Attach at least one text object to a path, then rename the object on the Layers panel.

12. Save your work, then examine the sample shown in Figure 39.

FIGURE 39
Sample Completed Project Builder 1

You've just completed your first class in Fireworks. Afterward, you meet with your boss to summarize some of the neat features. She is intrigued by the various ways you can change the alignment of text in Fireworks and has asked you to prepare a few samples for the next staff meeting.

1. Create a new document and name it **meandering_paths.png**.
2. Create a text object that is at least 15 characters long (you can use the font of your choice and as many words as you want).
3. Create a simple path, then attach the text to it. (*Hint*: You can use the Pen tool or a basic shape tool.)
4. Create text that describes the path alignment and the orientation settings. (*Hint*: Refer to Figure 40.)
5. Add a new layer, then copy the text on the path and the descriptive text from the old layer to the new one. (*Hint*: Press and hold [Alt] (Win) or [option] (Mac), then drag the object.)
6. Change the alignment and orientation settings and update the descriptive text accordingly.
7. Repeat Steps 5 and 6.
8. Save your work, then examine the sample shown in Figure 40.

FIGURE 40
Sample Completed Project Builder 2

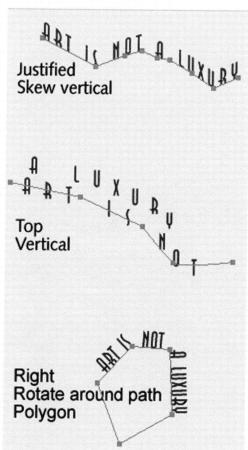

You can develop your design and planning skills by analyzing Web sites. Figure 41 shows a page from the Rock and Roll Hall of Fame Web site. Study the image and answer the following questions. Because dynamic Web sites are updated frequently to reflect current trends, this page might be different from Figure 41 when you open it online.

1. Connect to the Internet and go to *www.course.com*. Navigate to the page for this book, click the Student Online Companion, then click the link for this unit.

2. Open a document in a word processor, or open a new Fireworks document, then save the file as **rocknroll**.

3. Explore the site and answer the following questions. (*Hint*: If you work in Fireworks, use the Text tool.) For each question, indicate how you determined your answer.

   ▪ What vector shapes does the page contain?

   ▪ What fills or strokes have been added to vector shapes?

   ▪ Do objects appear to have been manipulated in some manner? If so, how?

   ▪ Do objects or text overlap? If so, list the order in which the objects could appear in the Layers panel.

   ▪ Has text been attached to a path?

   ▪ What is the overall effect of the text?

FIGURE 41
Design Project

Your group can assign elements of the project to individual members, or work collectively to create the finished product.

Your team serves on the Education Committee for Cultural Consequence, a cultural anthropology group. The group is constructing a Web site that examines facial expressions and moods in people around the world. The committee is in charge of developing emoticons—a shorthand method of expressing moods—for the Web site. The images will be in the style of the smiley face. You can use the facial expression of your choice in developing the emoticon.

1. Choose an emotion and the emoticon that conveys that feeling.
2. Obtain at least two images for the expression you've chosen. You can obtain images from your computer, from the Internet, from a digital camera, or from scanned media. You can use images from the Web that are free for both personal and commercial use (check the copyright information for any such file before downloading it).
3. Create a new document, then save it as **emoticon.png**.
4. Choose a canvas color other than white.
5. Create a new layer named **Faces** and copy the images you've obtained to the new layer.

6. Create a new layer and name it with the emotion you selected in Step 1.
7. Create the emoticon on the layer created in Step 6 using tools on the Tools panel, and apply fills and strokes to them as desired. (*Hint*: The emoticon in the sample was created with the Ellipse tool and the Pencil tool with a Basic Soft Rounded tip setting.)

FIGURE 42
Sample Completed Portfolio Project

8. Create a text object that identifies the expression. (*Hint*: The text in the sample is Pristina.)
9. Save your work, then examine the sample shown in Figure 42.

chapter

2

WORKING WITH
OBJECTS

1. Work with vector tools.

2. Modify multiple vector objects.

3. Modify color.

4. Apply filters to objects and text.

5. Apply a style to text.

Understanding Vector Objects

Fireworks offers a number of vector tools you can use to create vector objects. There are many benefits to working with vector objects. For example, you can modify the properties of a vector path at any time—its shape, size, fill, and stroke—without affecting the quality of the image. This editability makes vector objects easy to work with and adds flexibility to your Web graphics.

After you create an object, you can use a variety of features to transform it into a visually interesting graphic. Many of the tools in Fireworks let you alter or enhance the object. You can combine multiple objects to create entirely new shapes using various Combine Path commands. You can also modify a graphic's appearance by adjusting the alignment and grouping of multiple objects. You can change a path's color by filling it with a solid color, gradient color, or a texture, or by adjusting the stroke appearance.

The Stroke, Fill, and Filters sections on the Property inspector maximize your ability to experiment. You can create various combinations of strokes, fills, and filters, and turn them on or off in your document at will. An object's overall appearance varies depending on the order in which effects appear in the Filters list on the Property inspector.

Tools You'll Use

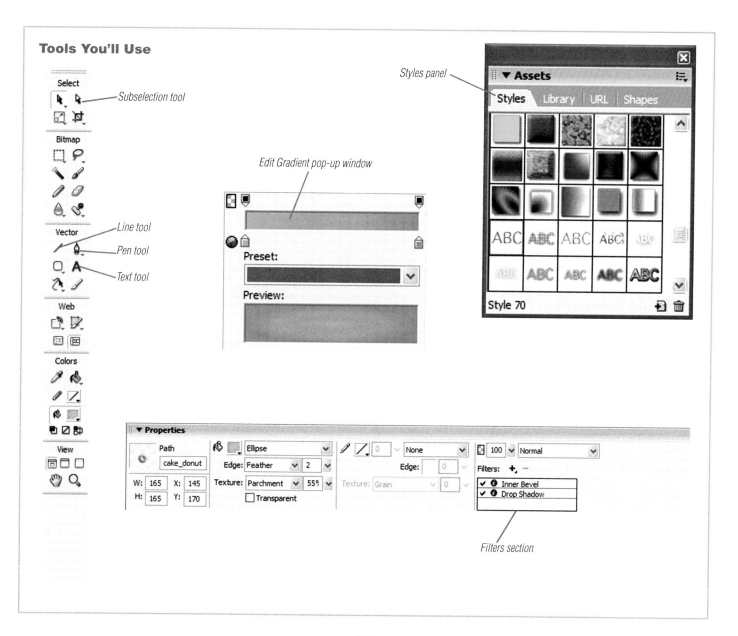

Select

— Subselection tool

Bitmap

Vector

— Line tool

— Pen tool

— Text tool

Web

Colors

View

Styles panel

Assets

Styles | Library | URL | Shapes

ABC ABC ABC ABC ABC

ABC ABC ABC **ABC** **ABC**

Style 70

Edit Gradient pop-up window

Preset:

Preview:

Properties

Path		Ellipse			0	None			100	Normal	
cake_donut		Edge: Feather	2			Edge:	0		Filters: + —
W: 165 X: 145		Texture: Parchment	55%		Texture: Grain	0		✔ ❶ Inner Bevel
H: 165 Y: 170		☐ Transparent						✔ ❶ Drop Shadow

Filters section

2-3

WORK WITH
VECTOR TOOLS

What You'll Do

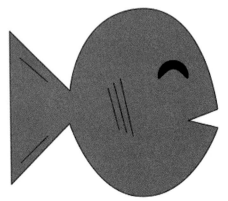

 In this lesson, you will create and modify paths and objects using vector tools.

Understanding Vector Tools and Paths

A vector object can be a straight or curved path, or a group or combination of open, closed, straight, or curved paths. When you create a vector object, path segments connect the anchor points of a path. Paths can be open or closed. The points of an open path do not connect; the start and end points of a closed path do connect.

QUICKTIP

The basic Rectangle shape has a Rectangle roundness setting on the Property inspector, which you can use to create a rounded rectangle basic shape.

You can draw free-form paths using the Vector Path and Pen tools. The Pen tool creates a path one point at a time. The Vector Path tool creates paths in one

Making additional points with the Pen tool and Subselection tool

To create a path with the Pen tool, you click the canvas to create corner points. You can create a curve point as you draw the path by dragging the mouse pointer as you click the canvas. If the newly created path is still selected, you can convert a corner point to a curve point by dragging the point with the Pen tool to create a curve point handle. If you want to convert a corner point that is on an existing path, select the path with the Subselection tool and then drag the point until curve point handles are visible.

motion. Fireworks automatically inserts anchor points as you drag the pointer on the canvas. Regardless of its initial shape, a vector object's path is always editable.

If the path of an object has curves, such as a circle, ellipse, or rounded rectangle, the circular points are known as **curve points**. If the path has angles or is linear, such as a square, a star, or a straight line, the square points are known as **corner points**. Figure 1 shows points selected for various objects. When you edit a vector object, you add, delete, or move points along the path; adjust the point handles; or change the shape of the path segment.

Using the Pen Tool and the Subselection Tool

You can add or delete points on a segment using the Pen tool. Modifying the number of points on a path allows you to manipulate it until you have created the exact shape you want. For example, adding points allows you to maneuver the path with greater precision, whereas deleting points simplifies the path's editability. If you want to move points on a path, you can use the **Subselection tool**. You can also use the Subselection tool to select the points of an individual object that has been grouped or to create a curved point.

QUICKTIP

To connect two unconnected paths, select the Pen tool, click the end point of one path, and then click the end point of the other path.

Each anchor point has one or more **point handles**; point handles are visible when you edit a curved path segment, but not when you edit a straight path segment. You can modify the size and angle of a curve by adjusting the length and position of the point handles. You can use both the Pen tool and the Subselection tool to create and modify point handles on curved paths, or to convert curve points into corner points and vice versa.

FIGURE 1
Points on paths

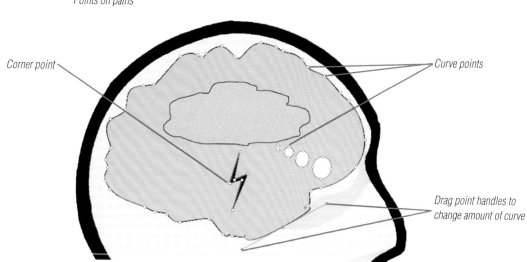

Corner point

Curve points

Drag point handles to
change amount of curve

The two-dimensional curves in a vector object are known as **Bézier curves**, named after the French engineer who developed the mathematical formulas to represent three-dimensional (3D) automobile shapes. Figure 2 shows how you can manipulate a vector object by dragging its point handles.

As you become more familiar with using vector objects, you can experiment with more intricate vector modifications using the **Path scrubber tools**, which alter a path's appearance based on the pressure and speed with which you apply the stroke, and the **Reshape Area tool**, which pulls areas of the path to a boundary.

FIGURE 2
Modifying a vector path

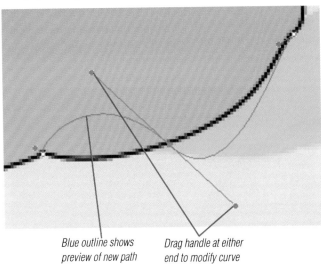

Blue outline shows preview of new path

Drag handle at either end to modify curve

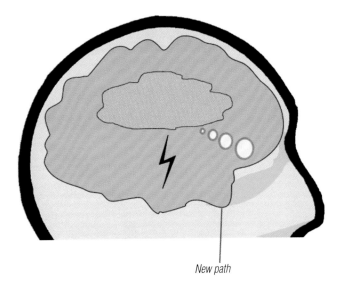

New path

FIGURE 3
Selecting a stroke category

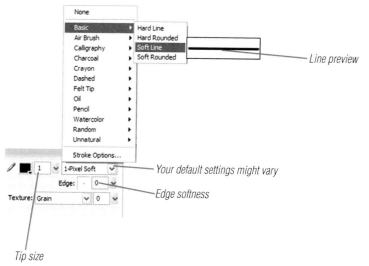

Line preview

Your default settings might vary

Edge softness

Tip size

FIGURE 4
Creating a shape using the Pen tool

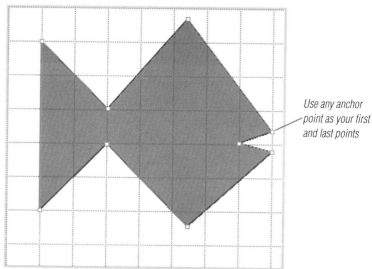

Use any anchor
point as your first
and last points

Create an object using the Pen tool

1. Create a new document, set the Width to **300**, set the Height to **275**, verify that the canvas color is white, then save it as **fish.png**.

2. Click **View** on the menu bar, point to **Grid**, then click **Show Grid**.

   TIP You can use the grid to help align objects on the canvas.

3. Click the **Pen tool** on the Tools panel.

4. Click the **Fill Color box** on the Property inspector, type **#3399FF** in the hexadecimal text box, then press **[Enter]** (Win) or **[return]** (Mac).

5. Click the **Stroke Color box** on the Property inspector, type **#000000** in the hexadecimal text box, then press **[Enter]** (Win) or **[return]** (Mac).

6. Click the **Stroke category list arrow**, point to **Basic**, click **Soft Line**, then verify the remaining settings shown in Figure 3.

   TIP You can preview stroke graphics in the Stroke category list.

7. Click the canvas in the locations shown in Figure 4.

   TIP Close the path by clicking your first anchor point.

You created a new document, set properties for the Pen tool, and created a closed path.

Use the Pen tool and the Line tool to modify a path

1. Position the **Pen tool** 🖊 over the top corner point, then click and drag the point to create a smooth curve, as shown in Figure 5.

   The sharp point smoothes into a curve, and the point handles are visible.

2. Repeat Step 1, but click and drag the bottom corner point, then click a blank part of the Fireworks window to deselect the vector object.

   > TIP Remember that you can undo your changes if you're not satisfied with the results.

3. Press and hold the **Rectangle tool** 🔲 on the Tools panel, then click the **Ellipse tool** 🔾.

4. Click the **Stroke Color box** 🖊🔲 on the Property inspector, then click the top-left black color swatch in the color pop-up window.

5. Repeat Step 4 for the Fill Color box 🖌🔲.

6. Press and hold **[Shift]**, then draw the circle shown in Figure 6.

   > TIP Press and hold [Shift] to draw a perfect square or circle.

7. Click the **Line tool** ✏ on the Tools panel, then drag the pointer on the canvas to create the lines shown in Figure 7.

You modified an object using the Pen tool and the Line tool.

FIGURE 5
Converting a corner point to a curve point

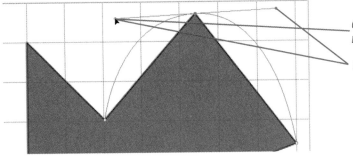

Click corner point and drag handles to create a smooth curve

Point handles

FIGURE 6
Circle object

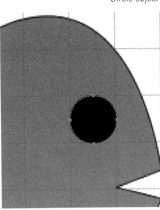

FIGURE 7
Creating lines using the Line tool

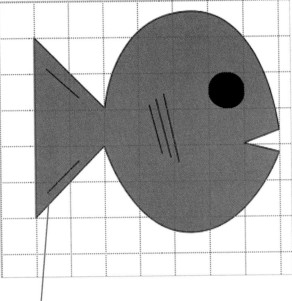

Click and drag the Line tool to create a line

FIGURE 8
Dragging a point handle

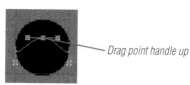

— *Drag point handle up*

FIGURE 9

Modified vector objects

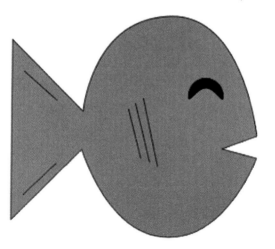

Use the Subselection tool to modify an object

1. Click the **Subselection tool** ▶ on the Tools panel, position the pointer ▶ over the lower-middle point of the black circle, then click the **point**.

   TIP   Click View on the menu bar, then click Zoom In if you want a larger view while you work.

2. Drag the point to the position shown in Figure 8, then click a blank part of the Document window to deselect the object.

   TIP   You can also press [Ctrl][D] (Win) or ⌘[D] or ⌘[Shift][A] (Mac) to deselect an object.

3. Click **View** on the menu bar, point to **Grid**, then click **Show Grid** to turn off the grid.

4. Compare your image to Figure 9, then save your work.

5. Close fish.png.

You modified an object using the Subselection tool, and then closed the document.

MODIFY MULTIPLE
VECTOR OBJECTS

What You'll Do

Existential
Pastries

the HOLE is the ESSENCE

In this lesson, you will create, copy, align, and combine paths of vector objects using the Punch command. You will also group objects.

Aligning and Grouping Objects

Using vector shapes allows you to work with many individual objects at the same time. The Align commands on the Modify menu allow you to align two or more objects with each other: left, centered vertically, and so on. You can open the Align panel to further align, distribute, size, and space multiple objects or to align a vector object's anchor points.

You can also use the Group command on the Modify menu to configure objects on the canvas. The Group command allows you to combine two or more objects to make a single object. You can group any objects in your document: vector images, bitmap images, text, and so on. Fireworks preserves each individual object's shape and its placement in relation to the other objects. After you group objects, you can modify properties of the group as a whole; for example, by changing fill color or by applying a stroke. If you

want to change any one of the objects, you can ungroup the objects, apply the change, and then regroup them. For example, if you want to change the stroke of one object in a group of vector shapes, you must first ungroup the objects before you can modify the individual stroke. However, if the grouped object consists of text and another vector object or bitmap image, you do not need to ungroup the objects to edit the text.

Combining the Paths of Multiple Objects

Fireworks offers six commands for combining paths: Join, Split, Union, Intersect, Punch, and Crop. Each command produces a different result. You must select two or more ungrouped vector objects before you can apply a combination command to them. The Combine Paths commands are described next and most are illustrated in Figure 10.

Join—The Join command allows you to combine the paths of two or more objects to create a single merged object that includes all the points of both paths. If the two objects are both closed, the new path is a **composite path**; if the objects are open, the new path is a **continuous path**. You can also use the Join command to join two open selected points. The first example in Figure 10 shows all four objects joined.

Split—You can split apart the paths of two or more objects that had been combined using the Join command. The Split command creates two or more simple objects and paths. Because the Split command is based on the joined path, and not the original objects, it is not the same as performing Undo.

Union—The Union command creates a path that is the sum total of all the selected paths.

If two paths overlap, the nonintersecting areas are also included. If the selected paths have different fill, stroke, or effects properties, the new path assumes the properties of the lowest object in the stacking order, or the lowest layer on the Layers panel. The union example in Figure 10 shows all four objects combined, with the same properties as the triangle.

FIGURE 10
Sample Combine Path commands

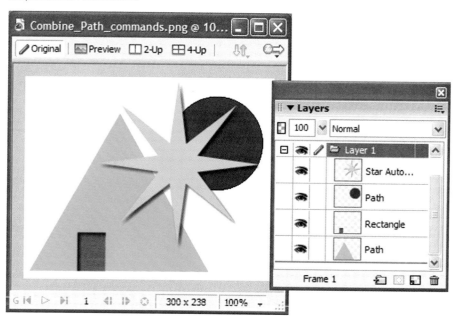

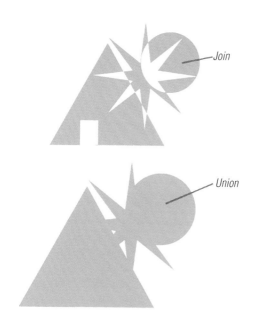

Join

Union

Intersect—The Intersect command creates an object consisting of the area that is common to all of the selected paths. If the selected paths have different fill, stroke, or effects properties, the new path assumes the properties of the lowest object in the stacking order. In the intersect example shown in Figure 10, the intersection is the area shared by the star and the circle hand. The properties are the same as the circle's properties.

Punch—The outline of the topmost object carves through all of the lower selected images. In Figure 10, the *shape* of the star appears to slice through the circle below it. The fill, stroke, and effects properties are unaffected in the areas not being punched.

Crop—The area of the top path is used to remove the areas of the paths beneath it. While the area of the top object defines the object's shape, the fill, stroke, and effects properties of the objects placed further back

are retained. In the crop example in Figure 10, the shape of the top object, the rectangle, has the properties of selected path beneath it, the triangle.

QUICKTIP

Use the Group command if you want your objects to maintain independent fill, stroke, and effect settings. If you want to be able to manipulate the paths of two or more objects after you combine them, use the Join command instead of the Group command.

FIGURE 10
Sample Combine Path commands (continued)

Intersect

Punch

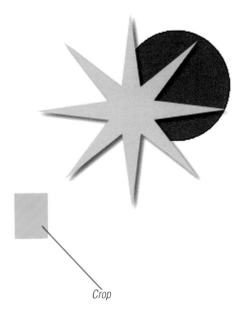

Crop

FIGURE 11

Layers panel and Ellipse tool properties

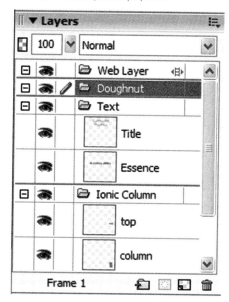

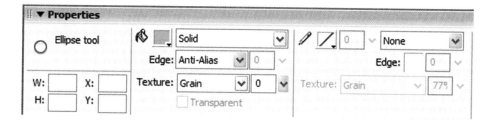

1. Open fw2_1.png, then save it as **pastries.png**.

2. Insert a layer above the Text layer on the Layers panel, double-click the layer name, type **Doughnut**, then press [**Enter**] (Win) or [**return**] (Mac).

   TIP You can name other objects on the Layers panel in the same manner, or you can name selected objects on the Property inspector.

3. Click the **Ellipse tool** ⬭ on the Tools panel.

   TIP You can modify the properties of basic shapes on the Property inspector; to modify Auto Shapes properties, open the Auto Shapes panel from the Window menu.

4. Click the **Stroke Color box** ✎ ■ on the Tools panel, then click the **Transparent button** ☑ on the top of the color pop-up window, if necessary.

5. Click the **Fill Color box** ◈ ■ on the Tools panel, type **#E5B900** in the hexadecimal text box, then press [**Enter**] (Win) or [**return**] (Mac).

6. Make sure that the Property inspector is open and that the Edge and Texture values in the Fill section are 0, then compare your Layers panel and Property inspector to Figure 11.

(continued)

7. Display and expand the Info panel, position the pointer ✛ on the canvas at approximately 130 X/170 Y, press and hold **[Shift]**, then drag the pointer until both W and H text boxes on the Property inspector display 165.

> TIP If necessary, you can enter 165 in the width and height text boxes on the Property inspector after you create the circle.

8. Compare your image to Figure 12.

You created a circle and set its diameter.

Copy an object

1. Verify that the circle is selected, click **Edit** on the menu bar, then click **Copy**.

2. Click **Edit** on the menu bar, then click **Paste**.

   A duplicate Path object appears on the Layers panel.

   > TIP You can also press [Ctrl][C] and [Ctrl][V] (Win) or ⌘[C] and ⌘[V] (Mac) to copy and paste a selection.

3. Click the **Fill Color box** 🪣▪ on the Property inspector, then click the top-left black color swatch in the color pop-up window.

4. Double-click the **W text box** on the Property inspector, type **44**, repeat for the H text box, then press **[Enter]** (Win) or **[return]** (Mac).

5. Compare your image to Figure 13.

You copied an object and changed its properties.

FIGURE 12
Newly created circle

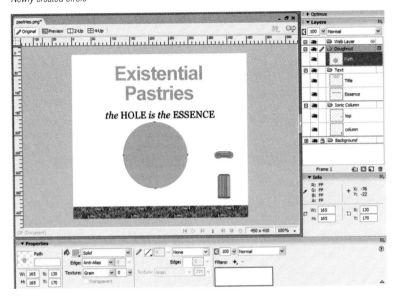

FIGURE 13
Modified object

the HOLE *is the* ESSENCE

FIGURE 14
Aligned objects

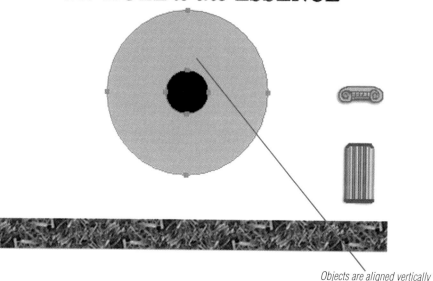

the HOLE is the ESSENCE

*Objects are aligned vertically
and horizontally*

1. Click the **Pointer tool** ![pointer] on the Tools panel, then verify that the black circle is selected.

2. Press and hold **[Shift]**, then click the **yellow circle** to select both objects.

3. Click **Modify** on the menu bar, point to **Align**, then click **Center Vertical**.

4. Click **Modify** on the menu bar, point to **Align**, click **Center Horizontal**, then compare your image to Figure 14.

   The black circle is perfectly centered on the yellow circle.

(continued)

Cloning, copying, and duplicating

You can replicate any object using the Copy/Paste, Clone, or Duplicate commands on the Edit menu, or by pressing and holding [Alt] (Win) or [option] (Mac) and then dragging the object on the canvas. Each menu command creates an identical object and places it above the original on the Layers panel. The Copy/Paste and Clone commands replicate the object directly on top of the original object on the canvas. The Copy command places a copy of the object on the clipboard, which you can use to paste the object in other open files or in other programs. You can also use Copy/Paste commands to copy items on the Frames or Layers panels. The Duplicate command offsets the copied object 10 pixels down and to the right of the original.

5. Click **Modify** on the menu bar, point to
Combine Paths, click **Union**, then notice the
combined object.

   The black circle is no longer visible.

6. Click **Edit** on the menu bar, then click **Undo
Union Paths**.

7. Click **Modify** on the menu bar, point to
Combine Paths, click **Punch**, then compare
your image to Figure 15.

   The paths combine to form a donut.

8. Click the **Edit the object name text box** on
the left side of the Property inspector, type
cake_donut, as shown in Figure 16, then
press [**Enter**] (Win) or [**return**] (Mac).

   Fireworks renames the object.

*You aligned two objects and then combined their
paths. You also undid a Combine Paths command.*

FIGURE 15
Objects combined by the Punch command

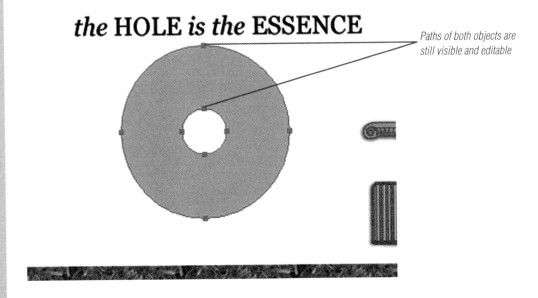

*Paths of both objects are
still visible and editable*

FIGURE 16
Renaming an object

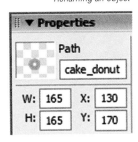

FIGURE 17
Object being moved

FIGURE 18
Grouped objects

Existential Pastries

the HOLE *is the* ESSENCE

Selection handles for a single grouped object

1. Verify that the Pointer tool ![pointer] is selected, then click the **top object** in the Ionic Column layer on the Layers panel.

2. Drag the top object on top of the column object, as shown in Figure 17.

3. Press and hold [**Shift**], then click the **column object** to select both objects.

   The selection handles for both objects are visible.

4. Click **Modify** on the menu bar, click **Group**, then notice that the object on the Layers panel is renamed Group: 2 objects.

   TIP You can also press [Ctrl][G] (Win) or ⌘ [G] (Mac) to group objects.

5. Drag the grouped object under the circle, as shown in Figure 18.

   The selection handles for a single object are visible.

6. Change the name Group: 2 objects to **full_column**.

7. Save your work.

You grouped and moved objects.

MODIFY COLOR

What You'll Do

Existential Pastries

the HOLE is the ESSENCE

In this lesson, you will apply a gradient fill to the cake_donut object, and then modify the fill.

Understanding Fills and Gradients

After you create a vector shape, you can modify its appearance by changing its interior, or **fill**. The Property inspector provides powerful tools for enhancing fills in objects. You can apply several kinds of fills to an object, including solid, gradient, web dither, and pattern. Some of the available fill patterns are shown in Figure 19.

A **solid fill** is the color swatch or hexadecimal value that you specify in the color pop-up window or in the Color Mixer. If you want to ensure that the colors in your document are Web-safe, you can use a **Web Dither fill**. A Web Dither fill approximates the color of a non-Web-safe color by combining two Web-safe colors. **Pattern fills** are bitmap images that have complex color schemes and textures. Fireworks offers dozens of preset patterns from which to choose, or you can create a pattern in Fireworks or another program and then add it to the list. A **gradient** consists of two or more colors that blend into each other in a fixed design. You can select from several preset gradient fills, which you can apply to an object by choosing a fill category or by selecting the Gradient tool on the Tools panel. The Gradient tool, located as a tool option under the Paint Bucket tool, fills an object with the selected gradient, just as the Paint Bucket tool fills an object with the selected color.

> **QUICK**TIP
>
> You can transform or skew a fill's pattern or gradient by adjusting the width, position, rotation, and angle of the fill handles. The gradient adjusts to the contour of the path.

Whether you select a pattern or gradient as a fill, it becomes the active fill color visible on the Tools panel and on the Property inspector. There may be times when you apply a pattern or a gradient and instantly attain the look you want. You can also experiment by modifying the pattern or gradient, for example by adding a transparent gradient, adding an edge or texture, and adjusting the respective amounts of each. The sophisticated styling you add to objects when you choose a pattern fill type can mimic real-world lighting, surface, and depth, and can have quite a dramatic result, as shown in Figure 20.

You can change gradient colors, including preset gradient colors, at any time without affecting the appearance of the gradient. The Edit Gradient pop-up window allows you to modify gradient colors and the transition from one color to the next by manipulating the color swatches beneath the **color ramp**. The color ramp creates and displays the range of colors in a gradient, including their transparency.

FIGURE 19
Pattern categories

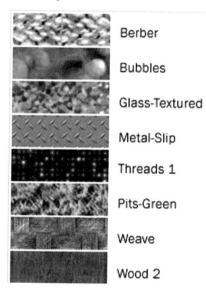

Berber

Bubbles

Glass-Textured

Metal-Slip

Threads 1

Pits-Green

Weave

Wood 2

FIGURE 20
Combining pattern and texture

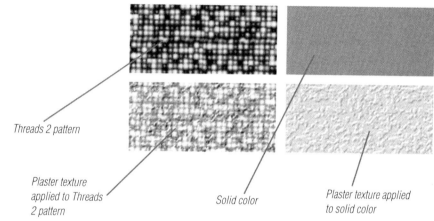

Threads 2 pattern

Plaster texture applied to Threads 2 pattern

Solid color

Plaster texture applied to solid color

Apply a gradient to an object

1. Click the **cake_donut object** to select it.

2. Click the **Fill Category list arrow** on the Property inspector, point to **Gradient**, then click **Ellipse**, as shown in Figure 21.

   An ellipse gradient is applied to the object, as shown in Figure 22. Gradient fill handles also appear on the gradient.

3. Click the **Fill Color box** 🪣 ▪ on the Property inspector, click the left color swatch beneath the color ramp, type **#E5B900** in the hexadecimal text box, then press [**Enter**] (Win) or [**return**] (Mac).

4. Repeat Step 3 for the right color swatch, but type **#FF8000** in the hexadecimal text box, press [**Enter**] (Win) or [**return**] (Mac) to close the color pop-up window, then compare your color ramp to Figure 23.

5. Click a blank part of the Fireworks window to close the color ramp.

6. Click the **Edge list arrow**, click **Feather**, double-click the **Amount of feather text box**, then type **2**.

7. Click the **Texture list arrow**, click **Parchment**, click the **Amount of texture list arrow**, drag the slider to **55**, click a blank part of the Fireworks window, then verify that the Transparent check box is not selected.

8. Compare your image to Figure 24.

   The new gradient colors and texture are applied to the object.

You selected and modified gradient colors, and applied a texture to an object.

FIGURE 21
Fill and gradient categories

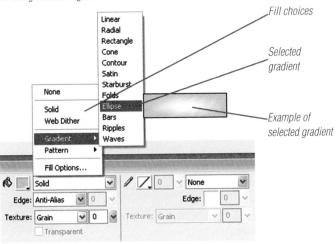

Fill choices

Selected gradient

Example of selected gradient

FIGURE 22
Gradient applied to object

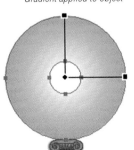

Opacity swatch adjusts transparency

Color ramp shows currently selected gradient colors

Color swatch opens color pop-up window

FIGURE 23
Edit Gradient pop-up window

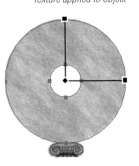

Preset:

Preview:

Click list arrow to select present color combinations

Gradient color preview

FIGURE 24
Texture applied to object

FIGURE 25
Adjusting fill handles

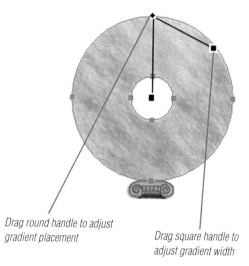

Drag round handle to adjust
gradient placement

Drag square handle to
adjust gradient width

Transform an object and its gradient

1. Verify that the cake_donut object is selected.
2. Click **Modify** on the menu bar, point to **Transform**, then click **Rotate 90° CW** to rotate the object.

   The gradient handles flip position.
3. Drag the fill handles to the positions shown in Figure 25.

   The placement and shading of the gradient is altered.
4. Click a blank part of the Document window to deselect the cake_donut object, then compare your image to Figure 26.
5. Save your work.

You rotated the object and adjusted the fill handles to change the gradient.

FIGURE 26
Modified gradient

the HOLE *is the* ESSENCE

Understanding basic colors in the Color Mixer

The Color Mixer displays the color palette of the values of the active solid color, which you can also view in the Fill Color box or Stroke Color box on the Tools panel or on the Property inspector. You can edit color values to create new colors by changing the values for each color component of a color model. You can define colors in five different models: RGB (red, green, blue); Hexadecimal (Fireworks default), which has values similar to RGB; HSB (hue, saturation, and brightness); CMY (cyan, magenta, yellow); and Grayscale. The color model you choose depends on the medium in which the graphic will appear. Generally, the models Fireworks offers are geared toward screen-based and Web-based computer graphics, with the exception of the CMY or Grayscale models. If you want to use a Fireworks-created graphic in print media, you might want to export the graphic into another program that has additional print-specific color models, such as Macromedia Freehand or Adobe Photoshop. All file formats exported by Fireworks are based on the RGB color model.

APPLY FILTERS TO
OBJECTS AND TEXT

What You'll Do

 In this lesson, you will add filters to objects, including text, and change the order of filters in the Filters list.

Understanding Filters

In addition to using the Fill and Stroke sections of the Property inspector, you can use the Filters section to customize the appearance of objects in your document. The Filters section includes the effects found on the Filters menu, as well as bevel, emboss, shadow, and glow effects. For example, you can sharpen, blur, and add the appearance of depth or dimension to an image. The features in the Filters section are similar to filters, labs, or renders used by other graphics programs, such as Adobe Photoshop or advanced 3D landscaping programs, such as Corel Bryce.

Fireworks calls these **Live Filters** because you can always edit and preview changes to them even after you have saved, closed, and reopened the document. The Filters section lets you experiment with multiple effects. You can add, edit, delete, or hide filters in the Filters list at your convenience. Figure 27 shows the options available in the Filters section.

QUICKTIP

To edit a filter, select the object(s) to which the filter is applied, then click the Info icon or double-click the Filters list in the Filters list to open its pop-up window or dialog box.

Just as you can move objects on the Layers panel to change their appearance in your document, you can modify the overall look of an object by changing the order of filters. Figure 28 shows how changing the stacking order of filters in the Filters list can produce very different results. Each macaw has the same settings and filters applied to it, but in a different order.

QUICKTIP

To move a filter, drag it to a new position in the Filters list.

Using the Filters Menu

The Filters menu contains commands that correspond to many of the features found in the Filters section. However, be aware that some of the effects you add from the Filters menu do not appear in the Filters section of the Property inspector and you cannot alter their settings after you apply them. You can edit or remove these filters only in the current work session—more precisely, you can *undo* these filters, not edit them. After you save or close the document, the Undo actions are lost, and the filter is permanently applied to your document.

FIGURE 27
Filter categories

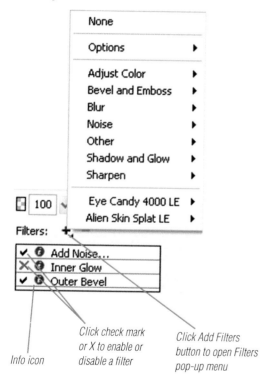

Info icon

Click check mark or X to enable or disable a filter

Click Add Filters button to open Filters pop-up menu

Filters and File Size

Although enabled filters generally contribute to increased file size, disabling a filter instead of deleting it does not significantly add to file size. Some filters, such as the Blur, Blur More, and Gaussian Blur filters, may actually decrease file size because blurring an object decreases the total number of colors in the graphic. The fewer colors used in your document, the less storage space required—hence, smaller file size.

Understanding Transparency

You can adjust the transparency of an image or effect in your document by varying its opacity settings. Fireworks adjusts transparency in terms of percentage, just as it uses percentage settings to adjust the amount of texture in strokes and fills. The **opacity setting** determines if your image is completely opaque (100%) or completely transparent (0%).

FIGURE 28
Rearranged filters in the Filters list

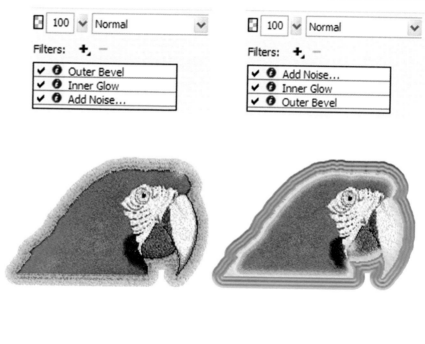

Apply filters to objects

1. Select the **cake_donut object**, then click the **Add Filters button** + on the Property inspector.

2. Point to **Bevel and Emboss**, then click **Inner Bevel**.

   The Inner Bevel pop-up window opens.

3. Enter the values shown in Figure 29, then press **[Enter]** (Win) or **[return]** (Mac) to close the Inner Bevel pop-up window.

4. Click the **Add Filters button** + on the Property inspector.

5. Point to **Shadow and Glow**, then click **Drop Shadow**.

6. Enter the values shown in Figure 30, then press **[Enter]** (Win) or **[return]** (Mac).

   With these filters applied, the cake_donut object now appears to have depth and dimension.

7. Click the **full_column object**, then repeat Steps 4, 5, and 6.

   > TIP To delete a filter, select the effect in the Filters list in the Filters section of the Property inspector, then click the Delete Filters button.

8. Deselect the full-column object, then compare your image to Figure 31.

You applied filters to the full_column and cake_donut objects to give them the illusion of three-dimensionality.

FIGURE 29
Inner Bevel pop-up window

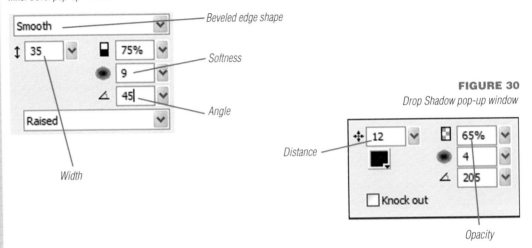

FIGURE 30
Drop Shadow pop-up window

FIGURE 31
Filters, added to objects

FIGURE 32
Rearranged effects

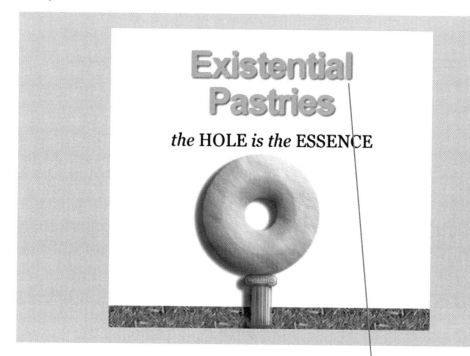

*Drop Shadow effect appears
more subtle*

Apply filters to text

1. Click the **Title text object**, click the **Add Filters button** ✚ on the Property inspector, point to **Bevel and Emboss**, then click **Raised Emboss**.

2. Press **[Enter]** (Win) or **[return]** (Mac) to accept the default settings in the Raised Emboss pop-up window, then deselect the object.

3. Click the **Title text object**, click the **Add Filter button** ✚ on the Property inspector, point to **Shadow and Glow**, then click **Drop Shadow**.

4. Double-click the **Distance text box**, type **2**, accept the remaining default settings, then deselect the object.

5. Select the **Title text object**, drag the **Drop Shadow filter** to the top of the Filters list, deselect the objects, then notice the difference in the text.

6. Compare your image to Figure 32, then save your work.

You added filters to a text object, and then rearranged the filters in the Filters list to create a more subtle visual effect.

APPLY A STYLE
TO TEXT

What You'll Do

In this lesson, you will apply a style to text and add a new text style to the Styles list.

Using Styles in Documents

Styles are preset attributes, such as color and texture, that you can apply to objects and text. Fireworks manages styles on the **Styles panel**, which you can open from the Window menu. Fireworks comes with two types of styles, text and object. Text styles differ from object styles in that they contain text-specific properties, such as font, size, and style, but you can apply text and button styles to any object. Figure 33 shows a style applied to two different objects. You can create your own style and then save it as a custom style in the Styles panel. When you create a custom style, you can save many of the properties associated with fills, strokes, effects, and text. You can also import or export preset or custom styles.

Figure 34 shows a new style added to the Styles panel. Many text styles change the font style and font size when you apply them.

> **QUICK**TIP
>
> You can apply the attributes from one object to another by selecting the object with the attributes, clicking the Copy command on the Edit menu, selecting the target object, and then clicking the Paste Attributes command on the Edit menu.

Applying a style to a bitmap object

You cannot apply every style to a bitmap object. For example, a bitmap object will not pick up a style that contains certain colors, textures, or strokes. However, if the style contains filters that have color or pixel attributes, such as Noise, Glow, or Inner Bevel, the bitmap will assume those attributes.

Using Plug-ins

A **plug-in** adds features to an application. You can install plug-ins from other software applications into Fireworks. Some plug-ins augment existing features. For example, Fireworks includes a sampling of effects from two Alien Skin products: Eye Candy 4000 LE and Alien Skin Splat LE. (Additional information about Alien Skin plug-ins is available at *www.alienskin.com*.) You need to install the correct plug-ins, software drivers, and modules before you can import files from scanned or digital cameras. Note that plug-ins are platform-specific: for example, the TWAIN module (Win) or Photoshop Acquire plug-in.32 (Mac) are needed to import images from a scanner or digital camera.

Using Adobe Photoshop Plug-ins and Features

Adobe Photoshop plug-ins and other import features are often of interest to Fireworks users. The Fireworks Preferences dialog box allows you to extend the functionality of the program by accessing certain Photoshop features. For example, the Folders tab of the Preferences dialog box contains options for Photoshop plug-ins, textures, and patterns. The Import tab allows you to determine how Fireworks translates Photoshop layers and text—by sharing layers across frames or allowing you to edit text after you import it.

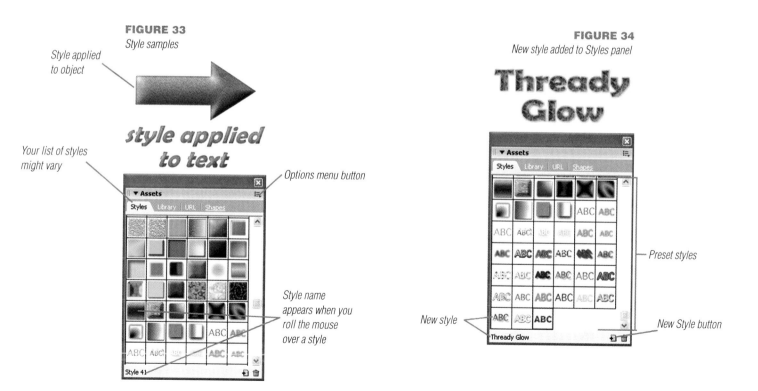

FIGURE 33
Style samples

Style applied to object

Your list of styles might vary

Options menu button

Style name appears when you roll the mouse over a style

FIGURE 34
New style added to Styles panel

Preset styles

New style

New Style button

Apply a style to text

1. Click **Window** on the menu bar, then click **Styles**.

   TIP   Make sure that the Styles panel is undocked and expanded or fully visible in a panel docking area.

2. Click the **Text tool** A on the Tools panel, then enter the values shown in Figure 35.

3. Click the middle of the **column**, then type **The cake is commentary**.

   TIP   If your text block does not automatically resize to fit the text, drag a blue sizing handle until the words fit.

4. Click **Style 70** in the Styles panel, as shown in Figure 36.

   The text changes size, color, and has a filter applied to it.

5. Compare your text to Figure 37.

You applied a style to a text object.

FIGURE 35
Text properties

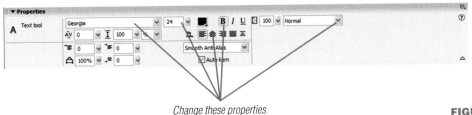

Change these properties

FIGURE 36
Selecting a style in the Styles panel

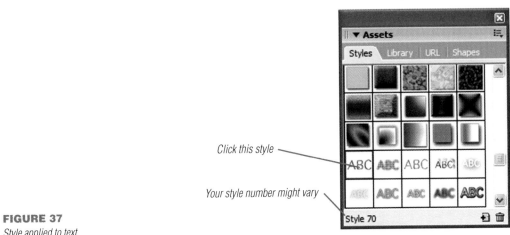

Click this style

Your style number might vary

FIGURE 37
Style applied to text

FIGURE 38
New Style dialog box

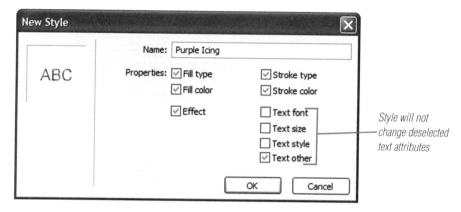

Style will not change deselected text attributes

FIGURE 39
Customized style applied to text

Create a custom style and align objects

1. Select the object you just created, double-click the **Font Size text box** on the Property inspector, type **20**, click the **Color box** ▪, then type **#9900FF** in the hexadecimal text box.

2. Click the **Add Filters button** ➕ on the Property inspector, point to **Shadow and Glow**, then click **Glow**, click the **Color box** ▪, click the white color swatch, press **[Enter]** (Win) or **[return]** (Mac), then deselect the text object.

3. Click the **Options menu button** ☰ on the Styles panel, then click **New Style** to open the New Style dialog box.

4. Double-click the **Name text box**, type **Purple Icing**, deselect the Text font, Text size, and Text style check boxes, compare your dialog box to Figure 38, then click **OK**.

   A new style, Purple Icing, is added to the bottom of the Styles panel.

5. Click **Select** on the menu bar, then click **Select All**, to select all the objects in the document.

6. Click **Modify** on the menu bar, point to **Align**, then click **Center Vertical**.

7. Click **Select** on the menu bar, then click **Deselect**.

8. Compare your image to Figure 39, save your work, then close the file.

You created a new style and added it to the Styles panel, and then you aligned objects.

Create a vector object and modify its path.

1. Open fw2_2.png, then save it as **confection.png**.
2. Select Layer 1, deselect the objects, select the Pen tool, then set the following properties: Fill color: #66CC99 and Stroke: Black Pencil 1-Pixel Soft, 1 px.
3. Using the large white gumdrop as a guide, draw a triangle that approximates the gumdrop's height and width.
4. Convert the corner points to curve points, using Figure 40 as a guide.
5. Use the Subselection tool to increase the height of the object, approximately half the distance to the document border.
6. Drag the object to the lower-left corner of the canvas.
7. Rename the object **Gumdrop**.
8. Save your work.

Align and group objects.

1. Use the Pointer tool to drag the purple circle in back of the multicolored circle.
2. Align the two objects so that they are centered vertically and horizontally.
3. Group the two circles.
4. Move the grouped circles to the top of the right stick, then group them with the stick.

5. Rename the grouped object **Lollipop**.
6. Save your work.

Combine objects' paths.

1. Click the right green wing, then use the arrow keys to move it up and left to merge it with the left green wing.
2. Select both the left and right wings.
3. Combine the paths of the two objects, using the Union command.
4. Rename the combined object **Insignia**.
5. Save your work.

Apply a gradient to an object and modify the gradient.

1. Select the Gumdrop object and apply a Ripples gradient to it.
2. Edit the gradient, and change the left color swatch to #006600.
3. Modify the right gradient by dragging the right fill handle to the lower-right corner of the gumdrop. (*Hint*: The fill handle should resemble the hands of a clock set to 4 o'clock.)
4. Add the following fill properties: Edge: Anti-Alias and Texture: Grain, 25.
5. Save your work.

Apply filters to objects.

1. Select the Insignia object.
2. Apply an Inner Bevel filter with the default settings.
3. Add a stroke with the following settings: Stroke: Black Pencil 1-Pixel Soft, 1 px.
4. Drag the Insignia object to the middle of the Gumdrop object. (*Hint*: Move the Insignia object on the Layers panel, if desired.)
5. Apply an Inset Emboss filter to the Gumdrop object with the default settings.
6. Save your work.

Apply a filter to text.

1. Select the Text tool with the following properties: Font: Times New Roman, Font size: 22, Color: Red, Bold, and Italic. (*Hint*: Change the Fill type to Solid.)
2. Position the pointer in the upper-left corner of the canvas, then type **Sugarless Tastes Great**.
3. Apply a white Glow filter to the text. (*Hint*: Click the Shadow and Glow command on the Filters pop-up window to access the Glow option, then change the color to White and the Halo effect to 1.)
4. Save your work.

Apply a style to text.

1. Open the Styles panel.
2. Select the text.
3. Apply Style 1 to the text. (*Hint*: Substitute a different style, if desired.)
4. Save your work.

FIGURE 40
Completed Skills Review

Add a new style.

1. Change the Font color to #66FFCC and the Font size to 28.
2. Edit the Inner Bevel filter in the Filters section to the following settings: Bevel edge shape: Sloped and Width: 8.

3. Add a new style to the Styles panel, name it **Snow**, and do not have the style affect Text font, size, or style.
4. Compare your document to Figure 40.
5. Save your work.

You're in charge of office security at your business. In the last four months, several employees, including the owner, have neglected to engage their screen savers when they've left their desks for lunch, meetings, and so on. So far, friendly reminders and rewards haven't done the trick, so you're going to e-mail the same obnoxious attachment to everyone. You'll develop a simple, but effective, message using Fireworks vector tools and effects.

1. Create a new document that is 504 × 246 pixels with a white background, then save it as **remember_me**.

2. Create a rounded rectangle that fills the background, and apply the following properties to it: Fill: Pattern: Paint Blue, Edge: Anti-Alias, Texture: Grain, 25, and Stroke: None.

3. Add an Inner Glow filter with the following properties: Width: 8, Color: White, and Softness: 8, then lock the Background layer.

4. Create and name a new layer **Ruler**, then using Figure 41 as a guide, draw a rectangle that has a Linear gradient, then adjust the swatches on the color ramp as follows: Left and Right: #CCCCCC and Middle: #FFFFFF. (*Hint*: Click beneath the color ramp to add a color swatch.)

5. Add a black 1 px Pencil 1-Pixel-Hard stroke and Inner Bevel filter with default settings.

6. Use the Line tool to create evenly spaced hash marks that resemble those on a ruler, then group the ruler objects.

7. Create the following text in the font and filters of your choice: **don't rule out computer security**. (*Hint*: The text in the sample is bold Eras Medium ITC and has a Raised Emboss effect applied to it.)

8. Create **clean up your act** text in the font and color of your choice and apply at least one filter to it using settings of your choice. (*Hint*: The text has Glow and Raised Embossed filters applied to it.)

9. Save your work, then compare your document to Figure 41.

FIGURE 41
Sample Completed Project Builder 1

Impact Potions, a new energy drink aimed at the teen market, is sponsoring a design contest. They want you to introduce the drink by using the design in an ad window on other teen Web sites. They haven't decided on the container yet, so you can create the bottle or can of your choice.

1. If desired, obtain images that will reinforce your message delivery and enhance the vector shapes you will create. You can obtain an image from your computer, from the Internet, from a digital camera, or from scanned media. You can use images from the Web that are free for both personal and commercial use (check the copyright information for any such file before downloading it).

2. Create a new document and save it as **impact_potions**.

3. Create a beverage container using the vector tools of your choice, apply a fill, style, or stroke, and combine paths as necessary. (*Hint*: The side grips on the can in the sample were created using Punch commands.)

4. Create a label for the container, applying fills, strokes, styles, transparency, and filters as necessary. (*Hint*: The label text has been attached to paths.)

5. Create text for the ad applying fills, strokes, styles, transparency, and filters, as desired. (*Hint*: The Aristamp text in

the sample has the Glow and Inner Bevel filters applied to it.)

6. Rename objects or layers on the Layers panel as appropriate.

FIGURE 42
Sample Completed Project Builder 2

7. Experiment with changing the order of filters in the Filters list.

8. Examine the sample shown in Figure 42, then save your work.

One of the many advantages to using Fireworks for your images is the ability to combine vector and bitmap images into one document. For a performance artist, such as the country musician Dwight Yoakam, an official Web site can reinforce both the artistic message and mood. Photographs and Fireworks-generated images combine to convey the feel of an old-time café and street scene. Many images also link the viewer to other pages within the site. Because dynamic Web sites are updated frequently to reflect current trends, this page might be different from Figure 43 when you open it online.

1. Connect to the Internet and go to *www.course.com.* Navigate to the page for this book, click the Student Online Companion, then click the link for this chapter. (*Hint*: Click Two Doors Down Club (Home Page), if necessary.)
2. Open a document in a word processor, or open a new Fireworks document, then save the file as **yoakam**. (*Hint*: Use the Text tool in Fireworks to answer the questions.)
3. Explore the site and answer the following questions:
   - When they were created in Fireworks, which objects could have been grouped?
   - Do objects appear to have been combined?
   - Identify gradients, textures, styles, or other effects applied to objects.
   - Are there objects that appear to be a combination of vector shapes, which include photographic images, objects, or that appear to have an effect applied to them? (*Hint*: Visit the site during the day and during the night and note the differences.)
4. Save your work.

FIGURE 43
Design Project

Your group can assign elements of the project to individual members, or work collectively to create the finished product.

Vintage Wheels, a classic car club, is known for the unusual prizes the club awards to winners of their road rallies. To promote the rallies, the prizes are shown on the group's Web page. Your group has been selected to design and promote this year's grand prizewinner: a custom belt buckle. The only requirement is that the buckle honor a classic car and be large enough to be seen from a distance. You can select the classic auto of your choice.

1. If desired, obtain an image for the buckle. You can obtain an image from your computer, from the Internet, from a digital camera, or from scanned media. You can use images from the Web that are free for both personal and commercial use (check the copyright information for any such file before downloading it).

2. Create a new document and save it as **classic_buckle**.

3. Create two or more vector objects for the buckle and add fills, styles, strokes, or transparency to them. (*Hint*: The ovals in the sample have a combination of Inner Shadow, Inner Bevel, and Outer Bevel filters applied to them.)

4. Apply at least one Combine Paths command to the objects.

5. Create text as desired and apply fills, styles, and filters to them.

FIGURE 44
Sample Completed Portfolio Project

6. Examine the sample shown in Figure 44, then save your work.

IMPORTING, SELECTING, AND MODIFYING GRAPHICS

1. Work with imported files.

2. Work with bitmap selection tools.

3. Learn about selection areas.

4. Select areas based on color.

3 IMPORTING, SELECTING, AND MODIFYING GRAPHICS

Understanding Importing

Whether you want to create a simple image or a complex Web site, having the right graphic is crucial to the success of your project. Many times, the graphic you need may have been created in another application. Fireworks makes it easy to access such a graphic—regardless of whether it was created within the Macromedia application suite in a program such as FreeHand, created in another progam, such as Adobe Illustrator, or downloaded from a digital camera or scanner.

Fireworks allows you to import several types of files, including vector and bitmap files, as well as HTML tables. Being able to work with many different file types in the same document has obvious advantages. Fireworks lets you control file size by merging and flattening objects in your document, which combines pixels of different bitmap images or converts vector objects into bitmap images.

After you import a bitmap image, you can use an assortment of tools to select the pixels on that image. You can select pixels based on an area or on color. After you select pixels, you can manipulate them independently. For example, you can select and edit a defined set of pixels or blend a selection into surrounding pixels.

Tools You'll Use

Marquee tool

Lasso tool

Magic Wand tool

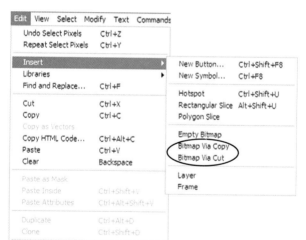

WORK WITH IMPORTED FILES

What You'll Do

In this lesson, you will import graphics with different file formats into a Fireworks document.

Considerations for Importing Files

If you use mostly vector objects in your documents, you can change their dimensions and appearance without affecting the quality of the graphic. When you import several bitmap images or vector or text objects created in other programs into your document, you may need to weigh the advantages of using the new images against the disadvantage of increasing your file size. In addition to other factors, such as color depth, the number of bitmap images in a document affects file size.

Using Different File Formats

Fireworks offers several ways to acquire an image for use in your document. For example, you have already seen that you can copy and paste or drag and drop images from one native Fireworks .png file to another. Fireworks also has many features that maximize your ability to work with different file formats created in different programs, such as being able to copy and paste a graphic open in a different application into your

Fireworks document. In this example, because the copied graphic is placed on the Clipboard, you can paste it into your document as you would any other copied object. Dragging and dropping a selection from within Fireworks or between applications offers an additional advantage. Whenever you copy a selection, the selection is placed on the Clipboard, which consumes resources from your computer to store it. In contrast, using the drag-and-drop method saves memory.

Another easy way to acquire an image is to import a file with a compatible file format. Because individual elements in bitmap images are not editable, importing bitmap files is a relatively straightforward process. However, importing vector files offers the distinct advantage of being able to edit the individual paths that make up the graphic. Depending on the complexity of the original graphic, as well as its native format, Fireworks may import the graphic as a single grouped object or as an ungrouped collection of individual editable objects. You can import vector objects into

Fireworks from many vector programs, including FreeHand, Adobe Illustrator, and CorelDRAW. Figure 1 shows the import file types available in the Import dialog box.

QUICKTIP

You can select Photoshop conversion options, such as layers and text, by opening the Preferences dialog box from the Edit menu, and then clicking the Import tab. For vector-based files, you can select a wide range of options in the Vector File Options dialog box that opens when you import the file.

For some files, when you open a file that was created in another program, you may be able to save the changes you've made to the file in the extant file format. For example, you can open a JPEG or GIF file, modify it, and use the Close or Save commands to save it as a JPEG or GIF. In that instance, you modify and save in the original file format. However, Fireworks recognizes non-editable modifications, such as adding new objects or Live Effects, and also prompts you to save the document as a .png file, which preserves the original file for a different use. For other files, such as some vector file formats that were created in other programs, the original

FIGURE 1
Import dialog box

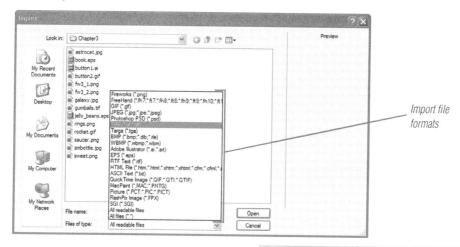

Import file formats

Understanding image resolution

For an image displayed on a computer screen—on the Web, attached to an e-mail, or inserted in a slide presentation—the unit of measurement is in **PPI** (pixels per inch). The standard resolution setting for Web images is 72 PPI, which is directly related to the display capability of computer monitors. The same picture that looks fabulous in a Web page often appears blurry when you enlarge it in a computer program because the same number of pixels is being spread over a larger number of inches. That picture also looks fuzzy when you print it because the on-screen resolution is too low for printing detailed tone transitions.

file is not affected regardless of the changes you make. In that case, the file that you open automatically is saved as a native Fireworks .png document when you click the Close, Save, or Save As commands on the File menu. To create a file in another format that you saved as a Fireworks .png document, you can select an export file format and export the file.

You can determine how Fireworks imports an Adobe Photoshop document by selecting different options on the Import tab of the Preferences dialog box shown in Figure 2. For a vector-based file, you can select options when you import the file in the Vector File Options dialog box, also shown in Figure 2. For example, in the File Conversion section of the

Vector File Options dialog box, you can determine whether to flatten layers or retain them. You can change settings in the Render as Images section to determine the number of individual objects Fireworks will import. In some cases, you might not need to edit the vector file, or you might simply prefer to import the file as a single bitmap image.

FIGURE 2
Import options

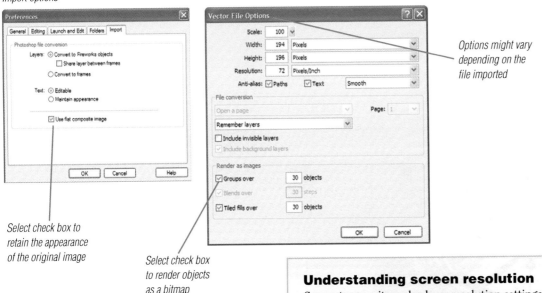

Options might vary depending on the file imported

Select check box to retain the appearance of the original image

Select check box to render objects as a bitmap

Understanding screen resolution

Computer monitors also have resolution settings that refer to the number of pixels contained across the horizontal and vertical axes—that is, how densely packed the pixels are on the screen. For example, a monitor set at a resolution of 1024×768 can display 1024 dots on each of 768 lines, totaling around 786,400 pixels. In contrast, a resolution of 800×600 displays less than half that amount of pixels. You can easily notice this when you change the resolution of your computer monitor: the lower the resolution, the larger the image appears, but it displays less detail than it does at a larger resolution.

FIGURE 3
Imported GIF

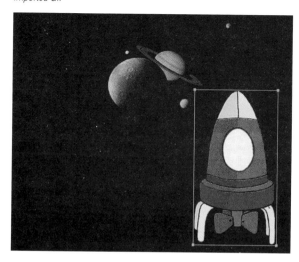

FIGURE 4
Imported Fireworks file

Import a .gif file

1. Open **fw3_1.png**, save it as **horizons.png**, then verify that the Info panel is open.

2. Change the name of Layer 1 on the Layers panel to **Spaceships**.

3. Click **File** on the menu bar, click **Import**, then navigate to the drive and folder where your Data Files are stored.

4. Click the **Files of type list arrow**, then click **All readable files** (if necessary) (Win).

   TIP   You might need to scroll down the list to find the file type.

5. Click **rocket.gif**, then click **Open**.

6. Position the **import pointer** ⌐ on the canvas at approximately 353 X/143 Y, then click the mouse to import the file.

   TIP   If you can't position the mouse just where you want it, enter the precise coordinates in the X and Y text boxes on the Property inspector after you click the mouse.

7. Compare your image to Figure 3.

You imported a GIF file into a Fireworks document.

Import a Fireworks .png file

1. Click **File** on the menu bar, then click **Import**.

2. Double-click **saucer.png**.

3. Position the **import pointer** ⌐ on the canvas at approximately 65 X/290 Y, then click the mouse.

4. Compare your image to Figure 4, then save the file.

You imported a Fireworks file.

Import a vector file as editable paths

1. Click the **Background layer** in the Layers panel, click the **New/Duplicate Layer button** at the bottom of the Layers panel, then change the name of the new layer to **Book**.

2. Click **File** on the menu bar, click **Import**, then double-click **book.eps** to import it.

   The Vector File Options dialog box opens.

   TIP If the imported file was created in a program that is also designed for print media, such as Macromedia FreeHand or Adobe Photoshop, Fireworks converts the original color mode from print colors, such as CMYK, to RGB mode, which uses colors designed for the Web.

3. Compare your dialog box to Figure 5, then click **OK**.

4. Position the **import pointer** ⌐ in the upper-left corner of the canvas, click the mouse, then compare your image to Figure 6.

   The book appears on the canvas and the object appears on the Layers panel as a grouped object.

You imported a vector file into a Fireworks document.

FIGURE 5
Vector File Options dialog box

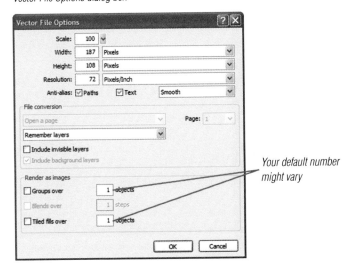

Your default number might vary

FIGURE 6
Vector file imported as a group

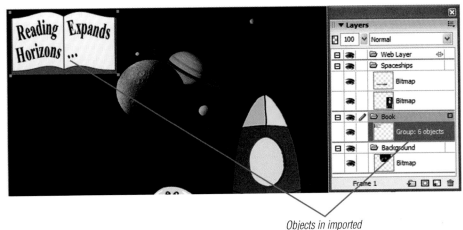

Objects in imported vector file are grouped

FIGURE 7

Imported vector objects ungrouped

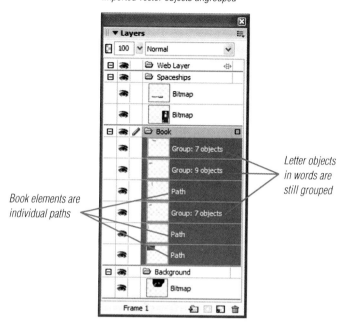

Book elements are
individual paths

Letter objects
in words are
still grouped

FIGURE 8

Modified object

Move word here

Edit an imported vector object

1. Verify that the books object is selected, click **Modify** on the menu bar, then click **Ungroup**.

   TIP You can also ungroup objects by pressing [Ctrl][Shift][G] (Win) or ⌘[Shift][G] (Mac).

2. Drag the bottom border of the Layers panel until all the layers are visible (if necessary), then compare your Layers panel to Figure 7.

   TIP You might need to collapse the Property inspector or drag the right border of the horizons.png Document window to the left to match Figure 7.

   Some individual paths are ungrouped, while other objects remain grouped (the individual letters). You could ungroup all the objects if you wanted to edit individually (for a total of 26 objects).

3. Click a blank part of the canvas to deselect the objects, click the **Group: 9 objects object** on the Layers panel to select the word **Horizons**, then drag the selected word to the location shown in Figure 8.

4. Click the **Book layer** on the Layers panel to select all the objects on the layer, click **Modify** on the menu bar, then click **Group**.

   The numerous book objects are regrouped into one object.

5. Save your work.

You ungrouped and modified an object, and then regrouped the objects.

WORK WITH BITMAP
SELECTION TOOLS

What You'll Do

In this lesson, you will use the marquee tools to select and change pixels in an image.

Understanding Pixel Selection Tools

Being able to select the precise pixels is the crucial first step to altering or editing parts of an image. Fireworks offers several ways to select and manipulate pixels in an image. This lesson covers some of those ways. When you select pixels on an image, Fireworks creates a flashing perimeter, known as a **marquee selection**, around the pixels. (This perimeter is also referred to as "marching ants" because of the way it looks.) Marquee selections are temporary areas of selected pixels that exist until you modify the pixels themselves, for example, by cutting, copying, or recoloring them.

You can save and recall a bitmap selection, but only one selection at a time. You cannot save bitmap selections in your document when you close it. In this lesson, you use the Marquee, Lasso, and Magic Wand tools to select and manipulate pixels in different ways. You can also use the selection tools in combination to select a complex area.

After you create a marquee selection, you can transfer it to another bitmap by clicking another bitmap object on the same or on a different layer. You can copy or cut a pixel selection into the layer of a document by using the Bitmap via Copy or Bitmap via Cut Insert command options on the Edit

Moving marquee selections

To move a marquee selection after you have created it, click any of the bitmap selection tools and drag the marquee on the canvas. To move a marquee selection while you are creating it, create an initial marquee, press and hold [Spacebar], move the selection to another area of the canvas, then release [Spacebar] and continue drawing the marquee.

menu. For example, if you select pixels and then click the Bitmap via Cut command, Fireworks cuts the selected pixels from the original bitmap and then pastes them as a new object on the active layer. Similarly, when you create a bitmap using the Bitmap via Copy command, Fireworks copies the selected pixels and pastes them as a new object on the active layer.

Using the Marquee Tools

Marquee tools select pixels on an image in a specific shape. The properties available for the marquee tools are shown in Figure 9.

You can press and hold [Shift] to constrain your rectangle or oval marquee to a square or circle. Use the Fixed Ratio style to constrain the height and width to a precise ratio and the Fixed Size style to set the marquee to an exact dimension.

Using the Transformation Tools

The transformation tool group consists of the Scale tool, Skew tool, and Distort tool. The Scale tool resizes an object, the Skew tool slants an object along the horizontal or vertical axes, and the Distort tool alters the size and proportion of an object and is useful for creating perspective in an object. Figure 10 shows skew and distort samples. When you select an object with any of the transformation tools, sizing handles surround the object. You can use these handles to transform the object. You can also use any transformation tool to rotate an object. The transformation tool pointer appears when you position the pointer over a sizing handle; the rotation pointer appears when you position the pointer in between the sizing handles or outside the object.

FIGURE 9
Properties for the marquee tools

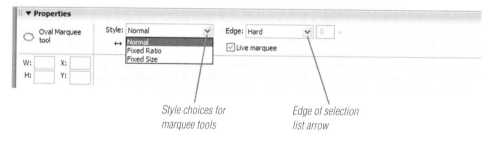

Style choices for
marquee tools

Edge of selection
list arrow

FIGURE 10
Skew and distort samples

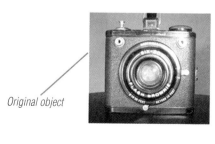

Original object

Skewing slants object evenly

Distorting slants points
independently

Select pixels using the Marquee tool

1. Click the **Background layer** on the Layers panel, click the **New/Duplicate Layer button** , then change the name of the new layer to **Galaxy**.

2. Open galaxy.jpg.

3. Click the **Marquee tool** on the Tools panel, then verify that the Info panel is open.

4. Verify that **Normal** is the selected style in the Style list on the Property inspector and that **Anti-alias** is the Edge of selection setting.

5. Place the **pointer** $+$ on the canvas at approximately **40 X/6 Y**, then drag a rectangle that surrounds the galaxy, as shown in Figure 11.

6. Click **Edit** on the menu bar, click **Copy**, click **Edit** on the menu bar, then click **Paste**.

   The copied pixels are not noticeable because they are pasted on top of the original image on the canvas. The selection appears as the top object on the Layers panel.

7. Click the **Show/Hide Layer icon** next to the original bitmap on the Layers panel (the bottom one), then compare your image to Figure 12.

You set properties for the Marquee tool, created a rectangular marquee selection, and copied the selection.

FIGURE 11
Using the Marquee tool

FIGURE 12
Rectangular marquee selection

Anti-alias edge
appears sharp

FIGURE 13

Using the Oval Marquee tool

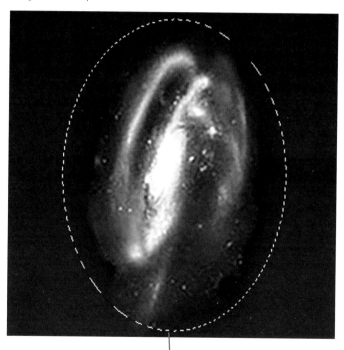

Create marquee by dragging
down and to the right while
pressing [Alt] (Win) or
[option] (Mac)

1. Click the **Show/Hide icons** next to both galaxy bitmaps on the Layers panel to hide the rectangular selection and show the original image, respectively.

2. Press and hold the **Marquee tool** on the Tools panel, then click the **Oval Marquee tool**.

3. Verify that **Normal** is the selected style in the Style list on the Property inspector, click the **Edge of selection list arrow**, click **Feather**, double-click the **Amount of feather text box**, then type **20**.

4. Place the **pointer** in the middle of the canvas (180X/175Y), press and hold **[Alt]** (Win) or **[option]** (Mac), then drag down and to the right to create an oval marquee around the galaxy, as shown in Figure 13.

   Pressing and holding [Alt] (Win) or [option] (Mac) allows you to draw a marquee from the center point outward.

5. Drag the marquee or use the arrow keys to reposition the oval around the galaxy (if necessary).

   TIP You can reselect the marquee as many times as necessary. Notice that the marquee appears to be cropped when you release the mouse button if you extend it beyond the canvas.

   (continued)

6. Click **Edit** on the menu bar, point to **Insert**, then click **Bitmap Via Copy** to copy the selection.

7. Click the **Show/Hide Layer icon** next to the original bitmap on the Layers panel to hide it, then compare your image to Figure 14.

You set properties for the Oval Marquee tool, created an oval marquee selection, and then created a new bitmap from the original.

Transform a selection

1. Resize the galaxy.jpg Document window to make it smaller, then drag it to another part of the Fireworks window so that it, the horizons.png Document window, and the Info panel are all visible.

2. Verify that the oval bitmap is selected, click the **Pointer tool** on the Tools panel, then drag the selection from galaxy.jpg to the location in horizons.png shown in Figure 15.

3. Close galaxy.jpg without saving changes.

4. Maximize the horizons.png Document window, then click the **Scale tool** on the Tools panel.

   Rotation handles appear around the selected objects.

   | TIP   You can press and hold [Alt] (Win) or [option] (Mac) to scale an object from its center.

(continued)

FIGURE 14
Oval marquee selection

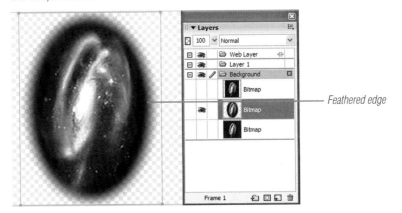

Feathered edge

FIGURE 15
Dropped selection

FIGURE 16

Rotating a selection

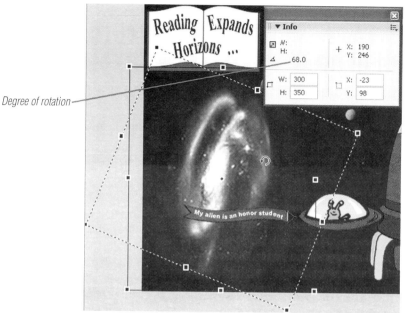

Degree of rotation

5. Place the **pointer** ✛ outside the object until the rotation pointer ↻ appears, drag the selection counterclockwise 68 degrees, as shown in the Info panel, compare your image to Figure 16, then release the mouse button.

6. Click the **Opacity list arrow** on the Property inspector, drag the slider to **60**, then press **[Enter]** (Win) or **[return]** (Mac).

   TIP If the Info panel covers the right side of the Property inspector, move or close it.

7. Click the **Pointer tool** ▸ on the Tools panel, then drag the **Book object** and the **Saucer object** to the locations shown in Figure 17.

8. Save your work.

You dragged and dropped an object, rotated it, and changed its opacity.

FIGURE 17

Moved objects

Understanding resampling

If the bitmap selection you are copying has a print resolution that differs from the document into which you want to paste, a Resampling dialog box opens, asking if you want to resample the bitmap. Choose Resample if you want to preserve the selection's original dimensions, which will adjust the number of pixels as needed to maintain the bitmap's appearance. Choose Don't Resample to retain the number of original pixels, which may affect the size of the graphic when pasted.

LEARN ABOUT
SELECTION AREAS

What You'll Do

In this lesson, you will select pixels in an image using the lasso tools.

Using the Lasso Tools

As you have seen, the marquee tools select an area of pixels in a preset shape. Using the lasso tools, you can define an exact pixel selection with precision. The Lasso tool works well on images that appear to have curves, whereas the Polygon Lasso tool works well on images that have straight lines or asymmetrical outlines. With the Lasso tool, you create the marquee as you draw it on the canvas—its accuracy is linked to your tracing ability. The result is similar to the result obtained with tools such as the Pencil tool—what you draw is what you get, which might or might not be a good thing. Using the Polygon Lasso tool is similar to using the Pen tool—you create your marquee by clicking the mouse as you go along, although the final marquee does not contain points and is just like the other marquees you create.

Adding and subtracting pixels

To add pixels to an existing lasso selection, press and hold [Shift], then drag a new marquee. The pixels you select are added to the previously selected marquee.
To subtract pixels from a marquee, press and hold [Alt] (Win) or [option] (Mac). Fireworks deletes the areas where the marquees overlap. To select just the intersection of marquees, create the first marquee, press and hold [Shift][Alt] (Win) or [Shift][option] (Mac), then create the second marquee. You can add or subtract pixels using other bitmap selection tools in much the same manner. Note that pressing [Shift] as you use the Polygon Lasso tool constrains the lines that you can draw to 45-degree angle increments.

Using Select Menu Commands

Using commands on the Select menu, you can adjust a pixel selection after you create it, as shown in Figure 18. You can edit the set of selected pixels, or add pixels to or subtract pixels from the selection marquee. The Select Inverse command selects all of the pixels except the ones enclosed by the marquee. Other commands, such as Expand Marquee or Contract Marquee, allow you to enter the number of pixels that add to or subtract from the selection's border. Creating a marquee can be a grueling process. Fortunately, after you are satisfied with a selection, you can use the Save Bitmap Selection and Restore Bitmap Selection commands to save it and recall it at any time during the current editing session or after the file has been saved, closed, and reopened.

FIGURE 18

Applying Select menu commands to a selection

Original selection —

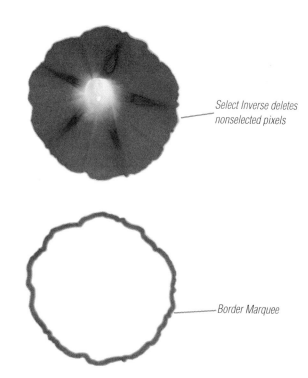

— Select Inverse deletes
nonselected pixels

— Border Marquee

Select pixels using the Lasso tool

1. Open astrocat.jpg.
2. Click the **Zoom tool** 🔍 on the Tools panel, click the canvas until you can view the image in detail, then drag the borders of the Document window until the entire image is visible.

   You might need to adjust the magnification settings a number of times before you are satisfied.

   > TIP You can also increase magnification by clicking the Set magnification icon on the bottom of the Document window and then clicking a magnification setting from the Set magnification pop-up menu.

3. Click the **Lasso tool** 🔗 on the Tools panel, click the **Edge of selection list arrow** on the Property inspector, click **Feather**, double-click the **Amount of feather text box**, then type **1**.
4. Drag the **pointer** 🔗 along the perimeter of the cat, as shown in Figure 19, then notice the areas where the marquee is off the mark.

   Because the Lasso tool is sensitive to even the slightest deviations from the path you are drawing, the accuracy of your marquee will vary.

   > TIP You can change the pointer of most tools to a crosshair by pressing [Caps Lock], which can make it easier to see the pixels you want to select.

   (continued)

FIGURE 19
Creating a marquee with the Lasso tool

Drag pointer along perimeter of image

Understanding magnification and the Zoom tool

You can increase the magnification of any area on the canvas. To change the magnification in preset increments, click the Zoom tool on the canvas or click a magnification setting in the Set magnification pop-up menu on the bottom of the Document window. To set a magnification between 6% and 6400%, use the Zoom tool to drag a zoom selection box on the canvas. The amount of magnification is based on the size of the zoom selection box. To zoom out of a selection, press and hold [Alt] (Win) or [option] (Mac), then click the canvas.

FIGURE 20
Marquee created with the Polygon Lasso tool

Marquee is
less erratic

5. Click **Select** on the menu bar, then click **Deselect**.

TIP You can also remove a marquee by drawing another one, by clicking an area outside the selection with a marquee or lasso tool, or by pressing [Esc].

You selected pixels on an image using the Lasso tool.

Create a selection using the Polygon Lasso tool and save it

1. Press and hold the **Lasso tool** on the Tools panel, then click the **Polygon Lasso tool** .

2. Create a selection by clicking the **pointer** along the perimeter of the image, make sure you connect the start and end points, then compare your image to Figure 20.

TIP You can readjust your wrist or reposition the mouse on a flat surface in between clicks, which may ensure a more accurate selection.

3. Click **Select** on the menu bar, then click **Save Bitmap Selection**.

4. Type **Kitty** in the Name text box, then click **OK**.

You selected pixels on an image using the Polygon Lasso tool, and then saved the selection.

Transform a selection

1. Click **Select** on the menu bar, click **Expand Marquee**, type **10** in the Expand by text box (if necessary), then click **OK**.

   The marquee expands 10 pixels in each direction.

2. Click **Select** on the menu bar, click **Contract Marquee**, type **20** in the Contract by text box, then click **OK**.

3. Click **Select** on the menu bar, click **Restore Bitmap Selection,** then click **OK** in the Restore Selection dialog box.

   The original marquee selection is restored.

4. Click **Select** on the menu bar, click **Smooth Marquee**, type **10** in the Sample radius pixels text box (if necessary), click **OK**, then compare your image to Figure 21.

   TIP   Fireworks removes pixels to smooth out the jagged points on the marquee.

5. Click **Select** on the menu bar, click **Restore Bitmap Selection,** then click **OK**.

   TIP   You can hide the marquee display by clicking the Hide Edges command on the View menu.

6. Click **Select** on the menu bar, click **Select Inverse**, then press **[Delete]**.

7. Click **Select** on the menu bar, click **Restore Bitmap Selection**, then click **OK**.

8. Click **Edit** on the menu bar, then click **Copy**.

9. Close astrocat.jpg without saving changes.

You applied different marquee commands to transform the selection, and then restored the original marquee.

FIGURE 21
Result of Smooth Marquee command

Smoothing
removes pixels

Importing, Selecting, and Modifying Graphics   Chapter 3

FIGURE 22
Results of numeric transform

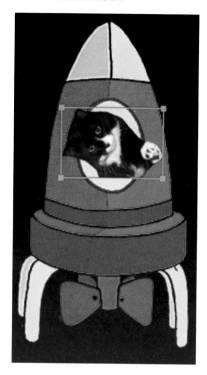

FIGURE 23
Repositioned and rotated selection

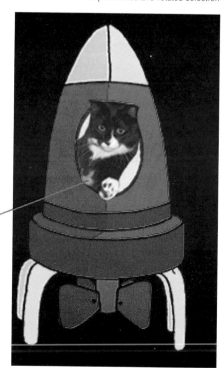

*Position cat image
in window frame*

Transform a copied selection

1. Click the **Pointer tool** on the Tools panel, then click the **large rocket object** on the canvas.

2. Click **Edit** on the menu bar, then click **Paste**.

3. Click **Modify** on the menu bar, point to **Transform**, then click **Numeric Transform**.

   The Numeric Transform dialog box opens, where you can scale an object by a percentage, resize it by pixels, or rotate an object.

4. Verify that **Scale** is selected in the drop-down list and that the **Scale attributes and Constrain proportions check boxes** are selected.

   The padlock indicates that the object will be resized proportionately.

5. Double-click the **width percentage text box**, type **50**, then click **OK**.

6. Drag the **cat image** on top of the rocket window, then compare your image to Figure 22.

7. Click the **Scale tool** on the Tools panel, position the **rotation pointer** outside the object, then drag the pointer clockwise to **−73** degrees, as indicated on the Info panel.

8. Click the **Pointer tool** on the Tools panel, then drag the image to the location shown in Figure 23.

9. Save your work.

You transformed the copied selection.

SELECT AREAS BASED ON COLOR

What You'll Do

In this lesson, you will add select areas of color using the Magic Wand tool, merge layers, and then flatten the image.

Using the Magic Wand Tool

The marquee and lasso tools select pixels by enclosing them. The Magic Wand tool allows you to select similarly colored areas of a bitmap image. The Magic Wand tool includes edge and tolerance settings. **Tolerance** refers to the range of colors the tool will select. The higher the setting, the larger the selection range. The Magic Wand tool works well on areas of strongly defined color, such as photographic images.

> **QUICKTIP**
>
> Depending on your graphic, you might find it more efficient to add pixels to a Magic Wand selection by pressing and holding [Shift], rather than increasing the tolerance setting and reclicking the bitmap.

The tolerance setting also affects the pixels selected when you click the Select Similar command on the Select menu. The Magic Wand tool selects pixels of contiguous color tone, not contiguous pixels on the image. When you use the Select Similar command, any matching pixels on the image are selected. Figure 24 shows four selections. The photo on the left shows the pixels selected with a low tolerance setting and those selected at that setting using the Select Similar command. The photo on the right demonstrates the same principle at a higher tolerance setting.

Merging and Flattening Objects and Layers

After you start creating, copying, or importing vector and bitmap objects in a document, your Layers panel can quickly fill up and appear unruly. Although creating and collapsing layers can help manage the large number of objects, you can also flatten or merge the objects you create into a single image, just as grouping objects assembles them into a single arrangement. Flattening and merging objects and layers helps to manage objects, layers, and file size. However, you can no longer edit individual objects after you flatten or merge them.

The Merge Down command on the Modify menu merges selected objects with the bitmap object that lies beneath the lowest selected object. The Flatten Selection command on the Modify menu flattens two or more objects, even if they are on different layers (the top object moves to the bottom-most object), converting them to bitmap objects. If you want to move all your objects to a single layer and remove all other layers, you can use the Flatten Layers command.

FIGURE 24
Sample Magic Wand and Select Similar selections

Select Similar command selects more green pixels

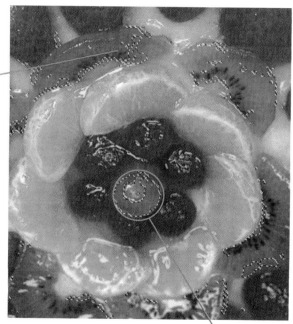

Select Similar command selects pixels in more colors

Tolerance 16 selects some green grape pixels

Tolerance 64 selects nearly all of grape

Select and copy pixels using the Magic Wand tool

1. Click the **bitmap object** (with the planets) on the Background layer to select it.

2. Click the **Magic Wand tool** on the Tools panel, double-click the **Tolerance text box** on the Property inspector, type **64**, click the **Edge of selection text box**, then click **Anti-alias** (if necessary).

3. Click the center of the small green moon, click **Edit** on the menu bar, point to **Insert**, then click **Bitmap Via Copy** to copy the selection.

   Although you cannot see the copy on the canvas (because it is directly on top of the original), notice that a new layer is created on the Layers panel.

4. Click **Select** on the menu bar, click **Deselect**, click the **Pointer tool** on the Tools panel, click the **copied bitmap** on the canvas, then drag it to the location shown in Figure 25.

5. Click the **Add Filters button** on the Property inspector, point to **Adjust Color**, then click **Hue/Saturation**.

6. Click the **Colorize check box** to select it, enter the values shown in Figure 26, then click **OK**.

   The colors change in the copied selection.

You selected pixels using the Magic Wand tool, and then copied, moved, and changed the color of the selection.

FIGURE 25
Pixels selected and moved with the Magic Wand tool

Move copied
selection here

FIGURE 26
Hue/Saturation dialog box

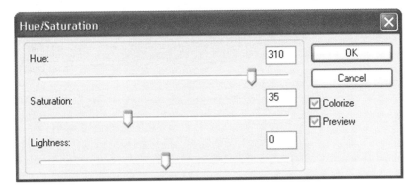

FIGURE 27
Selected pixels

All yellow pixels are selected

FIGURE 28
Modified bitmap selections

Pixels modified after being copied

Pixels modified after being selected

FIGURE 29
Flattened layers

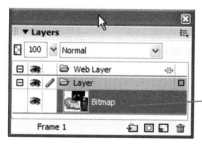

Bitmap and vector objects flattened onto one layer

Select and alter pixels

1. Click the **rocketship bitmap object**, click the **Magic Wand tool** on the Tools panel, then click the right yellow half of the nose cone.

2. Click **Select** on the menu bar, click **Select Similar**, then compare your image to Figure 27.

3. Click **Filters** on the menu bar, point to **Blur**, then click **Zoom Blur**.

4. Double-click the **Amount text box**, type **50**, double-click the **Quality text box**, type **20** (if necessary), then click **OK**.

5. Click **Select** on the menu bar, click **Deselect**, then compare your image to Figure 28.

You added similar pixels to a selection, and applied a filter to it.

Merge and flatten objects and layers

1. Click the **Pointer tool** on the Tools panel, then click the purple planet object.

2. Click **Modify** on the menu bar, then click **Merge Down** to merge this layer with the layer below it.

3. Click **Modify** on the menu bar, then click **Flatten Layers**.

4. Click the **Layer layer**, click **Modify** on the menu bar, click **Flatten Selection**, compare your Layers panel to Figure 29, save and close your work, then exit Fireworks.

You merged and flattened objects and layers.

Import files.

1. Open fw3_2.png, then save it as **sweet_essence.png**. (*Hint*: Because the canvas is narrow, readjust the size of the Document window if desired.)
2. Verify that the Info panel is open.
3. Change the name of Layer 1 to **Small Bottle**.
4. Import smbottle.jpg, placing the import cursor on the upper-left corner of the canvas.
5. Center the small bottle on the blue bottle so that it appears to be floating inside it.
6. Import sweet.png, placing the import cursor on the upper-left corner of the canvas.
7. Move the text to the bottom of the canvas.
8. Save your work.

Edit an imported vector object.

1. Create a new layer and change the name to **Jellies**.
2. Import jelly_beans.eps, accepting the default import settings, and placing the import cursor on the upper-left corner of the canvas.
3. Regroup the objects, then resize them so they fit across the top of the canvas.
4. Save your work.

Use the marquee tools.

1. Hide the Background layer, then select the text bitmap object.
2. Select the Marquee tool, verify that the Style is Normal and the Edge is Anti-alias, then draw a rectangular marquee around the text object.

3. Copy the selection using the Bitmap Via Copy command. (*Hint*: Use the Insert command on the Edit menu.)
4. Hide the original text bitmap on the Layers panel, then note the selected area.
5. Delete the copied rectangular marquee selection.
6. Save your work.

Transform a selection.

1. Show the original text bitmap, then select the Oval Marquee tool.
2. Set the Edge to Feather 10 pixels on the Property inspector, then draw an oval marquee around the text object.
3. Select the inverse of the selection and then delete it.
4. Deselect all objects, select the Scale tool, select the oval bitmap object, then rotate the oval bitmap object –90 degrees (clockwise). (*Hint*: View the rotation angle on the Info panel.)
5. Center the text bitmap selection on top of the small blue bottle.
6. Select the Background layer on the Layers panel.
7. Save your work.

Use the lasso tools.

1. Open rings.png, then select the Lasso tool.
2. Set the Edge to Feather 1 pixel on the Property inspector, adjust the magnification setting as desired, then create a marquee around the center ring.
3. Deselect the marquee.

4. Select the Polygon Lasso tool, then create a marquee around the two adjoining green rings to the left of the orange ring.
5. Save the bitmap selection.
6. Save your work.

Transform a selection and a copied selection.

1. Expand the marquee 5 pixels.
2. Contract the marquee 15 pixels.
3. Smooth the marquee 10 pixels.
4. Restore the bitmap selection.
5. Select the inverse of the bitmap selection, then deselect it.
6. Restore the bitmap selection.
7. Copy and paste the object to the sweet_essence.png document.
8. Close rings.png without saving changes.
9. Position the green rings selection so it appears to be floating near the bottom of the bottle on the left.
10. Save your work.

Use the Magic Wand tool.

1. Open gumballs.tif, then select the Magic Wand tool.
2. Adjust the Tolerance to 32 and the Edge to Feather 1 pixel.
3. Click the middle of the orange gumball, then click Select Similar.
4. Add pixels as necessary to the selection. (*Hint*: Press and hold [Shift].)

5. Drag and the drop the selection in the first bottle in the sweet_essence.png document. (*Hint*: If prompted to sample the selection, click Resample.)

6. Repeat for the yellow, white, and pink gumballs. (*Hint*: Work with each gumball separately.)

7. Close gumballs.tif without saving changes.

Select and alter pixels.

1. Using Figure 30 as a guide, resize and change the layer position of the gumballs.

2. Select the white gumball object, then apply a Hue/Saturation effect to it with the following settings: Colorize check box selected, Hue: 260, Saturation: 40, and Lightness: 5.

3. Save your work.

Merge objects and flatten layers.

1. Click the Jellies layer on the Layers panel, then merge down the layer. (*Hint*: Use the Modify menu.)

2. Click the Small Bottle layer on the Layers panel, then flatten the layers.

3. Select all the objects, then flatten the selection.

4. Save your work, then compare your image to Figure 30.

FIGURE 30
Completed Skills Review

You and your friends are going to partici-pate in a charity auction by creating a one-of-a-kind jacket. You are going to col-lect hundreds of different buttons and sew, staple, and glue them in solid cover-age over a jean jacket. The auction has a Web site, so you will use your Fireworks skills to create the background for a Web page announcing this item.

1. Obtain images of buttons and/or jean jackets in different file formats that will convey something unique about your jacket. You can obtain images from your computer, from the Internet, from a digital camera, or from scanned media. You can use images from the Web that are free for both personal and commercial use (check the copyright information for any such file before down-loading it).
2. Create a new document and save it as **mybuttons.png**.
3. Create a background image using any of the images you've obtained or create one using vector tools and applying a fill, stroke, style, or effect to it. You can also adjust its transparency. (*Hint*: The background in the sample is a rectangle filled with the Impressionist-Green pattern.)

4. Import the following files and the files you obtained in Step 1 into your document or open and select them using the bitmap selection tools.
   ▪ button1.ai
   ▪ button2.gif
5. Create visual elements using the images in your document, changing their size, color,

and other properties as needed. (*Hint*: Various buttons have been skewed or distorted.)
6. Flatten the layers and selections in your document, if desired.
7. Save your work, then examine the sample shown in Figure 31.

FIGURE 31
Sample Completed Project Builder 1

You're driving a moving truck across the country with a friend, and to occupy the time when you're not driving, you will use your new digital camera to take photographs. To memorialize this road trip, you will create a Web page dedicated to your adventure.

1. Obtain images that will fit your theme. You can obtain images from your computer, from the Internet, from a digital camera, or from scanned media. You can use images from the Web that are free for both personal and commercial use (check the copyright information for any such file before downloading it).
2. Create a new document and save it as **roadtrip.png**.
3. Import the files into your document or open and select them using the bitmap selection tools.
4. Create an interesting arrangement of your images, changing their size, color, and other properties as needed. (*Hint*: The lights of the long building in the example were selected using the Select Inverse command.)
5. Flatten the layers and selections in your document as necessary.
6. Save your work, then examine the sample shown in Figure 32.

FIGURE 32
Sample Completed Project Builder 2

Before you can build a visual element of a Web page, you need the visuals. As a designer, you'll want to be able to access as many images as possible to create a meaningful visual experience. Because dynamic Web sites are updated frequently to reflect current trends, this page might be different from Figure 33 when you open it online.

1. Connect to the Internet and go to *www.course.com*. Navigate to the page for this book, click the Student Online Companion, then click the link for this unit.
2. Open a document in a word processor, or open a new Fireworks document, then save the file as **mountainclimb**. (*Hint*: Use the Text tool in Fireworks to answer the questions.)
3. Explore the site and answer the following questions:
   - Identify different techniques that could have been used to isolate photographs.
   - Is a cropping technique evident? If so, identify.
   - How do the images affect the site design?
   - How are photographic images and illustrations used in the site?

- Who is the target audience for this site, and how does the design reinforce that goal?
4. Save your work.

FIGURE 33
Design Project

Students from the entomology department at a local college are preparing an educational Web site for the reluctant public. The group, Give a Bug a Break, wants to show how beneficial insects are to the ecosystem and our lives. Your group is in charge of developing a sample template the group can show to potential sponsors.

1. Obtain images of insects, and choose an insect to feature in the document. You can obtain images from your computer, from the Internet, from a digital camera, or from scanned media. You can use images from the Web that are free for both personal and commercial use (check the copyright information for any such file before downloading it).

2. Create a new document and save it as **mybug.png**.

3. Import the files into your document or open and select them using the bitmap selection tools.

4. Create an interesting arrangement of your images, changing their size, color, and other properties as needed. (*Hint*: The praying mantis has a feathered edge on an oval marquee and is placed on an oval vector object with inner bevel and emboss effects.)

5. Flatten layers and selections in your document as desired.

6. Save your work, then examine the sample shown in Figure 34.

FIGURE 34
Sample Completed Portfolio Project

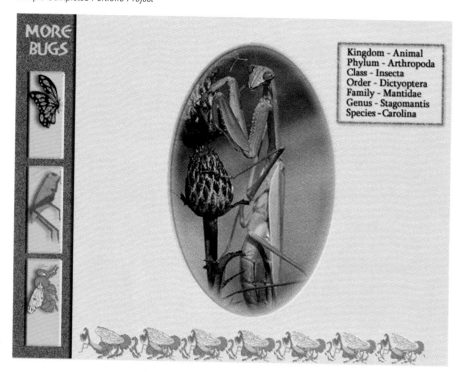

Chapter 3   Importing, Selecting, and Modifying Graphics

INTEGRATING
MACROMEDIA STUDIO 8

1. Set up the work environment.

2. Place Fireworks images into a Dreamweaver document.

3. Edit Fireworks images from a Dreamweaver document.

4. Insert and edit Macromedia Flash movies in Dreamweaver.

1 INTEGRATING
MACROMEDIA STUDIO 8 PRODUCTS

Introduction

The Macromedia Studio 8 suite of integrated Web development products includes Dreamweaver, Flash, and Fireworks. Used together, these tools allow you to create Web sites that include compelling graphics, animations, and interactivity. Recognizing that developing a Web site often involves team members with varying expertise (graphic designers, animators, programmers, and so on), Macromedia has designed these products so that they integrate easily.

This integration allows you to move from one tool to another as you bring together the elements of a Web site. For example, you can create a graphic image using Fireworks, import the image into Dreamweaver, and then edit the image starting from the Dreamweaver environment. While each of the products can stand alone, they have a similar look and feel, with common features and interface elements, such as the Property inspector, that allow you to transfer your skills from one product to another.

Tools You'll Use

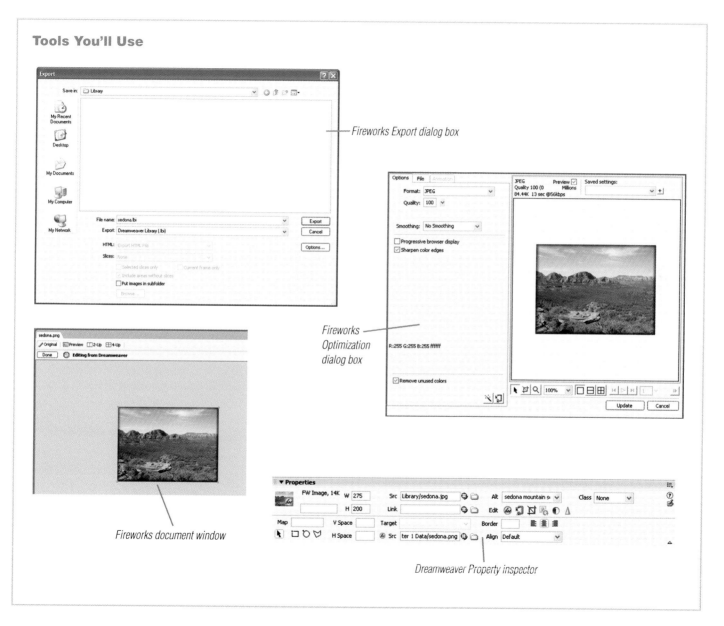

Fireworks Export dialog box

Fireworks Optimization dialog box

Fireworks document window

Dreamweaver Property inspector

SET UP THE WORK ENVIRONMENT

What You'll Do

 In this lesson, you will set up the work environment to facilitate integrating Fireworks images into a Dreamweaver document.

Setting Fireworks as the Primary External Image Editor

You can import a Fireworks image into a Dreamweaver document. Later on, when desired, you can edit the graphic by launching the Fireworks program from within Dreamweaver. This requires that you set Fireworks as the primary external image editor for GIF, JPEG, and PNG files in Dreamweaver. You can set the external image editor using settings in the Preferences dialog box in Dreamweaver.

Using Design Notes

When you export a Fireworks document or Macromedia Flash file to Dreamweaver, information about the original source file (PNG or FLA) is saved in a Design Notes file (MNO). For example, if you open air-plane.png in Fireworks and export it as air-plane.jpg, Fireworks creates a Design Notes file named airplane.jpg.mno. The Design

Notes file contains references to the source PNG file that created the exported file, which allows you to access the original PNG file for editing. You should save your Fireworks source PNG file and exported files in a Dreamweaver site. Saving in this location ensures that any developer shar-ing the site can access the source PNG file when launching Fireworks from Dreamweaver. Figure 1 shows the con-tents of a Design Notes file. The code indicates that the Fireworks source file (airplane.png) is located on the C: drive in a folder named Images.

Specifying Launch and Edit Preferences

The Fireworks launch-and-edit settings allow you to specify how to deal with source PNG files when editing Fireworks images from another program, such as Dreamweaver. You use the Fireworks

Preferences dialog box to specify one of the following launch and edit settings:

- Always Use Source PNG, which automatically launches the Fireworks PNG file specified in the Design Notes. Updates are made to both the source PNG file and the exported file.

- Never Use Source PNG, which automatically launches the exported Fireworks image. Updates are made to the exported image only.
- Ask When Launched allows you to specify whether or not to launch the source PNG file.

Setting up the Dreamweaver Site

Figure 2 shows the structure for the Web site you will be developing in this chapter. Initially, the site will contain only a Library folder that you will use to export a Fireworks image. As you work through the chapter, you will integrate Fireworks images and a Macromedia Flash movie into the site.

FIGURE 1
Contents of a Design Notes file

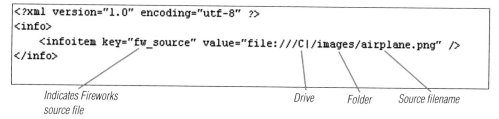

```
<?xml version="1.0" encoding="utf-8" ?>
<info>
    <infoitem key="fw_source" value="file:///C|/images/airplane.png" />
</info>
```

Indicates Fireworks source file   *Drive*   *Folder*   *Source filename*

FIGURE 2
Structure of the Web site

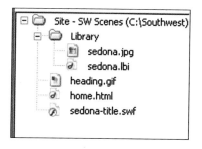

Designate the primary external image editor

This lesson requires that you have Dreamweaver 8 and Fireworks 8 installed on your computer.

1. Start Dreamweaver 8, then create a new HTML document.

2. Click **Edit** (Win) or **Dreamweaver** (Mac) on the menu bar, then click **Preferences**.

3. Click **File Types / Editors** to display the options shown in Figure 3.

4. Make sure that .png is highlighted in the Extensions column, that Fireworks is displayed in the Editors column, click **Fireworks** (if necessary), then click **Make Primary**.

   TIP If "Fireworks (Primary)" (Win) or "Fireworks 8.app (Primary)" (Mac) appears in the Editors column, Fireworks is already designated as the primary external image editor.

5. Click **.gif** in the Extensions column, make sure that Fireworks is displayed in the Editors column, then repeat for .jpg .jpe .jpeg.

6. Click **OK** to close the Preferences dialog box.

You used the Preferences dialog box to verify that Fireworks is the primary external editor for .png, .gif, and .jpg files.

FIGURE 3
Dreamweaver Preferences dialog box

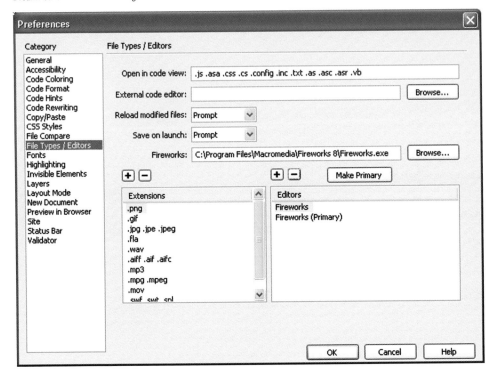

FIGURE 4

Fireworks Preferences dialog box

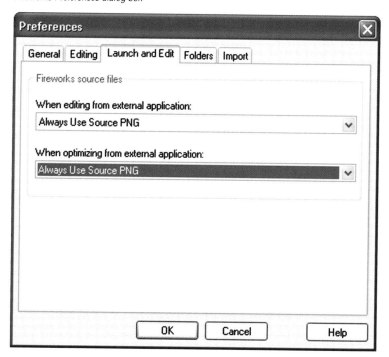

This lesson requires that you have Fireworks 8 installed on your computer.

1. Start Fireworks 8, then create a new Fireworks document.

   TIP To maximize your computer's use of resources, close other programs not relevant to the lessons.

2. Click **OK** in the New Document dialog box to accept the default values.

3. Click **Edit** on the menu bar, then click **Preferences** (Win), or click the **Fireworks menu**, then click **Preferences** (Mac).

4. Click the **Launch and Edit tab** to display the source file options.

5. Click the **When editing from external application list arrow**, then click **Always Use Source PNG**.

6. Repeat Step 5 for the When optimizing from external application option, then compare your dialog box to Figure 4.

7. Click **OK** to close the Preferences dialog box.

You used the Preferences dialog box to set the Fireworks launch and edit preferences.

Set up the Dreamweaver site

1. Using your operating system file management tool, create a folder where your Data Files are stored, then name it **Southwest**.

2. Create a new folder named **Library** in the Southwest folder.

3. In Dreamweaver, click **Site** on the menu bar, click **Manage Sites**, click **New**, then click **Site**.

   The Site Definition dialog box opens.

4. If necessary, click the **Advanced tab**, as shown in Figure 5.

5. Type **SW Scenes** in the Site name text box.

   (continued)

(continued)

FIGURE 5
Site Definition dialog box

Advanced tab

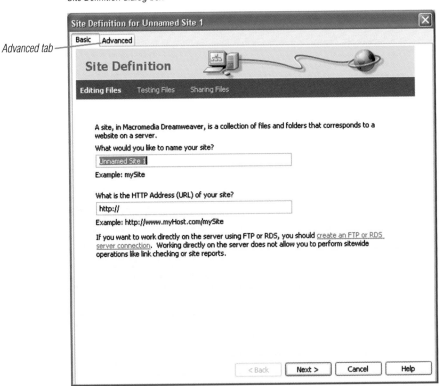

FIGURE 6

The completed Site Definition for SW Scenes dialog box

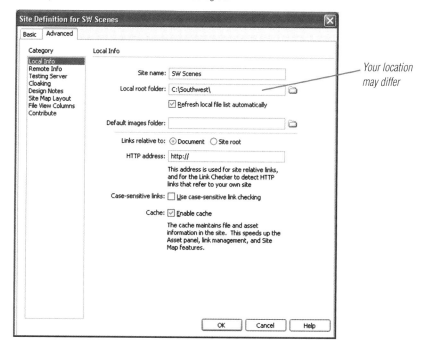

Your location
may differ

6. Click the **folder icon** next to the Local root folder text box, then navigate to the Southwest folder.

7. If necessary, double-click the **Southwest folder** to select it in the Choose local root folder for site SW Scenes dialog box, then click **Select** (Win) or **Open** (Mac).

8. Verify that your Site Definition for SW Scenes dialog box resembles Figure 6, then click **OK**.

9. Click **Done** to close the Manage Sites dialog box.

You created a folder for the Dreamweaver site and then used the Site Definition dialog box to specify a site name and location.

PLACE FIREWORKS IMAGES
INTO A DREAMWEAVER DOCUMENT

What You'll Do

In this lesson, you will place two Fireworks images into a Dreamweaver document.

Placing a Fireworks Image into Dreamweaver

You can place PNG, JPEG, and GIF images created in Fireworks directly into a Dreamweaver document. One method is to select the position in the document where you want the image to appear, and then use the Image command on the Insert menu to specify the image file to insert. Alternately, you can export an image from Fireworks into a Dreamweaver site folder.

Exporting an image in the Library folder of the site allows you to insert the image in a document as a library item. Then you can change the master library item and have it update all occurrences of the image throughout the site. To do this, create a folder named Library in the Dreamweaver Web site, then use the Export command on the File menu in Fireworks to specify the type of file to save (Dreamweaver Library or Image Only). When you export an image

Using Libraries

Libraries allow you to store items such as graphic images and text that you want to reuse or update throughout your Web site. When you place an item from the Library into a document, Dreamweaver inserts a copy of the item and a comment containing a reference to the original item. This makes it possible to update all occurrences of the item by merely changing the original item in the Library. An example of the use of a Library item would be a "Thought for the day" that appears in several locations in a Web site. Each day, this Library item can be changed, and all the pages that display it are updated to show the new item.

file as an image only, one file (.jpg or .gif) is created. When you export it to a Dreamweaver Library, two files are created, the image file and an .lbi file that contains information on the source filename and the dimensions of the image. Figure 7 shows the Dreamweaver Site panel after exporting a .gif file to the root folder and a .jpg file to the Library folder.

FIGURE 7

Site panel after exporting images from Fireworks

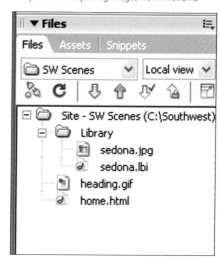

Export a Fireworks graphic as an image

1. In Fireworks, navigate to the location where your Data Files for this chapter are stored, then open **heading.png**.

2. Click **Window** on the menu bar, then click **Optimize** to open the Optimize panel, if necessary.

3. Verify that GIF is selected in the Export file format box in the Optimize panel.

4. Click **File** on the menu bar, then click **Export**.

5. Click the **Export list arrow**, then click **Images Only**, if necessary.

6. Select **Southwest** as the Save in (Win) or Where (Mac) folder, then compare your screen with Figure 8.

7. Click **Export**.

   TIP While you can use the Save As command on the File menu to save a file in a different file format, only the Export command creates an .MNO file.

8. Close heading.png without saving changes.

You used the Optimize panel in Fireworks to specify the export file type, and then you exported a Fireworks PNG graphic as a GIF image.

FIGURE 8

Export dialog box specifying the export type as Images Only

FIGURE 9

The Export dialog box specifying the export type as Dreamweaver Library

1. Open **sedona.png** in Fireworks.

2. Click **File** on the menu bar, then click **Export**.

3. Click the **Export list arrow**, then click **Dreamweaver Library (.lbi)**.

   TIP You cannot use the Save As command to create a library item.

4. Click **OK** when the message appears asking you to locate a Library folder, if necessary.

5. Navigate to the Southwest folder, double-click (Win) or click (Mac) **Library**, click **Open** (Win) or **Choose** (Mac), if necessary, then compare your dialog box with Figure 9.

6. Click **Export** in the Export dialog box.

7. Close sedona.png without saving changes.

You exported a Fireworks graphic to a Dreamweaver Library folder.

Insert a Fireworks image into a Dreamweaver document

1. Verify that the SW Scenes site in the Files panel is open in Dreamweaver.

2. Create a new HTML document and save it as **home**.

3. Click **Insert** on the menu bar, then click **Image**.

4. Click **heading.gif** to select the file, as shown in Figure 10, then click **OK** (Win) or **Choose** (Mac).

5. Type **Southwest Scenic Site heading** for the Alternate text in the Image Tag Accessibility Attributes dialog box, then click **OK**.

6. Make sure that the image is selected, then click the **Align Center button** ≣ in the Property inspector.

7. Click **File** on the menu bar, then click **Save**.

You created a Dreamweaver document and inserted a Fireworks image into it from a folder.

FIGURE 10
Specifying an image to insert

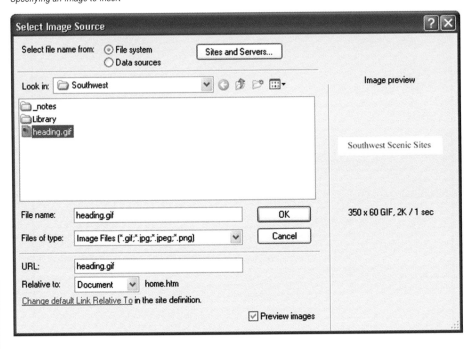

FIGURE 11

Inserting the image to the document

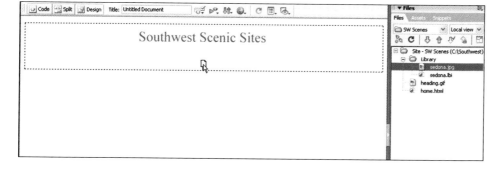

Insert a Fireworks image
from the Assets Library Folder
panel into a Dreamweaver
document

1. Point to the right side of the heading text image, then click to set an insertion point.

2. Press **[Enter]** (Win) or **[return]** (Mac).

3. Click **Window** on the menu bar, then click **Files** to display the Files panel, if necessary.

4. Click the **plus sign** (Win) or **side triangle** (Mac) next to the Library folder to expand the folder, then select **sedona.jpg**.

5. Drag **sedona.jpg** to the Document window beneath the heading.gif file, as shown in Figure 11.

6. Type **Sedona mountain scene** for the Alternate text in the Image Tag Accessibility Attributes dialog box, then click **OK**.

7. Save your work.

You inserted a Fireworks image from the Library folder into a Dreamweaver document.

EDIT FIREWORKS IMAGES
FROM A DREAMWEAVER DOCUMENT

What You'll Do

 In this lesson, you will edit a Fireworks image from a Dreamweaver document.

Editing a Fireworks Image from Dreamweaver

When you edit a Fireworks image from a Dreamweaver document, the Fireworks program is launched and the selected image is displayed. You complete the desired changes and then return to Dreamweaver without having to resave or reexport the edited image. The programs automatically update the image files. To perform this process, select the image in the Dreamweaver document, and then click the Edit Fireworks button in the Property inspector, as shown in Figure 12. The Fireworks program is launched, and the image appears in an edit window. After making your changes, click Done to return to the Dreamweaver document. If you need to make quick export changes, such as resizing the image or changing the file type, you can use the Optimize Image in Fireworks command to display the Optimize dialog box.

FIGURE 12
Edit button in the Property inspector

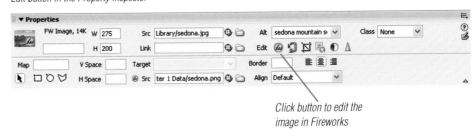

Click button to edit the image in Fireworks

FIGURE 13

The Editing from Dreamweaver window

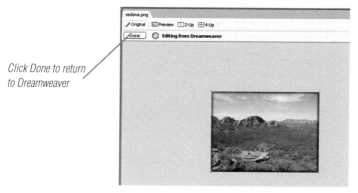

Click Done to return
to Dreamweaver

FIGURE 14

Changing the Quality setting

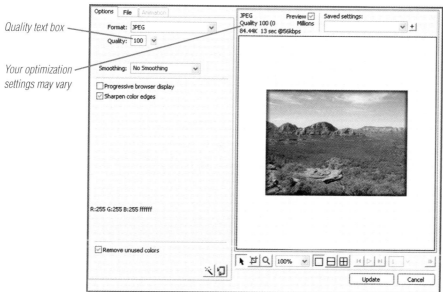

Quality text box

Your optimization
settings may vary

Edit a Fireworks image from Dreamweaver

1. Click the **sedona.jpg** image to select it.
2. Click the **Edit Fireworks button** 🖼 in the Property inspector.

   The image opens in Fireworks.
3. If necessary, click the **Pointer tool** 🔧 on the Tools panel, then click the **sedona image** to select it.
4. Click the **Add live filters button** ➕ in the Property inspector, point to **Shadow and Glow**, then click **Inner Glow**.
5. Accept the default values, then click a blank part of the Fireworks window.
6. Click **Done** in the Editing from Dreamweaver window, as shown in Figure 13, to return to the Dreamweaver document.

   The image in Dreamweaver displays the inner glow effect.

You edited a Fireworks image from Dreamweaver.

Optimize a Fireworks image from Dreamweaver

1. Verify that the sedona.jpg image is selected in Dreamweaver.
2. Click **Commands** on the menu bar, then click **Optimize Image in Fireworks**.
3. Double-click the **Quality text box**, then type **100**, as shown in Figure 14.
4. Click **Update**, then switch to Dreamweaver.

You changed an optimize property of a Fireworks image from Dreamweaver.

INSERT AND EDIT
MACROMEDIA FLASH
MOVIES IN DREAMWEAVER

What You'll Do

Southwest Scenic Sites

SEDONA, ARIZONA

 In this lesson, you will insert a Macromedia Flash movie into a Dreamweaver document and edit the movie within Dreamweaver.

Inserting a Macromedia Flash Movie into a Dreamweaver Document

You can easily insert a Macromedia Flash movie (.swf) into a Dreamweaver document. To do this, set the insertion point where you want the movie to appear, and then use the Media command on the Insert menu to select Flash as the media to insert. If the file is not in the root folder for the Web site, you are asked whether you would like to copy it into the root folder. It is

recommended that you copy the file to the root folder, so that it is accessible when you publish the site. When the insert process is completed, a placeholder appears at the insertion point in the document.

Viewing Information About the Movie

When you click the placeholder to select it, the Property inspector displays information about the movie, including the dimensions and the filename, as shown in Figure 15.

FIGURE 15
The Property inspector with a movie selected

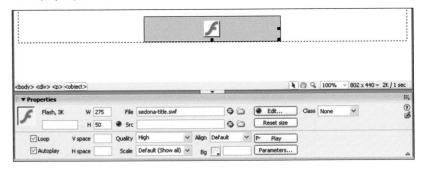

Setting an Image to Control the Movie's Playback

The Control Shockwave or Flash action feature of Dreamweaver allows you to specify an object, such as an image, to control the actions (play, stop, rewind, or go to a frame) of a Macromedia Flash movie. For example, you can specify that the movie plays when the mouse pointer rolls over an image. To do this, select the movie in the Dreamweaver document you want to control and name it in the Property inspector, as shown in Figure 16. You can select the object to control the movie and use the Behaviors panel to specify the type of action.

FIGURE 16

Naming the movie in the Property inspector

Movie name

Insert a Macromedia Flash movie into Dreamweaver

1. Click the insertion point to the right of the image.

2. Press **[Enter]** (Win) or **[return]** (Mac) to center the insertion point below the image, as shown in Figure 17.

3. Click **Insert** on the menu bar, point to **Media**, then click **Flash**.

4. Navigate to the location where your Chapter 1 Data Files are stored, click **sedona-title.swf**, then click **OK** (Win) or **Choose** (Mac).

5. If a "This file is outside of the root folder..." message appears, click **Yes**, then click **Save** when the Copy File As dialog box appears.

6. Type **Sedona Arizona caption** for the title in the Image Tag Accessibility Attributes dialog box, then click **OK**.

7. Save your work.

You inserted a Flash movie into a Dreamweaver document and copied the Flash movie to the root folder of the Web site.

FIGURE 17
Positioning the insertion point

Insertion point

1. Click the **Flash movie placeholder** to select it, if necessary.
2. Click **Play** in the Property inspector.
3. Click **Stop** in the Property inspector.
4. Click the **Loop check box** in the Property inspector to deselect it.
5. Double-click the **height box (H)**, type **100**, as shown in Figure 18, then press **[Enter]** (Win) or **[return]** (Mac).
6. Click **Reset size** in the Property inspector to restore the previous setting.
7. Save your work.

You played a Flash movie and changed its settings in Dreamweaver by turning off the Loop option, and then changing and resetting the movie height.

FIGURE 18

Changing the movie window height

Type new height here

Edit a Macromedia Flash movie from Dreamweaver

1. Click the **Flash placeholder** to select it, then click **Edit** in the Property inspector.

2. Navigate to the location where your Chapter 1 Data Files are stored, click **sedona-title.fla**, then click **Open**.

   TIP   If a Missing Font warning box opens, click Choose Substitute.

3. If necessary, click the **Pointer Tool** in the toolbox to select it.

4. Click **Frame 1** in the Heading layer.

5. Click **Sedona, Arizona** on the stage.

6. Click the **Color Styles list arrow** in the Property inspector, then click **Alpha**, if necessary.

7. Double-click the **Alpha Amount text box**, type **0** (if necessary), as shown in Figure 19, then press **[Enter]** (Win) or **[return]** (Mac).

8. Click **Done** in the Editing from Dreamweaver window.

9. Click **Play** on the Dreamweaver Property inspector.

10. Click **File** on the menu bar, point to **Preview in Browser**, then click **IExplore** (Win), or **Internet Explorer** (Mac).

    TIP   Your default browser may vary.

11. View the movie, then close the browser.

You edited a Macromedia Flash movie from Dreamweaver.

FIGURE 19
Changing the Alpha setting

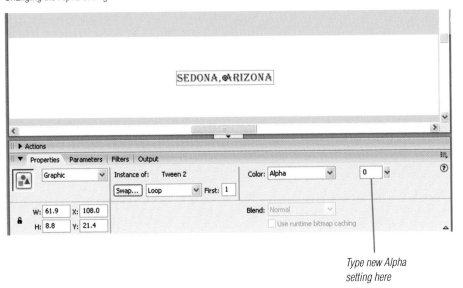

Type new Alpha
setting here

FIGURE 20

Naming a movie in the Property inspector

Name text box

Your path may differ

FIGURE 21

The completed Control Shockwave or Flash dialog box

1. Click the **Flash placeholder** to select it, click the **Name text box** in the left side of the Property inspector, type **sedonamv**, then compare your Property inspector to Figure 20.

2. Click the **Autoplay check box** in the Property inspector to deselect it.

3. Click the **sedona.jpg image** to select it.

4. Click **Window** on the menu bar, then click **Behaviors**, if necessary.

5. Click the **Add behavior button** ➕ in the Behaviors panel, then click **Control Shockwave or Flash**.

6. Make sure the Control Shockwave or Flash dialog box has the same settings as shown in Figure 21, then click **OK**.

7. Click **onClick** (below the Add behavior button), click the **list arrow**, then click **onMouseOver**.

8. Save the document.

9. Click **File** on the menu bar, point to **Preview in Browser**, then click **IExplore** (Win) or **Internet Explorer** (Mac).

   | TIP Your default browser may vary.

10. Point to the image to play the movie.

11. Point away from the image, then point to the image to play the movie again.

12. Close the browser, then save your work.

You set a bitmap image as the control for playing a Macromedia Flash movie.

Designate the primary external image editor.

1. Start Dreamweaver 8.
2. Display the Preferences dialog box and display the File Types / Editors option.
3. Verify that Fireworks is set for .png, .gif, and .jpg files.

Specify the launch and edit settings.

1. Start Fireworks 8.
2. Display the Preferences dialog box.
3. Set the Launch and Edit options to always use the source PNG when editing from an external application.
4. Set the Launch and Edit options to always use the source PNG when optimizing from an external application.

Set up the Dreamweaver site.

1. Create a folder where your Data Files are stored and name it **Foods**.
2. Add a folder within the Foods folder named **Library**.
3. Create a new Dreamweaver site named **Foods-for-Thought**, using the Foods folder as the root folder.

Export a Fireworks graphic as an image.

1. Open bread-heading.png in Fireworks.
2. Export the file as an image-only GIF file to the Foods folder.
3. Close the file without saving the changes.

Export a Fireworks graphic to a Dreamweaver site Library folder.

1. Open bread-photo.png in Fireworks.
2. Export the file as a JPEG file to the Library folder in the Foods folder.
3. Close the file without saving the changes.

Insert a Fireworks image into a Dreamweaver document.

1. Open the Foods-for-Thought site in Dreamweaver.
2. Create a new HTML document and save it as **food-home.html** in the root folder.
3. Insert the bread-heading.gif file into the document and enter **The Staff of Life heading** for the alternate text.
4. Center-align the heading across the document, then save your work.

Insert a Fireworks image from the Assets Library folder into a Dreamweaver document.

1. Place an insertion point below the heading.
2. Move the bread-photo.jpg file from the Files panel to the insertion point and enter **Photo of various breads** for the alternate text.
3. Save your work.

Edit a Fireworks image from Dreamweaver.

1. Select the bread-photo.jpg image and click Edit Fireworks in the Property inspector.
2. Add an inner glow effect to the image.
3. Click Done to return to the document.

Optimize a Fireworks image from Dreamweaver.

1. Select the bread-photo.jpg image, if necessary.
2. Display the Optimize Library dialog box. (*Hint:* Click the Commands menu.)
3. Change the quality setting to **75** and click Update.

Insert a Macromedia Flash movie into a Dreamweaver document.

1. Set an insertion point below the image.
2. Insert the bread-An.swf file below the photo image, and accept copying the image if asked.
3. Enter **Animation of the word Bread** for the title.
4. Save your work.

Play a Macromedia Flash movie and change the movie settings from Dreamweaver.

1. Select the Macromedia Flash movie placeholder.
2. Click Play, then click Stop.
3. Deselect the Loop feature.
4. Change the movie window height to **250**, then reset the size.
5. Save your work.

Edit a Macromedia Flash movie from Dreamweaver.

1. Select the movie placeholder, then click Edit.
2. Select the bread-An.fla file.
3. Create a motion animation that causes the word Bread to scroll in from the left side of the stage.
4. Click Done to return to the document in Dreamweaver.
5. Save your work.
6. Display the Web page in a browser and refresh the page.

Control a movie from within Dreamweaver.

1. Select the movie placeholder and name the image **breadmv**.
2. Deselect the Autoplay feature.
3. Select the bread-photo.jpg image.
4. Set the behavior of the image to control the playing of the breadmv movie with onMouseOver.
5. Save your work.
6. Display the document in a browser and point to the image to play the movie.
7. Compare your screen to Figure 22.
8. Close the browser.

FIGURE 22
Completed Skills Review

Integrating Macromedia Studio 8 Products

Ultimate Tours has asked you to develop a Dreamweaver Web site for their travel company. The site will include graphics exported from Fireworks and the Macromedia Flash animations that were developed in Flash Chapter 5 for the Ultimate Tours Web site.

1. Create a folder on your hard drive and name it **ULTours**, then create a folder within the ULTours folder named **Library**.

2. In Dreamweaver, create a new site named **Ultimate_Tours**, using the ULTours folder as the local root folder.

3. Open ultours_home.html and save it to the root folder for the ULTours folder.

4. In Fireworks, export ULTours-heading.png as an image-only file to the ULTours folder.

5. Export the ULTours-photo.png as a Library file to the Library folder.

6. In Dreamweaver, display the ultours_home.html document, insert the ULTours-heading.gif image, and provide alternate text.

7. Insert the ULTours-photo.jpg file to the right of the heading, provide alternate text, and center the heading and photo across the page.

8. Insert the ultimatetours5.swf file below the heading and provide a title.

9. Turn off the Loop and Autoplay features, then name the movie **ULTmv**.

10. Select the photo, choose to edit it in Fireworks, and add an inner glow effect.

11. In Dreamweaver, select the photo and set it to play the Macromedia Flash movie when the user points to the photo.

12. Save your work, display the document in a browser, then compare your image to the sample in Figure 23.

FIGURE 23

Sample completed Project Builder 1

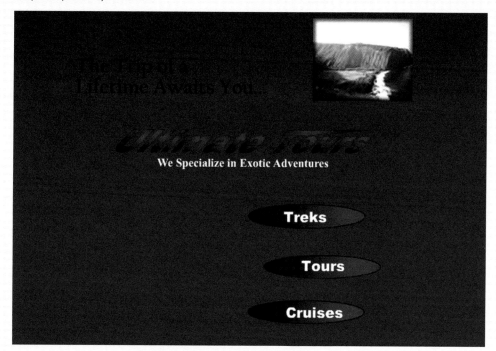

This project begins with the Striped Umbrella site created in Dreamweaver Chapter 5.

You have been asked to enhance the Striped Umbrella site by adding a Flash movie and changing a graphic image on the cafe page. Figure 24 shows the completed page for this part of the Web site. The idea is to replace the static crab logo image with a Flash animation that plays in the same space on the page.

1. In Macromedia Flash, create an animation using the cafe_logo.gif image. You decide on the type of animation, which could be a zoom or fade in; the entire crab moving; the crab claws moving; and so forth. (*Hint*: After importing the .gif file to the Library panel and placing it on the stage, you should set the stage size to the size of the graphic. You can use the Lasso tool to select the text and place it on another layer; and you can select parts of the crab and place them on separate layers to be animated individually.) Save the movie as **crab_Anim.fla** and publish it.

2. In Dreamweaver, display the Striped Umbrella site files in the Site panel.

3. Display the cafe.html page and delete the cafe_logo graphic on the page.

4. Insert the crab_Anim.swf file into the page where the cafe_logo graphic had been located.

5. Select the Flash movie placeholder and use the Property inspector to turn off the Loop and Autoplay features and to name the movie **crabmv**.

6. With the Flash movie placeholder selected, set it to play the animation when the viewer points to the crab. (*Hint*: Use the same process you would use to have the animation play when the viewer points to a photo on the page.)

7. Select the photo of the building, choose to edit it in Fireworks, and add an inner shadow effect. (*Note*: You can choose not to update the orginal .png file.)

8. Save your work.

FIGURE 24
Sample completed Project Builder 2

Crab is animated on mouse over

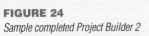

Figure 25 shows the home page of a Web site that was developed using Macromedia Dreamweaver, Flash, and Fireworks. Study the figure and complete the following questions. For each question, indicate how you determined your answer.

1. Connect to the Internet, and go to *www.course.com*. Navigate to the page for this book, click the Online Companion, then click the link for this chapter.

2. Open a document in a word processor or in Flash, save the file as **dpcIntegration**, then answer the following questions.
   - What seems to be the purpose of this site?
   - Who would be the target audience?
   - Identify three elements within the Web page that could have been created or enhanced using Fireworks.
   - Identify two elements on the page and indicate how you would use Fireworks to enhance them.
   - Identify an animation that could have been developed by Macromedia Flash.
   - Indicate how you would use Macromedia Flash to enhance the page.
   - What would be the value of using Macromedia Flash, Dreamweaver, and Fireworks to create the Web site?
   - What suggestions would you make to improve on the design, and why?

FIGURE 25
Design Project

PORTFOLIO PROJECT

This is a continuation of the Portfolio Project in Macromedia Flash Chapter 5. You will create a Web site in Dreamweaver, export graphic files from Fireworks, and import portfolio5.swf into the site. The home page of the Web site will include a heading and photo image (of your choice), as shown in Figure 26.

1. Create a folder on your hard drive and name it **Portfoliowebsite**, then create a folder within the Portfoliowebsite folder named **Library**.

2. In Dreamweaver, create a new site named **PortfolioWeb**, using the Portfoliowebsite folder as the local root folder.

3. Open portfoliohome.html and save it to the Portfoliowebsite site.

4. In Fireworks, export portfolio-heading.png as an image-only file to the Portfoliowebsite folder.

5. Export portfolio-photo.png as a Library file to the Library folder. (*Note*: You can provide a photo of your choice, if desired.)

6. In Dreamweaver, display the portfolio-home.html document, insert the portfolio-heading.gif image, and provide alternate text.

7. Insert the portfolio-photo.jpg file from the Library folder to the right of the heading, provide alternate text, and center the heading and photo across the page.

8. Insert portfolio5.swf below the heading and provide a title.

9. Turn off the Loop and Autoplay features, then name the movie **portfoliomv**.

10. Select the heading and edit it in Fireworks to apply a drop shadow.

11. Select the photo, choose to edit it in Fireworks, and add an inner glow effect.

12. In Macromedia Flash, edit the movie by adding a graphic that resembles a portfolio case to the initial screen.

13. In Dreamweaver, select the photo and set it to play the Macromedia Flash movie. (*Note*: If you specify an onMouseOver action, when the viewer points to the photo the movie will start playing and display the next screen. If the viewer points to the photo again, the movie will play from that point.)

14. Save your work, display the document in a browser, then compare your image to the sample in Figure 26.

FIGURE 26
Sample completed Portfolio Project

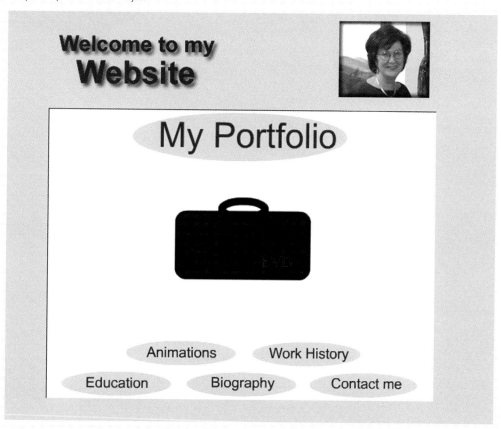

Read the following information carefully!!

Find out from your instructor the location where you will store your files.

- To complete many of the chapters in this book, you need to use the Data Files on the CD at the back of this book.

- All of the Data Files are organized in folders named after the chapter in which they are used. For instance, all Chapter 1 Data Files are stored in the chapter_1 folder. You should leave all the Data Files in these folders; do not move any Data File out of the folder in which it is originally stored.

- Your instructor will tell you whether you will be working from the CD or copying the files to a drive on your computer or on a server. Your instructor will also tell you where you will store the files you create and modify.

Copy and organize your Data Files.

- Use the Data Files List to organize your files to a USB storage device, network folder, hard drive, or other storage device.

- Create a subfolder for each chapter in the location where you are storing your files, and name it according to the chapter title (e.g., Dreamweaver Chapter 1).

- For each chapter you are assigned, copy the files listed in the **Data File Supplied** column into that chapter's folder.

- If you are working from the CD, you should store the files you modify or create in each chapter in the chapter folder.

- **Special instructions for Dreamweaver chapters:**

  - As you build each Web site, the exercises in this book will guide you to copy the Data Files you need from the appropriate Data Files folder to the folder where you are storing the Web site. Your Data Files should always remain intact because you are copying (and not moving) them to the Web site.

- Because you will be building a Web site from one chapter to the next, sometimes you will need to use a Data File that is already contained in the Web site you are working on.

Find and keep track of your Data Files and completed files.

- Use the **Data File Supplied** column to make sure you have the files you need before starting the chapter or exercise indicated in the **Chapter** column.

  - **Special instructions for Dreamweaver chapters:** Some of the files listed in the **Data File Supplied** column are ones that you created or used in a previous chapter, and that are already part of the Web site you are working on.

- Use the **Student Creates File** column to determine the filename you use when saving your new file for the exercise.

- The **Used in** column tells you where a file is used in a chapter.

Files used in this book

Macromedia Dreamweaver 8

Chapter	Data File Supplied	Student Creates File	Used In
1	dw1_1.html about_us.swf accommodations.swf activities.swf cafe.swf index.swf shop.swf spa.swf assets/pool.jpg assets/striped_u_background.jpg assets/striped_umbrella_banner.gif		Lesson 2
	dw1_2.html assets/striped_umbrella_banner.gif	about_us.html activities.html cafe.html cruises.html fishing.html spa.html	Lesson 5
	dw1_3.html dw1_4.html assets/blooms_banner.jpg assets/blooms_logo.jpg	annuals.html classes.html newsletter.html perennials.html plants.html tips.html water_plants.html	Skills Review
	dw1_5.html assets/tripsmart_banner.jpg	amazon.html catalog.html destinations.html kenya.html newsletter.html services.html	Project Builder 1
	dw1_6.html assets/book_bag_banner.jpg	books.html cafe.html corner.html events.html seasonal.html signings.html	Project Builder 2

Macromedia Dreamweaver 8 (continued)

Chapter	Data File Supplied	Student Creates File	Used In
	none		Design Project
	none		Group Project
2	dw2_1.html spa.doc assets/striped_umbrella_banner.gif assets/the_spa.jpg		Lesson 2
	dw2_2.html gardening_tips.doc assets/blooms_banner.jpg assets/garden_tips.jpg		Skills Review
	none		Project Builder 1
	none		Project Builder 2
	none		Design Project
	none		Group Project
3	questions.doc		Lesson 1
		su_styles.css	Lesson 2
	dw3_1.html assets/boardwalk.jpg assets/club_house.jpg assets/pool.jpg assets/sago_palm.jpg assets/sports_club.jpg assets/striped_umbrella_banner.gif		Lesson 4
	assets/stripes_back.gif assets/umbrella_back.gif		Lesson 6
	dw3_2.html assets/blooms_banner.jpg assets/daisies.jpg assets/lantana.jpg assets/petunias.jpg assets/verbena.jpg	blooms_styles.css	Skills Review
	dw3_3.html dw3_4.html assets/tripsmart_banner.jpg assets/lion.jpg assets/zebra_mothers.jpg	tripsmart_styles.css	Project Builder 1

Macromedia Dreamweaver 8 (continued)

Chapter	Data File Supplied	Student Creates File	Used In
	dw3_5.html dw3_6.html assets/book_bag_banner.jpg assets/reading.jpg	book_bag_styles.css	Project Builder 2
	none		Design Project
	none		Group Project
4	dw4_1.html assets/heron_waiting_small.jpg assets/striped_umbrella_banner.gif assets/two_dolphins_small.jpg		Lesson 1
		top.swf	Lesson 3
	assets/about_us_down.gif assets/about_us_up.gif assets/activities_down.gif assets/activities_up.gif assets/cafe_down.gif assets/cafe_up.gif assets/home_down.gif assets/home_up.gif assets/spa_down.gif assets/spa_up.gif		Lesson 4
	dw4_2.html dw4_3.html assets/boats.jpg assets/heron_small.jpg		Lesson 5
	dw4_4.html dw4_5.html dw4_6.html dw4_7.html assets/b_classes_down.jpg assets/b_classes_up.jpg assets/b_home_down.jpg assets/b_home_up.jpg assets/b_newsletter_down.jpg assets/b_newsletter_up.jpg assets/b_plants_down.jpg assets/b_plants_up.jpg assets/b_tips_down.jpg	top.swf	Skills Review

Macromedia Dreamweaver 8 (continued)

Chapter	Data File Supplied	Student Creates File	Used In
	assets/b_tips_up.jpg assets/blooms_banner.jpg assets/flower_bed.jpg assets/fuchsia.jpg assets/iris.jpg assets/water_hyacinth.jpg		
	dw4_8.html dw4_9.html dw4_10.html assets/giraffe.jpg assets/parrot.jpg assets/sloth.jpg assets/tripsmart_banner.jpg assets/water_lily.jpg		Project Builder 1
	dw4_11.html dw4_12.html dw4_13.html assets/book_bag_banner.jpg assets/books.jpg assets/grif_stockley.jpg assets/salted_with_fire.jpg		Project Builder 2
	none		Design Project
	none		Group Project
5	assets/cafe_logo.gif assets/cafe_photo.jpg assets/cheesecake.jpg		Lesson 3
	cafe.doc		Lesson 4
	gardeners.doc registration.doc assets/flower_bed.jpg		Skills Review
	assets/hat.jpg assets/pants.jpg assets/vest.jpg		Project Builder 1
	book club.doc assets/muffins.jpg		Project Builder 2
	none		Design Project
	none		Group Project

Macromedia Flash 8

Chapter	Data File Supplied	Student Creates File	Used In
1		workspace.fla	Lesson 1
	fl1_1.fla		Lesson 2
		tween.fla	Lesson 3
		layers.fla	Lesson 4
	*layers.fla		Lesson 6
	fl1_2.fla		Skills Review
		demonstration.fla	Project Builder 1
	fl1_3.fla		Project Builder 2
		dpc1.fla	Design Project
			Portfolio Project
2		tools.fla	Lessons 1-4
	fl2-1.fla		Lesson 5
		skillsdemo2.fla	Skills Review
		ultimatetours2.fla	Project Builder 1
		thejazzclub2.fla	Project Builder 2
		dpc2.fla	Design Project
		portfolio2.fla	Portfolio Project
3	fl3-1.fla		Lesson 1
	fl3-2.fla		Lessons 2-4
	fl3_3.fla		Skills Review
	**ultimatetours2.fla		Project Builder 1
		isa3.fla	Project Builder 2
		dpc3.fla	Design Project
	**portfolio2.fla		Portfolio Project

*Created in a previous Lesson or Skills Review in current chapter

**Created in a previous chapter

Macromedia Flash 8 (continued)

Chapter	Data File Supplied	Student Creates File	Used In
4	fl4-1.fla		Lesson 1
	fl4-2.fla		Lesson 2
	fl4-3.fla		Lesson 3
	fl4-4.fla		Lesson 4
	fl4-5.fla		
	*frameAn.fla		Lesson 5
	fl4-6.fla		Skills Review
	**ultimatetours3.fla		Project Builder 1
	ship.giv		
		summerBB4.fla	Project Builder 2
		dpc4.fla	Design Project
	**portfolio3.fla		Portfolio Project
5	fl5-1.fla		Lesson 1
	fl5-2.fla		
	fl5-3.fla		
	fl5-4.fla		Lesson 2
	fl5-5.fla		Lesson 3
	CarSnd.wav		
	beep.wav		
	fl5-6.fla		Lesson 4
	*rallySnd.fla		
	fl5-7.fla		Lesson 5
	fl5-8.fla		Skills Review
	**ultimatetours4.fla		Project Builder 1
	foghorn.wav		
		zodiac5.fla	Project Builder 2
		dpc5.fla	Design Project
	**portfolio4.fla		Portfolio Project

*Created in a previous Lesson or Skills Review in current chapter

**Created in a previous chapter

Macromedia Fireworks 8

Chapter	Data File Supplied	Student Creates File	Used In
1	fw1_1.png		Lesson 1
	pool.png	my_blue_heaven.png	Lesson 2
	fw1_1.png		Lessons 3 & 4
	fw1_2.png elbow.gif		Skills Review
	none	crystal.png	Project Builder 1
	none	meandering_paths.png	Project Builder 2
	none	rocknroll	Design Project
	none	emoticon.png	Portfolio Project
2	none	fish.png	Lesson 1
	fw2_1.png		Lessons 2–5
	fw2_2.png		Skills Review
	none	remember_me.png	Project Builder 1
	none	impact_potions.png	Project Builder 2
	none	yoakum	Design Project
	none	classic_buckle.png	Portfolio Project
3	fw3_1.png rocket.gif saucer.png book.eps		Lesson 1
	galaxy.jpg		Lesson 2
	astrocat.jpg		Lesson 3
	none		Lesson 4
	fw3_2.png smbottle.jpg sweet.png jelly_beans.eps rings.png gumballs.tif		Skills Review
	button1.ai button2.gif	mybuttons.png	Project Builder 1
	none	roadtrip.png	Project Builder 2
	none	mountainclimb	Design Project
	none	mybug.png	Portfolio Project

Integration

Chapter	Data File Supplied	Student Creates File	Used In
1	none		Lesson 1
	heading.png sedona.png	home.html	Lesson 2
	none		Lesson 3
	sedona-title.fla sedona-title.swf		Lesson 4
	bread-An.fla bread-An.swf bread-heading.png bread-photo.png	food-home.html	Skills Review
	ultours_home.html ULTours-photo.png ULTours-heading.png ultimatetours5.fla ultimatetours5.swf		Project Builder 1
	cafe_logo.gif cafe.html Striped Umbrella site files	crab_Anim.fla	Project Builder 2
	none	dpcIntegration	Design Project
	portfoliohome.html portfolio-heading.png portfolio-photo.png portfolio5.swf portfolio5.fla		Portfolio Project

Absolute path
A path containing an external link that references a link on a Web page outside of the current Web site, and includes the protocol "http" and the URL, or address, of the Web page.

ActionScript
The Flash scripting language used by developers to add interactivity to movies, control objects, exchange data, and create complex animations.

Aligning an image
Positioning an image on a Web page in relation to other elements on the page.

Alternate text
Descriptive text that can be set to appear in place of an image while the image is downloading or when users place a mouse pointer over an image.

Anchor point
Joins path segments to delineate changes in direction.

Animation
The perception of motion caused by the rapid display of a series of still images.

Anti-aliasing
Smoothes the edges of curved or diagonal lines, such as type, so that the appearance is not jagged.

Assets folder
A subfolder in which you store most of the files that are not Web pages, such as images, audio files, and video clips.

Assets panel
A panel that contains nine categories of assets, such as images, used in a Web site. Clicking a category button displays a list of those assets.

Background color
A color that fills the entire Web page, a frame, a table, a cell, or a document.

Background image
A graphic file used in place of a background color.

Balance
In screen design, balance refers to the distribution of optical weight in the layout. Optical weight is the ability of an object to attract the viewer's eye, as determined by the object's size, shape, color, and so on.

Bandwidth profiler
A feature used when testing a Flash movie that allows you to view a graphical representation of the size of each frame and the frame by frame download process.

Banners
Graphics that generally appear across the top of the screen that can incorporate the company's logo, contact information, and navigation bars.

Behavior
A preset piece of JavaScript code that can be attached to page objects. A behavior tells the page object to respond in a specific way when an event occurs, such as when the mouse pointer is positioned over the object.

BMP
Bitmapped file. A file format used for images that is based on pixels.

Body
The part of a Web page that is seen when the page is viewed in a browser window.

Border
An outline that surrounds a cell, a table, or a frame.

Broken links
Links that cannot find the intended destination file for the link.

Browser
Software used to display Web pages, such as Microsoft Internet Explorer, Mozilla Firefox, or Netscape Navigator.

Bullet
A small dot or similar icon preceding unordered list items.

Bulleted list
An unordered list that uses bullets.

Button Symbols
Objects in Flash that appear on the stage and that are used to provide interactivity, such as jumping to another frame on the timeline.

Cascading Style Sheet
A file used to assign sets of common formatting characteristics to page elements such as text, objects, and tables.

Cell padding
The distance between the cell content and the cell walls in a table.

Cell spacing
The distance between cells in a table.

Cell walls
The edges surrounding a cell in a table.

Cells
Small boxes within a table that are used to hold text or graphics. Cells are arranged horizontally in rows and vertically in columns.

Child page
A page at a lower level in a Web hierarchy that links to a parent page.

Class style
See Custom style.

Code and Design Views
A Web page view that is a combination of Code View and Design View.

Code Inspector
A window that works just like Code view, except that it is a floating window.

Code View
A Web page view that shows a full screen with the HTML code for the page. Use this view to read or directly edit the code.

Columns
Table cells arranged vertically.

Comments
Helpful text describing portions of the HTML code, such as a JavaScript function, that are inserted in the code and are not visible in the browser window.

Contents
The Macromedia Help feature that lists topics by category.

Controller
A toolbar that contains the playback controls for a movie.

Custom style
A style that can contain a combination of formatting attributes that can be applied to a block of text or other page elements. Custom style names begin with a period (.). Also known as a class style.

Debug
To find and correct coding errors.

Declaration
The property and value of a style in a Cascading Style Sheet.

Default base font
Size 3 (Dreamweaver). The default font that is applied to any text without an assigned size that is entered on a Web page.

Default font color
The color the browser uses to display text, links, and visited links if no other color is assigned.

Default link color
The color the browser uses to display links if no other color is assigned. The default link color is blue.

Defining a Web site
Specifying the site's local root folder location to help Dreamweaver keep track of the links among Web pages and supporting files.

Definition lists
Lists made up of terms with indented descriptions or definitions.

Delimited files
Database or spreadsheet files that have been saved as text files with delimiters.

Delimiter
A comma, tab, colon, semicolon, or similar character that separates tabular data.

Description
A short summary of Web site content that resides in the Head section.

Design notes
A file (.mno) that contains the original source file (.png or .fla) when a Fireworks document or Flash file is exported to Dreamweaver.

Design View
The view that shows a full-screen layout and is primarily used when designing and creating a Web page.

Diagonal symmetry
A design principle in which page elements are balanced along the invisible diagonal line of the page.

Document toolbar
A toolbar that contains buttons for changing the current Web page view, previewing and debugging Web pages, and managing files.

Document-relative path
A path referenced in relation to the Web page that is currently displayed.

Documents
Flash, Fireworks, and Dreamweaver files.

Document window
The large white area in the Dreamweaver workspace where you create and edit Web pages.

Domain name
An IP address expressed in letters instead of numbers, usually reflecting the name of the business represented by the Web site.

Down Image state
The state of a page element when the element has been clicked with the mouse pointer.

Download time
The time it takes to transfer a file to another computer.

DSL
Digital Subscriber Line. A type of high-speed Internet connection.

Embedded CSS style sheet
Styles that are part of an HTML page rather than comprising a separate file.

Enable Cache
A setting to direct the computer system to use space on the hard drive as temporary memory, or cache, while you are working in Dreamweaver.

Expanded Tables Mode
A Dreamweaver mode that displays tables with temporary cell padding and spacing to make it easier to see the table cells.

Export data
To save data that was created in Dreamweaver in a special file format so that you can bring it into another software program.

External CSS style sheet
Collection of rules stored in a separate file that control the formatting of content in a Web page. External CSS style sheets have a .css file extension.

External links
Links that connect to Web pages in other Web sites or to an e-mail address.

Favorites
Assets that are used repeatedly in a Web site and are included in their own category in the assets panel.

Files panel
A window similar to Windows Explorer (Windows) or Finder (Macintosh), where Dreamweaver stores and manages files and folders. The Files panel contains a list of all the folders and files in a Web site.

Fill
A solid color, a pattern, or a gradient applied to an object.

Flash Button Objects
Flash graphic and text objects that you can insert onto a Web page without having the Flash program installed.

Flash Player
A program that allows Macromedia Flash movies (.swf and .exe formats) to be viewed on a computer. This a free program from Macromedia.

Flash text
A vector-based graphic file that contains text.

Floating workspace
A feature of Macromedia products that allows each document and panel to appear in its own window.

Font combination
A set of three fonts that specifies which fonts a browser should use to display the text on a Web page.

Frame animation
An animation created by specifying the object that is to appear in each frame of a sequence of frames (also called a frame-by-frame animation).

Frame delay
The display time for each frame in an animation.

Frame-by-frame animation
Animation that creates a new image for each frame (also called Frame animation).

Frame label
A text name for a keyframe that can be referenced within ActionScript code.

Frames
Individual cells that make up the timeline in Flash or that contain an animation's images and objects in Fireworks.

Frameset
Multiple Web pages displayed together using more than one frame or window.

FTP
File Transfer Protocol. The process of uploading and downloading files to and from a remote site.

GIF file
Graphics Interchange Format file. A GIF is a type of file format used for images placed on Web pages that can support both transparency and animation.

Gradient
Two or more colors that blend into each other in a fixed design.

Graphic
Picture or design element that adds visual interest to a page.

Graphic Symbols
Objects in Flash, such as drawings, that are converted to symbols and stored in the Library panel. A graphic symbol is the original object. Instances (copies) of a symbol can be made by dragging the symbol from the Library to the stage.

Group
A command that manipulates multiple objects as a single selection.

Guide layers
Layers used to align objects on the stage in a Flash document.

Head content
The part of a Web page that is not viewed in the browser window. It includes meta tags, which are HTML codes that include information about the page, such as keywords and descriptions.

Headings
Six different styles that can be applied to text: Heading 1 (the largest size) through Heading 6 (the smallest size).

Hexadecimal value
A value that represents the amount of red, green, and blue in a color and is based on the Base 16 number system.

History panel
A panel that lists the steps that have been performed in a Macromedia application while editing and formatting a document.

Home page
Usually, the first Web page that appears when users visit a Web site.

Horizontal symmetry
A design principle in which page elements are balanced side-to-side across the page.

Horizontal and vertical space
Blank space above, below, and on the sides of an image that separates the image from the text or other elements on the page.

Hotspot
An area that you define in your document to which you can assign a URL (Web address) or other type of interactivity. A clickable area on a graphic that, when clicked, links to a different location on the page or to another Web page.

HTML
Hypertext Markup Language. A language Web developers use to create Web pages.

Hyperlinks
Graphic or text elements on a Web page that users click to display another location on the page, another Web page on the same Web site, or a Web page on a different Web site. Hyperlinks are also known as links.

Image map
A graphic that has one or more hotspots defined on it that, when clicked, serve as a link that will take the viewer to another location.

Import data
To bring data created in one software program into another application.

Index
The Macromedia Help feature that displays topics in alphabetical order.

Insert bar
Groups of buttons for creating and insert-ing objects arranged by category.

Instances
Representations of symbols after you drag them from the Library panel to the canvas or stage.

Interactivity
Allows visitors to your Web site to interact with and affect content by moving or click-ing the mouse.

Internal links
Links to Web pages within the same Web site.

IP address
An assigned series of numbers, separated by periods, that designates an address on the Internet.

ISP
Internet Service Provider. A service to which you subscribe to be able to connect to the Internet with your computer.

JavaScript
A Web-scripting code that interacts with HTML code to create dynamic content, such as rollovers or interactive forms.

JPEG file
Joint Photographic Experts Group file. A JPEG is a type of file format used for images that appear on Web pages. Many photographs are saved with the JPEG file format.

Kerning
An adjustment to the spacing between adja-cent letters or a range of letters.

Keyframe
A frame that signifies a change in the time-line of a Flash movie, such as an object being animated.

Keywords
Words that relate to the content of the Web site and reside in the Head section.

Layer (Fireworks)
An element that functions like a folder divided into sections that contain objects. A document can be made up of many layers.

Layers (Flash)
Rows on the timeline that are used to organize objects and that allow the stacking of objects on the stage.

Layout Mode
A Dreamweaver mode that is used when you draw your own table.

Leading
An adjustment to the amount of vertical space between lines of text.

Library
A panel containing graphic symbols, button symbols, and animation symbols. You can use multiple Libraries in a document and share Libraries between documents.

Local root folder
A folder on your hard drive, Zip disk, or floppy disk that holds all the files and folders for the Web site.

Looping
The number of times an animation repeats.

Mailto: link
An e-mail address that is formatted as a link that opens the default mail program with a blank, addressed message.

Main Timeline
The primary timeline for a Flash movie. The main timeline is displayed when you start a new Flash document.

Mask layer
A layer in a Flash document that is used to cover the objects on another layer(s) and, at the same time, create a window through which you can view various objects on the other layer.

Menu bar
A bar across the top of the program win-dow that is located under the program title bar and lists the names of the menus that contain commands.

Merge cells
To combine multiple cells in a table into one cell.

Merge Drawing Model
A drawing mode that causes overlapping drawings (objects) to merge, so that a

change in the top object, such as moving it, may affect the object beneath it.

Meta tags
HTML codes that include information about the page such as keywords and descriptions. Meta tags reside in the head section.

Morphing
The animation process of changing one object into another, sometimes unrelated, object.

Motion guide layer
A path used to specify how an animated object moves around the Flash stage.

Motion tweening
The process used in Flash to automatically fill in the frames between keyframes in an animation that changes the properties of an object such as the position, size, or color.

Movement
In screen design, movement refers to the way the viewer's eye moves through the objects on the screen.

Named anchor
A specific location on a Web page that is used to link to that portion of the Web page.

Navigation bar
A set of text or graphic links that viewers can use to navigate between pages of a Web site.

Nested table
A table within a table.

Non-breaking space
A space that is left on the page by a browser.

Object Drawing Model
A drawing mode that allows you to overlap objects which are then kept separate, so that changes in one object do not affect another object. You must break apart these objects before you can select their stroke and fills.

Objects
The individual elements in a document, such as text or images.

Onion skinning
A setting that allows you to view one or more frames before and after in the current frame.

Ordered lists
Lists of items that must be placed in a specific order and are preceded by numbers or letters.

Orphaned files
Files that are not linked to any pages in the Web site.

Over Image state
The state of a page element when the mouse pointer is over the element.

Over While Down Image state
The state of a page element when the mouse pointer is clicked and held over the element.

Panel groups
Groups of panels such as Design, Code, Application, and Files that are displayed through the Window menu. Sets of related panels are grouped together.

Panels
Components in Flash used to view, organize, and modify objects and features in a movie.

Panels
Individual windows in Dreamweaver that display information on a particular topic, such as Answers or History.

Parent page
A page at a higher level in a Web hierarchy that links to other pages on a lower level.

Path (vector object)
An open or closed line consisting of a series of anchor points.

Path (file location)
The location of an open file in relation to any folders in the Web site.

Persistence of vision
The phenomenon of the eye capturing and holding an image for one-tenth of a second before processing another image.

PICS
Platform for Internet Content Selection. This is a rating system for Web pages.

Pixels
Small squares of color used to display a digital image on a rectangular grid, such as a computer screen.

Playhead

An indicator specifying which frame is playing in the timeline of a Flash movie.

Plug-in

A module that adds features or enhancements to an application.

PNG file

Portable Network Graphics file. A PNG is a file format used for images placed on Web pages that is capable of showing millions of colors but is small in file size. The native file format in Fireworks.

Point of contact

A place on a Web page that provides viewers a means of contacting a company.

PPI

Pixels per inch.

Projector

In Flash, a standalone executable movie, such as a Windows .exe file.

Property inspector

A panel where properties and options specific to a selected tool or command appear. In Dreamweaver, a panel that displays the properties of the selected Web page object. You can change an object's properties using the text boxes, drop-down menus, and buttons on the Property inspector. The contents of the Property inspector vary according to the object currently selected.

Publish

The process used to generate the files necessary for delivering Flash movies on the Web.

Publish a Web site

To make a Web site available for viewing on the Internet or on an intranet.

Radial symmetry

A design principle in which page elements are balanced from the center of the page outward, like the petals of a flower.

Reference panel

A panel used to find answers to coding questions, covering topics such as HTML, JavaScript, and Accessibility.

Refresh Local File List Automatically option

A setting that directs Dreamweaver to automatically reflect changes made in your file listings.

Relative path

A path used with an internal link to reference a Web page or graphic file within the Web site.

Remote server

A Web server that hosts Web sites and is not directly connected to the computer housing the local site.

Remote site

A Web site that has been published to a remote server.

Resolution

The number of pixels per inch in an image. Also refers to an image's clarity and fineness of detail.

Rollover

An effect that changes the appearance of an object when the mouse rolls over it.

Root folder (local root folder)

A folder used to store all folders and files for a Web site.

Root-relative path

A path referenced from a Web site's root folder.

Rows

Table cells arranged horizontally.

Rule of Thirds

The rule of thirds is a design principle that entails dividing a page into nine squares and then placing the page elements of most interest on the intersections of the grid lines.

Rules

Sets of formatting attributes in a Cascading Style Sheet.

Sans-serif fonts

Block-style characters used frequently for headings, subheadings, and Web pages.

Scene

A timeline designated for a specific part of the movie. Scenes are a way to organize long movies by dividing the movie into sections.

Screen reader

A device used by the visually impaired to convert written text on a computer monitor to spoken words.

Script Assist

A feature found in the Actions panel which can be used to generate ActionScript without having to write programming code.

Seamless image

A tiled image that is blurred at the edges so that it appears to be all one image.

Search

The Macromedia Help feature that allows you to enter a keyword to begin a search for a topic.

Selector

The name or the tag to which style declarations have been assigned.

Serif fonts

Ornate fonts with small, extra strokes at the beginning and end of the characters; used frequently for paragraph text in printed materials.

Shape hints

Indicators used to control the shape of an object as it changes appearance during an animation.

Shape tweening

The process of animating an object so that it changes into another object.

Site map

A graphical representation of how Web pages relate to each other within a Web site.

Slices

A Web element that divides an image into different sections, which allows you to apply rollover behaviors, animation, and URLs to those areas.

Soft return

A shortcut key combination that forces text to a new line without creating a new paragraph by creating a <BR> tag.

Split cells

To divide cells into multiple cells.

Stage

That area of the Flash workspace that contains the objects that are part of the movie and that will be seen by the viewers.

Standard toolbar

A toolbar that contains icons for some frequently used commands that are also available on the File and Edit menus.

Standard Mode

A Dreamweaver mode that is used when you insert a table using the Insert Table icon or command.

State

Represents the button's appearance based on a mouse action. These include: Up, Over, Down, and Over While Down.

Status bar

A bar that appears at the bottom of the Dreamweaver or Fireworks document window. The left end of the status bar displays the tag selector, which shows the HTML tags being used at the insertion point location. The right end displays the window size and estimated download time for the page displayed.

Storyboard

A small sketch that represents each page in a Web site. Like a flowchart, a storyboard shows the relationship of each page to the other pages in the site.

Style Rendering toolbar

A toolbar that allows you to render a Web page as different media types (e.g., handheld).

Symbol

A graphic, animation, or button that represents an object, text, or combination group.

Table header

Text placed at the top or sides of a table on a Web page that is read by screen readers.

Tables

Grids of rows and columns that can be used either to hold tabular data on a Web page or as a basic design tool for page layout.

Tabular data

Data arranged in columns and rows and separated by a delimiter.

Tag Selector

A location on the status bar that displays HTML tags for the various page elements, including tables and cells.

Target

The location on a Web page that the browser displays in full view when an internal link is clicked or the frame that opens when a link is clicked.

Templates
Web pages that contain the basic layout for similar pages in the site.

Tiled image
A small graphic that repeats across and down a Web page, appearing as individual squares or rectangles.

Timeline
The component of Flash used to organize and control the movie's contents over time, by specifying when each object appears on the stage.

Timeline Effect
Pre-built animation effects (such as rotating, fading, and wiping) that can be applied to objects using a dialog box.

Tools panel
A panel in Flash, Dreamweaver, and Fireworks separated into categories containing tools and their options.

Tweening
The process of adding tweened instances and distributing them to frames so that the movement appears more fluid.

Unity
In screen design, intra-screen unity has to do with how the various screen objects relate. Inter-screen unity refers to the design that viewers encounter as they navigate from one screen to another.

Unordered lists
Lists of items that do not need to be placed in a specific order and are usually preceded by bullets.

Unvisited links
Links that have not been clicked by the viewer.

Up Image state
The state of a page element when the mouse pointer is not on the element.

Upload
The process of transferring files from a local drive to a Web server.

URL
Uniform Resource Locator. An address that determines a route on the Internet or to a Web page.

Vector graphics
Mathematically calculated objects composed of anchor points and straight or curved line segments.

Visited links
Links that have been previously clicked, or visited. The default color for visited links is purple.

Web design program
A program for creating interactive Web pages containing text, images, hyperlinks, animation, sound, and video.

Web server
A computer dedicated to hosting Web sites that is connected to the Internet and configured with software to handle requests from browsers.

Web site
Related Web pages stored on a server that users can download using a Web browser.

Web safe Colors
Colors that display consistently in all browsers and on Macintosh, Windows, and Unix platforms.

White space
An area on a Web page that is not filled with text or graphics.

Workspace
The area in the Dreamweaver program window where you work with documents, movies, tools, and panels.

WYSIWYG
An acronym for What You See Is What You Get, meaning that your Web page should look the same in the browser as it does in the Web editor.

XHTML
eXtensible HyperText Markup Language. The most current standard for developing Web pages.